Ingmar Bergman

INGMAR BERGMAN
Essays in Criticism

Edited by
STUART M. KAMINSKY
with Joseph F. Hill

OXFORD UNIVERSITY PRESS
London Oxford New York 1975

OXFORD UNIVERSITY PRESS

London   Oxford   New York
Glasgow   Toronto   Melbourne   Wellington
Cape Town   Ibadan   Nairobi   Dar es Salaam   Lusaka   Addis Ababa
Delhi   Bombay   Calcutta   Madras   Karachi   Lahore   Dacca
Kuala Lumpur   Singapore   Hong Kong   Tokyo

This book is dedicated
to my students

PREFACE

· ·

A number of problems arise in compiling a collection of articles and essays on Ingmar Bergman. First, there is the problem of evaluation. Since he was first recognized by English language critics in the late 1950's, Ingmar Bergman has been regarded as "great," a "master," who is to be praised when one likes his films and condemned for not living up to his potential when the individual viewer or reviewer does not like a particular film. Too much of what is written about Bergman is simply praise or condemnation, which gives us little insight into the man and his work though it may tell us quite a bit about the reviewer.

Film scholars, students, and serious viewers require a collection of works which deal with Bergman as a filmmaker from various analytic perspectives. There is no need at this point to prove that Bergman is an important filmmaker who merits attention. Nor, really, is there any reason to argue the quality of his work. Though some may not like what he does, those who do need no convincing of Bergman's quality and those who do not are not very likely to be swayed by another's insistence on quality.

With this in mind, we sought a collection of pieces which gave a variety of perspectives on individual films of Ingmar Bergman, pieces with an analytical base and not primarily evaluative. Each piece in the section on *Perspectives on Individual Films* was chosen both because it dealt with a specific film and because it provided a way to approach the film.

The next problem is that of scope. There have been some excellent books written on Bergman by, among others, Robin Wood, Birgitta Steene, and Jorn Donner, who are represented in this collection. Each has put forth a cohesive analysis from an individual perspective. Each has attempted to deal with all of the films of Bergman to the point at which the book was written. However, the present volume is not an attempt at biography. It is a presentation of points of view, approaches to a creator. In compiling the pieces we felt no need to include something on every film, but we did, however, feel a need to bring in viewpoints from various specific disciplines, including psychiatry, literature, philosophy, and theology.

A third problem relates to the question of length. For every one article of merit written on Ingmar Bergman, there are a dozen terrible ones, of the praise or condemnation variety described earlier. Even so, there are literally dozens and dozens of fine pieces on Bergman in both small-circulation journals and large-circulation magazines and in books. Choices must be made. Ours were on the basis of which pieces we felt demonstrated valuable approaches to the particular film in question and to Bergman in general.

As might well be inferred by what we have stated, we are committed to the concept of non-evaluative criticism. Since this collection is founded on that commitment it merits some explanation. We believe valuable criticism comes from analysis, not assertion of quality. If one analyzes a Bergman film for us that we do not like and gives us some understanding of it through his (the writer's) own disciplinary background we are more likely to change our attitude toward that film than if he simply tells us loudly that a movement is beautiful, an idea profound, an actor great. If we lean away from a film, regardless of what it is, no amount of assertion, scholarly bullying or critical posturing is likely to change our mind. On the other hand if we already agree with the writer, then there is no need to assert. Although some of the selections in the volume do display a strong bias in taste, the major portion of each is strongly analytical. Our inclination in general is to ignore the first three paragraphs of most articles on directors which are likely to be highly laudatory or strongly critical and move to the essence. The need for analysis, however, continues. Thus, even if we, as viewers, do not like a particular Bergman film, we can profit by an analysis. This then leads to an important point about selections for this volume.

There is but one piece in this collection which shows hostility for a Bergman work. That is the review of *The Virgin Spring* by Stanley Kauffmann which we have intentionally juxtaposed with a favorable analysis. We realize that while we can exclude negative reviews or articles which we generally find unhelpful, we cannot fully prevent critics with an affirmative response to a film from expressing that enthusiasm, an enthusiasm which is often stated in this collection as a critical evaluation. That must be accepted if a collection on Bergman is to exist. The concern of this collection, however, is not so much that you will come to love the films of Ingmar Bergman, but that you will, to a great extent, understand them.

The question of understanding as opposed to feeling often comes up in relation to the work of Ingmar Bergman in particular and more commercially oriented filmmakers in general. There are those who feel that it is somehow wrong to attempt to analyze a work which has been created as emotional entertainment, and surely, Bergman's films are primarily emotional. It is not unusual for students who see the films of Bergman to say that they like what they see but are unable to tell you what it is they like. All too often they fall back into the comfortable posture of the reviewer who simply describes a scene and says it is great, or gives us a theme—concern for the silence of God—and says it is important. In truth, the silence of God or any other of Bergman's themes of anguish and alienation can be found in a variety of popular films from *The Trip, The Last Movie,* and *Earthquake* to *Magnum Force.* It is not the existence of these themes in Bergman which is qualitatively unique. There is, however, something in the work of Bergman which is compelling for viewers, which makes his films the most written about and discussed, perhaps, of any filmmaker in history. Coming from this is the assumption of this collection that (a) the viewer will have an intellectual curiosity about why these films are so responded to, and (b) the viewer will want to know more about the films and Bergman's work so that he will have a broader insight into past and subsequent works by that filmmaker. It is assumed that the more one knows about Bergman (or any other creator) and his works the more he can appreciate those works.

There is one final and central reason for the study of Ingmar Bergman and it is we believe an undeniable one. In the 1950's, Bergman was the director who made film a respectable study, the director whose work caused scholars, intellectuals (and those who thought they were), and reviewers to accept that film could be considered as a continuing art. One might argue, as one of us does elsewhere (Kaminsky, *American Film Genres: Approach to a Critical Theory,* Pflaum/Standard, 1974), that in Bergman's films there is not necessarily more "art" than in those of George Roy Hill or William Friedkin, but that Bergman led the way to serious attention by audience and critics of the contemporary filmmaker.

Bergman continues to hold this position as touchstone director of the "art" film. He represented the director who could truly be considered the auteur, the author of his film. Bergman became the example of the director as creator who can express a personal vision in his work, though filmmaking is a collective creative act.

As of this writing, Bergman is very much an active director of plays and films. It is hoped that the critical perspectives presented here will be helpful in understanding and appreciating not only the existing films, but those yet to come.

STUART KAMINSKY
Evanston   JOSEPH F. HILL
February 1975

ACKNOWLEDGMENTS

Research on this book was conducted by Joseph F. Hill. This book exists because of the encouragement of John Wright, the introduction of Bergman's films to me by Jack Ellis, the suggestions of Father Gene Phillips of Loyola University, and the excellent resources of the Northwestern University Library.

EDITORS' NOTE

There are several problems in dealing with a variety of pieces from several countries on the work of Ingmar Bergman. First, titles of films vary from country to country. Second, the spelling of character names varies. There are also differences in spelling in general.

Instead of attempting to have all titles, character names, and spelling in these pieces conform to our choice, we have reprinted each piece as it was published. In the filmography at the end of the book all titles for each film are included so that there should be a minimum of confusion. Our decision to do this is based on three considerations:

1. Not knowing which of two or three titles is necessarily the best we see no reason to impose our views on other writers. And while we may think *Sawdust and Tinsel* is a better title than *The Naked Night*, that is just our opinion. Add to this that few of the titles are ever literal translations of Bergman's original and the problem is compounded.

2. Since the various films are released under different titles, the reader will encounter prints of the film and articles on the films with a variety of titles. Familiarity with the alternatives will be of value.

3. We assume the writers had valid reasons for their individual choices and we wish to respect their decisions.

CONTENTS

I

Overviews on a Career

1

A BIOGRAPHICAL NOTE

Birgitta Steene

. . . .

Ingmar Bergman is a playwright, theater director, and film-maker. Throughout his career he has remained faithful to both the stage and the screen, maintaining that "the theater is like a loyal wife, film is the big adventure, the expensive and demanding mistress—you worship both, each in its own way."[1]

Bergman's attraction to the stage and the screen seems to stem from an early age. He was only ten years old when he received his most memorable toy, a magic lantern and puppet theater, for which he made scenery and dolls, and wrote plays. When the couple in *The Devil's Wanton* relive their childhood, it is with the help of a similar apparatus. Bergman's love for the world of illusion was more than a child's fascination with playacting. Throughout his adolescence he used much of his pocket money to buy film for his *laterna magica* and film projector and he spent several nights a week at the cinema. He also attended the opera regularly but only seldom went to the theater. In 1935, however, he saw Olof Molander's epoch-making staging of Strindberg's *A Dream Play*, a production that was to leave a lasting impression on him.[2]

After passing his college entrance examination and doing his military service, Bergman began to study literature and art at the University of Stockholm. He wrote his literature thesis on Strindberg's *Keys to Heaven*, a composition that reads like a directorial stage copy, but he was more involved in amateur theater groups than in formal studies. He did not complete the work for his academic degree; nevertheless, his years at the University were invaluable, for they gave him an

From *Ingmar Bergman* (New York: Twayne Publishers, 1968), pp. 19-24. Reprinted by permission of Twayne Publishers, Inc.

opportunity to try out his creative and directorial talents and also led to his first contacts with film producers.

Bergman made his debut in the theater as director of a Christian "settlement workshop," Mäster Olofsgården. Among his productions were Strindberg's *Lucky Per's Journey* and *Macbeth*, his favorite Shakespeare play. The chairman of the Student Theater in Stockholm, who saw the production of *Macbeth*, invited Bergman to talk about his work. Soon he was busy staging Strindberg's *The Pelican* for the Stockholm University theater group. He became known among the students as a director with a magic touch but also a man of volatile temperament. One of the young actors in the workshop, Birger Malmsten (who later appeared in a number of Bergman's films, from *The Devil's Wanton* to *The Silence*), has recorded his early memories of Bergman: "His face always seemed to have an angry expression and he was considered to be very gifted but utterly crazy. He directed the play, holding a hammer in his hand, and he threw it from time to time at the young actors."[3]

By 1944 Bergman had left the University and now became a professional director at the City Theater in Hälsingborg, a city in the south of Sweden. The theater was on the verge of artistic and economic collapse, but in two years Bergman had transformed it into a very successful enterprise. He then moved on to the Gothenburg City Theater where his influence became equally strong. In 1952 he began a six-year directorship at the Malmö City Theater, one of the most modern playhouses in Europe, which during "the Bergman era" became known for its fine ensemble acting and well-balanced repertory, ranging from *Faust* to *The Merry Widow*. Many of the actors at the Malmö theater later became Bergman's favorite interpreters on the screen: Harriet Andersson, Bibi Andersson, Ingrid Thulin, and Max von Sydow.

Bergman's career in the theater culminated during the three years (1963–66) that he was head of Sweden's national stage, the Royal Dramatic Theater in Stockholm. All in all he has staged, between 1938 and 1966, some seventy-five productions, in addition to many television and radio plays. Among dramatists whose works he has produced we find Molière, Goethe, Ibsen, Strindberg, Chekhov, Pirandello, Brecht, Camus, Anouilh, Tennessee Williams, and Edward Albee.

Early in his career in the theater Bergman wrote plays for the stage. Relatively soon, however, he came to accept himself in the role of interpreter, which may have to do with the fact that for him "the theater represents . . . absolute objectivity." A stage director and a playwright are incompatible; the latter's approach is subjective while the director must learn to enter something more important than himself and become "a member in a large body, a member of a collective group and subordinated to the demands of discipline and humbleness."[4]

When Bergman announced his resignation from the Royal Dramatic Theater early in 1966, one drama critic wrote:

> It is difficult to hide a certain bitterness at Bergman's resignation. For he has given the Royal Dramatic a shot of vitamins of a kind seldom seen in its hundred and seventy-five years old history. . . . Ingmar Bergman's brief leadership charged our theatrical life with new areas of excitement. At last we got a creative temperament working with all the resources of power in his hands, a Swedish Jean Vilar who was not satisfied with directorial victories but wanted to transform our entire view of the theater. . . . One has always sensed the vision that lay before him, with a national theater that deserved that name. If I am to be honest, I would rather have done without some of his new films—no matter how good they might be—in order to have seen that vision realized.[5]

Bergman will continue to work in the theater as a guest director, but it is clear that one of the reasons for his resignation from the Royal Dramatic Theater was the fact that he wanted to devote more of his time to film-making. This is understandable since his career in the cinema has been even more remarkable than his contribution to the theater.

The Swedish film enjoyed its Golden Age in the early nineteen-twenties. With the arrival of sound, Swedish directors felt that the language problem prevented them from producing films for export. The lack of international competition may be one reason why the nineteen-thirties became a period of artistic decline in Swedish film-making, when trivial comedies and historical spectacles were produced with only the home market in mind. Finally, in the early nineteen-forties, came the first signs of an attempt to remedy the situation. Dr. Carl Anders Dymling, who was appointed managing director of Svensk Filmindustri, the leading movie company in Sweden, tried to encourage younger talents. Like Shakespeare who arrived in London at a time of fresh and vital interest in the drama, Bergman came upon the scene at a most opportune moment in the history of Swedish film-making.

Mrs. Stina Bergman, wife of the late playwright and novelist Hjalmar Bergman, who had assumed the task of talent scout for Svensk Filmindustri, became interested in Ingmar Bergman (no kin) after reading an appreciative review of one of his early stage productions.

Invited to the home of Mrs. Bergman, the young director appeared "shabby, ill-mannered and unshaven, with a derisive laughter that seemed to originate in the darkest corner of Inferno." But he also exuded "an unconcerned charm, which was so forceful that after a few hours' conversation I had to drink three cups of coffee in order to get back to normal."[6]

The result of the interview was that Bergman produced his first film script, *Torment (Hets)*, and was made the apprentice of Alf Sjöberg, who directed the film. With its cutting criticism of the autocratic Swedish school system, *Torment*—and its author—became a *cause célèbre*. A year later Bergman was allowed to direct his first picture, *Crisis (Kris)*. Since then he has directed one or two pictures a year. For most of them he has written the script. Making films has, says Bergman, "become a natural necessity, a need similar to hunger and thirst. For certain people to express themselves implies writing books, climbing mountains, beating children, or dancing the samba. I express myself by making films."[7]

Elsewhere Bergman has referred to film-making as "self-combustion and self-effusion." The creation of a film is an exacting work, "a tapeworm 2,500 meters long that sucks the life and spirit out of me. . . . When I am filming, I am ill."[8] No one can be unaware of Bergman's films as intensely personal statements, which, however, is not to say that they are highly private; it seems definitely a mistake to try to draw too close a parallel between his cinematic characters and actual people or to interpret his symbols only in terms of available biographical information.[9] Bergman's strength as an artist—apart from his unquestionable technical skill—lies in his ability to create characters who, although they are carriers of his personal ethics, have the abstract quality of people in a morality play, and to project these characters on a scene of great visual clarity and emotional intensity. Bergman is by no means a great and original thinker, but his themes and characters are banal in the sense that archetypes are banal, and in this lies their appeal to a large number of people. Siegfried Kracauer's theory of filmmaking, although dubious as a general thesis, certainly applies to Bergman: "What films reflect are not so much explicit credos as psychological dispositions—those deep layers of collective mentality which extend more or less below the dimension of consciousness."[10]

Turning from the immediate social reality around him, Bergman has focused his lens on an interior landscape, and much of his work emerges as an "allegory" on the progress of the soul—his own and, by inference, the soul of modern man. Citing O'Neill, Bergman has stated that any drama is worthless which does not deal with man's relationship to metaphysical questions. This artistic premise is no doubt connected with his personal background. As he once said to French film critic Jean Béranger: "To make films is to plunge to the very depth of childhood."[11]

Ernst Ingmar Bergman was born on July 14, 1918, the son of a Lutheran clergyman who later became court chaplain to the King of Sweden. Bergman's father often took his son on bicycle trips to the rural churches of Uppland, and while he preached the son would absorb the symbolic interior of the churches, their mural paintings and wood carvings, their popular renderings of biblical stories. Years later Bergman transformed some of these early memories into a play entitled *Wood Painting (Trämålning)*, which eventually became the film *The Seventh Seal (Det sjunde inseglet)*.

Bergman spent much of his childhood in the university town of Uppsala, staying with a widowed grandmother in a 14-room apartment, which was arranged then as it had been in 1890 when the grandmother moved in there as a bride. Bergman's other companion was an old servant, full of fairy tales and country stories. He experienced a great sense of security at his grandmother's place and later on in life when he wanted to describe a sense of completeness, he could do so by referring to this part of his childhood: "I know where I am, how I stand, who I am. . . . This feeling is identical to the sense of security, of seeing clearly and being sure that my vision of life was correct, that I had back there when I was a boy living with my grandmother in Uppsala."[12]

Bergman's tendency to bypass social problems—even in his earliest films society is abstracted to represent the destructiveness and evil of the adult world as opposed to the innocence of youth—for metaphysical questions probably received a new impetus during the nineteen-forties. Bergman's formative years as an artist coincided with the emergence of a new generation of Swedish writers whose mood was one of existential *Angst* and religious skepticism. The encounter with this "school of the forties" may have helped crystallize Bergman's own doubts about God although his pessimism was never as complete as that of the literary group. The Kafka fever that raged in Sweden about the same time may also have shaped Bergman's concept of a distant and silent God, of God as a need but not as fulfillment, and of modern man's rootlessness in a world of outmoded values. Yet, the brooding over questions of guilt and reconciliation, punishment and forgiveness that permeates both Kafka's and Bergman's work has its common denominator in the Protestantism and worship of the Father as a distant Power under which both artists grew up. To both of them the home offered protection, but also paralysis and isolation.[13]

Bergman has always admitted that he is deeply rooted in Swedish art and life. He belongs in fact to a category of artists that might be disappearing in the Western world: artists for whom the personal vision fuses with a feeling of national identity. Bergman needs his Swedish tradition and milieu, not only for inspiration but for a sense of security, without which he admits he could not work. He has often referred to the feeling of panic that can grasp him in a totally foreign surrounding, and he has never accepted offers to make films abroad although the financial benefits would probably be considerable. Typical is a passage from his brief essay, "A Page from My Diary," which describes a day during the shooting of *The Virgin Spring*, with everyone being somewhat downcast until two cranes appeared overhead and everyone dropped his work to watch. The company went back to work happy and enchanted by the experience and Bergman mentions his feelings of relief and security in this "Swedish" atmosphere and among these people; he decides at this time to reject an American film offer.[14]

NOTES

1. From an interview in *Filmnytt*, No. 6 (1950), p. 13.
2. "It is completely natural for artists to take from and give to each other, to borrow from and experience one another. In my own life, my great literary experience was Strindberg. . . . And it is my dream to produce *A Dream Play* some day. Olof Molander's production of it in 1934 was for me a fundamental dramatic experience." *Four Screenplays of Ingmar Bergman*, p. xix.
3. Quoted in Gunnar Oldin, "Ingmar Bergman," *The American-Scandinavian Review*, XLVII (Autumn 1959), p. 142.
4. From a lecture in Uppsala on February 23, 1959. Quotation from a résumé in *Upsala Nya Tidning*, February 24, 1959.
5. Bengt Jahnson, "Bergmans avgång," *Dagen Nyheter*, November 28, 1965.
6. Quoted in Gunnar Oldin, "Ingmar Bergman," *The American-Scandinavian Review*, XLVII (Autumn 1959), pp. 152-53.
7. Ingmar Bergman, "Self-Analysis of a Film-Maker," *Films and Filming*, September 24, 1956, p. 19.
8. *Time*, March 14, 1960 (cover story on Ingmar Bergman), p. 62.
9. See Marianne Höök, *Ingmar Bergman* (Stockholm: Wahlström & Widstrand, 1962).

10. Siegfried Kracauer, *From Caligari to Hitler* (Princeton: Princeton University Press, 1947), p. 6.
11. Jean Béranger, "Renaissance du cinéma suèdois," *Cinéma 58*, No. 29 (July-August 1958), p. 32.
12. Alan Cole, "Ingmar Bergman. Movie Magician," *New York Herald Tribune*, November 8, 1959.
13. Cf. Jörn Donner, *The Personal Vision of Ingmar Bergman* (Bloomington: Indiana University Press, 1962), p. 212.
14. Ingmar Bergman, "A Page From My Diary," reprinted in a program distributed at the foreign showing of *The Virgin Spring* (Stockholm: Svensk Filmindustri, 1960), n.p.

2

THE TORMENT OF INSIGHT
Children and Innocence in the
Films of Ingmar Bergman

Stuart M. Kaminsky

In the films of Ingmar Bergman, children live in a world of tormented innocence. They are surrounded by tortured adults who cannot or will not communicate to them the reasons for their anguish. Distrustful, the children seek their own answers by observing and eavesdropping on the adult world. They try, as they develop understanding, to personify and simplify good and evil. Like heroes of Greek tragedy, they are driven by curiosity, a need to know. Bergman's children are constantly reaching out to touch and communicate with an adult world which they cannot understand. If the child does make contact, either by his own experience or a shared experience, his protective innocence is torn away and he must face the insight which he has only vaguely sensed. He must face the realization that God does not exist or does not communicate, that terrible things are possible because man is unprotected, that death exists as a frightening and final end. This, to Bergman, is what it means to become an adult. As an adult, the former child can only find solace for his lost innocence in the acceptance of love, a love which Bergman tells us can range from pure animal passion to almost-spiritual devotion. If a child is unable to accept this insight, he grows into an even more tortured adult without innocence, clinging to childhood fears which cannot sustain him, unable to accept or seek the solace of love.

The problem of youthful loss of innocence emerges artistically in *Summer Interlude* (1950), develops in *Summer with Monika* (1952),

Portions of this essay originally appeared in *Cinema Journal*, Vol. 13, No. 2 (Spring 1974). Reprinted by permission of *Cinema Journal* and the author.

Secrets of Women (1952), *Wild Strawberries* (1957), *The Magician* (1958), and *The Virgin Spring* (1959). It culminates explicitly in *Through a Glass Darkly* (1961). Bergman then begins the painful personal examination of the child who cannot or will not accept tormented adult insight because he has never communicated with the adult world and has, if forced to face insight, retreated into childhood attempts to personify evil. This exploration begins tentatively in *Winter Light* (1962). Bergman then plunges deeply into it in *The Silence* (1963), reacts with an anguished hopelessness in *Persona* (1966), and comes to a shattering, painful conclusion in *The Hour of the Wolf* (1968). In a real sense, *The Silence*, *Persona*, and *Hour of the Wolf* can be viewed as the "Johan trilogy," in which we see the artist struggle from boyhood to adult suicide without having come to terms with his loss of innocence, without having accepted the hope of love which Bergman had considered in *Through a Glass Darkly*.

Before a child can begin the tortured path to insight, he must first be born. Bergman's films are filled with pregnant women, repopulating an earth which the male figures with whom Bergman so often identifies do not want. Bergman's men, his artists, fear the responsibility of children, for the child must live a life of meaningless anguish. This situation exists most clearly in Evald in *Wild Strawberries* and Johan in *Hour of the Wolf*. We also feel that it must have been David's attitude toward his own children in *Through a Glass Darkly*. The pregnant women in Bergman's films either reject the burden of pregnancy and its physical responsibility (*Monika, The Virgin Spring*) or they come to accept the responsibility with the possible compensation of love (*Brink of Life, Wild Strawberries, Hour of the Wolf*).

An examination of some of Bergman's revelations about his view of childhood and innocence supports these conclusions as does a study of the specific films.

Marie's problem in *Summer Interlude* (1950) concerns her inability to come to terms with her loss of innocence, a loss thrust on her with the death of Henrik following their summer together. When she reads Henrik's diary, she knows that the wall she has built around herself has not really insulated her from human contact, has not allowed her to escape feeling and pain. In the flashback story of her summer with Henrik, she is, at the age of fifteen or sixteen, confident, sure of her art as a ballet dancer, aware of the sinister possibilities of Uncle Erland, but unafraid. Henrik, only slightly older, is tormented by the possibility of death, a possibility which Marie never acknowledges. For Marie, their summer together is without torment or responsibility, really without understanding. She simply feels and enjoys, living in innocent make-believe which is possible only for such young people in Bergman films. When Henrik dies, her innocence flees. She is lost, bewildered. She curses God, but sees no way to turn. Uncle Erland proposes that she build a wall around herself with his help. She accepts and finds as she grows older that Uncle Erland's way has been false, that only in the acceptance of love, in her case with David the reporter, can she find solace.

Summer with Monika (1952) deals with the same loss of innocence and in many ways parallels the story of Marie and Henrik. The difference is that Monika and Harry do not live in a protected world of innocence and there is no art or intellectual understanding for them to flee to when their innocence is taken away and painful insight comes.

Harriet Andersson and Lars Ekborg as Monika and Harry in *Monika.*

When we meet Monika, we feel she is already deprived of most of her innocence, aware of life and pain, but masking it with romantic illusion. She clings to this illusion at the end of the film. Having abandoned her husband and child, she seeks another man who can sustain her make-believe a little longer. In the midst of her romantic idyl on the island, Monika fights to sustain her illusion, willing to steal, lie, or starve to keep it going. Her view is constantly romantic. She tells Harry that she is pregnant and reacts like a character in one of the cheap films she loves. She smiles, hugs Harry, and then behaves as if her announcement has no consequences in the real world. However, it causes Harry, totally innocent, to begin to peel away his illusions. He begins to feel the weight of responsibility and the need to accept it. His moment of crisis comes when they return to the city; he begins to hold down a job and go to school, the baby comes, and he discovers Monika's infidelity. His innocence crumbles. He is unprotected, burdened by responsibility, determined to go on with his life but unsure of what it means.

In *Monika* there is also the embryonic motif of childhood hostility toward an adult world with which the child cannot communicate. In one curious scene, Hasse, Monika's brother who appears to be about ten years old, plays a bitter trick on his father, creating a small explosion before him in the rubble of their squalid courtyard. This is never expanded or explained, but presented for us to conclude, probably, that the boy is attempting to punish the adult, get back at him for pains inflicted about which we are told nothing.

Secrets of Women (1952) opens with a scene expressing the burden of responsibility for children that preys on Bergman. The mothers are out calling for the children, obviously afraid that something has happened to them, relieved when they find them well. The children are a responsibility which helps bind the women of the film to their husbands. In the first of the three stories told in flashback, Kaj, just before his seduction of Marta, finds a doll in the water and fishes it out, placing it conspicuously on the ground near the beach house at the same point where, as we had already seen, Marta would be searching for her temporarily missing child. Kaj's wife, we have been told, is pregnant. For both, the doll is a reminder of the responsibility which will later face Marta and of the fact that her action is one of an attempt to retain childhood innocence. She accepts Kaj's seduction because she is on the brink of accepting her own insight and compromise and he is a reminder of her make-believe world of the past.

When Marta finishes her story, Bergman returns us to the island before the next story begins. Each story is preceded by the appearance of the children. It is not even clear whose child is whose. The children are there together and constantly evident. One of the children breaks in to announce that "Peter says angels have propellers." There is no reaction from the mothers, who ignore the remark. It is, quite simply, a child's attempt to relate his real world with the fantasy world of God, fear, and lip-service good intentions.

In the second story, when Rakel discovers that she is pregnant she walks by the river and encounters a mother with a baby. Rakel smiles and the baby returns the smile in what appears to be a conventional film encounter between a romantic expectant mother and a pleasant infant. However, at that moment, a crippled old man appears and the baby responds to him with the same smile it had given Rakel. The sight is disconcerting to the girl, reminding her of the fact that life is cruel, that age and death are inevitable. There is no such understanding or even hint of it in the infant. In her apartment as she waits to go to the hospital, there are multiple hints about the future, the passing of time. Time and clocks intrude on her consciousness. A dark, indistinct figure appears at her door and retreats.

The theme of youthful innocence and the possible redemption of love played upon in *Monika* and *Summer Interlude* appears in *Secrets of Women*. Throughout the telling of the stories of romantic crisis, disillusionment, and acceptance, Rakel's teenage sister has sat without listening. At the end of the film, the girl runs away with the young man who is destined to become, like other men in the film, an extension of the Lobelius business empire. Rakel tells the eldest Lobelius about the runaways, but he makes no attempt to stop them. They will, he says, spend a summer—figurative or literal—together, come to the end of their innocence, and accept the adult world. He and Bergman know this is inevitable, but they do not wish to deprive the young people of that summer, the brief time between the fears of childhood and the pain of adulthood, when they can experience innocent love.

In *Sawdust and Tinsel* (1953) Bergman continues to explore his view of the young child. Albert, the ringmaster, talks to Anne about spending time with his wife and children, but there is no warmth or real affection in what he says. This is evident when he first encounters his older son, age nine, in his wife's shop. Albert is uncomfortable and the child coldly observant. "You're my father," says the boy. Albert nods. They understand each other and have no more to communicate. The child will allow no insincere sympathy or affection. Later, the boy listens at the door while Albert and his wife are talking. The boy is absorbing, storing information, trying to form pictures of good and evil.

In *Smiles of a Summer Night* (1955), Fredrik Egerman's love for his young wife Anne is born out of his wish to sustain himself by association with youthful innocence. He wants to feel, live that summer before the pain of insight and adulthood, but it is too late for him. His

wife, still innocent, cannot relate to him as a lover, cannot give him
that which he needs to give him comfort. Anne is a child who plays
with dolls, has no function, remains a vrigin. Fredrik's son Henrik is
the innocent with whom Anne is naturally matched. They both sustain
themselves by make-believe. Henrik's make-believe involves his romanticized love for Anne, his role playing as man-of-God. It is innocent
make-believe because Henrik and Anne, for all their childish torment,
have no insight into the real reason for the need to love, a need emerg
ing from man's loneliness.

In an exchange between father and son which looks forward to a
more serious exchange between father and son on the same subject in
Through a Glass Darkly (in fact, the father will be played by the same
actor, Cunnar Bjornstrand), we find:

> HENRIK: So young men cannot love.
> FREDRIK: Yes, of course. A young man always loves himself, loves his
> self-love, and his love of love itself.
> HENRIK: (ironic) But at your mature age, of course, one knows
> what it means to love.
> FREDRIK: I think so.
> HENRIK: (ironic) That must be wonderful.
> FREDRIK: It's terrible, my son, and one doesn't know how to stand it.
> HENRIK: Are you being sincere now, Father?

Henrik's irony drops and father and son come briefly together in a
moment of honesty.

As Frid, the groom, later tells Petra, the young lovers are "smitten"
by love as "both a gift and as a punishment."

Children and innocence are not a main theme in *The Seventh Seal*
(1956), but the film ends with a child being told to, and trying to,
understand the adult world. Jof describes the characters being led off
by death: "They dance away from the dawn and it's a solemn dance
toward the dark lands, while the rain washes their faces and cleans the
salt of the tears from their cheeks." The description is an attempt to
extract some meaning from the act of death, some salving understanding. Bergman tells us that Jof's "son Mikael, has listened to his words"
and "crawls up to Mia (his mother) and sits down in her lap."

To Bergman, Isak Borg in *Wild Strawberries* (1957) is an adult who
has never come to terms with his loss of innocence and the terror it
revealed to him. Isak tells us early in the film that he detests "emotional outbursts, women's tears, and the crying of children." The tears
of children are a reminder of Isak's lost youth, his departed innocence,

and a reminder of his unhappiness as a child. At the end of the film, however, he tells us that "Whenever I am restles or sad, I usually try to recall memories from my childhood to calm down." The contradiction is that whatever pleasant memories he has are of the time of ignorant youth which he never fully enjoyed. He is touched by the young people he picks up on the road who project the soothing innocence which Isak seeks in his fantasy.

A particularly revealing note on Isak's fascination with childhood comes from Bergman himself and gives us increased understanding of Bergman's conception of other children in his films. An article by Charles Turner in the May 1960 issue of *Films in Review* dealt with Victor Seastrom, the Swedish director who played Isak. The article was written as a memorial to Seastrom and, perhaps, for this reason Bergman contributed some excerpts from the diary he had kept while directing *Wild Strawberries*. "I cannot escape," wrote Bergman, "that the old man is a strangely aged child, who, at birth, was bereft of parents and brothers and sisters, a child who unceasingly sought a security which was unceasingly denied. Therefore, he strongly rejects all insincere sympathy or affection. He abhors those who grasp at him with soft, coddling hands, and he scorns half-hearted pity."

The entry tells us much about Isak, but also looks forward to the coldly staring children of *The Silence, Persona,* and *Winter Light* and the adult-child, Johan, in *Hour of the Wolf.*

In *Wild Strawberries,* we also encounter the adult tormented by life, unable to accept love, resisting the responsibility for bringing life into the world. When Marianne, Isak's daughter-in-law, corners Evald, her husband, to discuss her pregnancy, Evald responds that he does not want to create another potentially tormented human being, a being which will give him earthly responsibilities, bind him to life. "This life," he says, "disgusts me and I don't think that I need responsibility which will force me to exist another day longer than I want to." While Bergman understands Evald, ultimately he has us side with Marianne who calls Evald a coward. Life cannot be avoided.

In *The Magician* (1958), the innocent is Sanna, the servant girl, who Bergman tells us is "about sixteen." Her first words remind us of the honest responses of the children in *Sawdust and Tinsel* and *Winter Light.* "I think," says Sanna of Vogler and his troupe, "they are dangerous people and we must guard ourselves against them." Sanna senses the assault which Vogler and those he has brought can make on her, an assault that can destroy her innocence and bring her into the adult world. Sanna is afraid. Fear permeates her actions. She "cries in confused anguish" when Simson, Vogler's coach driver, and Sara, the other maid, come together, touch hands, obviously indicate that they will have a sexual relationship, the kind of relationship that symbolizes the end of innocence that threatens Sanna. It is at this point that Vogler's grandmother "moves to the chair next to Sanna and nudges her." She becomes Bergman's instrument of magic and wisdom to ease Sanna into the adult world instead of having her experience it with the jarring pain of Marie in *Summer Interlude*. Uncle Erland brought a false message of solace. The grandmother brings a real, difficult message of love as necessity and salvation.

The grandmother says she is a witch and responds to Sanna's cries: "Now go along to bed and the witch will give you a gift. Do what I say, little ant. I only want the best for you."

Later, the grandmother goes to Sanna's room and presents her with an ear, "a gift to console you."

> GRANDMOTHER: It's an ear. And if you whisper your wishes into this ear, you'll get what you ask for. But only on one condition.
> SANNA: What kind of condition?
> GRANDMOTHER: You can only wish for things that live, are living, or can become alive.
> SANNA: I don't understand what you mean.

The grandmother offers Sanna the understanding that she can learn to cope with life by accepting life and what it offers in terms of physical love, love of a woman for a man or a woman for a child. Again, the message is essentially the same as that given to Albert by Frost at the end of *Sawdust and Tinsel* or David to Minus, as we will see, in *Through a Glass Darkly*. Sanna is not quite convinced, still in fear, unable to deal with her roused sexual feelings and fear of the unknown.

The grandmother puts her message into song, a song of love which drives away Sanna's fear and lets her sleep, but before she sleeps "the room is filled by a white light which disappears almost immediately. Sanna awakens."

> SANNA: Now it will thunder.
> GRANDMOTHER: Far away.
> SANNA: I'm not afraid of thunder. (Sleeps.)

The lightning flash, much like the sudden light behind Pastor Ericsson in *Winter Light*, is a flash of understanding, of insight. Sanna realizes that after the light will come something fearful—life, understanding—but she is unafraid, ready to accept.

In his screenplay, Bergman describes a scene at the end of the film in which "Sanna has accepted the grandmother's advice and plunged into life unafraid of both the sexual and metaphysical challenge.

In *The Virgin Spring* (1959), Bergman further explored and dramatized both his concepts of inquiring: terror filled childhood and youthful innocence at the brink of understanding and insight. Even though he did not write the screenplay, he most certainly chose to make the film accommodate his thinking and artistic development.

The child in the film is the young brother of the herdsmen who rape the girl. The girl (played significantly by Birgitta Pettersson, the same actress who played Sanna) who is raped is Bergman's "innocent."

At first the boy is eager, interested, curious concerning his brothers and their plan to trap the girl. He helps willingly, but when she is raped and murdered he becomes frightened. His world of terror and fear has become real. Death, about which he knows nothing, can come swiftly, meaninglessly. He tries to cover the gril's body with dirt and leaves, but cannot bring himself to finish. He is fascinated and repulsed by the corpse. He is unable to eat, to cope with the process of living. All he can do is register fear, a fear which cannot be overcome by the beating and threats of his brothers. The boy has no insight, only fear and horror. The beggar tries to comfort the boy at the farmhouse by telling him that, in some way, he is one with the outside world. The boy is uncomforted by the words of the man "who may have been a priest." It is too late for the boy to accept a vague metaphysical answer. His life has been closed like a telescope. His initiation, insight, and death come within a day, before he can even begin to understand them.

Karin, the girl, too experiences insight and death, sex and pain, within a single day—actually, in the space of a few minutes. Like Sanna, we see her on the verge of sexual knowledge and insight, close to a loss of protective innocence and ignorance. She is unafraid of the herdsmen, of whom we, the audience, are immediately afraid. She is confident of her power, her control, her beauty, her youth. Her death comes almost the instant she realizes that life and sex are deadly, not games. She dies a symbolic virgin. She dies before she comes to the knowledge of life which Ingeri, the pregnant servant, well understands. In a tragic way, Ingeri is to Karin as Petra is to Anne in a comic way in *Smiles of a Summer Night*, but in *The Virgin Spring* the relationship is bitter, not understanding. The cleansing, mystical water which flows in the spring beneath Karin's body at the end of the film represents to Bergman the memory of innocence, which is all too brief. This echo of flowing water as a reminder of loss of innocence appears in subsequent films even more strongly than in those which came before *The Virgin Spring*. Bergman's artists—in *Through a Glass Darkly*, *Persona*, *Hour of the Wolf* and *Shame*—surround themselves with water, live on islands, as Bergman himself does, to try to protect at least their memory of innocence.

Through a Glass Darkly (1961) brings Bergman's concept of youthful innocence and the hope for a salving love to a clear artistic and intellectual statement. Karin, in a sense, has been resurrected from *The Virgin Spring*, robbed of innocence, forced to try to see and accept the God everyone tells her is there, a literal God which both she and Bergman find impossible to accept. She goes mad trying to reconcile her feelings and knowledge with her fear. It is Minus, fifteen years old, who becomes the focus of the film. In their first talk together, Karin mocks Minus's attempt to be serious about the need for their father's success: "And no need to put on such an air of injured innocence. I love you, little Minus. But it's horrible how tall you've grown."

Karin realizes that her brother is still innocent, has not yet faced the crisis she is facing, is concerned about things which are not of real importance. Her reference to his growth—Bergman says in his screenplay that "Karin puts her arm around her brother. It's rather uncomfortable since he's tall and walks brusquely with an impatient gait."—points out that he is on the verge of coming to physical manhood and understanding, and is "impatient" to get there.

Minus is in agony about the sound of his sister and her husband making real love in the room next to his, as Henrik was in agony about his thoughts of his father and Anne making love. Like Henrik, Minus's view of love and sex is unreal. In the play he puts on for his father, Minus romanticizes, talks of his "heart's betrothed." The scene is remarkably like that in Chekov's *The Seagull* in which the romantic and innocent young man puts on a play for his actress mother. Both plays end in humiliation for the young playwrights.

"What is life," says Minus in his play, "to a real artist?" To Bergman and to Minus's father David it is everything, the source of all anguish. David, at the end of the play, "feels he should applaud." There is no communication, no attempt at communication between disillusioned father and innocent, romantic son.

"Think," says Minus, "if for just once in my life I could talk to Daddy. But he's so absorbed in his own affairs."

David and Minus do begin to talk tentatively and cautiously as Minus shows signs that he is moving into manhood.

MINUS: Last summer I found it as easy to walk on my hands as on my feet. Now I've grown so tall I can't keep my balance any more.

DAVID: Same thing with me.

MINUS: Ah. You mean spiritually. I understand.

Minus is proud of himself for understanding, which he does, but he does not yet feel. He stalks along beside his father.

DAVID: Are you writing anything yourself nowadays?

MINUS: Plays.

DAVID: May I read them?

MINUS: No, thanks. (Pause) Sorry, I didn't mean to hurt your feelings. But so far I think they're rotten.

DAVID: Have you written much?

MINUS: This summer I've put together thirteen three-acters and an opera.

DAVID: Whew.

MINUS: Yes, it pours out. The devil it does. Isn't it that way with you too?

DAVID: No.

MINUS: What did you think of Karin's and my play, yesterday evening? Honestly.

DAVID: I couldn't see anything wrong with it.

MINUS: I thought it was shit.

Minus's growth, physical, artistic, and emotional, is evident, but his father neither wants to nor can help him to take the last step which will cause him lasting pain.

Later, when Minus finds himself unable to help his spiritually tormented and increasingly psychotic sister, he goes to his room "throws himself on his knees on the floor and clasps his hands, bends his head and presses his hands to his lips" whispering "God . . . God . . . help us." When no answer comes, and it never does in a Bergman film, Minus goes back to his sister, tries to comfort her.

"Minus is sitting somewhere in eternity with his sick sister in his arms," says Bergman. "He is empty, exhausted, frozen. Reality, as he has known it until now, has been shattered, ceased to exist. Neither in his dreams nor his fantasies has he known anything to correspond to this moment of weightlessness and grief. His mind has forced its way through the membrane of merciful ignorance. From this moment on, his senses will change and harden, his receptivity will become sharpened, as he goes from the make-believe world of innocence to the torment of insight."

It is a precise, concise statement of Bergman's view of the moment of the loss of protective innocence. The film then turns to and ends with another discussion between Minus and David.

> MINUS: Reality burst and I fell out. It's like in a dream, though real. Anything can happen—anything Daddy.
> DAVID: Yes, I know.

For the first time in the film, father and son touch, really communicate. David answers his son's statement that he cannot live with this new understanding by saying: "Yes, you can. But you must have something to hold on to." Minus asks if it is God that he should believe in, but David does not respond.

"No Daddy," he concludes, "it's no good. God doesn't exist in my world." He calls for proof of God to contradict his statement. David answers that his own hopes lie in "the knowledge that love exists as something real in the world of men." To Minus, the words are "Terribly unreal." Minus gets his father's permission and runs away, looks out at the vast, deep and, possibly, cleansing water and finds solace in the fact that he has communicated with his father, has begun to come to adulthood with the possibility of further balm in the words of love given to him.To himself and to us Minus whispers, "Daddy spoke to me."

Now whether we interpret "Daddy" as a mystical representation of God or anti-God, or simply accept what has happened without interpretation, the hope of love does touch Minus. It is true that Minus does not fully understand this communication from the intellectual adult, just as Johan does not fully understand the communication from Ester at the end of *The Silence*, but in *Through a Glass Darkly* the message of the possibility of love is affirmative, a real hope. This statement, a refinement of that given to Marie by the ballet master, to Albert by Frost, to Henrik by Fredrik Egerman, to Sanna by Vogler's grandmother, is the closest Bergman can come to an affirmation of existence, outside of the possible compensations of art which, according to the artists in his films, he does not find fully satisfying either.

This affirmation of love as compensation for the loss of the make-believe of innocence is vague, certainly as vague for Bergman as for us. Following his clearest statement of it in *Through a Glass Darkly*, Bergman appears to have stepped back, re-examined his view of children even more personally, and come to an even less affirmative conclusion.

Starting with *Winter Light* (1962), the youthful innocents, teenagers on the verge of insight, disappear and Bergman moves back,

seems to begin again, picking up the darker, tortured thread of child-
hood only hinted at in *Secrets of Women, Monika, Sawdust and
Tinsel, The Seventh Seal, Wild Strawberries,* and *The Virgin Spring.*
Even in *Smiles of a Summer Night,* although he says nothing, we
might wonder what we are to assume is going on in the mind of little
Fredrik, Desiree's (and probably Fredrik's) small son.

Winter Light also raises the question of how frightened adults deal
with, communicate with, and view equally frightened children. The
question also becomes one concerning the failure of adults to find love
and the concurrent failure to communicate with children. The child
exists in stark honesty to plague the adult consciousness, point a finger
of guilt.

In *Winter Light* when Thomas, the pastor, says "Let us now pray
together, even as our Lord Jesus hath taught us," Bergman tells us in
his screen play that "Doris Apelblad, who is only five, yawns and kicks
her legs; she is like a regular pendulum. Her mother takes her hands
and holds them. At the same time, she grimaces disapprovingly. The
pendulum stops for the moment. Thomas kneels."

Doris does not accept or even listen to the false ritual before her.
She is living, vibrant. Her tongue touches the front of the pew, tactile
and alive. Her reaction is honest, alive, a small but real challenge to
the formalized ritual before her in which few of the participating
adults believe.

Later Thomas goes with Marta to her classroom. He sits at a desk as
Doris had sat, or rather squirmed, in a pew. A boy comes in and proceeds to give an honest sermon to the pastor, unlike the false one
Thomas had given. In the screenplay the conversation is longer than
in the finished film.

The boy says he is ten years old, has no intention of being confirmed;
in response to the pastor's question about what he will be when he
grows up, the boy "shifts his glance and looks Thomas straight in the
eyes with an expression of indulgent disdain" as he replies that he intends to be a spaceman.

The child is repeating Doris's message that religious ritual and spiritual incomprehensibility are worthless and false. To be a spaceman is
to live in the future, believe in it, to go metaphorically into God's
heaven and challenge him or replace him.

Thomas understands and smiles.

In *The Silence* (1963) Bergman gave his fullest attention to the
problem of communication between adult and child and what the

adult had, if anything, to offer the child, the child who lives in fear and confusion.

Robin Wood points out the trauma in Bergman's childhood that epitomized his fear. According to Wood:

> In *Hour of the Wolf* the artist Johan Borg (Max von Sydow) describes a childhood punishment that has affected all his subsequent development: he was locked in a completely dark cupboard in which, he was told, there lurked a small creature who would bite his toes off. When he was at last released (after experiencing the most extreme terror) his father asked him how severe a beating he deserved, and he (Bergman) asked for it to be as severe as possible. Questioned about this story in an interview, Bergman said that it was taken from a personal experience: "This happened forty or forty-two years ago, and not just once. It was a ritual. It's amazing I came out of it with my life."

Punishment of self to drive away the demons of fear, fear of the unknown, stays with Johan, who as an adult concludes that there is nothing that can drive away fear. I believe that the boy Johan we see in *The Silence* is also the boy we see in *Persona* and the adult Johan we see in *Hour of the Wolf*. It is Bergman taking himself from tortured boyhood to the torment of adulthood in which he as an artist cannot come to terms with his fears, cannot find consolation in life.

It is both interesting and significant that we find the adult Johan's last name is Borg, the same as that of the old man in *Wild Strawberries*. When we leave Johan he is, like Isak, at the end of his life, but there is no memory of wild strawberries and joys of youth, only that which we see in *The Silence* and *Persona*. Bergman's diary entry about the character Isak which I have already quoted (see the middle of page 16) is painfully applicable to Johan in the three films to which we now turn.

In *The Silence*, Johan is ten years old, as was the boy in *Winter Light*. The film opens with his trying to see what is happening around him. He looks at us, touches the glass of the train window in which he is riding, has an intellectual contact with his aunt Ester and a tactile, emotional one with his mother, Anna, but his face is blank; he gives no sign that these contacts have meaning for him. His aunt is sick and he is sent out of the compartment. He looks in through a window, a barrier between him and those whom he is supposed to love and who are supposed to love him. He turns to look out the train window at the fantasy of passing images, the light and darkness, the row of passing

tanks—industrial, warlike, phallic. He is enclosed by glass, isolated as
he watches the world around him, tries to make sense of it. He is
frightened by the conductors and returns to his mother.

Gunnel Lindblom (left) as Anna, Jorgen Lindstrom as Johan, and Ingrid
Thulin as Ester in *The Silence*.

The opening sequence is a compression of that which happens
throughout the film, in which Johan is torn between the smothering
affection and sexual oppression of his mother and the intellectual
promise of his aunt. He wanders through the hotel, finding at a slower
pace the same things he had seen in the train.

Johan identifies with the dwarfs he encounters, seeing them as stifled
adults, perhaps images of how he sees himself. He encounters erotic
art, sees the tanks in the street, is confronted by the black image of
death (and religion) in the old waiter as he had been by the conductor
on the train. Johan is cast out by the dwarfs who realize that he is not
really one of them. The boy rejects the waiter and his images of death,
his old man sexual symbolism of castration and repression. Johan's
amulet is his gun which he turns phallically on all that challenges him.
When the dwarfs reject him, he urinates on the hotel wall, showing in

an act of sexual-scatological defiance his anger with the adult world he cannot understand.

He is vaguely aware of the sexual trap he is in. He knows his mother is with the waiter. He cannot read to his aunt, an intellectual act, but he can try to escape creatively in a puppet show. In the show he has Punch beat Judy, a substitute for his mother and the other adults with whom he cannot communicate, who frustrate and confuse him. Punch is frightened and talks in a funny language. The moment is artistic, cathartic. The boy breaks and cries, but he is careful to hide his tears behind the chair. His emotions, like his mother, have betrayed him, hurt him, confused him. He goes to his aunt for comfort, and she tries to give him all that is in her power to give, intellectual understanding. She is a translator and she promises to try to communicate with him, give him words in the foreign language.

The boy's frustration is communicated in rudimentary art, in the puppet show and in the drawing he makes of the face with fangs. He tries to hide by reading the fairy tales of Lermontov. He escapes, as best he can, in artistic expression. At the end of the film, Johan leaves with his mother and finds himself again in a train compartment with her. Whereas at the beginning he clung to her and the potentially sick and erotic affection she gave, he now turns to the intellectual communication of his aunt, the words in a foreign language. According to Bergman, the film ends as "Johan's face is pale with the effort of trying to understand the strange language. This secret message."

The adult world remains a mystery to Johan at the end of the film. He is confused, trying to communicate with adults, perhaps increasingly aware that he may have to do without emotional communication and settle for intellectual understanding.

The next time we see Johan is in *Persona* (1966). The filmic images that pass before us on the screen at the start of the film have much in common with the images that flickered past Johan through the train window at the start of *The Silence*. When the images slow down, stop like the train, we see Johan, the same actor although he is not identified by name as Johan. Before him is Lermontov's tales, between him and us, between him and the central core of the film, there is a glass, a barrier to direct contact and communication, a glass like a train window or the conscious lens of a camera. Three years have passed since *The Silence*. He is thirteen. He appears dead when we first see him, as, perhaps, he has been dead in Bergman's mind until this film when he was emotionally able to resurrect him. As he did at the beginning of *The Silence*, the boy looks at us, touches the glass barrier, seems to try to communicate with us. We come behind him and see him touching the glass, trying to communicate with, make sense of the changing face of a woman or women. It may be the two women he will see in the film, Elisabeth and Alma, but it could also be his mother and aunt or a combination of all four. The visual implication is that he will try to learn from, understand the two women he will see before him.

Two children are seen within the central narrative of the film, both about the age of Johan. Both children appear to Elisabeth, the actress who has decided not to speak, to retreat from life. One child is her son, whom we see in a photograph. She tears up the picture, refuses to try to communicate with him. It is not a strange hatred which makes her tear the picture, but a realization with Bergman of the horror of existence she cannot communicate to her son or anyone. In the films of Ingmar Bergman, the withdrawn intellectuals and artists who bitterly see the horror of existence are paired with a vibrant, outgoing figure, an almost earth mother or earth daughter figure who knows what life is and is willing to face it. In *Wild Strawberries*, for example, Marianne fills this role opposite Evald. Marta and Thomas are another such pair in *Winter Light*. In *Persona*, Alma seems to fill such a role, but the outcome is strikingly different. It is more a matter of Alma changing and seeing through Elisabeth's eyes, than Elisabeth and, possibly, Bergman and his audience accepting some hope of love from Alma. The other child Elisabeth sees is in a photograph too. The boy is the same general age as her son and Johan who, in a sense, is her son. The boy in the second photograph is a Jew being marched to a concentration camp by a Nazi. (In my opinion there is an intentional link between the tanks and impending war in *The Silence* and the real war in *Shame* in which the protagonist is a Jew like the boy in the photograph. In *Shame* the situation is such that total chaos has taken over. Bergman seems to be destroying his world.) In *Persona* the Jewish boy is seen by Elisabeth as one who has come to full horror, the terrible realization of life that she has held within her, away from her own son although she knows she cannot protect him.

At the end of the film, Johan seems to have gotten nowhere. The glass barrier is still before him. Bergman has been unable to give him an answer as he is unable to give himself an answer.

In *Hour of the Wolf* (1968) we again see Johan. He is now an adult, but he still has no answers. He still seeks personification of evil in drawing people with fangs. His childhood fears have become adult fears. Johan has observed life and come to a realization of its horror. This horror manifests itself in a childhood madness of horror films in which he is tortured by vampires, ghouls, and zombies and in which he, himself, almost becomes a Frankenstein monster.

The puppet show in the *Hour of the Wolf* is a bizarre re-creation of Johan's puppet show in *The Silence*. The words of the puppet are indistinct, as if in a foreign language, but the puppet is real, a live person. The art is no longer a childhood escape, but an instrument of further torture.

Johan sees those about him—including his wife who wants to help him and offers him a child as parasites, a horrible responsibility, an imposition on him as an artist who can give them no answers, and a torment to him as a human being who has no answers for himself.

The solace of love given by David to Minus in *Through a Glass Darkly* is of no use to Johan. His wife offers it simply, beautifully, but he cannot accept it. Johan is driven by his love of Veronica Vogler, an actress, an illusion which both draws and repels him, giving him the false promise of escape and the certainty of humiliation like that of his art. In *Persona* Johan had watched a battle between an actress named Vogler and an emotional, earthly woman named Alma. The promise or at least the hope of love had not been clearly rejected, but it certainly had not been accepted. In *Hour of the Wolf*, Johan is torn between the actress who is clearly illusionary and parasitic, both a vampire and a ghoul, and Alma who offers him love which he rejects. Johan can accept neither.

There is one child in *Hour of the Wolf*. Johan mentions a son from a previous marriage. We never see the boy. There is only one reference to him. The boy we do see is a vampire-like creature in a dreamlike story Johan tells Alma. Johan says that he killed the boy while fishing. The boy had come up to him, hovered frighteningly, threatening behind him, counted three fish as if in mockery of the trinity, and attacked Johan when told to leave. We see with Johan the body of the boy in the water, bloody and haunting. The occurrence is almost certainly no more real than Johan's other horror nightmares in the film, but it does represent a symbolic killing of his son, a son who, as Evald had said in *Wild Strawberries*, forces him to remain alive is a responsibility, a vampire-like responsibility with which he cannot cope. Like Bergman, Johan has turned to his art as solace for, sublimation of, his inability to understand life and, when faced directly, his inability to accept the hope of love.

The prospect of Alma's coming child is not a joy to Johan, but the burden of further responsibility, further holding him to a life which is meaningless. When he shoots Alma, he is trying to destroy the child and the continuation of the cycle of life. Johan's death is a suicide, but he is also murdered by his fears.

Bergman does not have Alma die. We know that she will live and have the child. The cycle will go on. At both the beginning and end of the film a voice questions Alma. The voice is Bergman's and ours asking her what sustains her, what hope can she have.

Her answer is quiet, almost a shrug. It is not presented as a philosophical statement. She endures. She exists. She loves. Even if all else is taken away Bergman cannot deny that people endure and love exists. That, says Bergman, is all we have to sustain us.

3

SEXUAL THEMES IN THE FILMS OF INGMAR BERGMAN

Richard A. Blake, S.J.

. . . .

The rape scene in *The Virgin Spring* (1960) was at first considered too vivid for American audiences, and so was cut from the prints released in this country. What was left was an unmistakable suggestion of the evil intentions and activities of the three goatherds, but the violence and brutality of the act were cut out. American critics who had seen the Swedish or German prints were horrified, for the carefully constructed balance between the ruthless violence of the crime and the brutality of the father's revenge was gone. The original version proposed the theme that evil drives the righteous to take evil means to right the wrong, but the American audience was told that evil precipitates greater evil. If Bergman can be described as "making a statement" in his films, the deletion of a few feet of "obscene" material changes the content of the statement appreciably.

What is often enough lacking from the endless discussion and litigation on obscenity and censorship in films is a reflection on the film medium itself. Film cuts close to the skin of reality. Even at its most artistic, film gives the illusion that it is presenting real people, doing real things. In a documentary film this is certainly true; the film is a recording device and by structuring and commenting upon "reality" the filmmaker can frequently make a powerful statement on the human condition.

At the other end of the spectrum, however, is a highly artificial medium. Characters come to life under the urgings of a scriptwriter, professional actors breathe their own life's breath into them, and directors

From *Sexual Behavior*, Vol. I, No. 5 (August 1971), pp. 35-43. Reprinted by permission of Interpersonal Publications, Inc. and the author.

like Bergman refine their personalities. In *The Virgin Spring* the audience is not watching a record of a sexual assault in medieval Sweden, rather it is watching an artist's reflection on the human condition, imaged in terms of a senseless rape.

The problem is that most people watch movies as entertainment only, and, as a result, discussions on censorship often center on film as offering material for the voyeur. Nudity and sexual activity are treated as though they were glimpses of reality and the debate centers on the questions, "What right does the filmmaker have to subject us to this kind of material?", or conversely, "What right does a censor have to deprive me of this kind of experience?" The fact that film is an art form, using light and shadow images to communicate an idea, seems lost.

An investigation of the films of Ingmar Bergman may help to illustrate this point. His treatment of sexuality is frank, graphic, and at times even revolting, but his stature as a filmmaker is so overpowering that no one could seriously accuse him of pandering. Two themes are apparent in his metaphorical use of human sexuality: (1) sexual behavior reveals man's inner striving for love and communion with others, and (2) sterility and impotence are signs of the artist's inability to create and thus fulfill his inner needs.

Torment

The very first Bergman script to be produced, *Torment* set the pattern for many of his later films. In one of the key scenes, the hero, Jan-Erik, is trying to study for an examination which will qualify him for the university. He has just been rejected by Bertha, the girl at the tobacco store, and as he tries to concentrate on his studies he is torn between the books and his eagerness to return to her. On the desk is a human skull, and as he draws closer to the inevitable decision he stands and the camera reveals on the wall behind the desk a figurine of a nude torso of Rubens' proportions. In that image the major theme of Bergman's work is captured: the choice is between love and death, and each man takes his pick.

On the brink of exhaustion, Jan-Erik has a dream in which the love-death alternatives are presented to him a second time. Caligula, a malicious Latin teacher, appears with his textbook and begins to question him, but as he does Bertha also appears and beckons him; Caligula is not moved and Bertha finally turns away. With intense satisfaction Caligula announces that he will have to execute Jan-Erik for being insufficiently acquainted with dead languages. He leans over the boy and lowers his pen menacingly toward his forehead, as though the pen were the instrument of execution.

Bergman does use sex as a metaphor for love, but he is quite careful to avoid identifying the two. Phallic images are inevitably associated with Caligula. The pointer he wields in the classroom is a symbol of power which he uses to intimidate and dominate the boys in his class. Early in the film, he asks Bertha to open a box of cigars for him, he takes one and then tells her to light it for him. When he has exercised this dominance over her, he notices that she has cut her hand in the process. Ceremoniously he takes her hand and sucks the blood from the wound, thus suggesting vampirism in addition to his cruelty; he draws life from the wounds he inflicts on others. His sexuality involves power and domination, not love.

During the next few years many of Bergman's film heroes follow Jan-Erik in their quest for ideal love which will bring them fulfillment and happiness. But in each case some misfortune strikes the young lovers and dashes their plans. Society in its many guises, usually represented by a parent or another member of the older generation, enters into a conspiracy to destroy even the possibility of love.

Summer Interlude

In 1950, at the age of thirty-two, Bergman made *Summer Interlude* (also entitled *Illicit Interlude*) and seems to have come to grips with his world. In this neglected masterpiece, the heroine, Mari, is a moderately successful ballerina who reflects on her life through a series of flashbacks. She had one love in her life when she was sixteen, and as she looks into her make-up mirror she realizes that that was indeed a long time ago. During that summer of happiness, Mari faces the typical Bergman alternatives of love or death. In the family home she is haunted by the memory of her dead mother, whom she is supposed to resemble. Henrik, too, lives with an aunt who is dying of cancer, but she refuses to die. Happiness for both the young people can be found only outside the death filled atmosphere of their families. In a hidden cove they share wild strawberries with one another, and this image, for Bergman, always indicates a gift of happiness and immortality. They play on the beaches like children, they kiss at first tentatively, and finally share their love fully in sexual union.

At this peak of happiness, as the autumn winds start to blow across the island, Henrik takes one last dive into the chilly waters, strikes the rocks and dies. This is typical of the early Bergman: Mari is crushed and bitter. She says, "If there were a God, I'd spit in his face." Taking the advice of an uncle, again a voice of death, she "builds a wall around herself" and dedicates herself to her dancing. She dates a journalist, named Nystrom, but broods on the memory of Henrik.

In one of the loveliest scenes Bergman ever filmed, Mari confronts reality and herself head-on. After a dress rehearsal she sits in front of her make-up table, unhappy with her mask and costume and at the same time lacking the courage to step out of her dancer's role and rejoin the world she left for the stage. The ballet master visits her, and, significantly he is dressed for the part of Dr. Copellius in *Tales of Hoffmann*; in the opera he is the optician who gave eyes to the doll-maker, so that his dolls could come to life as real women. Through this conversation she realizes her plight; she removes the make-up with a sense of joy, and she resolves to allow Nystrom to enter the wall she has built.

Nystrom, as presented in the film, is far from an idealized lover. By Henrik's standards, he is quite ordinary, a bachelor who has grown coarse through years in a newspaper office. By the standards of the ballet, he is simply a misfit who does not understand the world of art. But what Mari has realized in her reflections and memories is that she is a real woman, nearing thirty and with the end of her career fast approaching. Her memories of Henrik were overly romantic and unrealistic, simply because he has been dead for thirteen years. Nystrom is real, and alive, and he loves her. In a final scene, she rushes over to him as she is preparing for her entrance in *Swan Lake*, stands on points and kisses him. She has been able to bring him into her world.

What is new in the ending of *Summer Interlude* is the element of acceptance, both of the self and of the beloved. Only when Mari was honest enough to face herself and understand who she was and how destructive her romanticized dreams were, could she open herself to a new sexual relationship and a new life. When she realized that she could love Nystrom despite his very obvious limitations as a human being, then she could receive the love he had to give her. The schoolgirl fantasies are gone for Mari, and she is ready to accept the real world.

Secrets of Women

The theme of acceptance gives Mari a way out of her self-enclosure in *Summer Interlude*, but in *Secrets of Women* (also released as *Waiting Women*) the theme is central. The wives of four brothers are waiting on an island for the arrival of their husbands, and each in turn tells a story about her marriage.

In the final episode, which is the most pointed of the three, a wealthy couple on the brink of middle age are returning from a formal dinner and are imprisoned in an elevator overnight. The dialogue is as witty as anything Bergman ever wrote, and in the course of their conversation they discover that they have let their marriage deteriorate into a businesslike relationship. He has been too concerned with his company to notice her at all; her playful teasing reveals more than a bit of contempt for his pomposity and impracticality. Their pretenses are shattered, and in a solitude of the elevator they sexually reaffirm their relationship. They resolve to spend the day together like honeymooners, but just as they enter their apartment he remembers an important business appointment. There is anger and frustration, of course, but the sexual imagery has revealed the nature of their marriage: love will be an almost accidental element in their lives. When they experience it, they are grateful but they really can't plan for it or expect it. Modern society doesn't permit that kind of love and fulfillment for busy people. The couple learn that they must accept this kind of existence, because, given the personalities and circumstances of their lives, they have much to be grateful for.

Romantic expectations from love are not deflated that easily, and as the husbands and wives dance in the living room of their summer home the son of the eldest couple elopes with the sister of one of the wives. As they plan their escape, he delivers a manifesto of youth in which he condemns the mercantile interests of his father and the idiocy of the university. They escape in a motorboat, but have great difficulty starting the motor. As two of the older generation watch from the porch of the house, they conclude that all young people must have their chance to test the ideal world. Remarkably, the lines do not convey cynicism, but a sincere wish that they find the love they expect. By ending with the two generations involved in the same dramatic action, Bergman seems to hint that this kind of love that the older people have come to accept is at least enough to bring new life into the world, and maybe the younger people will have better luck in realizing their idealized version of love and life.

Smiles of a Summer Night

A real turning point in the career of Ingmar Bergman came when he won an award at the Cannes Film Festival with his *Smiles of a Summer Night*, released in 1955. This comedy of manners is an ultimate statement of many of his earlier themes. After an introductory passage which takes place in the city, the principals gather for a week-end party at the estate of an actress. As foil for the turn of the century formalities and posturings of their employers, the maid and coachman react to one another instinctually and simply; they meet, flirt, rendezvous outdoors away from the artificiality of the house, make love, talk and finally resolve to marry. The relationship is natural and uncomplicated; but knowing the history of the two, their lasting fidelity to one another will have to be defined with some flexibility.

Bjorn Bjelvenstam as Henrik Egerman, and Ulla Jacobsson as Anne Egerman in *Smiles of a Summer Night.*

The Count and Countess Malcolm have been experiencing some strain in their marriage. He has cast himself into the role of a military Don Juan, and she confesses that she pays him back in kind. As in earlier films, the gun takes on sexual implications: before an encounter with his wife, he is pictured at his own shooting range and we find that he has great pride in his marksmanship. At the end of the film there is no stunning conversion of either partner. He perhaps summarizes their relationship best when after they confess their need and love for one another, he promises "to be faithful in his way."

The central figure in the film however is the pompous lawyer, Fredrik Egerman, whose child bride of two years remains a virgin. The mismatch is so obvious that the sexual metaphor merely underlines the sterility of their relationship. If they are to find love and life, it obviously will not be with one another. Fredrik keeps portraits of his young wife, as though reducing her to a thing to be looked at.

But Fredrik has been having an affair of some duration with a famous actress, Desirée. When her troupe comes to a local theatre, Fredrik comes to renew their acquaintance. In a device characteristic of Bergman, there is the ritual undressing before each other; she invites him to watch her bathe and he falls in the mud and has to undress in her house. All pretense and posturing is thus destroyed and they see one another for what they really are. With this understanding of one another there is a possibility that their relationship will be a source of life for both of them, for a little boy appears, whom Desirée calls "Fredrik," but she refuses to say whether Fredrik Egerman is the father. When he questions her ability to be a mother, she slaps him.

The young wife is obviously unhappy and miscast in her role as mistress of the household. She dresses like a little girl, has no duties around the house, and treats her husband like a father. The maid tells her she even looks like a virgin, and moments later the two of them giggle like schoolgirls and wrestle on the bed, in a scene which heightens the sense of frivolity and sterility she has experienced in her nonsexual marriage.

At the summer house, she is comically thrust into the arms of her stepson, whom she has been unwilling to recognize as her true love. As they elope on speeding horses, she smiles and drops the veil from her head. Fredrik watches but makes no attempt to stop them. He picks up the fallen veil and thinks of what might have been. As the action continues through a comic duel between Fredrik and the Count, it becomes clear that Fredrik and Desirée have at last recognized that they really love one another. He needs her and she is willing to accept him for all his comic pomposity.

Wild Strawberries

Wild Strawberries (1957) explores human need for love with a depth and delicacy rarely seen in the motion picture. The elderly Isak Borg is a famous bacteriologist, who retraces the geography of his youth on his way back to his university to receive a jubilee award. At the outset, he admits that he has become an "old pedant" and has gradually allowed himself to withdraw "almost completely from society." In this film there is a reversal of the usual Bergman dramatic action; there is no idealized love which must be refocused in terms of reality, nor is there a frantic questing for life through love. On the contrary, Isak has forgotten all about love and his salvation, if we may borrow the term from theology, will consist precisely in his discovery of what he has missed in life. He never realized before that despite his professional success he is a failure as a person, and in fact little more than a dead man.

Images of death cluster around Isak. In the opening dream sequence he sees himself being drawn into a coffin by the corpse who turns out to be himself. His wife and all his brothers and sisters are dead; only his ninety-six year old mother survives, but he does not visit her often. His son, Evald, is a professor of medicine, and, like his father, has so given himself to his work that he has little time to be human.

The women, however, function as life images in the film. Marianne is Isak's daughter-in-law, and she is now living with Isak, because Evald demanded that she have an abortion. She bears life within her, and in the course of the dramatic action communicates this life to both Isak and Evald. At the end of the journey, Isak makes the startling discovery that he likes her, and Evald consents to having the child. Almost reluctantly the two men accept the life that love, imaged by Marianne, gives them.

On the journey, Marianne and Isak pick up Sara, a young hitchhiker and her two traveling companions, one a medical student and the other a student-pastor. Her presence looses a chain of memories of youth, when Isak loved his cousin Sara and planned to marry her. In another flashback, however, we learn that Sara found Isak cold, distant, and only willing "to kiss in the dark," and so she married another. The great revelation to Isak is that he had indeed loved her, but had refused to be hurt by losing her. He simply withdrew into himself and his work, and by so doing had effected spiritual suicide.

His own marriage imaged this inner death. In a dream he recalls having discovered his wife in the act of adultery, and she says that he is too cold even to be upset by this; she predicts his response: "There is nothing to forgive." In the same dream, he is asked to examine a woman whom he pronounces dead. With that she opens her eyes and laughs derisively in his face. He has so drawn away from woman, the source of life, that he has lost his ability even to distinguish life from death, and fittingly, since he has failed his examination in diagnosis, he is sentenced to a punishment of loneliness.

In the closing sequence it is cousin Sara who approaches Isak in the wild strawberry patch and leads him by the hand to the edge of the lake, where his mother and father are fishing in the bright sunlight. This is about as close as Bergman will ever come to a positive image of "salvation" and it is significant that it was the lost love who brought him there. It seems clear that Bergman is insisting that if salvation comes at all to a person, it will be through love, communion with another person, or at least, since that is so difficult for Isak, a recognition of the fact that love is all important in human living.

The Seventh Seal

The Seventh Seal, released in 1956, one year before *Wild Strawberries*, puts a new twist on the theme of life through woman and inaugurates the "theological period" of his work, a body of films that will extend through 1963 with *The Silence*. In *The Seventh Seal* Bergman begins to associate woman as the source of life with God, and the sexual relationship as the metaphor which best describes the relationship between man and God.

In *The Seventh Seal* the knight, Antonius Block, is returning to his home and wife after a futile experience on the Crusades. He has failed to find the knowledge of God that he so desperately wanted, and the journey motif here is readily understood as a journey toward God. He talks about the first days of his marriage as a form of paradise, but when he returns he finds a rather plain and aging woman who greets him coldly and shyly, but who prepares a meal for him and his friends. Perhaps the God that he finds is a mirror image of his wife, cold, aloof, distant, but at least willing to serve.

The black plague rules the countryside and images of death are everywhere; a personified figure of Death comes to claim his victims and the churches foster panic with their icons of a suffering Jesus, murals of plague victims going to hell because of their unknown sins, and their persecution of a girl suspected of witchcraft. At the climax of the film, Death enters the Knight's home and claims everyone for his dark realm. The only survivors are Jof and Mia, and their baby son, who have been portrayed throughout the film as the perfectly loving couple, giving life to one another and fostering new life in the person of their son. All the victims are, as far as the script tells us, childless. Bergman is then consistent in his use of sexuality to illustrate the life and death polarity in human experience.

Through a Glass Darkly

In his trilogy, *Through a Glass Darkly* (1961), *Winter Light* (1962), and *The Silence* (1963), Bergman uses the sexual metaphor almost exclusively as he tries to grapple with the experience of God in man's life. Before he made the trilogy, Bergman stated that "religious questions are continually alive for me," a fact which is scarcely surprising since his father was a pastor of the Court in Sweden. But at the end of the work, after years of trying to fit his experience and knowledge of human love into a Procrustean bed of traditional concepts of the Christian God, he reached a new conclusion: "My basic concern in making them (the trilogy) was to dramatize the all-importance of communication, of the capacity for feeling. They are not concerned—as many critics have theorized—with God or his absence, but with the saving force of love. Most of the people in these films are dead, completely dead. They don't know how to love."

In the unfortunate coda to *Through a Glass Darkly*, David, the author and father of Karin and Minus, tries to propose to his son the theme of the Johannine Gospel, "God is love," as a way out of the absurdity of this world. Neither Bergman nor Minus seem convinced by this explanation: Minus runs on the beach and Bergman repeats the entire sermonette through a sleazy church organist, Blom, in *Winter Light*. Throughout the trilogy both concepts, God and love, receive severe scrutiny.

Karin and her husband have been unable to express their love sexually for some time as the film begins. She has had a series of breakdowns and it appears that her condition will deteriorate. But while she cannot accept her husband, she is tormented by an almost pathetic need for love. The atmosphere becomes progressively charged with sexual overtones whenever she is together with her brother. In a scene deleted from the American print, Minus comes upon her as she is changing from her bathing suit; he stares at her and she smiles at him. As they travel to a dairy together, she continually embraces him, and resentful and disturbed by her physicality he spills the milk he is carrying and complains about how disgusting women are. Later, when they are left alone together on the island, she discovers him looking at pictures in a pornographic magazine, mocks him for it, and insists that they go through the pictures together while they comment on the qualities of the various models.

Later that afternoon, she begins to lose contact with reality. She hides in an attic room of the house and waits for God to come out of the closet to her. The attitude of prayer she assumes involves kneeling, bent over with both forearms clasped between her knees. Eventually she rushes out of the house and hides in an abandoned boat, and when Minus comes to look for her she pulls him brutally down upon herself.

Her frenzied quest for love, or God, has brought her self-destructive drive to the surface; the incest fails to satisfy her and may have destroyed Minus. As she drifts further from the real world she again retreats to the attic, and at last imagines that God has come to her but he appears in the form of a spider who attempts to rape her, crawls across her breast and face, and climbs up the wall. When God finally does appear to her, it is in the form of a destructive presence, whom she must repel.

Both God and love became repulsive for her, and the tragedy for Karin, and one might imply for all men, is their desperate need for both. Karin, like so many of Bergman's people, cannot learn to love in the real world or accept the God of the tradition who reveals himself "through a glass darkly" (1 Cor. 13:12). Like so many people whom Bergman refers to as "dead," Karin must give up and opt for etherized living rather than life; as they take her back to the asylum she makes her husband promise that they will discontinue treatments and leave her alone.

Winter Light

In *Winter Light* Bergman returns to the theme of God is love. A pastor, Thomas, suddenly discovers that he has lost his faith in God. His wife died many years ago, and he keeps pictures of her, which have as much the same meaning for him as religious icons have for the devout. He remembers her in ideal terms, and likewise he looks back on his memories of a "comfortable God," who has now been taken away from him. He proclaims his freedom from God, and scoffs at the icons in his church. Shut off from both God and love, he is a figure of death.

Marta, the local schoolteacher, represents life for him. She continually asks him to marry her and offers her love to him, but he cannot or will not accept. He remains chained to the image of the past and his dead wife. In the same way, he has lost the security-blanket God, and refuses to accept the God which he finds in his present circumstances. In a highly ambiguous ending, Thomas decides to continue with the afternoon service even though Marta is the only one present in the church. Marta is, in this last scene at any rate, a surrogate for God; a living, present reality that one can love and thus gain life from. This is not a particularly pleasant prospect, for Marta is scarcely an ideal woman, so neither can Thomas be overjoyed at the prospect of making a leap of faith toward a God whose presence in his life has been at best a mixed blessing.

The Silence

While the sexual motif in *Winter Light* is simple and unified, in *The Silence* it becomes terribly complex. The sexual relation is again a metaphor for human communication; but in a world where God is silent, or absent, or irrelevant, such communication is slight indeed. The original title for this conclusion to the trilogy was *God's Silence*, but rather than invite misunderstanding and too much concern with "theological questions" the title was pruned. Even with no reference to any kind of divinity, the film remains a powerful statement of modern man's inability to reach his fellow man.

The little boy, Johan, is the thematic core of the work. He journeys through an unknown land with his mother, Anna, and her sister, Ester. Ester is a translator by profession and is dying of tuberculosis. They stop in a hotel in a city where they cannot speak the language. Johan is closely associated with his mother: he washes her back as she bathes, she rubs him with cologne and kisses the palms of his hands, then they take a nap together. He assumes the fetal position next to his naked mother, which would indicate that their relationship is purely instinctive and sensuous.

Anna feels a revulsion for her dying sister, and partly from a motive of revenge leaves her in the suite, goes to a bar and does not discourage a waiter who flirts with her. Later, she goes to a theatre and watches a couple copulate in the row in front of her; she leaves immediately to find the waiter. They make love in an empty church. During a second meeting with the waiter, she expresses her satisfaction that they cannot speak the same language. Ester breaks in on the couple, and as Anna screams the accusation of jealousy at her sister, the waiter approaches her and they asume a position for anal intercourse. Like Karin in *Through a Glass Darkly* Anna lives in a frenzy trying to find love and life, but her drive is mindless and aimed more at self-gratification than personal self-giving, and as a result she submits herself to degradation rather than love.

The opposite seems to be the trouble with Ester. Her world is exclusively one of the mind, and fulfilling love for another person is quite impossible. There are hints that she suffered an incestuous experience with her father, which has closed her in upon herself. She says that when she was fertilized she smelled like dead fish, and as she drinks and reads alone in her room she masturbates. All the sexual images converge to underscore a theme of loneliness and inability to love. For her, in the midst of her illness, death and sterility are one. The only affection she seems to have is an unhealthy love for her sister, but the Lesbian relationship, physically at any rate, cannot lead to life, and this for Bergman is the whole point of love.

Johan's affection shifts the center of gravity toward the dying aunt. At first only his mother was permitted to touch him, but during the course of the evening in the hotel he draws a picture for his aunt, shares her meal, and finally as Anna prepares to take him home and leave Ester to die, Johan embraces the dying aunt. Significantly too as the mother and child are on the train the film ends with Johan reading "Words in a Foreign Language," a note left to him by Ester, which points out the words that she learned during their stay in the hotel. Johan is Bergman, or Everyman, continuing the journey torn between a life of the senses and a life of the intellect, trying to make some sense out of the broken fragments of thought that dying intellectuals leave for us. Is love possible? Johan does not know; he has yet to experience it. Is there something, like a God, which can make the world make sense for him? Again he is not sure. At least we know that the journey and the search will go on.

All These Women

While *The Silence* does put the period to the theme of love and life versus death theme in many senses, it would be a mistake to stress the discontinuity and ignore the fact that problems of communication continue to intrigue him. The sexual relationship remains as the basic metaphor for human communion, but beginning with *All These Women* (1964) sexuality becomes more and more involved with the problem of the artist trying to continue his creative vocation. This theme is not new to Bergman since fourteen years before *All These Women*, Mari in *Summer Interlude* found in her dancing a way to escape love and life. The human person, striving to be creative, finds the perfect metaphor in human sexuality, and with this point of view in mind we can arbitrarily begin the second section of this analysis of the sexual metaphor in Bergman's works.

In *All These Women* Felix is a highly creative cellist, whose creativity may be portrayed in the fact that he keeps a wife and six mistresses, one for each day of the week. Cornelius is an effeminate music critic who visits this household and in his attempt to discover the intimate personal details of the life of the cellist peeks through keyholes and even sleeps with the mistresses. However, by giving him the theme music of "Yes, We Have No Bananas," as a ribald comment on the action, Bergman mocks the sexual or creative power of the critic. By the use of this musical device, Bergman tells us that the critic tries frantically to violate the privacy of the artist, but is ridiculous in his ineptitude and impotence. As his attempts to meet Felix become more desperate, Cornelius finally disguises himself as a woman, which indicates his willingness to sacrifice his manhood for a story. When Felix dies rather than compromise his art, a new young cellist moves in to inherit the harem, and so the story repeats itself.

Jarl Kulle as Cornelius, and Gertrud Fridh as Traviata in *Now About All These Women.*

Persona

The sexual metaphor is repeated in what may be Bergman's finest work, *Persona* (1966). In this film an actress, Elizabeth Vogler, is suddenly stricken with an emotional impasse which drives her to a state of partial catatonia. She refuses to speak. Her blockage as an artist is imaged in her refusal of the role of mother; she has a child but despises it and refuses to function as its mother. In effect, she has backed away from all forms of human creativity. The nurse assigned to care for her confesses a strange sexual experience she had on a beach with two adolescent boys which led to an abortion. She is capable of life and communication, but is unwilling or unable to bring it to fruition. The two women grow close to one another during the therapeutic process and in one of the dream sequences there is even a hint of a Lesbian relationship. In another dream the nurse receives Elizabeth's husband, indicating the completeness of the sharing of the two women. At the end of the film there is only a hint of the cure for Elizabeth, but at least she has confronted her inner turmoil and may, it is hoped, return to a full artistic career.

Hour of the Wolf

No such hope is present in *Hour of the Wolf* (1968) for in this film the artist gradually loses his ability to confront himself or reality. The narration is introduced by his wife, Alma, who is bearing his child, but the life that she carries remains only a potentiality. He cannot paint and is tortured by the thought of losing his artistic power. In his fantasies he returns to the memories of a former mistress, Veronica, who appears as an ideal of art and love that has long ago left him. Near the end of the film she appears as a naked corpse, perhaps the memory of his faded artistic talent, who comes to life before him, and as he embraces her, she mocks his futile efforts at lovemaking, or in the metaphorical sense, his artistic pretensions. He is thoroughly emasculated for the encounter, made up with a cupid's bow mouth and a silk dressing gown. He is subjected to the laughter of all the residents of the castle for his efforts. He finds himself inept both sexually and artistically. What is more, in his visit to the strange castle he finds the distinction between reality and the world of his fevered imagination becoming more and more vague.

Shame

Much the same is the encounter with reality that Jan Rosenberg faces in *Shame* (1968), except in this case the confusion comes not so much from the tortured imagination as from the irrational war that engulfs the country. He is a concert violinist, who because of some unspecified emotional problem is no longer able to play. Both he and his wife Eva want children, but have not had any; both art and the sexual relationship are futile for them.

As the war rages, the mayor of the town, who has influence with the occupation forces, befriends them. When Jan falls asleep from drinking too much wine, the mayor persuades Eva to enter into a sexual relationship with him. Since it is merely a physical relationship, he leaves a wad of bills on the bed, which Jan discovers. His impotence is then affirmed, and in an act of revenge he allows the mayor to be captured and executed by enemy troops. Since he has lost sexual control over his wife, it is obvious that his control over his art has gone, and in the following scene the army sacks his house and smashes his violin. With both art and self-respect gone from his life, Jan becomes brutalized to the point where he can murder a wounded soldier for a pair of shoes. Society has created an atmosphere for modern man in which neither art nor love is possible; what is left is a panorama of death.

Passion of Anna

In *Passion of Anna* (1969) the alternatives are not quite clear. Andreas is a writer who has apparently not done much writing in the recent past. He lives alone and forms a casual relationship with Eva, which lasts only a few weeks, and, as the story progresses, forms a more lasting relationship with Anna; but neither strikes roots deep enough to restore his desire to write. In the final scene, Anna nearly repeats the accident which killed her former husband and Andreas leaves her in the car and paces back and forth on the road, unable to follow her or to leave her. His lack of decisiveness in his relationship with her mirrors his inability to grapple with his writing. It is quite likely that he will never be able to write anything.

Summary

In this rapid survey of some of the works of Ingmar Bergman, it should be abundantly clear that he never uses his portrayal of human sexuality as a clinical study of the male-female relationship. Always it fits into the larger meaning of his artistic expression; it is an image which reveals in a most powerful and personal way the value of communication and art in man's attempt to find a meaning in his life. The human person, according to Bergman, is not the atomic unit of society; rather he is a component seeking a reality beyond himself, either in love for another person or in artistic expression. In the enunciation of this theme, the sexual metaphor provides the most fruitful comparison.

4

INGMAR BERGMAN AND GOD

Gene D. Phillips, S.J.

. . . .

When the French film-maker François Truffaut was first exposed to the films of Swedish director Ingmar Bergman he said: "Here is a man who has done all we dreamed of doing. He has written films as a novelist writes a book. Instead of a pen he has used a camera. He is an author of cinema." Bergman himself has said: "The motion picture, with its complicated process of birth, is my method of saying what I want to say to my fellow men."

Bergman has used his camera to compose a continuing essay on man's relationship to God in the context of the problem of evil. Two things have influenced Bergman's film-making. One is his background in the theater, which accounts for his expert handling of the repertory of film actors he has built up.

The other is his early upbringing as the son of an Evangelical Lutheran pastor, which accounts for his preoccupation with the more somber side of religious truth in his films. As early as 1948, in *The Prison* (American title: *The Devil's Wanton*), one of his characters reflects that "if one can believe in God, there is no problem; if one cannot, there is no solution."

During the next decade, however, Bergman made a series of comedies which dealt mainly with the battle of the sexes, underlining the need for compromise between male and female. These included *A Lesson in Love* (1954) and *Smiles of a Summer Night* (1955). With *The Seventh Seal* (1956), however, he embarked on a series of films dealing with the problem that the existence of evil poses for the believer. As film critic Anthony Schillaci has written, this new series of film went

Portions of this essay originally appeared in *The Clergy Review*, Vol. 52, No. 10. Reprinted by permission of the author.

a step beyond the line quoted above from *The Prison*. For it is the peculiar torment of the characters in the films beginning with *The Seventh Seal* that they *do* believe in God, but still have a problem, the problem of evil.

Bergman describes his process of making a film as grasping hold of "a brightly colored thread sticking out of the dark sack of the unconscious. If I begin to wind up this thread, and do it carefully, a complete film will emerge." The thread from which he spun *The Seventh Seal* was the story of a disillusioned medieval knight, Antonius Bloch (Max von Sydow) returning to Sweden from the Crusades to find a plague ravaging the land.

Bloch's wavering faith places him somewhere between the agnosticism of his squire, Jons (Gunnar Björnstrand), and the simple faith of the traveling juggler and his wife named Jof and Mia (Bibi Andersson) whom Bloch meets. Bloch wishes that he could either believe as they do or abandon belief as Jons has done. He muses, "Why can't I kill God within me? Why does he live on in this painful way even though I curse him and want to tear him from my heart? Why, in spite of everything, is he a baffling reality that I can't shake off? I want knowledge, not faith."

When the black-caped figure of Death comes to claim him as a victim of the plague, Bloch wins from him in a game of chess the right to do one meaningful deed before he dies since he considers that his life has been meaningless. Bloch chooses to save Jof, Mia, and their small child Mikhael from the plague. Whether or not they symbolize the Holy Family, as some critics have conjectured, Bloch's gesture enables him to face Death with resignation.*

In the final scene Jof and Mia are playing with their son on a hillside in the only scene in which Bergman symbolically allows sunshine to brilliantly bathe the otherwise gray landscape. They see Bloch and others, their hands clasped in a dance of death, disappearing over a distant horizon. Paraphrasing the Apocalypse, from which the film's title comes, Jof says that the rain will wash their faces and cleanse the salt tears from their cheeks.*

---

* Cf. Apocalypse v, I-viii, 5 (passim): The Lamb who was slain to ransom men for God is the only one worthy to open the scroll sealed with seven seals. Before the Lamb breaks the last seal, the narrator sees those "who have come out of great tribulation" to have the Lamb as their shepherd forever. "And he will guide them to springs of living water; and God will wipe away every tear from their eyes. When the Lamb opened the seventh seal, there was silence in heaven," and the prayers of the saints rose as incense up to God.

In *Wild Strawberries* (1957) we have another man nearing the end of what he considers a futile life. This time it is the elderly Dr. Izaac Borg (Victor Sjöström) traveling to the University of Lund to accept an honorary degree for his services to humanity. His journey becomes a recapitulation of his journey through life, as he visits familiar old landmarks on the way to Lund. It is also a journey to self-knowledge as his reminiscing slowly makes him aware how he has served others at the cost of neglecting his own family. His daughter-in-law, while driving him to the University, tells him that his son Evald (Gunnar Björnstrand) also a doctor, wants her to have an abortion because Evald does not want to bring new life into a corrupt world.

They pick up three teenagers along the way: two boys and a girl. The girl (Bibi Andersson) reminds him of his first love, whom he lost to his brother. He begins to understand how, ever since, he has been a coldly ambitious person. He sees too how his own subsequent unhappy marriage is responsible for his son's cynicism. In confronting his memories and making peace with the past, Dr. Borg is also able to reason with his son when he reaches journey's end. One is reminded of Antonious Bloch's prayer of resignation in *The Seventh Seal:* "Have mercy on us, for we are small, frightened, and ignorant."

The problem of God's existence and his permission for evil in the world comes up in *Wild Strawberries* in the form of the two teenage boys, one a divinity student, the other an artist, who constantly argue about these points. They could both represent Bergman himself, the artist who explores his theological doubts in his own films. At one point the divinity student gets angry and strikes the artist. The artist replies that this is not a very convincing argument for the existence of God.

Yet in many of Bergman's films belief in God is reaffirmed only after a character has been dealt a staggering blow which brings him literally to his knees in resignation to the God he cannot hope to understand in this life. This is true of *The Virgin Spring* (1960), which won a U.S. Academy Award. The film is based on the medieval tale of a young girl who is raped and murdered on her way to Mass by two brutish shepherds. When the girl's father (played by Max von Sydow, who was also Antonius Bloch) discovers the deed he reverts from his Christian beliefs to his pagan ways and brutally kills not only the two shepherds but their younger brother who had no hand in their crime. Then, kneeling near his daughter's body and realizing how his own crime has matched that of the shepherds, he prays, "You saw it, God. The death of an innocent child, and my vengeance. You permitted it,

and I don't understand you. Yet I now ask you for forgiveness—I do
not know of any other way to reconcile myself with my own hands. I
don't know of any other way to live."

A spring of water then bubbles forth from where his daughter's body
had lain. After this strong affirmation of God many thought that Bergman would now begin to examine the more positive aspects of religious
belief. Instead Bergman next mounted a trilogy which shows how people who fail to reconcile themselves with other human beings cannot
reconcile themselves with God. "Most of the people in these three
films are dead, completely dead," he explains. "They don't know how
to love or to feel any emotions. They are lost because they can't reach
anyone outside of themselves."

The three films are *Through a Glass Darkly* (1961), which won an
Academy Award; *Winter Light* (or *The Communicants*, 1963); and
The Silence (1964). Some critics were somewhat dismayed because
the characters in the three films get further and further out of touch
with God and man in each succeeding film. Yet the fact that the films
treat the loss of faith rather than the finding of faith is no reflection on
Bergman's own beliefs. The theme of each film would be the same had
they been made in reverse order. As they stand, the need for human
and divine love is stressed more strongly in each film in proportion to
the absence of both in the characters of each film.

Through a Glass Darkly is the key to the trilogy.* It concerns Karin
(Harriet Andersson), a young wife slipping into schizophrenia. Throughout her life she has never known true human love, and therefore develops a distorted notion of what the love of God is.

Her mother died when she and her brother Minus were small; David (Gunnar Björnstrand), her father, is a novelist who, like Dr. Borg
in *Wild Strawberries*, has neglected his family for his work; Martin,
her husband, is a well-meaning but inadequate person who has never
been able to establish a meaningful relationship with her. Karin con-
ceives a desire to know God as he really is, echoing the words of Antonius Bloch, the Knight in *The Seventh Seal*: "I want knowledge, not
faith."

At the climax of the film, Karin experiences a hallucination in which
she sees God as a huge spider trying to ravish her. Since Karin identified human love with sexual love, which for her seemed a selfish and

* These lines from St. Paul appear as a preface to the film: "For now we see
through a glass darkly, but then face to face. Now I know in part; then I shall
understand fully, even as I have been fully understood. So faith, hope, and
love abide, these three; *but the greatest of these is love.*" I Cor. xiii, 12-13.

devouring experience, her distorted image of divine love is a magnified version of this.

In the film's final scene David comforts his son by telling him that God is love and that we know divine love through loving other human beings. For the first time David is able to communicate with his own son, as each seeks to help the other get over the shattering experience of Karin's final madness. For Karin the knowledge of God available to us in this life, "through a glass darkly," was not enough. For Minus there is a genuine wonder about the new-found love between him and his father which, as David has indicated, is a reflection of the love of the Father: "My father talked to me," he says with astonishment as the film ends.

In turning to Bergman's next film one is reminded of Tennyson's lines in the prologue to "In Memoriam":

> We have but faith: we cannot know;
>   For knowledge is of things we see;
>   And yet we trust it comes from thee,
> A beam in darkness: let it grow.

In *Winter Light* the Pastor (Gunnar Björnstrand, David in *Through a Glass Darkly*) fears that the beam of faith in his life is flickering and dying. Bergman symbolizes this in the gray "winter light" in which the film is photographed. The Pastor is an unsympathetic man, out of touch with man as well as God, who can find no consolation to offer to a fisherman obsessed with anxieties, or to the man's family once the fisherman has killed himself in despair. The Pastor finally confides his desolation to a crippled church sexton, who reminds him of Christ's desolation on the Cross as they stand in a darkened church before evening devotions. The sexton then switches on the lights for the service and we see a close-up of a blazing chandelier. For the first time in the film the pervading winter light is dispelled. The Pastor resolutely begins the service: "Holy, holy, holy, the earth is filled with the glory of God." The Pastor will carry on, resigned that his darkness will be illuminated by an occasional beam of light: "A beam in darkness: let it grow."

The third film of the trilogy uses a different metaphor for God's absence from people's lives. *The Silence*, says Bergman, refers to "God's silence, negative print." God does not speak to those who have turned away from him if they refuse to hear, one might infer. The original script has more references to God's silence in the lives of such people than the English version of the film has.

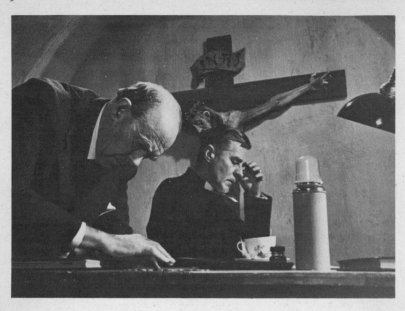

Kolbjorn Knudsen as the church warden, and Gunnar Bjornstrand as Tomas Ericsson in *Winter Light.*

Two sisters, Ester and Anna, are traveling through Timoka, a strange land, with Anna's son. They have to break their journey because of Ester's increasing illness. They do not understand the language of the country, but they seem to be better able to communicate with the local people in gestures than they are with each other in words. They have not gotten along since the death of their father (Father?) years before. Ester (Ingrid Thulin) is more intellectual than her sister; Anna (Gunnel Lindblom) more sensual: neither is a whole human being. Each is locked in her private hell: Ester is an alcoholic and Anna is promiscuous. Yet each somehow needs the other. Roger Manvell comments, " 'Hell together is better than hell alone,' the ultimate darkness is to be solitary."

Anna finally decides to leave Ester behind to die among strangers. Ester gives Anna's little boy a scrap of paper on which she has written two words of the language of Timoka, which Ester has been studying. On the train journey back to the father's house, the lad studies the two words: "heart" and "hand." A heart with which to love and a hand to reach out to others are two things of which the boy has seen little evidence in the disastrous lives of his mother and aunt. There is an implicit hope the lad will profit by what has happened to them, as the insane Karin's family are drawn together after her horrible experience in *Through a Glass Darkly,* and the murdered Karin's family learns to turn to God after her tragedy in *The Virgin Spring.*

Persona (1966) presents a situation similar to that of *The Silence.* A nurse (Bibi Andersson) is hired to help an actress (Liv Ullmann) to get over a period of depression which made her stop speaking her lines in the middle of a performance. Since then she has lapsed into silence. The nurse is less intellectual and more earthy than the actress and begins pouring out her own sordid past to the actress. The nurse strips away her own mask (*persona* in Latin) and achieves a certain relief and peace from dropping her pose as an aloof professional woman and admitting her own failures. This the actress refuses to do though she eventually is able to go back to the stage.

Shame (1968) also presents us with the problem of the artist who can no longer communicate through his art because he is unable to relate to others on an interpersonal level. Jan and Eva Rosenberg (Max von Sydow and Liv Ullmann) are both professional musicians who live on a remote island, where they have taken up farming until the war in progress on the mainland is over and they can return to the practice of their art. But more than war prevents them from personal fulfillment. Their marital life has grown stale and sterile, and it is therefore not surprising that their union has borne no fruit, that they remain childless.

When the war at last invades their island, Jan goes berzerk and descends to brutal and violent behavior in his frantic scramble to protect himself and his wife, culminating in his senseless shooting of an already wounded young deserter to obtain his boots. Seeking to escape the island with other refugees in an open boat whose motor fails, Jan and Eva are left to drift through the foggy waters, a compelling image of their purposeless lives throughout the picture.

Shame ends with Eva's half-hearted musings about whether God's failure to intervene in people's lives is partially responsible for man's earthly shame and misery. Although Bergman typically leaves this question open, critic John Fitzgerald is probably right in surmising that God's silence is a reminder that He refuses to intrude on man's free will, but that He nevertheless continues to make his presence felt in the very doubts about Him and His Providence that nag Eva and so many of Bergman's characters back to the *Seventh Seal's* Knight, and onward to the anguished magistrate in *The Ritual* (1969).

Although *The Ritual* was originally done for Swedish television, it
is very much an integral part of Bergman's canon. A small town magistrate (Erik Hell) is called upon to try a trio of actors who have been
arrested for performing an allegedly obscene routine which they call a
"ritual." At least two of the actors have religious problems. One says
that he is his own God: "I create my own angels and demons." Another, the only female member of the group (Ingrid Thulin) says, "I
play at being a saint and a martyr. That's why I call myself Thea,"
which is a Greek word for goddess.

Erik Hell as the judge, and Gunnar Bjornstrand as Hans in *The Ritual*.

But the magistrate seems to have his own spiritual conflicts. In the
film's key scene, one which recalls the confessional sequence in *The
Seventh Seal*, the magistrate confesses to a priest (played by Bergman
himself) that because of the sinfulness of his own life he does not feel
qualified to pass judgment on others. He is a non-believer, but prays
anyway because it relieves his inner anguish. He further believes that
"people can pardon each other, that there is mercy on earth."

One feels that Bergman here is giving his own reflections on his approach to film-making. As an artist he creates his own angels and demons in his films, i.e., characters who represent the forces for good and

evil at work in man; but he does not feel that he can judge his characters, only explore their behavior and look upon his fellow human beings with the compassion one hopes for from God. Significantly, the magistrate dies of heart disease and is never able to sit in judgment on the actors' performance.

Andreas, the hero of *The Passion of Anna* (1970), is also an indecisive person. A writer, he furthermore recalls Jan, the violinist in *The Shame*, for he too is a dried-up artist and, in addition, is likewise played by Max von Sydow. Here too the artist's loss of creativity is directly related to the sterile personal relationships which he has developed with the people in his life. He finally seeks to form a lasting attachment with Anna (Liv Ullmann). But, having failed to do so, he can neither give her up nor continue to strive for the growth of a genuine love between them—as evidenced by the film's final scene in which Andreas paces back and forth on the road nearby while Anna sits in her car waiting for him; he is incapable of either walking on without her or rejoining her to continue the journey of life. Andreas's emotional life has clearly been eaten away by what was referred to earlier in the movie as "cancer of the soul."

In *Cries and Whispers* (1972) Bergman continues to portray man as questing for peace and joy in a world that seems for the most part to offer only anxiety and pain. The film focuses on a group of women who live a claustrophobic existence in a large country mansion from which they seldom venture out-of-doors, an indication of the intense interior world in which they exist. Agnes (Harriet Andersson) is dying of cancer (of the soul, one infers, as well as of the body), and her two sisters have come to be with her in her last days.

The three sisters, we learn from flashbacks, are victims of self-delusions in which they take refuge from the failures of their lives. Agnes, a spinster, prefers to believe that there is a close emotional attachment between her and her sisters, but this is belied by the superficial nature of their kindness to Agnes, even in death. Karin (Ingrid Thulin) apparently is a devoted wife and mother but in reality she ignores her family, and she despises her husband to the point where she masochistically wounds her genitals with a fragment of glass before inviting him to their bed. Maria (Liv Ullmann) is ironically named, for she is a coquette who desperately needs to have her attractiveness reaffirmed by a steady succession of male admirers.

The only one of the four women in the house capable of any degree of love and self-giving is Anna, the devoted servant of Agnes. Yet even she has unsatisfied emotional needs, for she in effect transfers her maternal instincts, frustrated by the death of her daughter, to caring for Agnes. Even the minister who comes to read prayers over the dead Agnes seems, like the parson in *Winter Light*, to be attempting to resuscitate his own feeble faith more than to provide religious solace for the bereaved.

Basically, Bergman seems to be saying in his films, when we look at them as a group, that the coexistence of good and evil is all that we can hope for from our fragmented existence. Moreover he seems to imply that life is easier to bear when one is willing to take the risk of communicating with others and seeking union with them. One cannot hope to establish a relationship with God by bypassing fellow human beings.

But Bergman avoids being explicit in stating messages or meanings in his films. In his preface to the published edition of *Cries and Whispers* he says, "As I turn this project over in my mind it never stands out as a completed whole. What it most resembles is a dark flowering stream: faces, movements, voices, gestures, exclamations, light and shade, moods, dreams; nothing fixed, nothing really tangible other than for the moment, and then only appearing to be. A dream, a longing or perhaps an expectation, a fear, in which that to be feared is never put into words—I could go on indefinitely describing key and color, but we shouldn't be any wiser."

His chief interest, then, is to present the problems of human existence for filmgoers to ponder in order that they can come to their own conclusions, for he does not pretend to be able to make anyone any wiser. When he is asked the general purpose of his films he replies with a parable about the medieval artists who contributed their efforts to the building of the great cathedrals: "I want to be one of the artists in the cathedral on the great plain. I want to make a dragon's head, an angel, a devil—or perhaps a saint—out of stone. It does not matter which; it is the sense of satisfaction that counts. Regardless of whether I believe or not, whether I am a Christian or not, I would play my part in the collective building of the cathedral."

5

THE WORLD WITHOUT, THE WORLD WITHIN

PERSONA   Robin Wood

. . . .

> If (and how shall they not?) the sensitive and imaginative freely let their
> "hearts lie open" to the suffering of the world, how are they to retain any
> health or faith for living?"
>
> F. R. LEAVIS: *Wordsworth in Revaluation*

Art comments on life. But does it? Even tragedy, traditionally held
highest of the arts, with pretensions to illuminating the significance of
human existence, leaves huge areas, and huge possibilities, almost un-
touched. Those areas have always existed, but in our century they have
extended themselves enormously in the artist's consciousness. He can
no longer, for example, shut his consciousness off from the fact of
needless and appalling (not "tragic" because utterly unredeemed) suffering; nor can he keep at a manageable arm's length the possibility
that human existence *has* no significance. Shakespeare approached
such issues in *King Lear*; but even Lear *learns* something about himself, and the fate of a Lear (leaving aside differences between fiction
and reality) is more endurable to contemplate than that of the slaughtered women and children of Vietnam.

In the William Klein episode of *Far From Vietnam* a man stands
in a street howling a nonsense-chant on the word "Napalm." It comes
across as an expression of the rawest agony, as if the agony of the victims were finding expression through the chanter's full exposure of
himself to the fact of unredeemed and most extreme physical suffering.
His condition has the helpless abandonment of insanity, and strikes

one as perhaps the only valid response. It is not art but there is a sense in which it goes beyond art—beyond experience that can be ordered and organized and placed in "meaningful" perspective. The true artist, who feels himself committed to being, in some sense, the conscience (= consciousness) of the human race, feels himself increasingly driven in this way beyond what art as we have always understood it can readily assimilate (Eliot put it very succinctly a long time ago in "Prelude IV"). Total exposure to the meaninglessness and chaos the twentieth century has discovered (or thinks it has discovered—we mustn't assume too readily that it is the last word) cannot but be detrimental to the artist, yet no one who *is* an artist can refuse it. It can lead to a collapse into total incoherence, or to a hardening and toughening of the sensibility, driving a sensitive mind like Godard's, for example, to the artistic shambles of *Made in USA*, and to that too-ready acceptance of the association of vitality with brutishness in his "adoption" of Lemmy Caution, the adoption of a protective covering of insentience. The effects of all this are manifest as a pervasive and determining influence on the arts today. The popular cinema, because of its artistically conservative nature, has been the last stronghold of the traditional concept of art. But it, too, has been fundamentally, if indirectly, affected, and it is probable that no one, now, will be able to give us a *Rio Bravo* (not even Hawks, as *El Dorado* is there to prove).

Anyone who has seen *Persona* will understand at once when, in the context of the above remarks, I salute it as one of the most courageous films ever made. It bears, of course, a much stronger resemblance to a work of art than the Napalm "poem" in *Far From Vietnam*; but in it one can see the whole traditional concept of art—an ordering of experience towards a positive end, a *wholeness* of statement—cracking and crumbling even as, half-way through the film, the image cracks and crumbles. Breakdown, due to the sort of total exposure I have suggested, is both theme and form—that is to say, it is experienced both by the characters and by the artist, the "formal" collapse acting as a means of communicating the sensation of breakdown directly to the spectator. Useless to talk of the sudden mid-way reminder of the medium (the depicted projector-breakdown) in terms of the Brechtian (or Godardian) alienation effect. What Bergman does here has nothing in common with the continual and delicate—at times near-subliminal—play of distanciation devices with which Godard preserves the spectator's analytical detachment. Bergman, on the contrary, draws the spectator into the film, demanding total emotional involvement: the pre-credit and credit sequences shock and disturb rather than detach; the fiction that follows up to the mid-way point engrosses, with nothing either to distance or distract us from a moral and psychological exploration of the characters and their relationship, via the emotional-intellectual processes through which we customarily experience fictional narratives. The breakdown, when it comes, is, in terms of its emotional effect, far more closely analogous to the mid-way revelation in *Vertigo* or the shower murder in *Psycho* than to anything in Godard: in all these cases, our developed relationship to the film is shattered abruptly, and we are left gropingly to construct a new one. (Besides, *Vertigo*'s cumulative ambiguities regarding what is, in fact, "real," offer interesting thematic parallels with *Persona*.)

During the film's climactic sequences the two women seem to merge, their identities to become interchangeable; much has been written, reasonably enough, about the film along these lines. One can discuss this interchangeability another way, by saying that most people find it possible—even inevitable—during the film to identify with both Alma and Elizabeth: their consciousnesses find a common denominator in the consciousness of the spectator. Alma is the obvious identification figure: her "representative" quality is plain from the outset; the main body of the film begins and ends with her; it is through her consciousness that we study the withdrawn and enigmatic Elizabeth. Some have been driven to interpret the film as entirely subjective from Alma's viewpoint (which offers a comfortingly easy Eight-and-a-Halfian way out of the difficulties of deciding what is "real" and what is fantasy). However, there are two key scenes where Elizabeth is alone and where we share her consciousness, very painfully and acutely, learning perhaps more about her withdrawal than Alma ever learns: the scene where she watches the self-immolation of a Buddist monk on television, and the scene where she studies, with fascinated horror, a photograph of Jewish women and children being rounded up by Nazis. Elizabeth recoils—and her response is communicated to us very powerfully and directly—from the horror of existence itself: the horror of a life in which the sort of sufferings and outrages pointed to by the two examples are not merely possible but *everyday*; the horror of a humanity in which the tendencies that make such outrages possible are inherent and ineradicable. In Elizabeth's withdrawal—her refusal to take any further part in such a life and such a humanity—we are brought close to the Napalm "poem": one is passive, the other active protest, but both primarily communicate impotence and despair. What we watch, and are made to share, is an overwhelmingly emphatic identification with the suffering contemplated.

Elizabeth's motivation for withdrawal has, of course, other aspects, some more pervasively present than her exposure to the fact of suffering. The choice of *Electra* for her moment of decision is suggestive: the play associates cruelty and horror with the tangle of sexuality (already juxtaposed in the credit-sequence), and, being a play, adds the further dimension of Elizabeth's uncertainty as to what is real and what acted—what we mean and what we think we mean.

The film is not so much about an exchange of identities on the personal level, as about a merging of two representative consciousnesses, or the process whereby the protective façades people erect to defend themselves from reality are broken down. Alma's "normality," and its precarious and illusory nature, are touchingly observed and described. She represents our daily selves: Elizabeth our deeper and acuter awareness. The nurse's uniform is itself a mask, an assumed identity, Alma's image of herself as she wants to appear, both in the world's eyes and in her own: she reassumes it in the film's climactic sequences (either in reality or in imagination or both) in a final attempt to re-establish the identity that has by now irretrievably crumbled. Other details sketch in Alma's surface-identity (at the start of the film, the only one she is aware of): as she stands before the psychiatrist, the camera moves down to show her hands clasped behind her back, the stance of a good, obedient schoolgirl before the headmistress; introducing herself in her chatty-and-efficient-young-nurse manner, she tells Elizabeth that she is 25, engaged to be married, and that her mother was also a nurse.

The precariousness of Alma's protective façade is immediately apparent in her desire to give up the case. She tells the psychiatrist that she "may not be able to cope—mentally"; Elizabeth's refusal to speak or act shows "great strength," and clearly frightens her; without realizing it, she feels it as a personal threat. The other woman's silence, in fact, begins to break down Alma's defenses at once. As she tries to settle down, restless, for the night, she murmurs that "You can do almost anything you like." She will marry Karl-Henrik: "It's a nice safe feeling. So is work, in a different way." But she sounds quite unconvinced by either. The girl's unease is communicated to the audience by the restless switching off and on and off again of the light; we are brought very close to her by the almost imperceptible rise in the lighting a moment after it is finally switched off, her face becoming dimly visible as our eyes become used to the darkness—we are there in the room with her.

Gradually, Alma's certainties collapse as Elizabeth's response to reality communicates itself to her. On the beach among the rocks, Alma reads aloud to Elizabeth from a book she has with her. The passage states that hope of salvation is merely the crystallization of our realization of ourselves and reality, the proof of our awareness and our desolation. Alma asks Elizabeth if she believes that. Elizabeth nods slowly, with an effect of absolute certainty, as if the words had expressed her own thoughts; Alma, with an effect of much less certainty, insists that *she* doesn't. At the dinner table Alma describes a home for retired nurses and expresses her admiration for those who devote their whole lives to something they believe in. Our sense of the somewhat hollow conventionality of her words, of the large areas of the human personality left unfulfilled by a life devoted to good works, is intensified by the silence into which they fall: Elizabeth's silence. That silence leads Alma on to reveal herself, not only to Elizabeth, but to herself. She begins to talk of experiences she has buried away, to confront their full implications for the first time. Her description of prolonged sexual intercourse with a young boy on the beach (involving also a female acquaintance and another boy), during which all inhibitions were thrown off, is certainly one of the screen's great monologues. Bibi Andersson's performance is extraordinary. As Bergman has said, she "makes the scene so remarkable because she tells the story in a voice which carries a tone of shameful lust, and I've no idea where she got it from." It is important that there is no recourse to flash-back illustration and that much of the monologue is filmed in medium or medium-long shot: the "shameful lust" is there in the way Alma crouches in the armchair as much as in her voice. The experience described, considered in itself, seems a kind of sensual paradise, a sudden revelation of the possibilities of physical ecstasy; but the detached filming of it, with Elizabeth and her silence present in the frame much of the time, encourages us to place it in a context of human complexities—Alma's relationship with Karl-Henrik and the ensuing abortion—that prevents us from seeing it so simply. What Alma is led to discover during the course of the film is quite simply what is within herself, and potentially within all of us: fear that existence may be meaningless; uncertainty as to where "acting" stops and "being" begins; sexual confusion (Eliot's "may and may not, desire and control"); resort under pressure to "primitive" savagery. The second half of the film conveys a sensation of sinking into a dark, perhaps bottomless abyss of uncertainties, both for the women and for the spectator.

Elizabeth's withdrawal is no solution: we see her defeated at every turn. The psychiatrist understands, and seems deadened by her knowledge—the human being withdrawn into a hard shell of clinical detachment, yet unable to keep the bitterness out of her face and voice, speaking to Elizabeth with an emotional brutality that betrays a resentment of the other woman's preservation of a certain sensitivity. Silence, she tells Elizabeth, is itself a "role"; and Elizabeth, while she remains alive, cannot stop affecting other lives and inflicting pain. Her very refusal to take part in life becomes, however unwittingly, a positive action with unforeseeable and uncontrollable consequences. In fact, she finds it impossible just to do *nothing*. There is, for example, the letter she writes about Alma, which Alma reads and interprets as a sign of utter heartlessness, feeling that she has been exploited. One cannot quite see it like that. Elizabeth has shown Alma a sort of half-pitying affection, and has listened to her with a sympathetic attention not devoid of an assumption of superiority—Elizabeth, after all, *knows* more. The letter is to her psychiatrist, on whose part Elizabeth can assume an understanding not unlike her own and in whom she would feel free to confide without hesitation. The fact that Alma is a nurse in the same hospital tells somewhat against this, but one cannot feel that Elizabeth has committed any outrage against the moral code of confidences if one looks at the matter from her point of view. Looked at from Alma's point of view, on the other hand, it seems very different, because Alma is so much more deeply involved in the relationship than Elizabeth. The incident suggests the inevitability of pain in human intercourse. Consciously, Elizabeth is not guilty of deliberate cruelty. Unconsciously, however? She does, after all, leave the letter unsealed. Even the "aware" Elizabeth can't control her unconscious. There is also Elizabeth's ambiguous smile when Alma at last breaks. Is it cruel—the superior being's pleasure in watching the girl's discovery of anguish? Or is she laughing at the absurdity of everything, because, if it's all meaningless, then pain doesn't matter, it's of no more account than happiness? Her silence preserves the ambiguity and thereby inflicts further pain.

The thematic movement of *Persona* is, up to half-way, expressed through a clearly developed, meticulously observed "naturalistic" fiction: one could list at length the details of psychological insight manifest in the *mise-en-scène*. The moment when Alma, the nice, normal, altruistic young nurse, is forced to confront her own potential for cruelty in the incident with the broken glass completes the exposition of her discovery of reality (the reality of herself) through her experience of Elizabeth. At that point Bergman chooses to disrupt the film. The opening shots, showing technical details of film projection, constitute some warning of what is going to be done to us, but they don't really prepare us for the shock, engrossed as we are in the narrative. After the depiction of the projector-breakdown, the "naturalistic" drama is resumed, but we can no longer feel in quite the same relation to it: our sense of security has been (like Alma's) irreparably undermined, and from here on we have the constant feeling that *anything* may happen. As the second half develops, doubts begin to grow, at first almost imperceptibly but by the end very powerfully, about the nature of what we are watching.

In fact, we can narrow the area of uncertainty down to a long section of five consecutive episodes. There are, to be sure, moments of doubt in the first half of the film, but it is still possible to say there that it is Alma's doubt that is involved, not ours. Elizabeth's whispered words to Alma about going to bed before she falls asleep at the table are accepted by Alma as hallucination at the time—she immediately repeats them herself, implying that they have not been spoken aloud. Elizabeth's visit to Alma's room at night is given a dream-like quality by the hazy lighting and the music. (Bergman's increasing fondness for refusing to direct the audience's emotional reactions to "real" action by the use of incidental music seems to be largely applicable to *Persona*, where music is generally—not quite always—used to characterize the scenes that are non-"real.") Both incidents are denied by Elizabeth the next day, and there is no reason for us not to believe her; both are readily understandable as wish-fulfillments by Alma, who at that stage of the film wants Elizabeth as a combined elder-sister-and-lover, and also wants to merge identities with her, attracted by her frame, her beauty, her mysteriousness.

The section where there is real doubt begins with Alma in bed, tossing in a half-sleep, and ends with her waking up: tempting, of course, to interpret it all as dream, but not quite possible. For one thing, at the start of the section she is in her nightdress in bed, and when she wakes up she is fully dressed, at a table: a *series* of dreams, perhaps? But the way certain sequences are shot (particularly the visit of Elizabeth's husband, with Liv Ullmann's face in the foreground of the screen while Bibi Andersson and Gunnar Björnstrand make love in the background) suggests that, if we are watching a dream, it is as much Elizabeth's as Alma's. The five episodes are as follows:

1) The visit of Elizabeth's husband. Alma, tossing in bed, wakes up, switches on radio, hears a man's voice calling "Elizabeth," goes to the sleeping Elizabeth and comments on her puffy face and swollen, ugly mouth, hears the voice again and wanders out. Elizabeth opens her eyes, gets up, and follows. The husband (in dark glasses, which at

first make one think he is blind) greets Alma by Elizabeth's name, and makes love to her when, after initially denying it, she accepts the role. Elizabeth witnesses the whole encounter, mostly with her back to it, though at one point she guides Alma's hand to the husband's face.

2) Alma's twice-repeated story of Elizabeth's relationship with her child, filmed first with the camera on Elizabeth's face then repeated word for word with the camera on Alma's.

3) Alma talks nonsense-sentences to Elizabeth. Alma is in her nurse's uniform, which she has never worn at the summer house. The culminating sentence is "Many words and then nausea." This leads to:

4) The blood-sucking. The two women sit opposite one another at a table. Alma lays her bare arm on the table, her lips curl slightly with an erotic suggestiveness, when she gives her arm to Elizabeth, who

Liv Ullmann as Elisabeth Vogler (foreground), and Bibi Andersson as Alma in *Persona*. (Note: Sprocket holes showing at right of picture are shown at Ingmar Bergman's request.)

bites until the blood oozes out from under her lips. Alma strikes Elizabeth's (off-screen) face repeatedly and savagely. (3 and 4 should perhaps be thought of as a single sequence, because they are continuous; no time-relationship is suggested between the others, or between them and other events in the film.)

5) Back in the hospital room where Alma first saw Elizabeth. Alma in

nurse's uniform again. She holds Elizabeth tenderly and beseechingly, and persuades her to repeat after her the word *"Ingenting"* ("Nothing").

It seems to me clear that none of these incidents is to be thought of as literally "happening." Two of them (the husband's visit and the scene in hospital) are impossible on grounds of content; in common with these two, the others have a surreal, nightmare quality quite distinct from the crisp, lucid, objective tone of the "naturalistic" parts of the film. The doubt is as to the precise level of reality or unreality on which they are to be thought of as operating. Subjective fantasy? If so, whose? Bergman does not, I think, for reasons both thematic and formal, intend us to be able to answer such questions. By this point in the film the idea of the interchangeability of experience, of the identification of Alma with Elizabeth and of both with the spectator, has been carried about as far as it can go through an objective presentation of "real" actions. Bergman needs a means of finding a dramatic approximation for inner states of breakdown, disintegration and merging—at once the loss of identity and a kind of universal extension of identity. What we see on the screen is to be taken as interchangeable —as happening within (or beneath?) either woman's consciousness or both, an expression in actions of experiences taking place below the level of action. This makes these scenes virtually impossible to "explain" (and indeed if they could be neatly explained they would lose much of their point). One can, however, offer various pointers towards their interpretation.

1) Shortly before them comes the scene where Elizabeth looks at the Warsaw Ghetto photograph. It is important that we be reminded, at that point, of the extension outwards into "surface" existence, into the world of flesh-and-blood physical and mental suffering, of the film's central concerns. The relationship between the photograph of a public outrage and the psychic cruelty between the two women is very interesting: each has the effect, in a different way, of universalizing the significance of the other. Cruelty, exploitation, the desire to establish and express patterns of power and subjugation, all play their roles in the "hallucination" scenes that follow, on the level of psychic interaction: the roots of Nazism in the universal human psyche.

2) The suggestion of dream given by framing the episodes between Alma asleep and Alma waking is important: the release of suppressed fears and desires that characterizes dreams also characterizes these scenes. But the fact that we don't take them simply as dreams is important too: the transitions into and out of the "doubtful" section

are not abrupt, and the spectator is in no way adverted to "read" it differently from the rest of the film. We are to take it that what we see is *in some sense* really happening—locked in psychic conflict, the two women are really inflicting terrible psychological wounds on each other. 3) Each of the episodes can be seen as an attempt by Alma to master the world of experience Elizabeth's silence opens up to her, by dominating or possessing Elizabeth, each attempt culminating in a highly equivocal victory which is also defeat. In the first, she usurps Elizabeth's role in her relationship with her husband, only to discover the anguish and humiliation of incompatibility. It is natural to relate the scene of love-making back to Alma's story of her brief sensual fulfillment on the beach: the latter was an account of perfect satisfaction achieved by limiting the sexual relationship to merely animal experience, with all human complexities omitted; the scene with Elizabeth's husband epitomizes the imperfection of relationships involving emotional demands, the difficulties of yielding up consciousness of self. The episode of the twice-told story extends the idea of human incompatibility and separateness to motherhood. Alma tries to possess Elizabeth by entering her mind and memory, taking over her knowledge of her failure and cruelty as a mother, with which to denounce her. The first time the story is told we watch Elizabeth's disturbed face registering recognition of horrible truths she has buried from herself; the second time, we watch Alma's gradual realization that in taking over Elizabeth's mind she becomes Elizabeth, and thus is talking about herself—that the cruelty she is denouncing is something within *her* (the relevant reference back here is to her account of her abortion). The sequence culminates in the terrifying moment where Bergman merges the two faces—at first crudely, to give a distorted, split image, and then, even as Alma hysterically denies that she is Elizabeth, in a perfect image where it is impossible to detect where and how the faces are fused but which remains disturbingly unnatural. The third and fourth episodes show the breakdown of Alma's attempts to dominate the silent Elizabeth verbally, as her speech disintegrates into nonsense, followed by a recourse to the most direct physical intercourse of blood-sucking. Another equivocal victory-defeat: Alma dominates Elizabeth by inducing her by suggestion to satisfy her (Alma's) perverse desire, then reacts with horror and terrifying violence when she realizes the implications of having her blood drunk by the other woman. For this and the last hallucinatory episode, Alma has resumed her uniform in an effort to insist that her identity remains separate and undisintegrated; in the last sequence, this attempt to enforce a sense that things are unchanged is consolidated by the hospital setting. Alma induces Elizabeth to speak; but again the victory is equivocal, for the one word Elizabeth repeats—"Nothing"—epitomizes Alma's worst and ultimate fear, and her very means of mastering Elizabeth becomes the sign of Elizabeth's ascendancy over her.

Formally, the spectator's uncertainty as to the levels of reality is at least equally important: indeed, it is through this formal device that Bergman extends the film's thematic progress to the spectator. The disturbing perplexities to which the two women are exposed have their counterpart in our own inability to pin down and categorize the nature of what we are watching: Elizabeth and Alma? Liv Ullmann and Bibi Andersson? Images cast on a screen by light passing through a moving strip of film? The analogy between our experience and the imagined experience of the two characters is obviously incomplete, but the emotional effect offers, I think, a rough working equivalent. Bergman himself acknowledges the crudeness of art beside the complexities of existence in the film's very first images. After the film projector shots, we see a silent cartoon of a fat woman in a bathing costume washing her hands, framed as on a screen; the cartoon flickers jerkily, breaks down, starts up again. Bergman then cuts in a shot of real hands washing themselves, the image now filling the whole screen (i.e., the cartoon is shown as film, the hands as reality). A way, surely, of admitting, at the outset of one of the most complex films ever made, that, beside reality, art is as crude as are the jerky movements of the cartoon beside the flexible, organic motions of the real hands?

More than this, the breakdown constitutes Bergman's admission that he can't resolve the problems the film has raised. The last third of *Persona* gives us a series of scenes of uncertain reality and uncertain chronology; all are closely related, thematically, to the concerns established earlier in the film, and all carry us deeper into the sensation of breakdown due to full exposure to the unresolvable or unendurable. They come across as a series of tentative sketches, which are far from tentative in realization, of possibilities offered by the director who, because of his own uncertainties, denies himself the narrative artist's right to dogmatize, to say "*This* is what happened next." Given the universal implications of the subject-matter, the fact that we can no longer think in simple terms about "Alma and Elizabeth" (despite the fact that the characters keep their fictional identities to the end) compels us to feel what we are shown with unusual immediacy, as if naked experience were being communicated direct, instead of being clothed with the customary medium of characters-and-narrative. It is not a question of vagueness nor of artistic abdication, but of an extreme and rigorous honesty; each sequence is realized with the same intensity and precision that characterized the straight narrative of the first half.

The boy who appears at the beginning and end of the film need cause no bewilderment: we need not even go back to the ending of *The Silence*, where the same actor was struggling to master "Words in the Foreign Language," to grasp his function, though the continuity is clear. The slow build-up of the pre-credit sequence culminates in his stretching his hand towards the camera, as if trying to make out who we are, on the other side of the screen; the next shot, from behind him, shows him moving his hands on the screen over the merging faces of the two women. The universalizing identification of the characters with the spectator is thus established at once, together with the child's efforts (he is just past the verge of adolescence) to grapple with the perplexities of identity. The identifying of spectator with characters is complex: we are not only what the boy sees, we are the boy seeing. The near-subliminal flashes that punctuate the credits are also shown (like the tanks at the start of *The Silence*), as it were, through his eyes: with an effect of frightening confusion, they epitomize the tensions and anxieties to which the characters and the audience are to be exposed during the film. They anticipate key scenes: the burning priest, an erect penis (Alma's erotic story), the rocks shown later as she reads Elizabeth the book about "our desolation." It is easy to interpret the child-figure as a symbol for the growing and vulnerable part of the human psyche: one can if one wishes see him as an aspect of Bergman's own consciousness, but he is also universal, an aspect of ourselves. His reappearance at the end of the film contributes enormously to our sense of its ending, not with a negation, but with a question-mark.

The film offers no resolution: this is its most disturbing feature, and the one that—even more than its obviously innovatory qualities—sets it apart from Bergman's previous work. Gone are even the tentative gropings towards affirmation that ended *Winter Light* and *The Silence*. Instead, a complete openness: an openness expressed in the ambiguity of Alma's face as, dressed in her nurse's uniform again, she prepares to return to the world; the face of a woman irreparably broken, or ready to begin? (The closest parallel is perhaps the ending of Hitchcock's *The Birds*.) *Persona* excites, troubles and stimulates: it doesn't depress. For Bergman it is a great personal triumph of intelligence and character: the tendencies to self-pity, to masochism—a fascinated prodding of psychic sores—that disfigured certain of the earlier

films (*Sawdust and Tinsel, The Seventh Seal, The Face*) are here
quite subsumed into an identification with *universal* pain. One might
think of the Hopkins of the "Terrible Sonnets." "My cries heave,
herds-long, huddle in a main, a chief/Woe, world-sorrow; on an age-
old anvil wince and sing . . ." Bergman has been a great film-maker
from (at least) *Summer Interlude*, but *Persona* marks not only a new
phase in his development but a new extension of his genius, a further
dimension. Here for the first time one registers a Bergman film as the
work of a man fully and sensitively (hence very painfully) alive to the
pressures and tensions of the world we all have to live in, who has
been able through his courage and intelligence to convert a private
anguish into a universal witness, while remaining intensely human. He
exposes himself fully to the despair and horror that man must confront if there is ever to be a possibility of passing beyond. For all the
anguish and the sense of deep hurt, there is a marvellously sensitive
feeling, at once dynamic and compassionate, for human potentialities,
for the development of consciousness. Towards the end of the film
Alma, incoherently babbling nonsense-phrases, lets slip the words "A
desperate perhaps." And that is exactly what *Persona* is.

HOUR OF THE WOLF
. . . .

Hour of the Wolf derives from a script which Bergman wrote before
Persona, and provisionally entitled *The Cannibals*. Illness intervened,
and out of it grew *Persona*. Bergman then returned to the earlier sce-
nario, revising it extensively. As *Persona* broke new ground, one expected the new film to combine elements of the old and new Bergman, and such expectations are in the event confirmed. But the fact
that *Hour of the Wolf* is such a coherent and satisfying work, with no
sense of disparateness, also confirms the organic nature of Bergman's
œuvre, and warns one not to talk too glibly about "the old and the
new": *Persona* marked a new stage in Bergman's development, but
not at the cost of rejecting its predecessors.

The themes of *Persona* can be traced back readily enough through
Bergman's previous work to his early films. Apart from obvious innovatory features of style and method, what strikes one most in it—
and what is the outcome of the prolonged and rigorous self-disciplining

of the Trilogy—is its artistic impersonality: its distancing and universalizing of Bergman's personal concerns. If *Hour of the Wolf* may
strike one superficially as a pre-trilogy throwback, it is because of the
evidently close relationship between the protagonist (played, as in *The
Seventh Seal* and *The Face*, by Max von Sydow) and Bergman himself.
Yet comparison with *The Face* will demonstrate, I think, that the objectifying discipline is as strongly in control in *Hour of the Wolf* as in
Persona. The detailed objections to *The Face*—that it was at once too
explicit and too obscure, that certain subsidiary elements were neither
very interesting in themselves nor meaningfully integrated in the
whole, that the overall tone was unpleasant, at once frigid and strident
—add up to the primary objection that Bergman was not there sufficiently master of his material. No such objections can be raised against
Hour of the Wolf. Here, all the elements are perfectly integrated;
when the film becomes momentarily explicit (in Alma's final monologue), this is both in character and justified by the overall form; the
obscurities are for the most part meaningful *as* obscurities—the point,
that is, lies partly in their remaining obscure; and the film is made
with a spontaneity, a passion, and a sureness of expression that suggest, for all the blackness of the content, the work of an altogether
freer human being than the one who made *The Face.*

Much has been made of *Hour of the Wolf*'s references back to previous Bergman films, via characters' names and certain characteristic
incidents. What seems to me more interesting—and clearly related to
the increased objectification—is that this is the first Bergman film to
point to a wide (and non-Swedish) cinematic tradition outside his own
work. In view of his often expressed admiration for Fellini the film's
close relationship in subject, structure and method to *Giulietta degli
Spiriti* is perhaps not surprising, any more than is its complementary
self-sufficiency (Bergman clearly needn't fear accusations of plagiarism).
What *is* surprising is Bergman's use of the traditions of the American
horror film, from Whale and Browning to Hitchcock. Not only does the
Birdman (as Tom Milne has pointed out) bear an unmistakable resemblance to Lugosi's Dracula, but the face of Baron von Merkens, especially when photographed from below, as at the dinner party, distinctly
recalls in its contours Karloff's original Frankenstein creation. The mi-
nuscule but apparently human Tamino in the Birdman's "Magic Flute"
performance recalls Ernest Thesiger's homunculi in *The Bride of Frankenstein.* The general framework, with an outsider being initiated into a
close-knit, isolated and highly abnormal society, and especially the ending, where in the darkness and mud its members hideously exact a com-

munal vengeance, suggest *Freaks.* The old woman who peels off her face to reveal a decomposing skull and gaping eye-sockets evokes at once the two *Wax Museum* films and Mrs. Bates in *Psycho.* The pecking and jabbing Birdman suggests both *Psycho* and *The Birds,* and the shot of von Sydow passing through a corridor thick with sparrows and other wild birds looks like overt reference (hesitant as one is to associate such seemingly incompatible directors). There are further more generalized references: the castle interiors, for instance, especially in the later sequences, are strongly reminiscent of Hollywood Gothic, from Whale to Corman; the "cannibal" family suggests vampires, particularly in the way the lips of the father-figure's huge mouth draw back, and there is a reference to their "fangs" during the nightmarishly edgy and disquieting dinner-table conversation. It is impossible to be sure how many of these references are deliberate, and they nowhere interfere with the film's unity of tone: there is not a moment when we could be watching the work of anyone but Bergman. But by drawing on a popular tradition Bergman to a great extent depersonalizes the horrors, at the same time completely realizing the implicit relationship between the traditional horror figures and the psychological terrors for which they deputize.

Göran Persson has called the film "Bergman's *Psycho,*" and certainly it follows a similar progression into ever-deepening darkness and horror, to the ultimate disintegration of the personality. But perhaps, if we are to compare it with Hitchcock, it has more in common thematically with *Vertigo:* we have, again, the hero torn between the world of daily reality and another world, a fascinating abyss, which may represent a deeper and more potent reality or may be an illusion, but which leads by an inevitable process towards disintegration and death. The function of Alma, though she is a far "deeper" personality, is analogous to that of Midge in Hitchcock's film: both struggle to keep their men in the real world (see, for instance, Alma's efforts to interest Johan in her accounts), and their failure to do so is decisive to the development of each protagonist, hence of each film.

Alma has so far been comparatively neglected by the film's interpreters: this is a pity, as she represents its most striking new development. Alma is, quite simply, the most beautiful character in Bergman's whole work, and quite distinct from the "affirmative" characters of earlier films like *The Seventh Seal* and *Wild Strawberries.* In Alma we have a positive figure who is at once mature and convincing, a figure born out of the merciless honesty of *Winter Light* and *The Silence.* She is associated throughout with the idea of fruitfulness. We first see

her, big with child, at a table on which lies a heap of apples, some
half-peeled; among the objects she handles while unpacking Johan's
artist's equipment from the boat is a growing plant. The symbolism of
the blossoming apple tree, though quite simple and unequivocal in its
meaning, emerges naturally and unobtrusively. What we register first
is Alma's spontaneous delight in it, so that the tree is a means of char-
acterizing her as much as a symbol; when, on the first "manifestation"
to Alma (the appearance of the old woman), the tree is barren and
bare, the symbolism is allowed to make its effect without directorial
insistence. The fact of Alma's pregnancy is talked of little in the film,
apart from one key speech; but as a visual presence it assumes great
and pervasive importance. Alma, as wife and mother, convincingly
embodies the possibility of wholeness and health in life: Johan has
praised her as having "whole thoughts and feelings"—God "made her
in one piece"—and this is dramatically realized through Liv Ullmann's
performance. In a film showing ultimate disintegration, she stands for
its opposite, at least as an ideal whose attainability, though questioned,
is not decisively denied.

Alma is Pamina. The identification is made very plainly during the
puppet-theatre performance: at Tamino's words *"Lebt denn Pamina
noch?"* ("Is Pamina still alive?"), the camera settles on Alma's face,
and returns to it when the Birdman discusses the significance of Mozart's setting of the name afterwards. "The Magic Flute" connects
(indeed, virtually identifies) the perfected union of man and woman
with ultimate fulfillment and enlightenment: the Birdman describes
how in his setting Mozart separates the syllables of Pa-mi-na, so that
they become less a name than an incantation. The relationship of
Bergman's film to Mozart's opera is complex and important, containing at once a terrible irony and a positive assertion beyond irony's
reach. The irony is implied early, in Johan's remark (while showing
Alma the sketches of his "demons") that the Birdman, "the worst
of all," is "somehow connected with Papageno." Mozart's Papageno,
half-bird, half-human, is an entirely gentle and amiable child of nature; Johan's Birdman is also a "child of nature"—of a black and perverted nature, cruel, aggressive, destructive. In the extract from the
opera given in the film, Tamino stands in the darkness of ignorance
and confusion before the Temple of Wisdom, questioning unseen
powers about his destiny. Within "the loveliest and most disturbing
music ever written," Mozart distinguishes Tamino's restlessness and
yearning (set as recitative) from the unhurried and formalized responses of the off-stage chorus, accompanied by a melody of breadth

and mysterious serenity previously sung by the Priest of the Temple,
giving an effect of timelessness: the scene becomes a dialogue between
the human world of time (hence of doubt and anxiety) and a world
of serenity and illumination where time's tyranny has been overthrown.
Much is made in the film of Johan's acute awareness of time: there is
the transfixing counted minute (a striking example of Bergman's growing fondness for directly communicating emotional experience to his
audiences, as well as showing it), where we share Johan's sense of the
unendurable slowness of time and, simultaneously, his fear of its passing; and this gets its visual counterpart later as he strikes matches and
obsessively watches their burning. Tamino's question, *"Wann wird
das Licht mein Auge finden?"* ("When will my eye find the light?")
receives the answer, *"Bald, bald, Jungling, oder nie"* ("Soon, or
never"): for Tamino the answer proves to be "Soon," for Johan
"Never." The remainder of Mozart's opera is, for Tamino and the
listener, a steady progression into ever-intenser illumination; the remainder of Bergman's film, for Johan and the spectator, a descent into
ever-intenser darkness. In the latter half of *Hour of the Wolf* we see
no daylight (with the exception of the uncanny and unnatural light
of the over-exposed flashback). In one scene Alma-Pamina protects
with her hands a flickering candle-flame, in the midst of all-envelop-
ing darkness. It is in this scene that she talks of the coming child "in
all this awful darkness." The question may be asked, Why choose the
macabre Birdman to deliver, via Mozart, the film's most affirmative
statements? I think we must accept that, on one level, he speaks "out
of character": the affirmation is not felt as negated by the speaker, and
one senses Bergman himself very directly behind it. At the same time,
it has a valid dramatic function: one of the devil's supreme torments is
to hold up momentarily to the lost a glimpse of heaven in the midst
of hell.

The concept of wholeness becomes, then, through Alma and the
use of Mozart, a very real presence in the film; but it is of no more
efficacy against Johan's demons than is the candle-flame against the
surrounding blackness. Some have seen those demons as representing
the artist's imaginative creations over which, Frankenstein-like, he
loses control; or as the side of his personality out of which his art develops. Nothing could be further from the truth. The point is made
quite unequivocally that the demons are inimical to artistic creation
—their emergence in the first stretches of the film corresponds to a decline in Johan's art. What is more, their destruction of him as an artist
is closely paralleled by their destruction of his marriage relationship.

The connection is made in the film's one entirely happy scene—that in which Johan sketches Alma as she sits by the blossoming apple-tree, which links marriage, parenthood and creativity in an image of wholeness. It is the potentiality for wholeness that the demons destroy. They are the products of neurosis, embodiments of the power of the past over the present. It is a mistake to see *Hour of the Wolf* as essentially concerned with The Artist. Johan's speech on the "utter unimportance of art in the world of men," far from being central to the film, is a point where Bergman's personal concerns of the moment rather roughly intrude: it belongs with *Persona* and *Shame* rather than with *Hour of the Wolf*. Bergman uses Johan's art as a kind of shorthand for the creative side of the personality.

The information the film offers relevant to Johan's neurosis can be separated into four sections, and the sort of significance each has, the way it is to be taken, is carefully defined by formal or stylistic devices. Johan's account of his childhood punishment (locked in a cupboard in which he was led to believe there lurked a little creature that would bite his toes off) is given us as a straight statement without flashback or other illustration. We accept it as literal truth: here Johan is remembering the past *as it was*, not being haunted by it in distorted forms in the present. Secondly, by the same token, we accept the fact of Johan's past affair with Veronica Vogler. Thirdly, the flashback showing Johan's experience of murdering the boy is given a disturbing, heightened quality by the over-exposure that suggests nightmarish hallucination. Finally, there are the demons, emanations or projections from Johan's mind, and these include Veronica Vogler herself as she appears in the film—Bergman does not distinguish her from the rest. It is possible for the spectator to relate the parts so that they add up to a coherent and intelligible inner portrait; at the same time, in their presentation they are sufficiently disjunct to convey Johan's sense of unmanageable confusion.

The childhood experience is clearly formative. Two points especially emerge: an overwhelming terror of castration (the small creature biting off the toes), and the culminating emotional identification with the mother, against the father (who was responsible for the punishment): factors commonly associated in neurotic complexes with the development of fears of sexual inadequacy and with the possible formation of compensatory homosexual tendencies. The fantasy or hallucination of killing the boy combines various features relevant to this. The scene partly re-enacts the childhood punishment, the "small creature" biting Johan's foot. The most obvious interpretation of the scene is that it symbolizes an attempt to suppress homosexual tendencies. Johan is greatly disturbed by the boy's presence. The fishing-rod, in the position in which it is filmed, carries very obvious phallic overtones, and Johan's desperate and clumsy attempts to reel in are surely symbolic of an hysterical effort to deny sexual response. The boy then lies on his back in an attitude of erotic invitation; Johan leans over him, then begins to shake him violently. Near the beginning of the film, as he shows Alma the sketches of the demons, Johan says of the one he describes as "practically harmless," "I think he's homosexual." We identify him, I think, with Heerbrand, the man who, almost immediately after Johan's story of the boy, brings him the gun with which he tries to kill Alma. But what seems to unsettle Johan most in the boy's behaviour is the way in which he inspects, critically and perhaps contemptuously, first Johan's sketches and then his catch of three fishes (Bergman's favourite Freudian phallic symbol—see *Prison* and *Waiting Women*). His fears of creative and sexual inadequacy are behind the panic into which the child throws him. Finally, we tend to associate the child with the mysterious boy—presumably Johan's son by a previous marriage or product of his affair with Veronica Vogler (the obscurity here seems unprofitable and annoying)—mentioned by Alma in her accounts ("50 kronor for your boy's birthday"): another "ghost" from Johan's past. What the scene enacts, in this complex way, is an attempt to destroy by violence the various half understood pressures from the past. But they lurk on, as it were, just below the surface, like the submerged body that refuses to sink.

From what we gather of the affair with Veronica Vogler (from remarks, and from the fantasy re-enactments) it was characterized by an exclusive and violent sensuality, suggesting that it was at once Johan's attempt to assert his sexual adequacy and an expression of his emotional incompleteness. He passed from it to the potentially complete relationship with Alma, but without having mastered all the arrested and warped aspects of his personality expressed through the affair with Veronica: so Veronica is both dead and alive, as she later appears to Johan in the castle. To reach her, he is forced to undergo a series of humiliations and trials (kissing the old Baroness' foot, watching the old lady remove her face, seeing the Birdman's semi-transformation, etc.) which again suggest a macabre inversion of the initiation of Tamino in "The Magic Flute." At the end of it is Veronica: not Alma-Pamina, whom he has tried to kill, firing three bullets at her. But Alma is virtually unscathed. It is Veronica who is, apparently, dead; and above her (as Göran Persson has pointed out to me) hang three lights which at first, in long-shot, look like apertures or bullet-holes. The ambiguity beautifully suggests the unresolved confusions of Johan's psyche, the inner divisions and conflicts of conscious and subconscious.

As for the demons, with their horror-film affiliations, I think it is vain to try to attach detailed significance to individuals: perverted and destructive, they typify all that lives on unmastered in Johan. We can see now, I think, why Papageno, representative of entirely natural and untrammelled sexuality, should become, seen through the distorting glass of Johan's fragmenting psyche, the monstrous Birdman. That the demons are not susceptible to more precise categorization is important: they are an expression of all that Johan doesn't understand within himself. Even the level of reality on which they exist is continually in question, and unascertainable: we feel to the end that there *may* be a castle on the other side of the island with real people in it, seen through varying degrees of subjective distortion.

The "reunion" with the dead-alive Veronica culminates in Johan's ultimate sexual humiliation. His make-up, the masks of the Great Lover, mockingly applied by the Birdman, now smeared grotesquely over his face, he looks up from his love-making to find the demons watching, gloating with hideous laughter. What we see on the screen is an amazingly vivid and concrete depiction of mental breakdown. Johan is cruelly forced to confront his shattered inner self: "The glass is shattered," he says. "But what do the splinters reflect? Can you tell me that?" His lips go on moving, the voice obliterated. The camera tracks in until his face, slipping out of focus, seems to decompose before our eyes, to dissolve to water—just under the surface of which floats the corpse of the boy. Johan has been driven to a partial self-understanding: he sees just enough, I think, to grasp the strength of the destructive forces within him, so that all he can do is surrender to them—to surrender all that side of him that responded to Alma, and to the idea of wholeness. Bergman shows us neurosis proliferating like an evil growth, developing out of the small creature biting Johan's toes into the demons who in the end totally devour him.

Perhaps the most important thing in *Hour of the Wolf*, and what relates it most closely to *Persona*, is Alma's partial sharing of Johan's inner experiences. In *Persona* Elizabeth's horrified apprehension of reality was gradually communicated to her nurse, so that the girl's defenses of conventional "normality" were shattered. Here, Johan's increasing awareness of inner horrors is communicated, through the medium of her love for him, to Alma. The sharing is only partial. The greatest obstacle to the psychoanalytical cure of neurosis is the patient's inability to *want* to be cured—his tendency to cling on jealously to his neurosis as if it were his most precious possession. Hence there comes a point at which Johan refuses Alma further access to his world, and from that moment he is lost ("If only I could have been with him the whole time" are almost her last words in the film). Most disturbing of all is Alma's final self-questioning about her failure to save him: did her acceptance of the demons in fact accelerate their domination? Or did her jealousy prevent her from entering into Johan's inner world far enough? We are left pondering the efficacy of personal relationships, even at their most committed. Like *Persona, Hour of the Wolf* is a film that calls everything into question. At the beginning Alma sat outside at a table, in daylight. At the end she is indoors, surrounded by darkness. The child is still unborn.

The film begins and ends with Alma. On Bergman's own admission, the story of Johan Borg is very personal: that crucial punishment was repeatedly administered to Bergman as a child. Alma and the framework—emotional as much as formal—that she provides is the mature artist's means of distancing, hence mastering, all those unmanageable elements whose presence has so often flawed Bergman's work. The very fact that the film shows Johan's destruction suggests—coming as it does from the present active, open and assured Bergman—the completeness of the mastery.

SHAME

. . . .

> *We're quite definitely living in a twilight world. But I don't know when the darkness will descend.*
>
> BERGMAN

At the beginning of his essay on John Galsworthy—one of the very few statements about criticism that really mean anything to me—D. H. Lawrence insists on the critic's obligation to make explicit the standards by which he judges. It is time to lay one's cards openly on the table. I can see no purpose in the individual life beyond the complete realization of one's humanity. The most *basic* urge may be that of self-preservation, but, if one is thinking in terms of the quality of life,

Liv Ullmann as Eva Rosenberg in *The Shame*.

the mean and meagre instinct to preserve oneself is insignificant beside the creative urge. By the creative urge I mean all that drives us on towards the full expression of our human potentialities, the whole constructive, growing side of our natures, at once dynamic and responsive. And the standards by which one judges life must also be, at root, the standards by which one judges art. We live in a society whose main characteristics all tend towards the inhibiting and perverting of human creativity, and there is little sign that things are likely to improve in any foreseeable future. How to come to terms with this is the central human problem today, and one that the artist, through his creative functioning, must feel in a particularly acute form.

Such considerations as these determine my admiration for Bergman, and especially the Bergman of the Trilogy and after. *Winter Light,* *The Silence* and *Persona* are the record of an artist's struggle towards the full realization of his humanity, all his energies concentrated to that end. My appreciation of these films, and of *Shame,* my deep gratitude to Bergman for them, is greatly intensified by considering them in the context of cinema in the late 'sixties—the world of *Weekend*, of *Belle de Jour*, of *Boom*, of *Rosemary's Baby*. These are all films of distinction (the degree varying enormously), but in comparison with them, Bergman's films are the work of a man who, whatever his disabilities and limitations, at least *wants* to be human.

Comparison between *Shame* and *Weekend* is virtually inevitable: both are centrally concerned with the obsolescence of the civilized European sensibility. Godard's is the more obviously extraordinary work: significantly, it is formally and stylistically adventurous where *Shame* (in relation not only to Godard but to *Persona*) is reactionary. Bergman has never (except perhaps in *Prison*) shown any inclination to be *avant-garde*, and the "advanced" aspects of *Persona* were determined solely by the content: they are not evidence of a desire for deliberate formal experiment, but purely the expression of Bergman's sense of breakdown and disintegration. Godard's achievement is to be above all *modern*, not in any self-consciously *avant-garde* manner but by nature. It is an equivocal achievement, and Bergman does not and cannot share it. Between *Shame* and *Weekend* exists an impassable barrier.

Bergman is a great artist in the great civilized European tradition; Godard has aligned himself with the forces that have rejected that tradition and are now speeding its perhaps final disintegration. Godard's openness towards a "brave new world" adumbrated by the guerrilla-cannibals of *Weekend* would be unthinkable for Bergman. *Weekend* moves from the ineffectual, ludicrously incongruous farmyard recital-lecture on Mozart to the percussion improvisations of the solitary, absorbed guerrilla; the essential progress of *Shame* is from Jan Rosenberg's yearning dream about performing the slow movement of the 4th Brandenburg Concerto to his final withdrawal from contact at the end, irredeemably lost as a human being but equipped now for survival (if anyone is to survive). To me (and I suppose to Bergman) most of the more "advanced" aspects of contemporary art—action-painting, aleatory and electronic music, *musique concrète*, William Burroughs—are comprehensible only as evidence of disintegration. Perhaps I am wrong, and the arts are, as many claim, struggling towards a new synthesis; but it is obvious that it will be a synthesis that will leave out of account all that has been of central importance in the western cultural tradition hitherto: in a word, humanity. The values of *Shame* are above all human values; the values of *Weekend* are something else, I'm not sure what—and not sure that Godard is sure. Godard's early work abounded in references to the arts, a desperate and essentially

external attempt to relate himself to a tradition; Bergman has never
needed to refer, because he is an integral part of the cultural tradition,
its product and, at present, one of its greatest representatives. The role
of Bach in Bergman's recent work (there are references in every film
from *Through a Glass Darkly* on, except for *Hour of the Wolf,* where
Mozart takes over) is far more integral than the "cultural" references
in Godard, a matter of profound inner commitment rather than
would-be alignments. Nevertheless, the cultural tradition counts for
something in Godard's work up to and including *Masculin-Féminin,*
where it finds its most touching defender in the person of Paul (Jean-
Pierre Léaud). When Godard killed Paul off at the end of that film,
he took perhaps the most decisive single step of his career so far. One
recognizes, and honours, the courage of such a renunciation, even
while reflecting that Godard's ability to make it tells us something essential about his human limitations. If *Weekend* is the product of his
peculiar genius, it is also the product of his peculiar deficiencies; and if
Shame is Bergman's *Weekend,* then it is *Weekend* made by a human
being. Godard is both superhuman and subhuman, often simultaneously, but never quite human.

In placing so much emphasis on the arts, and on the "cultural tradition," I know I run the risk of being dismissed by many as an Ivory
Tower aesthete, clinging to a position of hopeless insulation. Certain
British journalist-critics, writing of *Shame,* have seemed to imply that
Bergman's alleged obsession (Obsession: any serious concern you don't
happen to share) with the idea of the irrelevance of art to the great
mass of mankind is invalid or at least not very interesting: a bit "old
hat," perhaps. One would like to ask these people why they are critics: art to them would appear to be no more than a kind of game,
merely marginal in relation to human life. For anyone capable of making real contact with a work of art (as opposed to a casual or dilettant-
ish pleasure or displeasure), the arts stand for very much more than
themselves. They are (as I. A. Richards said of literature) our "store-
house of recorded values." They are the tangible definition of the civilized tradition of which we are still more or less members, whether
we like it or not: a tradition consisting not only of artists and their
works but of the developing collective sensibility that, in their dis-
tinctive and particularized forms, they express. And this is precisely the
spirit in which Bergman handles the theme of art and its "utter unimportance in the world of men" (*Hour of the Wolf*) in his recent
films.

The reception of *Shame*—one of the very few films of recent years

that really matter—by the majority of reputedly "serious" British journalist-critics fills me with an emotion I can only call disgust. To use a
film of such passion and intelligence, so patently central to contemporary experience, as a pretext for condescending witticisms, or simply
to evade the issue, is to abdicate from all critical responsibility. The
following remarks can be taken as representative, in tone as well as in
actual content: "We are left at the end confirmed in our initial assumption that the husband and wife are people we know all too well
from other Bergman films and do not really want to know at all" (John
Russell Taylor, The Times). ". . . the paraphernalia of this anony-
mous war, a cold Vietnam of the far north, seems to have been assem-
bled as yet another frozen testing ground for artistic sensibility" (Penelope Houston, The Spectator). "I have not found Ingmar Bergman's
later films appealing . . . Jan is a coward who, like most cowards, can
easily become a bully. For some reason beyond my understanding, Eva
appears to love him" (Penelope Mortimer, The Observer: it can stand
as a fair enough comment on Mrs Mortimer's "understanding"). "I
find them [Bergman's films] adolescent, pretentious, silly, and visually
undistinguished" (Richard Roud, The Guardian). Nice to know that
Britain's leading Godard adulator finds Bergman adolescent. Mr Roud
falls back on a quotation from a colleague who admires the film, and
adds, ". . . Just let me plead *nolo contendere* and slip out by the near-
est exit." This facile attitude of "It may be one of my blind spots" de-
grades criticism to a level where debate becomes impossible. I am familiar with such tactics from my experience of school pupils, but most
outgrow them by the Sixth Form. Whether or not art matters any
longer, these people effectively demonstrate that criticism doesn't, as
they practise it. In themselves, of course, they don't matter, and one is
tempted simply to ignore them. But, insofar as any critics influence so-
called "educated" taste, it is these, and their ignominious failure is
particularly significant in relation to the kind of wider issues films like
Shame and *Weekend* are about. One can study what the phrase "cultural disintegration" means in the total absence of serious values demonstrated in most of the reviews of *Shame*. As I sit writing this there is
a record of the Brandenburg Concertos on the gramophone, and I can
see my children playing in the garden; men, women and children—
families like mine—are being burnt and blasted to death in Vietnam,
and I have absolutely no idea what may be happening to me and the
few people I love ten years, five years, two months from now. *Shame*
is central to the experience I am living at this moment, and at most
moments.

The immediately striking fact about *Shame,* if one comes to it from Bergman's previous work, is that it neatly reverses the somewhat simplified scheme of his films I took as my starting-point: for a great deal of its length the leading characters are in the home that has become their permanent one (even if they are still, essentially, displaced persons); journeys in the first half of the film are abortive attempts at flight, all of which end in a return to the house, and the journey at the end is a voyage to nowhere. The film breaks new ground for Bergman in a number of obvious ways, but this fundamental reversal suggests the depth and extent of the development. The feeling for a possible human normality is stronger, and the value placed on it higher, than in any previous Bergman film; yet we find, even stronger than in *Hour of the Wolf,* the pessimism that sees that precious normality as at the mercy of uncontrollable forces so great that their power and extent can only be guessed at. The tragic strength of *Shame* arises out of the fusion of these two developments.

A possible normality: Bergman certainly does not present us with ideal characters or an ideal marriage. Eva (Liv Ullmann) is perhaps as close to an ideal human being as is compatible with necessary human imperfection; even she cannot entirely preserve her personal integrity amid the messy confusion in which existence involves her. Jan (Max von Sydow) emerges as very un-ideal from all the situations in which we see him, though Bergman reminds us at several points that we never see him in the environment or occupation in which he lived in peacetime, and in which his weaknesses would have been much less exposed. It is one of the film's great strengths that Bergman can show us, in the first part, a character who is selfish, cowardly, hypochondriac, emotionally immature and lacking in self-awareness, and nonetheless convince us that his marriage to a woman of strength, tenderness and warmth has genuine possibilities. For all Jan's failings one is made to feel that, under favourable circumstances, the Rosenbergs could achieve a relationship of real value.

When writing about *The Silence* I suggested that a concept of normality can only exist in relation to a defined social framework. In *Shame* normality is associated with tradition. Love, tenderness, sympathy, the sense of marriage itself, the desire for family, are felt as dependent upon a context of civilized values. Jan feels love for Eva as he watches her buy fish from a fisherman-friend beside a quiet stream; as she completes the purchase and returns to the car, she loosens her hair. They have come from an isolated existence at their cottage where a state of constant tension apparently holds them separate; it is their contact with a seeming stability and order, in the tenuous but representative form of a solitary fisherman, that relaxes them. At Jan's declaration that he was in love with her, Eva blossoms. On the ferry in company with Mayor Jacobi (Gunnar Björnstrand) and his wife, in the town as they deliver trays of lingon berries, at an antique shop where they drink and buy wine, we see the relationship take on meaning and value. And all the time Bergman keeps present for us the forces of social disintegration. The fisherman tells Eva of an invasion scare; there are troop transports on the ferry, and the Jacobis are on their way to visit their son, who is in the army; the streets are full of armoured cars; the antique dealer has been called up and is in uniform; there are only a few bottles of wine left.

The scene in the antique shop, the characters surrounded by varied emblems of civilization, is very beautiful, the attitude complex but defined with great exactness. Bergman's humanity is nowhere clearer than in his presentation of the antique dealer. We see him as a man insulated from reality, politically ignorant and uncommitted, shut up amid relics of the past, hoping to convince the military authorities that his weak foot is bad enough to ensure him a safe office job, or perhaps get him discharged. Yet we cannot but view him with sympathy and a certain respect: he is a civilized and gentle human being. Then there is the Meissen musical ornament, useless, artificial, unjustifiable in a world where people starve to death, are tortured, persecuted, massacred; yet by virtue of its very uselessness embodying the concept of civilization in its purest form. The other objects we are shown add other aspects to this concept: the painting of a royal family group, absurdly obsolete yet indicative of a past stability; the battered but undaunted-looking figurehead from the final scenes of *Persona*, an emblem at once of human endurance and the ravages of time. Amid these, the three characters sip wine together, the sense of civilized communion balanced by the sense of valediction, the antique dealer's intuition that not only his life but his way of life is nearing its end.

A cultural tradition sufficiently represented by the antique dealer and his Meissen ornament would seem at best touchingly fragile, at worst merely trivial. Bergman extends the concept much further in the following scene, arguably the most beautiful in all Bergman's films, and consisting mostly of an almost static medium shot of Liv Ullmann as she and Jan, having dined off the fish, drink the wine at a table under a tree. The core of the film is the human reality of Eva, our sense of her needs and her potentialities. In a scene whose naturalness suggests partial improvisation, Bergman allows the actress and the character to reveal themselves to us: the "meaning" of *Shame*, one might say, is Liv Ullmann herself. Under the influence of their fleeting, fragile contacts with civilized stability, the creativity of the pair begins to blossom again: Eva will resume her learning of Italian, Jan wants them to make music together once more, for half-an-hour every morning. This revival of creative potentialities also manifests itself in a mutual tenderness and contact: they begin to be able to say things to each other with an intimacy they clearly haven't achieved for a long time. Nature plays a crucial role in the scene: the tree, the fresh air, the gentle sunlight, the daisies decorating the table, one of which Jan removes at the end as they go into the house to make love—the entirely natural and beautiful culmination of the feeling of the whole scene. The rich complex of inter-related ideas that underlies this part of *Shame* is also to be found in Yeats:

> How but in custom and in ceremony
> Are innocence and beauty born?
> Ceremony's a name for the rich horn,
> And custom for the spreading laurel tree

The author of "A Prayer for My Daughter" would surely have admired Bergman's film deeply. The poignant sense of precariousness—the vulnerable infant "under this cradle-hood and coverlid" set against the "haystack- and roof-levelling wind"—is nearly as strong; simply in *Shame* we are fifty years further into the future that filled Yeats with such deep dread.

The parallel is completed by Eva's own desire for the children that will fulfil her as a woman ("Then we'll be a family"). The defeating of her natural instincts for motherhood and family, and the consequent maiming of her potential for living, are movingly suggested during the film from her desolating decision (or realization) after the first experience of invasion that "we'll never have any children," through her finding of the dead baby after the massacre, and her urge to "mother" the young deserter whom Jan brutally shoots, to her account of her dream in the directionless open boat as the film ends. Her need for motherhood, and its implicit but deeply felt association with "custom and ceremony" and nature, provides a focal point for all the film's positive feeling for the civilized tradition.

The beauty of the long take at the table is inseparable from our sense of precariousness—of the way the beauty is threatened both by external forces (the war) and internal (Jan's character). The depth of

Eva's humanity, her adequacy as the vessel for Bergman's positive sense
of life, is evidenced by the fact that her absolutely clearsighted awareness of Jan's failings so little inhibits her capacity for tenderness towards him, her natural emotional generosity. In the course of the film
we watch, in Jan's development, the external and internal forces of
disintegration act upon one another and fuse. Defending *Les Cara-
biniers*, Godard said that the film that needed to be made about the
concentration camps, and probably never would be made, was a film
about, not the victims, but the guards. Bergman has gone one better,
and made a film showing a possible continuity between the two roles.
He mentions the camps, too, apropos of *Shame:* "I have wondered
how I would have sustained the experience of a concentration camp,
of being forced into such a damnable position" [interview in *Films and
Filming*]. In the first part of *Shame*, Jan's role is equivalent to that of
concentration camp victim: the emphasis is on the terrifying helplessness of human beings caught up in events they can neither evade nor
control. Then, after the long central scene with Jacobi that is the film's
turning-point, we see Jan develop to the stage where he would be perfectly fitted for the role of guard. The complex logic of this development is revealed by Bergman with an extraordinary acuteness of perception, through what is surely Max von Sydow's finest performance.
The premise that war does terrible things to people ceases to be merely
a phrase and takes on a concrete and specific reality. But it is too simple to talk just about "the pressures of war": what happens to Jan is
determined by their complex interaction with features of his character
and his marriage relationship—even, and decisively, by Eva herself. We
see that the possibility of Jan's achieving dignity or any human fullness
is dependent on his relationship with Eva; the moment when he discovers her infidelity with Jacobi effectively deadens his human potential. The infidelity itself has intricate causes, and love for Jacobi is not
among them: the unsatisfactoriness of the marriage makes it possible,
weakening Eva's instinct for final commitment to one man; with this
goes the frustrating of her maternal impulses. Through Jacobi she is
getting Jan the civilized comforts he needs to hold him together; for
her lover himself she feels no more than a weary compassion, cradling
his head on her breast like a mother. The shocking abruptness of the
scene where Jan and Eva quarrel furiously as they dig potatoes—a quarrel in which Jacobi figures prominently—becomes comprehensible when
one deduces what has been happening since the interrogation in the
school. Bergman sees that people don't cease to be affected by devel-

opments in their closest personal relationships because there is a war on: the film cannot be reduced to a schematic study of the *direct* brutalizing effects of war.

Jan kills Jacobi less for the money (which at that stage appears of little use) than for revenge. Again, the motivation is complex. His own sexual uncertainties, arising from his inability to give Eva a child, are part of it; so is his sense that Jacobi has broken his last hold on his own humanity. From that point on we watch him harden into an insentient being, his human potentialities stripped down to the base, basic instinct of mere self-preservation. He withdraws totally from contact. The moment in the devastated woods when Eva falls and Jan doesn't stop to help her up compares revealingly with the scene in *Weekend* where the wife is raped by a passing tramp and her husband squats apathetically by the roadside. The effect of the latter is primarily of a macabre, sardonic humour: Godard's characters were never human, their insentience being in the data from the outset. The moment in *Shame* expresses with the greatest simplicity the sense of utter loss in relation to the possibilities defined in the early scenes. Godard can't afford to allow emotion into his film, any more than he can allow a real sense of physical pain, or how could he make his cannibals acceptable? Near the end of *Shame*, as they wait on the stony beach for the boat, Eva asks Jan how they are to continue living if they can no longer talk to each other. He makes no answer.

The study of Jan's degeneration is obviously central to the film, but the theme is given extra dimensions through the characters of Jacobi and Filip. We watch both attempting to preserve what they can of human values within situations they can do no more than modify, with no hope of affecting the issues radically. Jacobi is forced by his position into an assumption of apparent personal authority which in fact he has to exercise in the ways expected of him. He can commute an execution by firing squad to penal servitude for life, and get Jan and Eva sent to the safety of his office; but he has had to make examples of them in a way he knows to be unjust, and he has to deal with the mass of alleged collaborators with some show of retribution in which innocent and guilty will suffer alike. Eva says she feels she is in a dream and it's not *her* dream but someone else's: we are never allowed the satisfaction of identifying the dreamer, of attributing blame. *All* the characters are enclosed in the "dream."

Bergman's maturity is nowhere more evident than in his treatment of Jacobi. In imposing himself upon Eva as a lover, Jacobi uses his position and his knowledge of her situation in a way that is obviously corrupt, knowing that she doesn't love him. Yet his need for Eva cannot possibly be seen as mere lust. She is his link with civilized values, with the possibility of tenderness, integrity and warmth: we see him, when he has sent the couple home from their interrogation, thinking about her as he sits in his cold office huddled in his overcoat, pulling the inadequate electric fire closer with his stick, completely isolated amid the dehumanizing drabness of his surroundings and his situation. Jacobi helps the Rosenbergs because he wants Eva, but also as an expression of his wider need to relate himself to values the war has rendered obsolete, to the cultural tradition and the artists who ought to be its highest representatives. There is nothing heroic about him, but his failure to adjust to the demands for ruthlessness imposed on him by circumstances testifies to his humanity, thereby appearing a strength rather than a weakness. He dies because he cannot cease to be a civilized human being.

The same could be said of Filip's suicide at the end of the film, though Filip is one of the "terrible idealists" of whom Jacobi expresses such fear, and the man by whose authority he is killed. Filip is the fisherman from whom Eva buys the fish at the beginning of the film. Bergman's development of the character is very elliptical. He appears in only four scenes, but his appearances imply the complexity of his predicament. The second time we see him is when, gun slung over shoulder, he witnesses the arrest of the suspected collaborators at the village shop: a scene filmed in a single long-shot without dialogue, ending with Filip walking into close-up so that we at last see his face, drawn and determined. His situation is revealed through his treatment of Jacobi during the long central scene. He likes and respects the man, is willing to involve himself in what, from the point of view of "terrible idealism," is corrupt behaviour by allowing Jacobi to buy his life. He knows Jan has the money, and does all he can to force him to hand it over. In compelling Jan to carry out the execution personally, he is both making a last attempt to get him to relinquish the money, and punishing him for removing the last hope of saving Jacobi. The gesture with which he leads Jacobi to execution—a restrained compassionate patting of the head—is the more moving for being unstressed by any directional "pointing." During the same scene, however, it is Filip who unleashes the violence that destroys the Rosenbergs' house and smashes their piano and Jan's violin. We feel that he carries personal responsibility for the destructiveness, and for the death of Jacobi, yet that he is part of a complex of larger movements beyond his control. When, afterwards, Jan justifies himself to Eva by saying that Jacobi would have been shot anyway, even if the money had been surrendered, she breaks down partly because she can't with any conviction refute him.

When Filip turns up at the end as the boatman to whom Jan pays Jacobi's money, we accept his "opting-out" as the logical outcome of what we have seen of him previously. Here, and more strikingly in his suicide, lowering himself silently over the edge of the drifting boat, he becomes a yardstick by which we can measure the degree of Jan's dehumanization. In the world Bergman shows us, the "Shame" of which is quite simply the loss of everything that gives human life dignity and significance, suicide becomes an act of desperate affirmation, the only means left of acknowledging the value of human feeling by rejecting an existence that demands its forfeiture. Jan watches, unmoved, and turns aside to sleep.

Bergman's total mastery of style is confirmed by the fact that he now feels free to allow himself and his actors a certain degree of controlled improvisation. He has reached an ideal fusion of surface detachment and profound emotional impact. It is always the spectator's deepest responses that are touched, beyond any facile direct onslaught. Certain scenes where the issues are relatively clear-cut are filmed with great immediacy: those in which people are rushed like herds of cattle in and out of the school, to be interrogated or despatched. But in the scenes of more complex significance—Jan's shooting of Jacobi, his later shooting of the deserter—Bergman rejects any temptation to overwhelm us with immediate horrors, leaving us free to absorb all the implications. The "execution" of Jacobi, from the moment Jan moves towards him with the revolver, is filmed in a single take, with all the action in long-shot and Jan's back to us most of the time. Throughout it we can see the yard where the hens Jan so hilariously failed to shoot earlier have now been summarily decapitated; we can watch Eva's reactions, and register fully all that is happening to the marriage relationship; we are aware of Filip's presence. Instead of shocking us with the details of the physical horror at the core of the scene, Bergman encourages us to see it in the context of the film's development: *beyond* the physical pain, there is the horrifying sense of people—executioners, victims, bystanders—trapped in a progress of events they can't arrest or control or extricate themselves from. Similarly, the treatment of the shooting of the young deserter—the burst of machine-gun fire heard against a long-shot of Eva as she runs to stop Jan, or runs away (she clearly doesn't know which herself)—removes us from the immediate horror, which is vivid enough in our imaginations, to keep us aware of its wider significance.

Eva remains to the end the emotional heart of the film. Though not entirely untainted by a disillusionment both public and private, she retains to the end her humanity and sense of value. Bergman's feeling for the potential beauty and value of the individual existence gives *Shame* a dimension and an emotional maturity that *Weekend* quite lacks—and which Godard's films already lacked before his dismissal of the possibility of a "personal solution" in *Masculin-Féminin*. As Eva lies beside Jan in the boat, the dream she recounts—it is more a soliloquy than a communication, for Jan is beyond communication—poignantly places essential human needs against a reality that denies them, and recalls Jan's dream about playing Bach, at the start of the film, thereby making us aware of the distance that has been travelled. During the early scene where the couple drink wine under the tree, Jan tells Eva that he can change his character, that he isn't a determinist. On the word "determinist" the camera tracks in towards Eva's face, moving for the first time in what has already been a very long take. Eva doesn't know what a determinist is. Her sense of events as a dream in which they are helplessly swept along clearly suggests determinism, and the overall progress of the film confirms this. Yet what makes *Shame* so moving is the feeling that the determinism isn't quite absolute. None of the characters can arrest the general movement of events, but within that uncontrolled progress they have a limited freedom to make, to differing degrees, their individual protests, whether by action or example. If it is a "protest" film, the protest is not against any government, or even against war, but against the nature of existence itself: a protest both metaphysical and tragic. Liv Ullmann has become the medium for this protest, in *Persona*, in *Hour of the Wolf*, and above all here in *Shame*, Bergman's masterpiece to date and one of the greatest films of the last decade. It is Bergman's distinction to have established himself as a great, and central, artist in an age peculiarly inimical to great art. His greatest quality is his capacity for development, which is also the drive towards the attainment of human fullness. The journey from *Frenzy* to *Shame* is an extraordinary feat of courage and intelligence.

6

EACH FILM IS MY LAST

Ingmar Bergman

. . . .

Artistic creation always manifested itself to me as hunger. I acknowledged it with a certain satisfaction, but during my conscious life I never asked myself what caused this craving. In the last few years the hunger has diminished and been transformed into something else; now I am anxious to find out what the reasons for it were. I have an early childhood memory of my desire to show off achievements: proficiency in drawing, playing ball, the first swimstrokes. I had a strong need to draw the grownups' attention to these signs of my presence in the external world. I never felt that people took enough interest in me. When reality was no longer sufficient, I started to invent things: I entertained my friends with tremendous stories of my secret exploits. They were embarrassing lies, which failed hopelessly when confronted with the level-headed scepticism of the world around me. Finally I withdrew, and kept my dream world to myself. A child looking for human contact, obsessed by his imagination, had been quickly transformed into a hurt, cunning, and suspicious daydreamer.

But a daydreamer is no artist except in his dreams.

The need to be heard, to correspond, to live in the warmth of a community, was still there. It grew stronger the lonelier I grew. It goes without saying that film became my means of expression. I made myself understood in a language going beyond words, which failed me; beyond music, which I did not master; beyond painting, which left me indifferent. I was suddenly able to correspond with the world around

From *The Drama Review*, Vol. 11, No. 1, T-33 (Fall 1966), pp. 94-101. © 1966 by *The Drama Review*. Reprinted by permission. All rights reserved.

From two speeches published by Svensk Filmindustri. Translated by P. E. Burke and Lennart Swahn. Edited by Erika Munk.

Ingmar Bergman directing a scene in *Winter Light.*

me in a language spoken literally from soul to soul, in phrases which escaped the control of the intellect in an almost voluptuous way. With the whole stunted hunger of a child I seized upon my medium and for twenty years, tirelessly and in a kind of frenzy, I supplied the world with dreams, intellectual excitement, fantasies, fits of lunacy. My success has been amazing, but at bottom it is an insignificant sequel.

I do not underestimate what I may have achieved. I think that it has been and perhaps still is of importance. But now I can see the past in a new and less romantic light; that is security enough for me. Today my situation is less complicated, less interesting, above all less glamorous than it was. To be completely frank, I experience art (not only film art) as insignificant in our time: art no longer has the power and the possibility to influence the development of our life.

Literature, painting, music, film, and theatre beget and bring forth themselves. New mutations, new combinations arise and are annihilated; the movement seems—seen from the outside—nervously vital. With magnificent zeal the artists project to themselves and to a more and more distracted public pictures of a world that no longer cares what they like or think. In a few countries artists are punished, art is considered dangerous and worth stifling and directing. On the whole,

however, art is free, shameless, irresponsible; the movement is intense,
almost feverish, like a snake's skin full of ants. The snake is long since
dead, eaten, deprived of his poison, but the skin is full of meddlesome
life.

If I have become one of these ants, I must ask myself if there is any
reason to continue my work.

The answer is yes. Although I think that the stage is an old, beloved
kept woman, who has seen better days. Although I and many other
people find the Wild West more stimulating than Antonioni and
Bergman. Although the new music gives us the sense of being suffocated by mathematically rarefied air. Although painting and sculpture,
sterilized, decline in their own paralyzing freedom. Although literature
has been transformed into a pile of words without any message or dangerous qualities. . . .

I think that people today can dispense with theatre, because they
exist in the middle of a drama whose different phases incessantly produce local tragedies. They do not need music, because every minute
they are exposed to hurricanes of sound passing beyond endurance.
They do not need poetry, because the idea of the universe has transformed them into functional animals, confined to interesting—but from
a poetical point of view unusable—problems of metabolic disturbance.
Man (as I experience myself and the world around me) has made
himself free, terribly and dizzyingly free. Religion and art are kept
alive as a conventional politeness toward the past, as a benign, demo-
cratic solicitude on behalf of nervous citizens enjoying more and more
leisure time. . . .

If I consider all these troubles and still maintain that I want to
continue to work in art, there is a simple reason. (I disregard the
purely material one.) The reason is *curiosity*. A boundless, insatiable
curiosity, that is always new and that pushes me onwards—a curiosity
that never leaves me alone and that has completely replaced my craving for community. I feel like a prisoner who, after serving a long term,
suddenly is confronted with turbulent life. I note, I observe, I keep
my eyes open; everything is unreal, fantastic, frightening, or ridiculous.
I catch a flying grain of dust, maybe it is a film—what importance does
it have? None at all, but I find it interesting and consequently it is a
film. I walk around with the grain of dust that I have caught with my
own hands. I am happy or sad. I jostle the other ants, together we accomplish an enormous task. The snake's skin moves.

This and only this is *my* truth. I do not request that it be valid for
someone else, and as a consolation for eternity it is of course rather

meager. As a basis for artistic activity during some future years it is completely sufficient at least for me. To devote oneself to artistic creation for one's own satisfaction is not always agreeable. But it has one great advantage: the artist lives exactly like every other living creature that only exists for its own sake. This makes a rather numerous brotherhood. . . .

THOU SHALT

Experience should be gained before one reaches forty, a wise man said. After forty it is permissible to comment. The reverse might apply in my case—no one was more certain of his theories and none more willing to elucidate them than I was. No one knew better or could visualize more. Now that I am somewhat older I have become rather more cautious. The experience I have gained and which I am now sorting out is of such a kind that I am unwilling to express myself on the art of the filmmaker. . . . The only real contribution the artist can make is his work. Thus I find it rather unseemly to get involved in discussion, even with explanations or excuses.

The fact that the artist remained unknown was a good thing in its time. His relative anonymity was a guarantee against irrelevant outside influences, material considerations, and the prostitution of his talents. He brought forth his work in spirit and truth as he saw it and left the judgment to the Lord. Thus he lived and died without being more or less important than any other artisan. In such a world flourished natural assurance and invulnerable humility, two qualities which are the finest hallmarks of art.

In life today the position of the artist has become more and more precarious: the artist has become a curious figure, a kind of performer or athlete who chases from job to job. His isolation, his now almost holy individualism, his artistic subjectivity can all too easily cause ulcers and neurosis. Exclusiveness becomes a curse which he eulogizes. The unusual is both his pain and his satisfaction. . . .

The Script

Often it begins with something very hazy and indefinite—a chance remark or a quick change of phrase, a dim but pleasant event which is not specifically related to the actual situation. It has happened in my theatrical work that I have visualized performers in fresh make-up but in yet-unplayed roles. All in all, split-second impressions that disappear as quickly as they come, forming a brightly colored thread sticking out of the dark sack of the unconscious. If I wind up this thread carefully a complete film will emerge, brought out with pulse-beats and rhythms which are characteristic of just this film. Through these rhythms the picture sequences take on patterns according to the way they were born and mastered by the motive.

The feeling of failure occurs mostly before the writing begins. The dreams turn into cobwebs, the visions fade and become grey and insignificant, the pulse-beat is silent, everything shrinks into tired fancies without strength and reality. But I have decided to make a certain film and the hard work must begin: to transfer rhythms, moods, atmosphere, tensions, sequences, tones, and scents into a readable or at least understandable script.

This is difficult but not impossible.

The vital thing is the dialogue, but dialogue is a sensitive matter which can offer resistance. The written dialogue of the theatre is like a score which is almost incomprehensible to the ordinary person; interpretation demands a technical knack and a certain amount of imagination and feeling. One can write dialogue, but how it should be handled, the rhythms and the tempo, the speed at which it is to be taken, and what is to take place between the lines—all that must be left out, because a script containing so much detail would be unreadable.

I can squeeze directions and locations, characterizations and atmosphere into my filmscripts in understandable terms, but then I come to essentials, by which I mean montage, rhythm and the relation of one picture to the other—the vital "third dimension" without which the film is merely dead, a factory product. Here I cannot use "keys" or show an adequate indication of the tempos of the complexes involved; it is impossible to give a comprehensible idea of what puts life into a work of art. I have often sought a kind of notation which would give me a chance of recording the shade and tones of the ideas and the inner structure of the picture. If I could express myself thus clearly, I could work with the absolute certainty that whenever I liked I could prove the relationship between the rhythm and the continuity of the part and the whole. . . . Let us state once and for all that the film script is a very imperfect *technical* basis for a film.

Film is not the same thing as literature. As often as not the character and substance of the two art forms are in conflict. What it really depends on is hard to define, but it probably has to do with the self-responsive process. The written word is read and assimilated by a conscious act and in connection with the intellect, and little by little it plays on the imagination or feelings. It is completely different with the motion picture. When we see a film in a cinema we are conscious that an illusion has been prepared for us and we relax and accept it with our will and intellect. We prepare the way into our imagination. The sequence of pictures plays directly on our feelings without touching the mind.

There are many reasons why we ought to avoid filming existing literature, but the most important is that the irrational dimension, which is the heart of a literary work, is often untranslatable and that in its turn kills the special dimension of the film. If despite this we wish to translate something literary into filmic terms, we are obliged to make an infinite number of complicated transformations which most often give limited or non-existent results in relation to the efforts expended. I know what I am talking about because I have been subjected to so-called literary judgment. This is about as intelligent as letting a music critic judge an exhibition of paintings or a football reporter criticize a new play. The only reason for everyone believing himself capable of pronouncing a valid judgment on motion pictures is the inability of the film to assert itself as an art form, its need of a definite artistic vocabulary, its extreme youth in relation to the other arts, its obvious ties with economic realities, its direct appeal to the feelings. All this causes film to be regarded with disdain. Its directness of expression makes it suspect in certain eyes, and as a result any and everyone thinks he's competent to say anything he likes, in whatever way he likes, about film art.

I myself have never had ambitions to be an author. I do not wish to write novels, short stories, essays, biographies, or treatises on special subjects. I certainly do not want to write pieces for the theatre. Film-making is what interests me. I want to make films about conditions, tensions, pictures, rhythms, and characters within me which in one way or another interest me. The motion picture and its complicated process of birth are my methods of saying what I want to my fellow men. I find it humiliating for work to be judged as a book when it is a film. Consequently the writing of the script is a difficult period, but useful, as it compels me to prove logically the validity of my ideas. While this is taking place I am caught in a difficult conflict between my need to find a way of filming a complicated situation and my desire for complete simplicity. As I do not intend my work to be solely for my own edification or for the few but for the public in general, the demands of the public are imperative. Sometimes I try a venturous alternative which shows that the public can appreciate the most advanced and complicated developments. . . .

The Studio

I stand in the half-light of the film studio with its noise and crowds, dirt and wretched atmosphere, and I seriously wonder why I am engaged in this most difficult form of artistic creation. The rules are many and burdensome. I must have three minutes of usable film in the can every day. I must keep to the shooting schedule, which is so tight that it excludes almost everything but essentials. I am surrounded by technical equipment which with fiendish cunning tries to sabotage my best intentions. Constantly I am on edge, I am compelled to live the collective life of the studio. Amidst all this must take place a sensitive process which demands quietness, concentration, and confidence.

I mean working with actors and actresses. There are many directors who forget that our work in films begins with the human face. We certainly can become completely absorbed in the aesthetics of montage, we can bring together objects and still life into a wonderful rhythm, we can make nature studies of astounding beauty, but the approach to the human face is without doubt the distinguishing quality of the film. From this we might conclude that the film star is our most expensive instrument and the camera only registers the reactions of this instrument. But in many cases the position and movement of the camera is considered more important than the player, and the picture becomes an end in itself—this can never do anything but destroy illusions and be artistically devastating. In order to give the greatest possible strength to the actor's expression, the camera movement must be simple, free, and completely synchronized with the action. The camera must be a completely objective observer and may only on rare occasions participate in the action. We should realize that the best means of expression the actor has at his command is his *look*. The close-up, if objectively composed, perfectly directed and played, is the most forcible means at the disposal of the film director, while at the same time being the most certain proof of his competence or incompetence. The lack or abundance of close-ups shows in an uncompromising way the nature of the director and the extent of his interest in people.

Simplicity, concentration, full knowledge, technical perfection must be the pillars supporting each scene and sequence. However, they in themselves are not enough. The one most important thing is still lacking: the intimate spark of life, which appears or fails to appear according to its will, crucial and indomitable.

For instance, I know that everything for a scene must be prepared down to the last detail, each branch of the collective organization must know exactly what it is to do. The entire mechanism must be free from fault as a matter of course. These preliminaries may or may not take a long time, but they should not be dragged out and tire those participating. Rehearsals for the "take" must be carried out with technical precision and with everyone knowing exactly what he is to do. Then comes the take. From experience I know that the first take is often the happiest, as it is the most natural. This is because the actors are trying to create something; their creative urge comes from natural identification. The camera registers this inner act of creation, which is hardly perceptible to the untrained eye or ear. I believe it is this which keeps me in films. The development and retention of a sudden burst of life gives me ample reward for the thousands of hours of grey gloom, trial and tribulation. . . .

Morality

Many imagine that the commercial film industry lacks morality or that its morals are so definitely based on immorality that an artistically ethical standpoint cannot be maintained. Our work is assigned to businessmen, who at times regard it with apprehension because it is concerned with something as unreliable as art. If many regard our activity as dubious, I must emphasize that its morality is as good as any and so absolute that it is almost embarrassing. However, I have found that I am like the Englishman in the tropics, who shaves and dresses for dinner every day. He does not do this to please the wild animals but for his own sake. If he gives up his discipline then the jungle has beaten him. I know that I shall have lost to the jungle if I take a weak moral standpoint. I have therefore come to a belief based on three commandments. Briefly I shall give their wording and their meaning. These have become the basis of my activity in the film world.

The first may sound indecent but really is highly moral:

THOU SHALT BE ENTERTAINING AT ALL TIMES

The public who sees my films and thus provides my bread and butter has the right to expect entertainment, a thrill, a joy, a spirited experience. I am responsible for providing that experience. That is the only justification for my activity.

However, this does not mean that I must prostitute my talents, at least not in any and every way, because then I would break the second commandment:

THOU SHALT OBEY THY ARTISTIC CONSCIENCE AT ALL TIMES

This is a very tricky commandment because it obviously forbids me to steal, lie, prostitute my talents, kill, or falsify. However, I will say that I am allowed to falsify if it is artistically justified, I may also lie if it is a beautiful lie, I could also kill my friends or myself or anyone else if it would help my art, it may also be permissible to prostitute my talents if it will further my cause, and I should indeed steal if there were no other way out. If one obeyed artistic conscience to the full in every respect then one would be doing a balancing act on a tightrope, and could become so dizzy that at any moment one could break one's neck. Then all the prudent and moral bystanders would say, "Look, there lies the thief, the murderer, the lecher, the liar. Serves him right"—never thinking that all means are allowed except those which lead to a fiasco, and that the most dangerous ways are the only ones which are passable, and that compulsion and dizziness are two necessary parts of our activity; that the joy of creation, which is a thing of beauty and joy forever, is bound up with the necessary fear of creation. . . .

In order to strengthen my will so that I do not slip off the narrow path into the ditch, I have a third juicy commandment:

THOU SHALT MAKE EACH FILM AS IF IT WERE THY LAST

Some may imagine that this commandment is an amusing paradox or a pointless aphorism or perhaps simply a beautiful phrase about the complete vanity of everything. However, that is not the case.

It is reality.

In Sweden, film production was halted for all of 1951. During my enforced inactivity I learned that because of commercial complications and through no fault of my own I could be out on the street before I knew it. I do not complain about it, neither am I afraid or bitter; I have only drawn a logical and highly moral conclusion from the situation: *each film is my last.*

For me there is only one loyalty: to the film on which I am working. What comes (or fails to come) after is insignificant and causes neither anxiety nor longing. This gives me assurance and artistic confidence. The material assurance is apparently limited but I find artistic integrity infinitely more important, and therefore I follow the principle that *each film is my last.* This gives me strength in another way. I have seen all too many film workers burdened down with anxiety, yet carrying out to the full their necessary duties. Worn out, bored to death and without pleasure they have fulfilled their work. They have suffered humiliation and affronts from producers, critics, and the public without flinching, without giving up, without leaving the profession. With a tired shrug of the shoulders they have made their artistic contributions until they went down or were thrown out.

I do not know when the day might come that I shall be received indifferently by the public, perhaps be disgusted with myself. Tiredness and emptiness will descend upon me like a dirty grey sack and fear will stifle everything. Emptiness will stare me in the face. When this happens I shall put down my tools and leave the scene, of my own free will, without bitterness and without brooding whether or not the work has been useful and truthful from the viewpoint of eternity. Wise and far-sighted men in the Middle Ages used to spend nights in their coffins in order never to forget the tremendous importance of every moment and the transient nature of life itself. Without taking such drastic and uncomfortable measures I harden myself to the seeming futility and the fickle cruelty of film-making with the earnest conviction that *each film is my last*.

7

INGMAR BERGMAN
An Interview

Charles Thomas Samuels

. . . .

STOCKHOLM, NOVEMBER 10, 1971

Aware that Ingmar Bergman is resolutely prompt and also that he would give me not a moment more than the three and one-half hours to which he had agreed, I arrived somewhat early at the Royal Dramatic Theater, where he had vacated his leadership but not a small office. Into this office, after a walk through seemingly endless corridors, I was ushered by a polite secretary who told me that Mr. Bergman would shortly arrive. While I waited, I examined the room, although one needed less time for that operation than I was granted.

Bergman's office is nearly as cold as the church in *Winter Light*, but here the austerity is secular and impersonal, rather than menacing. Moreover, the bare white walls are made radiant by light streaming in from the square and nearby seascape, which also bring in the noise of human bustle that served as background for our talk.

The room contains a pallet couch, fronted by a low coffee table (today offering two bottles of mineral water and a box of Droste chocolate), and a comfortable black leather chair, which Bergman first used but which he eventually gave up for the more rigid one that stands near the most important item of furniture: his desk. A color drawing of the theater hangs over the nearly empty bookcase (works by Strindberg, *Fellini Satyricon*, Lenny Bruce's *How to Talk Dirty and Influence People*, and a few others). The sole remaining ornament, also above the bookcase, is a child's toy: a stuffed red ant.

A few minutes after nine, Bergman strides in with hand extended.

From *Encountering Directors* (New York, Capricorn Books), pp. 179-207. Copyright © 1972 by Charles Thomas Samuels. Reprinted by permission of G. P. Putnam's Sons.

He seems uninterested in further introductions, but I am pleased that we can get down to business. During our talk, I am constantly amazed by the variety of expression that passes over his inherently bland face. This variety can no more be captured than the beautiful modulation of his voice, but both are so crucial to our encounter that I have departed from my usual methods in attempting to catch something of its manner, as well as our words.

Bergman discusses a scene with Elliot Gould and Bibi Andersson during shooting of *The Touch*.

From the beginning, I interrupted Bergman's sentences, sometimes completing them, sometimes anticipating a response that made me impatient to react. As the interview progressed, this became more frequent, and he also began to interrupt me. I have therefore reproduced nearly all the interruptions, whether of one man by the other or of one man by himself—I have also indicated (how I wish I could actually reproduce) some of the laughter with which Bergman increasingly punctuated the proceedings. For the man is passionate without being dour.

Although I have tried especially hard to capture much of the actuality of this interview, I have, as always, rewritten the text for readability. Bergman's heavily accented English, though very good, frequently falls into error when his mind outpaces his ease in the language. I saw no point in reproducing such errors, but one of them deserves remark. Whereas, midway in our talk, I put the word "tumultuous" in his mouth, what he actually said was "tumultarious," a portmanteau word, accidentally invented, that nonetheless perfectly describes a talk both "tumultuous" and "multifarious" in its concerns.

"Tumultariousness" is obviously meat and drink to Bergman. Even though our conversation absorbed him so that he inadvertently let it run an extra five minutes—thus, as frantic phone calls made clear, disarranging the meticulous schedule that is his daily regimen—when he escorted or rather trotted me to the elevator, he observed, with a broad and affectionate smile, "I think we had such a good talk, don't you?" Not only attending to film and theater business, he was in town that day, as I later learned, to make arrangements for his fifth wedding, which was to take place during the week.

SAMUELS: Mr. Bergman, I'd like to start with a rather general question: If I were asked to cite a single reason for your preeminence among film directors, I would point to your creation of a special world —the sort of thing we are accustomed to with great creative figures in the other arts, but rarely in film, and never to your degree. You are, in fact, very much like a writer. Why didn't you become one?

BERGMAN: When I was a child, I suffered from an almost complete lack of words. My education was very rigid; my father was a priest. As a result, I lived in a private world of my own dreams. I played with my puppet theater.

S: And—

B: Excuse me. I had very few contacts with reality or channels to it. I was afraid of my father, my mother, my elder brother—everything. Playing with this puppet theater and a projection device I had was my only form of self-expression. I had great difficulty with fiction and reality; as a small child I mixed them so much that my family always said I was a liar. Even when I grew up, I felt blocked. I had enormous difficulty speaking to others and—

S: I want to interrupt you for just a moment. This description of your childhood resembles one classic description of the genesis of a writer. Was it only the accident of the puppet theater that sent you the way of theater rather than of books?

B: No. I remember that during my eighteenth summer, when I had just finished school, suddenly I wrote a novel. And in school, when we had to write compositions, I liked it very much. But I never felt that writing was my cup of tea. I put the novel in my desk and forgot it. But in 1940, suddenly—in the summer—I started writing and wrote twelve—

S: Plays.

B: Yes. It was a sudden eruption.

S: May I offer an hypothesis about this so that you can react to it? Your skill as a writer and your need to express yourself in words are fulfilled more in the theater and cinema because in these arts one also embodies his words and even sees the audience's response to them.

B: My beginning was otherwise, because when I began writing, I was suspicious of words. And I always lacked words; it has always been very difficult for me to find the word I want.

S: Is this suspicion of words one of the reasons why Alma makes Elisabeth say "nothing" in *Persona?*

B: No. Yes. In a way. But that wasn't conscious on my part.

S: Because "nothing" is the truest word, one that asserts least.

B: I don't know. I have always felt suspicious both of what I say and of what others say to me. Always I feel something has been left out. When I read a book, I read very slowly. It takes a lot of time for me to read a play.

S: Do you direct it in your head?

B: In a way. I have to translate the words into speeches, movements, flesh and blood. I have an enormous need for contact with an audience, with other people. For me, words are not satisfying.

S: With a book, the reader is elsewhere.

B: When you read, words have to pass through your conscious mind to reach your emotions and your soul. In film and theater, things go directly to the emotions. What I need is to come in contact with others.

S: I see that, but it raises a problem I'm sure you've often discussed. Your films have emotional impact, but since they are also the most intellectually difficult of contemporary films, isn't there sometimes a contradiction between the two effects? Let me give you a specific example. How do you react when I say that while I watched *The Rite*, my feelings were interfered with by my baffled effort at comprehension?

B: Your approach is wrong. I never asked you to understand; I ask only that you feel.

S: *You* haven't asked me anything. I don't see you! I only see the film.

B: Yes, but—

S: And the film asks me to understand. Here are three performers under investigation for a spectacle that the authorities find obscene. The film continuously makes us wonder what the spectacle means, why the authorities want to suppress it, etc. These questions sit next to me. More and more, I feel them grab me by the throat—better, the head— so that I can't feel anything but puzzlement.

B: But that's you.

S: It's not the film?

B: No. *The Rite* merely expresses my resentment against the critics, audience, and government, with which I was in constant battle while I ran the [Royal Dramatic] theater. A year after my resignation from the post, I sat down and wrote this script in five days. I did it merely to free myself.

S: But then—

B: Excuse please. The picture is just a game, a way of kicking everyone's—not understanding—intellectual—

S: To puzzle the audience?

B: Exactly. I liked very much to write it and even more to make it. We had a lot of fun while we were shooting. My purpose was just to amuse myself and the audience which liked it. Do you understand what I mean?

S: I understand but—

B: You must realize—this is very important!—I never ask people to understand what I have made. Stravinsky once said, "I have never understood a piece of music in my life. I always only feel."

S: But Stravinsky was a composer. By its nature, music is nondiscursive; we don't have to understand it. Films, plays, poems, novels all make propositions or observations, embody ideas or beliefs, and we go to these forms—

B: But you must understand that you are perverted. You belong to a small minority that tries to understand. Ordinary people—and me, too. . . . Look, I have exactly the same feeling when I see a play. It is as if I were hearing a string quartet by Bartok. I never try to understand. I, too, am a little perverted, so I, too, on one level, control myself. Because I am a man of the theater, a professional, and this can—

S: Destroy spontaneous response?

B: Exactly. But it never does, because I feel that especially film. . . . You know, they always talk about Brecht's being so intellectual.

S: Whereas he's very emotional.

B: Yes. His own comments and those of his commentators come

between us and the plays. Music, films, plays always work directly on the emotions.

S: I must disagree. My two favorites among your films—though there are about ten that I think excellent—are *Persona* and *Winter Light*. Each of these films works as you say a film should, but neither is like *The Rite*. I'd therefore like to compare them so as to explore the problem of a film that is too puzzling to be evocative. Let me start with *Winter Light*, which I think your purest film. By the way, do you like it?

B: Yes.

S: Although the film raises questions about what the hero thinks and about what he and his mistress represent as different ways of life, the drama is so compelling, the images so powerful that we don't sit there—I didn't sit there, perverted though I am—and say, "What does this mean?" I was caught. *Winter Light* typifies one of the ways you are at your best; in it, the audience's concern for the fate of the characters is more intense than any puzzlement about their significance. Do you see what I mean?

B: Yes. But I think you are wrong.

S: Why?

B: Because . . . because . . . when you say, "I like *Winter Light* and *Persona*, and I think these are two of the best you have made," then you say "we," and then you confess "I" and "we," and you make generalizations, whereas for everyone, *Persona* and *Winter Light* are, I think, my most difficult pictures. So it is impossible for you to take this point of view.

S: I'll stop mixing "I" and "we"—

B: I must tell you, I must tell you before we go onto more complicated things: I make my pictures for use! They are not made *sub specie aeternitatis*; they are made for now and for use. They are like a table, or mineral water, or a flower, or a lamp, or anything that is made for someone who wants to use it. Also, they are made to put me in contact with other human beings, to whom I give them and say, "Please use them. Take what you want and throw the rest away. I will come back and make other new and beautiful things. If this was not successful, it doesn't matter." My impulse has nothing to do with intellect or symbolism; it has only to do with dreams and longing, with hope and desire, with passion. Do you understand what I mean? So when you say that a film of mine is intellectually complicated, I have the feeling that you don't talk about one of my pictures. Let us talk about the pictures, not as one of the best, or the most disgusting, or one of the stinking ones; let us talk about attempts to come in contact with other people.

S: I'm afraid I didn't make myself clear. We started with *The Rite*, and I said, "This is a film that I think. . . ."

B: I'm not interested in what you think! If you like, ask me questions! But I'm not interested in hearing what you think!

S: I'm not trying to tell you what I like or dislike for the purpose of giving you my opinion but for the purpose of raising questions. I won't say "I" anymore. Let's name a man X; I'll ask you about what X might want to know. Let's say that while watching *The Rite*, X isn't as emotionally—

B: No! It's clear! This is completely uninteresting! *The Rite* has been seen by millions of people who think. . . . It's completely uninteresting if one doesn't like. . . . You know, I live on a small island. The day after *The Rite* was shown on Swedish television, a man came to me on the ferryboat going to the island and said, "It was a nice play. Don't you think it was a nice play? My wife and I, we laughed and laughed, and we had a tremendous evening together." I was completely confused; as we would judge it, he had completely misunderstood the play. But he enjoyed himself! Perhaps he had been drunk; perhaps he had gone to bed with the old girl; perhaps he was being ironic. But he enjoyed coming to me and saying it was nice. Do you understand? So we must find some way of communicating. It's very important. If we continue this way, we will get nothing. We must find some sort of human communication, because if we don't, you only make me irritated and I just want to finish. You know, I can sit down here and discuss everything in an intellectual way. I can say the most astonishing things because I am perfect at giving interviews. But I think we could find another way—do you understand—a sort of human—

S: Haven't you noticed that I've ignored all my prepared questions?

B: Yes.

S: I have been trying to respond to what you say as you say it. I have been trying to communicate. Please, by all means, tell me when I seem to be going astray. But, my God, Mr. Bergman, I've told you. . . . Look, I have a job: interviewing and writing about you. You've done the most important job already: You've made the films. But despite what you've said, I think there are people who would like help in understanding your films. I want, to the best of my abilities, with whatever aid you'll give me, to work for those people.

B: Of course. I understand very well that you're trying to reach contact, but this way you've started will only keep us sitting like two puppets discussing absolute nonsense—to me, it is completely uninteresting and, to everybody, completely uninteresting. Please let's try—

S: Let me suggest two alternatives, and you say which you'd prefer.

B: No! Go on!

S: No! I want to make human contact also. Here are the two ways: A few moments ago, you said you met this man who liked *The Rite*, yet you were surprised because—

B: He didn't say he liked it; he said he had a nice evening. Perhaps he was being ironic. But I liked his way of approaching, you know. . . . It was sort of. . . . He used my play. He used it.

S: Wouldn't you care to know why he found it useful?

B: That is irrelevant. He used it! Why and how people use are interesting to hear—as with *The Touch*, which got extreme responses: People either liked it or hated it. I like to hear about *The Touch* because it was not the picture I intended to make—for many reasons—especially the actors. You know that actors often change a film, for better or worse.

S: May I ask you how the film differs from the one you intended?

B: I intended to paint the portrait of an ordinary woman, in which everything around her would be a reflection. I wanted her in close-up and the surroundings clear only when near her. I wanted the portrait to be very detailed and very lovely and true. But when I joined the actors, they liked the plot more than I did, and I think they seduced me away from my original plan. I can't say if the result is better or worse, but it is different. Bibi Andersson is a close friend of mine—a lovely and extremely talented actress. She is totally oriented toward reality, always needing motives for what she does. She is a warm, fantastic woman. To her, everything is important, so she asked that what I wanted out of focus or shadowed be made utterly clear. I'm not criticizing her; I admire and love her. But she changed the film. When I give an actor a part, I always hope that he will join in the creating by adding something I didn't intend. We collaborate. What Bibi Andersson did made the film more comprehensible for common people and more immediately powerful. I agreed with all her changes.

S: May I ask about a moment in the film that—I think—is very good? It sounds, from what you say, as if Bibi Andersson was behind it. Karin is giving breakfast to her family; everything is close-up, light, warm, gay. Suddenly, there is a jump cut to a long shot of her alone, drinking coffee, in an utterly quiet, utterly empty kitchen. This is a case in which the clarity of the surroundings immediately makes us understand her. Now we know why she goes to David.

B: I think this scene is mine, because the film was made about a woman I actually know. This transition from warmth to complete loneliness is typical of her whole life—and of every woman's life. That is why every woman laughs while watching that part of the film.

S: Do you ever do more than change a film for one of your actresses? Do you ever actually conceive of one to give her a chance to change? Let me give you an example. In *The Naked Night* Harriet Andersson plays a woman who epitomizes the power of sex. Then the next film you made, *A Lesson in Love*, casts her in the role of a tomboy who is afraid of sex. Did you make the later film at all to reverse her performance in *The Naked Night?*

B: I know my actors well. We all are closely involved with each other. I know how many parts each carries within him. One day I write one of the parts the actor can play but never has. Sometimes the actors themselves don't know that they can play it. But without actually telling me, they show me the parts they contain.

S: So it is possible for you to write a script because you realize that a particular actress is now ready to play a particular part.

B: Exactly. It's fantastic to be surrounded by so many actors, by so many unwritten parts. All the time the actors are giving you material; through their faces, through their movements, their inflections.

S: Do you sometimes reverse not only the actor but a whole film in the next one you make?

B: I think only a little bit in the relationship between *Through a Glass Darkly* and *Winter Light*.

S: Yes, that's a very interesting case. At the end of *Through a Glass Darkly*, Björnstrand communicates with his son, who had been longing for such an occurrence. The next year we go back to the movie house, and there is Björnstrand playing, in a sense, his own son, only now more desperately in search of communication with a father (God), who will not or cannot answer him.

B: I think that is fascinating, but I never had it in mind. You are right, but what you say astonishes me.

S: I'm not crazy?

B: No. No. No. You are completely right.

S: If you don't mind then, I'd like to get back to *Winter Light*. I want to ask you—ask you—something to see if I'm right. Isn't it true that whereas you are frequently concerned with the impossibility of attaining corroboration for one's faith, in *Winter Light* you show that the search for corroboration is itself the cause of harm?

B: All the time that I treated the questions of God and ultimate faith, I felt very unhappy. When I left them behind, and also abandoned my enormous desire to make the best film in the world—

S: To be God.

B: Yes . . . to . . . to—

S: Make the perfect creation.

B: Yes. To make the perfect creation. As soon as I said, here are my limits, which I see very clearly and which I will not jump over but only try to open up—technically—then I became unneurotic—

S: Like a research scientist?

B: Yes.

S: Isn't that how the drama operates in *Persona*? After the credit sequence, the film begins realistically. There is a woman in a hospital, suffering a sort of catatonic withdrawal. She is tended by a nurse. Then, as the film progresses, this realistic drama starts to break from inside (at one moment, the film itself shatters). Is it true that like a research scientist, you were investigating in *Persona* the limits that exist for an artist who wants his imitation of reality to be as true and as complex as reality itself? Don't you say, "Therefore, I will show where the limits are by declaring the artificialities that are my art and by showing them break down or break open at the point where they come closest to touching the truth?"

B: That's very interesting, but it's not what I intended. It's very simple: *Persona* is a creation that saved its creator. Before making it, I was ill, having twice had pneumonia and antibiotic poisoning. I lost my balance for three months. The summer before, I had written a script, but I told everyone it would be canceled because it was a complicated picture and I didn't feel up to it. I was going to Hamburg then to stage *The Magic Flute*, and I had to cancel that, too. I remember sitting in my hospital bed, looking directly in front of me at a black spot—because if I turned my head at all, the whole room began to spin. I thought to myself that I would never create anything anymore; I was completely empty, almost dead. The montage at the beginning of the film is just a poem about that personal situation.

S: With cuts from earlier Bergman films.

B: Because whenever I thought about making a new film, silly pictures from my old ones came into my head. Suddenly, one day I started thinking of two women sitting next to each other and comparing hands. This was a single scene, which, after an enormous effort, I was able to write down. Then, I thought that if I could make a very small picture—perhaps in 16 mm—about two women, one talking, the other not (thus an enormous monologue), it would not be too hard for me. Every day I wrote a little bit. I had as yet no idea about making a regular film, because I was so sick, but I trained myself for it. Each morning at ten I moved from the bed to the writing table, sat down, and sometimes wrote and at other times couldn't. After I left the hospital, I went to the seaside, where I finished the script, although I was still sick. Nevertheless, we decided to go ahead. The producer was very, very understanding. He kept telling me to go on, that we could throw it away if it was bad because it wasn't an expensive project. In the middle of July I started shooting, still so sick that when I stood up I became dizzy. Throughout the first week the results were terrible.

S: What did you shoot that week?

B: We started with the first scene in the hospital.

S: But not with the precredit sequence?

B: No, that came afterward. I wanted to give things up, but the producer kept encouraging me, finally telling me to move the company to my island. When we got there, slowly things picked up. The actresses and Sven Nykvist were fantastic; it was a fantastic collaboration. One day we made a scene that we all felt was good. That gave me courage. Then the next day, another scene; then many scenes. It grew, and we began to reshoot what hadn't worked. Exactly what happened and why it happened I don't know.

S: Here's a film you make immediately after thinking you'll never make another film again. You come back to life as an artist, step by step, growing in courage until you can face—utterly without fear—the problems, absurdities, and impossibilities of art itself. And you select as a surrogate an artist who suffers what you suffered, except that Elisabeth *wills* it; she chooses to stop being an artist.

B: Yes, because she is not sick.

S: Let me get at my point another way. When Elisabeth looks at television and sees a Buddhist monk immolating himself in Vietnam, several critics wanted to take this as an uncharacteristic expression of your interest in politics. But I think it must be related to the later scene—in her bedroom—when she studies the Cartier-Bresson photograph of the Jews being led out of the Warsaw ghetto. Both scenes dramatize the awe inspired in the artist when he faces true suffering—which, however, cannot escape some involvement with art, since both the monk and the Jews reach our consciousness through the art of the photographer.

B: Let me explain exactly what I tried to express in the first scene. The monk scares her because his conviction is so enormous he is willing to die for it. The photograph represents real suffering.

S: But it is, paradoxically, also art. And I find it suggestive that during the great scene in *Shame* when you show the people being herded in and out of buildings by the soldiers, you yourself recall the composition of Cartier-Bresson's great photograph. Didn't you feel the recollection?

B: In a way, yes. But I never thought of it. The scene you mention represents humiliation, which is the subject of *Shame*. The film isn't about enormous brutality, but only meanness. It is exactly like what has happened to the Czechs. They defended their rights, and now, slowly, they are being submitted to a tactic of brutalization that wears them down. *Shame* is not about the bombs; it is about the gradual infiltration of fear.

S: So that the low budget and consequent lack of large war scenes precisely reflect your theme.

B: Yes, but *Shame* is not precise enough. My original idea was to show only a single day before the war had broken out. But then I wrote things, and it all went wrong—I don't know why. I haven't seen *Shame* recently, and I'm a little afraid to do so. When you make such a picture, you have to be very hard on yourself. It's a moral question.

S: Why?

B: Certain things in life are impossible to represent—like a concentration camp.

S: Because the reality is too terrible?

B: Exactly. It is almost the same with war as with murder or death. You must be a hundred percent morally conscious in treating these things.

S: You must not simply shock.

B: Exactly. To see someone dying is false—

S: When we know he will get up after the performance.

B: In the theater it's not so bad because we accept all these conventions, but film is different.

S: Still, you are more successful in *Shame* than you acknowledge. For example, I think that the interview scene creates the horror of war without any false killings. Who are these soldiers? What do they want? How dare they televise their brutalization? How dare they humiliate other human beings in this way: *Life* goes to the end of Western civilization? [Bergman laughs heartily.] Where did you get the idea for this scene?

B: I don't know.

S: It was in the script? You didn't improvise?

B: It was in the script.

S: Do you improvise much at other times?

B: No. I improvise only when I have a plan. Improvising for itself is impossible.

S: Didn't you improvise the interviews with the actors in *The Passion of Anna*?

B: I'm sorry to say that those are very unsuccessful. I just wanted to have a break in the film and to let the actors express themselves. Bibi Andersson and Liv Ullmann improvised their interviews, but Max von Sydow and Erland Josephson had no idea what to say, so they said what I told them to. This led to two different films, and I no longer understand why I left the whole batch in, because I always realized that they wouldn't work. But I like *coups de théâtre*, things that make people wake up and rejoin the film. This time, however, it wasn't successful.

S: There are no *coups* in *Winter Light*; the rhythm is even. I want to ask another question about that film. When Von Sydow's drowned body is discovered, why is the shot so distant?

B: Because I always feel that something is more terrifying at a distance. Thus, in *Shame*, when Max shoots Björnstrand, we are far away, and I place the crime behind a wagon.

S: But we are close to Elisabeth when she sucks Alma's blood in *Persona*.

B: Because that isn't real.

S: It's an expression of their relationship rather than an event?

B: Exactly. It's not meant to be terrifying.

S: This brings me to a more general area. Do you exercise total control over camera placement and editing?

B: Yes. When I shoot, I know almost exactly how long a scene will take because I have a sort of rhythm inside that I try to re-create.

S: Do you ever shoot out of sequence, knowing how things will be put together?

B: I only do that when contingencies make it necessary. I always try to start at the beginning, shoot forward, and then reshoot later. I always reshoot the first days' work.

S: There are several possible explanations for Elisabeth's refusal to

speak in *Persona.* It is an act of great honesty; since she only imitates
the real suffering in the world, she decides not to get onstage night
after night and mock reality with her stage grief. It is also an act of ag-
gression against other people; her silence renders them helpless.

B: It is as the doctor in the films says, "Silence too is a role." Elisabeth lacks a sense of humor. Anyone who works in this profession must
keep from taking the theater too seriously; it is all a game.

S: Is that why you call *The Magician* a comedy?

B: Yes.

S: Because it is about the game of being an artist?

B: We artists represent the most serious things—life and death—but
it is all a game.

S: In *Persona,* why do you repeat the scene when Alma analyzes Elisabeth once with Alma on camera and again with Elisabeth on camera,
reacting?

B: Because both actresses are wonderful. First, I cut it in reverse
shots, but I felt that something was missing. I felt that a whole dimension was added by repeating the scene with the other woman on
camera.

S: Why does Alma break down and speak nonsense syllables before
she leaves the island?

B: She has been driven nearly insane by her resentments so that
words, which are no longer useful, can no longer be put together by
her. But it is not a matter of psychology. Rather, this comes at the
point inside the movement of the film itself where words can no
longer have any meaning.

S: Do you think that Elisabeth deliberately sent Alma off with the
letter [in which she discusses how she is using the nurse] in order that
the girl may read it?

B: I never thought about that. Perhaps.

S: Something like that happens often in your films. In *Through a
Glass Darkly,* for example, Karin learns how her father has been studying her when she finds his diary. In *The Passion of Anna,* Andreas
learns about Anna's lie by finding the letter she left in her purse. Etc.
Many of your characters leave evidence about themselves for the very
person who must not see it.

B: Letters and diaries are very tempting. I'm extremely, passionately
interested in human beings. Anything written or left behind tempts
me so much that I'd read it if I could. When my mother died—four
years ago—we discovered a diary that we had not known she was keeping daily since 1916! It was a fantastic act to read it because she wrote

in a microscopically small script, with many abbreviations. But suddenly we discovered an unknown woman—intelligent, impatient, furious, rebellious—who had lived under this disciplined perfect housewife.

S: I wouldn't dare to discuss your mother, but the characters in your films who leave evidence behind may, in a sense, be lying. After all, you yourself admit that words must arouse suspicion; the self we write about is an artistic construction.

B: Words . . . are . . . always . . . difficult. Now we're back to the beginning. The musician writes notes on a score, which are the most perfect signs that exist between creator and performer. But words are a very very bad channel between writer and performer.

S: And audience.

B: Yes, so I'm always suspicious of words.

S: Interesting fact, though: You use music less and less in your films. Why?

B: Because I think that film itself is music, and I can't put music in music.

S: Why did it take you so long to discover that?

B: Because I've been ambivalent.

S: In *The Touch* isn't the buzz saw that we hear when Karin comes to David's apartment and finds him gone your new way to use music?

B: I think everything on the sound track must complement the image—voices, noises, music; all are equal. Sometimes I feel very unhappy because I have still not found the solution to the problem of sound.

S: Isn't it true, however, that you use commentative sound more frequently now than in your earlier films?

B: Yes, it's true.

S: Another good example of this new use of the sound track is the fog horn in *Persona* that signals a movement out of the real world. One last question about that film: When Alma leaves, you hold for a moment on the wooden statue of a woman which we see again in *Shame, The Passion of Anna,* and *The Touch.* Why?

B: It's the figurehead from a ship. On the island where I live, I have her outside my house. She's a friend of mine, and I like her because she is made of hardwood. She represents something to me, for personal reasons.

S: How do you respond to the viewer who has caught such personal references—the reappearing figurehead, all the Voglers and Andreases, the discovered diaries and letters, the personal fear of birds that creates the climax of *Hour of the Wolf* but must be invoked even to explain small moments (like the bird dashing itself against the window in *The*

Passion of Anna)? What do you say to the person who keeps seeing these things but doesn't understand their significance? Bergman is sending messages, he thinks, but what are they and why?

B: Perhaps these things that mean so much to me also mean something to someone else.

S: You have no specific intention in repeating them?

B: No.

S: But do you see what this does to a spectator who follows you as if you were a writer? This problem has been brought on you by your own genius for creating a unique world that others wish to chart. And it's not a playful world either, like Truffaut's, with all his joking references to favorite directors and his playful casting of friends in minor roles. You don't joke in that way; even in your lightest comedy, the spectator never doubts that serious and typical issues are involved. Your admirers want to understand the layout of your world, to know the names and properties and even the importance of all these lakes, islands, rocks. What advice do you give us?

B: It's irrelevant. All these things are dreams—not necessarily ones that I have dreamed; rather fantasies. When you are dreaming. . . . Perhaps you remember your dreams?

S: Hardly ever.

B: But you know that you dream?

S: Of course. Otherwise I wouldn't sleep.

B: If you didn't dream, you would go mad.

S: Yes.

B: Every night you enter a world of people, colors, furniture, islands, lakes, landscapes, buildings—everything—that belongs to you alone. But if you remember your dreams and start telling them to other people, then maybe the other people will start to know you better.

S: Then it doesn't bother you when critics interpret you through these items?

B: Not at all. Not at all. And let me tell you, I learn more from critics who honestly criticize my pictures than from those who are devout.

S: Why then, very early in our interview, did you insist, "I don't care what you think"?

B: Because I had the feeling that we started with you trying to stress yourself. . . .

S: To make myself the subject of the interview?

B: No. You were so hidden. . . . I saw you had prepared very well, and you remained locked in your preparation. You knew we had little time; you wanted to start in a hurry. So you began to talk to me in a

way that was very hard for me to understand. Then I just said anything
to break through. Now I think we are in perfect communication. Perhaps our discussion is a little tumultuous, but I like it that way. Now
we sit down as two human beings, discussing things in a simple way.
When I was impolite and said, "I don't care what you think," I meant
it—because all the people who are important to me. . . . Buñuel once
said a wonderful thing: "I make pictures only for my friends." And
they influence me. They interfere, and I listen to them, and they help
me change things. But, you know, I hate the intellectual way of handling things that are very sensual, very personal to me. Do you understand what I mean? So I just said anything that would cut us down to
a level where we could communicate. I myself can't say that *Persona* is
my best picture. . . . Ten times a month people ask me, "Which is
your best picture?" but that is irrelevant to me because some of my
pictures are closer to my heart than others. When we meet and you
say, "This is good, and this is bad," I can't stand it, but if you say,
"This is closer to my heart; I feel this; I don't feel that," then I can
understand you.

S: Then we go on—to the other pictures. *Night Is My Future* is the
first film you directed from someone else's script and novel. When you
direct in that way, does it feel different from directing your own script?

B: Yes, in a way, but I'm used to it because in the theater I'm always
directing other people's scripts. Of course, I like it more in the theater
because that is my profession. In films, it's more difficult.

S: When you make such a film, under conditions that come close to
stage directing, are you therefore freed for more experimentation with
cinematic devices? For example, the opening scene in *Night Is My
Future*, in which the hero is blinded during target practice, seems more
cinematic than most things in your previous films.

B: The producer cut that whole sequence to pieces. When I made
that picture, I would have accepted an offer to film the telephone
book. I was a flop from the beginning. Then a very clever producer
came to me and said, "Ingmar, you are a flop. Here's a very sentimental story that will appeal to the public. You need a box-office success
now." I replied, "I will lick your ass if you like; only let me make a
picture." So I made the picture, and I'm extremely grateful to him—he
later let me make *Prison*. Every day he came to the studio and told
me, "No. Reshoot. This is too difficult, incomprehensible. You are
crazy! She must be beautiful! You must have more light on her hair!
You must have some cats in the film! Perhaps you can find some little
dog." The picture was a great success. He taught me—in a very tough

way—much that saved me. I will be grateful to him till my dying day.

S: He saved you from not communicating directly to the audience?

B: Yes. Yes. I was so frightened of the audience that I couldn't communicate.

S: Your next film, *Three Strange Loves*, contains a scene of childbirth. Such a scene recurs often in your films. Why?

B: I have nine children!

S: I have two, both of them sick now—unfortunately.

B: Yes? How?

S: A mysterious ailment. It began with my wife, stayed briefly with my elder daughter, and now my youngest has it most violently. Do you know what hives are? Red weltlike marks that appear on the skin. We now think we may know the cause. We've just built a new house, and the doctor thinks—this is weird!—that a chemical reaction has been set off between the vinyl asbestos tile and the concrete basement floor that somehow causes the emission of a thin gas to which they're all allergic.

B: That is terrible! Your wife is allergic, too?

S: My poor wife is working now for the first time in ten years, and just now she has to cope with the children's illnesses and her own and with getting someone to help out, since I'm not home. Every night the baby wakes up several times, yet my wife must go to work the next morning even though she hasn't slept.

B: It's terrible! Terrible!

S: In *Three Strange Loves*—

B: It started when you moved into the house?

S: No. That would be easy. It started eight months later. Maybe the chemical reaction took that long.

B: Have you tried a temporary move?

S: When she visited her parents in New York, it didn't improve. It's now systemic.

B: It sounds like an allergy that you can be vaccinated against.

S: Allergists can't do that unless they're certain of the cause.

B: Wouldn't sun and sea help?

S: We were in Cape Cod this summer, but it didn't help. We need to see a specialist. Mr. Bergman—

B: What torture! This is torture!

S: It's the uncertainty, more even than the disease itself. Mr. Bergman, in—

B: How did your wife react when the disease began?

S: She itched. But the medicine controls that. Mostly, she's upset for the children.

B: All of them are suffering now?

S: Except for the older child, who only had it two weeks. I didn't get it at all.

B: But your wife has it still?

S: Yes, but the medicine controls it.

B: Does the medicine make her tired?

S: No. But if she stops taking it, the hives return.

B: What is it called?

S: The medicine? Atarax.

B: Calcium or—

S: I don't really know the chemical composition.

B: It's very strange. You know, the relation between a small girl and her mother can be very strange and difficult. If the mother has a pain in the stomach, very often the child will feel the same pain for psychological reasons.

S: I don't believe in doctors, but—

B: Nor I.

S: But they say it's physical and, in this case, I think they're right.

B: The medicine doesn't help your daughter?

S: Only a little.

B: She itches?

S: Yes. And she comes to sleep with us in the middle of the night because she's wakened by it.

B: Terrible!

S: And she's such a good little girl that she feels guilty for spoiling our sleep.

B: Very difficult! It is—

S: Mr. Bergman, why did you make personal appearances in *Three Strange Loves* and in *Secrets of Women?*

B: Lack of extras! [Laughter.]

S: You were saving money?

B: Yes. [Laughter.]

S: Why did you decide at this particular point in your career to make so stylized a comedy as *Smiles of a Summer Night?*

B: I thought it was time for a box-office success, and although everyone disagreed with me, I was convinced that this picture would succeed. Moreover, I have always liked the *pièce bien fait* (Marivaux and Scribe) with its strategical plot construction. In a way, this film is just a play that I desired to write. I hadn't the money to produce it, so I got someone to let me make it into a film.

S: In fact, some people have criticized your films for being too theatrical—particularly the early ones. How do you answer this charge?

B: I am a director.

S: But aren't the two forms different?

B: Completely. In my earlier pictures, it was very difficult for me to go from directing in the theater to directing films. I didn't succeed in making the change. But this is not important.

S: Apropos, is that why you use a narrator in your first film, *Crisis*, and a sort of stage manager who addresses the audience and asks us to use our imaginations—unnecessarily, since cinema shows all it wants to—in your second film, *It Rains on Our Love?*

B: Yes. Until *Summer Interlude*. . . . I don't know how many pictures I had made before it—

S: Nine.

B: Nine. Well, I had always felt technically crippled—insecure with the crew, the cameras, the sound equipment—everything. Sometimes a film succeeded, but I never got what I wanted to get. But in *Summer Interlude*, I suddenly felt that I knew my profession.

S: Do you have any idea why?

B: I don't know, but for heaven's sake, a day must always come along when finally one succeeds in understanding his profession! I'm so impressed by young directors now who know how to make a film from the first moment.

S: But they have nothing to say. [Bergman laughs.] Still, I'm very interested in why—and I agree that it is—*Summer Interlude* is a turning point. Might the breakthrough, which you perceive as technical, be related to content? Because this seems to me your first film to achieve true complexity. At the end of *To Joy* the conductor tells the hero, who has just suffered the loss of a beloved wife, that he should find consolation in music, and we close on the strains of Beethoven's "Ode to Joy." *Summer Interlude* has a similar conclusion, but it is far more complicated and ambiguous. The heroine dances off to her new lover, having put the past idyll behind her, but we perceive this as an accommodation rather than a solution. Grief is not facilely transcended.

B: Your question is difficult. I will try to. . . . I don't understand. You are puzzled when the conductor tells the hero to play?

S: No. I'm saying that the conclusions of these two films are similar but—

B: And of *Winter Light*.

S: Yes—but *Summer Interlude* is the first excellent example of this theme, because for the first time you don't seem to feel the need of a simple conclusion. And I think this is crucial to your success. For example, even *Smiles of a Summer Night*, which you call a *pièce bien fait*, is distinguished not by neatness, but by ambiguity. The plot is resolved, but not the problems of the characters. Moreover, though a comedy about love, the film is also a drama about death: Before the lovers flee, you show a medieval clock striking the hour through a parade of wooden figures [recalling the end of *The Seventh Seal*], in which the most prominent is death.

B: That whole film is about destruction. *Smiles of a Summer Night* is much darker than it appears. I made it during one of my most depressing periods, when I myself was near death. Like *Persona*, it saved its creator. Often one makes a tragedy in a good mood and, when in a bad mood, turns to comedy. It is also true, as you say, that in *Summer Interlude* I start to accept life as a compromise. Before you do that, life is difficult and heavy, and things go wrong; at the moment you accept your limits and see them clearly, you have a greater desire to create and more joy in creation.

S: But how could you, in that state, make a film like *A Lesson in Love?*

B: Oh, that's just a *divertissement*. I had just finished *The Naked Night* and was living with Harriet Andersson at a small seaside hotel. She liked to sunbathe on the beach, and I liked to sit down—

S: In the shade?

B: No. It was a fantastic hotel, exactly like the one in *Mr. Hulot's Holiday*. There was a small tower in it where I used to sit and read. I had just divorced my third wife, though I still liked her very much, and, therefore, began writing about her. In fourteen days I finished the script, and fourteen days later we began shooting the picture. The whole thing was just for fun—and money. I was very poor at that time, you know. I already had lots of children and a lot of women, and money had to be paid out. A good deal of my filmmaking in earlier years came from lack of money.

S: "Women and children are hostages to fortune."

B: [Laughs uproariously.]

S: Were any of the scenes in *A Lesson in Love* that portray the couple before they're married made in imitation of American "screwball comedy"?

B: No, but I had seen them all, so perhaps unconsciously. . . . You know, I have never been scared of being influenced. I like to use others' styles. I don't want to be unique. I am a cinemagoer. I have no complexes on this subject.

S: Is that because you're sure that you'll always be yourself?

B: Yes.

S: Particularly in the scene where Eva Dahlbeck beats up her former lover, I was reminded of a Rosalind Russell picture.

B: That scene was a one-act play I had written long before and just put in there because it was funny. I wrote it in imitation of the one-act comedies by Chekhov.

S: Back to *Smiles of a Summer Night*. Normally, you show that the woman is wiser than the man in successful heterosexual love, almost like a mother to him. Yet in this film you seem to be arguing that men and women should marry people their own age. Hadn't you previously suggested, in effect, that all women are older than men? Why the new issue of compatibility in ages?

B: Perhaps you are right.

S: That's one of the reasons I don't feel too optimistic about the lovers' future; hence, I am not too happy at the conclusion. She is far too young and innocent for him. Am I right?

B: Yes, I think so.

S: This film is paradoxical, so much more complicated than it seems.

B: You know, a French critic compared it to *Rules of the Game*, so I wanted to see the film. When an American producer, who wanted to make me a present, asked me to choose one, I requested a print of Renoir's film to put in my private *cinémathèque*. I think it's an extremely bad picture. It is badly acted. Renoir is a very overrated director. He has only made one good picture: *The Human Beast*.

S: You liked that?

B: Wasn't it good?

S: It's awful!

B: It's awful? I saw it when I was twenty, and it made an enormous impression on me. It's not good?

S: No. No. I happen to like *The Rules of the Game* very much, but I think I can guess why you don't. Most of the film was improvised, and there is a tremendous effect of casualness.

B: It is irritating. It lacks style. I can't understand its humor, its complete lack of sensuality. The hunt is good, though.

S: Stupendous. The greatest thing in the film is when the hunters beat the trees to flush the rabbits out. *There* is real brutality! But back to your film: The more often I see *Smiles of a Summer Night*, the angrier I become at Egerman. His wife is dying for him to possess her, yet he is prevented by his own stupid ideas about the possible ways of living with love.

B: He is stupid. He is immature. He misunderstands his affair with the actress. He is a fool.

S: If you could have shot this in color, would you have?

B: No. Because it is more fascinating to shoot in black and white and force people to imagine the colors.

S: Why have you switched to color recently?

B: At the beginning, it was painful, but now I like it. It's more sensual—now that we've learned to use it.

S: *The Passion of Anna* is gorgeous, but—my God!—*All These Women* looks like a bad MGM musical.

B: We started by reading all the books, and we tried to do the right things, but it is—

S: Tutti-frutti.

B: Yes. Yes. [Laughter.] In *The Passion of Anna* we decided to use no blue at all—

S: Yet one feels so cold: gray, but not blue.

B: Exactly.

S: Do you work in color now—to any degree—because you feel that the audence demands it?

B: No. I like it.

S: Why, at the beginning of *The Passion of Anna*, do you show Liv Ullmann using a crutch?

B: All the time I was writing the part I knew Liv Ullmann must play it, and I knew that the crutch would have a powerful effect on Liv Ullmann's feelings.

S: Doesn't it also symbolize the way in which Anna uses her "happy marriage" as a crutch?

B: Of course. But that is a second reason.

S: Why did you make Anna dream a dream from *Shame?*

B: Things sometimes happen for strange reasons. When we made *Shame*, we built that house on the island and landscaped the grounds —all with government permission because, since the island is a sort of animal preserve, you aren't allowed to build houses there without a permit. When the film was finished, the producer told me that we had to tear the house down, and I begged him not to. I told him I would make another picture there even though I had no idea of making one; I just didn't want to lose that house. Inside, I had a strange feeling that I had not succeeded in *Shame*, and I wanted to recreate the film in the place where it had failed. You know, the atmosphere in *The*

Passion of Anna is exactly like that of *Shame:* killing, brutality, anonymity, people's sense of their utter helplessness before brutality. Liv Ullmann plays the same role in both films, and the woman in *Shame* might have dreamed the same dreams that Anna dreams. Originally, I indicated the intimate link between the two films through the dialogue, but I eventually cut it out. When Bibi Andersson first comes to Max von Sydow, I had him say, "Two people who disappeared in the war used to live in this house."

S: Why do you make Max von Sydow an archaeologist and then link that not to a former but to a subsequent film? In *The Touch*, Elliott Gould is also an archaeologist.

B: I have always been fascinated by digging and looking for things.

S: You also dig—for the truth about people—

B: Some sort of truth.

S: All right: a truth.

B: No! No! No! No! Excuse me. I dig for secret expressions and relations that we hide—

S: Behind our faces. Thus you put the camera right up close to see if you can get through the face. But you also seem to me to be aware that the hidden truth revealed by means of an actress' face is also a lie because it is art.

B: Please don't talk about the truth; it doesn't exist! Behind each face there is another and another and another. The actress' face gives you, in enormous concentration, that whole series of faces—not at a single moment, but at different moments in the performance or, sometimes, during a long close-up. In each thousandth part of a second an actor gives you a different impression, but the succession is so rapid that you take them all as a single truth.

S: That's the way film itself works: a succession of individual frames perceived by the eye as one moving image.

B: The two things are almost the same; you are right.

S: And in both cases, you pick the ones you want from all the separate expressions and thus make a single truth. So, finally, we get not the truth revealed through the actress' face but your selection of all the instances of it that she has expressed to you.

B: Everything you do in pictures is selection. People who now go out and shoot everything are perverting cinematographic art.

S: You select from the things you've caught with the camera, but you also impose by providing dialogue.

B: That's because I place my people in stylized surroundings and situations where they can express things that are complex and secret—

and emotionally stimulating to the audience. Every second in my pictures is made to move the audience.

S: Do you decide exactly how we are to be moved, what we are to feel?

B: No. No. Only that you feel something.

S: Why do you use so much dialogue in your films?

B: Because human communication occurs through words. I tried once, to eliminate language, in *The Silence*, and I feel that that picture is excessive.

S: It's too abstract.

B: Yes.

S: I want to move to *The Silence*, but one last question about *The Passion of Anna*. What is the meaning of the last line: "This time his name was Andreas."

B: [Laughter.] We will be back.

S: I don't understand. It can mean that she's a man-eater, because her first husband was also named Andreas, or it can mean that another human being has been destroyed in the world, "This time his name is Andreas," or that another Bergman character has been destroyed, this time named Andreas.

B: I will tell you; it's much simpler. It means a sort of giving up: "*This* time his name is Andreas." You must feel behind the meaning another that you cannot define. For me, it expresses a feeling of boredom.

S: I don't understand.

B: I mean, "*This* time his name is Andreas"; but I will be back, and *next* time my character will have another name. I don't know what it will be, but this boring character will be back.

S: Also you?

B: Yes. [Hearty laughter.]

S: You know, I think *The Silence* proves my point. Look, I'm not going to try to defend myself anymore, but you should understand that I do disapprove of the totally intellectual response to film—

B: You know, one of my best friends, who lives a completely intellectual life, is emotionally crippled. He's very tight, but I like him extremely because he's so unhappy and nice and, inside, warm. He's his own enemy all the time. Everything I dislike he likes; and everything he likes I dislike. Yet I find it so fascinating to study his reactions, which are always enormously intelligent. His second or third reaction may be emotional, but even that is controlled.

S: I never have only an intellectual reaction.

B: Yes, now that we have spoken awhile, I see that you are extremely emotional.

S: But I must talk to you intellectually because we are discussing your art. . . . Nevertheless, what displeases me about *The Silence* is the exclusiveness of its appeal to our intellects. It gets whiter and whiter as it goes on, bleaching out until I can't see anything. This fits the theme, but it also starves me. I don't hate *The Silence*, as, for example, I hate a film like *Crisis*, which is of no interest whatever, but I hate it. All it leaves me with are questions: For example, why does the boy look at the picture of the nymph and satyr?

B: This film is very. . . . What shall I say about *The Silence?* I think it is about the complete breakdown of illusions. . . . It's very difficult to tell you. . . . It's about my private life. . . . It's an extremely personal picture.

S: Which is why it doesn't communicate.

B: I think that's true. It is a sort of personal purgation: a rendering of hell on earth—my hell. The picture is so. . . . It is so strange to me that I do not know what it means. I saw it some weeks ago, so it is rather clear in my mind now. Some of the scenes I liked so much that I was astonished.

S: Such as?

B: One of the best scenes I have ever made is the short meeting between the waiter and Alma in the darkness while the radio is playing Bach. He comes in, pronounces the name Johann Sebastian Bach, and she says, "The music is beautiful." It is a sudden moment of communication—so clean.

S: Also clear.

B: Completely clear. This picture has too many personal references to me and to my life and experiences so that today—ten years later—it seems as if it were made by someone else. But that scene does not.

S: There are two paradoxes about the autobiographical nature of the film. One is the odd excess of impersonal, even routinized symbolism, largely Freudian. For example, when the waiter bites off the head of the hot dog, certain members of the audience can't resist pointing to the castration symbol.

B: It isn't. The actor I used for the part was a wonderful old man who was sick at the time—owing to a thrombosis, he had lost his memory and couldn't even recall his lines. He even forgot things that were taking place in his life while we were making the film. He had become completely childlike. But his face was so wonderful. So I told him to do whatever he wanted to do, to invent his own business. That was improvised by him to be playful with the boy.

S: All right, but the film is full of perverse sexuality: the dwarfs dressing the boy in girl's clothes, the masturbation, the loveless sex, etc.

B: This is hell—perversion of sex. When sex is completely totally isolated from other parts of life and all the emotions, it produces an enormous loneliness. That is what the film is about: the degradation of sex.

S: And war.

B: Yes, because brutality and cruelty are waiting outside.

S: Ready to break through in *Shame*.

B: In 1946, I spent a few weeks in Hamburg, and in Paris and Grenoble, in 1949; all, places where the war had been intense. The hotel in *The Silence* is exactly like ones I lived in. The film has to do with so many things that frighten me—

S: What about the scene where the boy urinates against the hotel corridor wall?

B: He is purging his troubles, his stress. Now he feels a little more courageous.

S: By being naughty, he asserts himself.

B: Yes.

S: Let me move to another kind of difficult film, *The Magician*. Every time I see it I feel differently toward it. Sometimes I love it; other times I hate it.

B: Can't you make up your mind and love the picture? Because it was made with so much vitality and pleasure. You know, I was in a very good mood when I made that film.

S: That's not the way it appears.

B: I'm sorry. We felt the whole time that we were playing a game.

S: Here, I think I *am* speaking for other people. After we've seen *The Magician*, we can't understand why it is called a comedy. At the end of the film, we look at each other and say—

B: "What sort of comedy is this?" A black comedy.

S: That won't do. At least, the moments that are meant to play humorously against the others aren't funny. For example, the whole subplot involving the servants—

B: That was more developed in the original; for reasons I prefer you not to report, I had to cut most of those scenes. You are right that this part of the film is very unsuccessful.

S: *The Magician* seems both to attack and to exploit theatricalism.

As a result, I don't know quite how to feel about your apparent surrogate, Vogler. Or is this doubt what I'm supposed to feel?

B: Yes. I don't want you to know how to feel.

S: Even more troublesome is the magician's conception of himself as a priest.

B: He *used* to think of himself as a priest. Once he was idealistic; now he simply does the tricks, without any feeling. The only completely integrated man in the film is Vergerus. He's the one I like, not the magician.

S: Why, then, do you make him a fool?

B: Because he is a fool.

S: Then why do you like him?

B: I like his dream of finding out the truth about magic.

S: You like his innocent scientism?

B: And his passion.

S: But he's an intellectual, a rationalist.

B: Yes, but. . . .

S: And you don't like intellectuals.

B: No. I do, I do. I do very much . . . and—

S: What differentiates the intellectuals you like from those you don't?

B: A good intellectual, in my opinion, is one who has trouble with his emotions. He must doubt his intellect, have fantasies, and be powerfully emotional.

S: Tell me, are you hostile to people who seem completely sure of themselves?

B: I am very suspicious of them. But, you know, I meet many fishermen and farmers on the island, who are completely free because their lives are so tough and close to them that they are extremely verbal. They are often crazy, but they are sure of themselves because they know their profession. And I always only work with actors who are—in a special way—self-possessed.

S: But your characters are never like that.

B: Not very often.

S: Why?

B: Because . . . it's very difficult to say in English . . . I think one day perhaps . . . I think that in my new film, *Whispers and Cries*, I have created one character who is self-possessed, but she's not intellectual.

S: But why do you generally not create such characters, though you say you like them in real life?

B: To create such a human being, you must be extremely powerful as a writer. I am not yet so powerful because I have so many things that are. . . .

S: Would you like to create someone like Portia in *The Merchant of Venice?*

B: Someone like a Solzhenitsyn character.

S: Let me ask you about *The Touch* now. I am not someone who hated or loved it; I had mixed feelings. I loved the true perceptions about people in the first part of the film, and Karin, by the way, comes very close to being a self-possessed character. In fact, one of the film's points is the limitation of her sort of strength, which David lessens. Do you want us to like him?

B: David is . . . it's very difficult to answer that question.

S: Why should I care about him?

B: David and the husband both were created as parts of Karin's life, but then the actress wanted to make the story truer to her heart—wanted more light shed on characters who were made to remain in the shadows. Critics have been very unfair to Elliott Gould. He's excellent; he makes much more of the part than there is in it. The guilt for the film's failure is mine. Nevertheless, I think the critical reaction was ridiculous because this film was not made for anything else than to. . . . No. That's not true. I can't understand the critics' aggressiveness.

S: I don't know about the others. For me, the problem is this: Throughout the film, you show that David is doing Karin some good. Church bells often ring when they meet. You include the obtrusive symbol of the madonna, which is being devoured by termites; David tells Karin that the termites are as beautiful as the madonna they destroy—

B: It is very simple. In the beginning of the picture, when it is still romantic, there is a lot of music and beauty. From the middle of the picture, all music, bells, and so forth cease. When he returns to her after his absence, everything has changed. His beard is off; everything is naked, hard, real.

S: But aren't we meant to feel that even the bad things in their affair have made her a better person?

B: That's because David has brought her suffering and change. She has resources and talents that he brings out.

S: Must one always suffer to develop? Isn't it possible to watch the film and say that she was just as talented before he showed up? One of the loveliest scenes occurs when she is looking at herself in the mirror. Her husband comes to embrace her, and then, without a word from him, she walks into the bedroom and prepares herself for what is obviously their favorite sexual position. This seems to be poise, richness, understanding.

B: That's true. That's true.

S: I think there's nothing that David does for her that is equally important.

B: Exactly. But you must remember that in the church she tells him that she could live with both men and make a meaningful and proper life. She is much more alive than anyone else. She knows she has enough warmth and human resources to make both men happy and create a new sort of life. She has a richness which he has made her understand.

S: Why, then, in the scene when she goes to his apartment and discovers he's left does she press her hand on the broken glass?

B: There you have an exact example of the difficulty between actress and director. I invented that, but Bibi Andersson could not perform it. An actress can do something unsuited to her and make it believable, but Bibi Andersson is so integrated a person that, for her, it is impossible to play something she doesn't believe in.

S: As the author, what did you intend as Karin's motive when she wounds her hand?

B: The pain in her soul is so extreme that she wants to localize it in her body.

S: But it looks different. She enters the room and is dismayed by his absence, yet in the midst of her anguish, she shows signs of exhaustion: She yawns. So, to restore her involvement with the pain, she inflicts a wound on herself.

B: But that is Bibi Andersson.

S: For whatever reason, the scene suggests that David had always appealed to her as a way of quickening her feeling *because* he brought her pain.

B: The whole scene is wrong.

S: It is like a note struck in a piece of music that brings the wrong overtone to the following notes.

B: I quite agree. I'm not very happy about it. It can't be cut out, but it is seductive and wrong. You always have the script, your intention, and the actress. All the time, a fight goes on among these things. It is very fascinating, this struggle. Often it makes things come alive. An example is *Persona*.

S: But *Persona* is not realistic so it can absorb what in *The Touch* becomes a destructive falsity.

B: You are exactly right.

S: This brings me to *The Seventh Seal*, which I also find unbalanced between realism and expressionism. Before I begin, are you willing to offer your opinion about *The Seventh Seal?*

B: *The Seventh Seal* was made in thirty-five days. Most of it was shot in the woods right outside the studio. Everything in it was done in an enormous hurry, and I like it because it expresses a sort of craftsmanship. It's very theatrical and complicated. Some parts of the picture I still like. It is very close to me. When we were making it, each morning brought a new catastrophe because we had to make it cheap and quick. For the beach scenes, we had only three days on location! The actors carried the cameras. We borrowed costumes from the theater. It was all done in a hurry, but with enormous enthusiasm. We were happy even to be able to produce some images each day. For example, the scene with the flagellants was shot from eight A.M. to seven P.M. of a single day.

S: Are you satisfied with that scene?

B: I like it, but of course, I had no time to reshoot anything or even to produce enough shots for the sequence.

S: It does seem to be awfully stagy.

B: Of course it is.

S: You wanted that? These religious people are also putting on a show?

B: That was not my intention. I only wanted it done quickly.

S: Was the script written quickly, too?

B: No. It started as a small one-act play. This picture is enormously theatrical, but I don't care. It was such a fantastic time. We never slept. We only rehearsed and shot. When Raval is dying in the forest, he asks for water, for pity, and he cries, "I'm dying, I'm dying, I'm dying." When we shot that moment, suddenly the sun came out!

S: A miracle.

B: [Laughter.] A miracle.

S: You had fun making it, but it's troubling for the spectator. For example, why does all-powerful death have to resort to such low trickery?

B: The whole film is based on medieval pictures in a Swedish church. If you go there, you will see death playing chess, sawing a tree, making jokes with human souls. It's like a Mexican peasant game that takes death as a joke. Only suddenly does he become terrible.

S: Let me get at the problem another way. It does seem that the sensibility of the medieval artist is totally different from the sensibility behind this film.

B: That's not true. Say anything you want against *The Seventh Seal.* My fear of death—this infantile fixation of mine—was, at that moment, overwhelming. I felt myself in contact with death day and night, and my fear was tremendous. When I finished the picture, my fear went away. I have the feeling simply of having painted a canvas in an enormous hurry—with enormous pretension but without any arrogance. I said, "Here is a painting; take it, please."

S: And internationally, people did.

B: Yes.

S: So you were vindicated.

B: Thirty-five days!

S: Time is running out. Where shall I go? Let me turn to that magnificent early film, *The Naked Night.* Were you consciously imitating Strindberg in that film?

B: Strindberg? I must tell you that I am a specialist on Strindberg, and I don't find anything Strindbergian in that film. People who don't know Strindberg so well. . . . We do. We have a great Strindberg tradition in this theater; I have produced many of his plays; I have devoted my professional life as a stage director to Strindberg; my version of *The Dream Play* is in its third year, and this is the second time I have staged it. I have staged several of his plays three times each. To me, there is no sign—

S: Let me point to one moment that—

B: No. The picture has something to do with Emil Jannings's *Variety* [a German film directed by E. A. Dupont in 1925].

S: Why?

B: Because it was the first picture I acquired as a collector. It fascinated me so much that I consciously imitated it.

S: *The Naked Night* marks the start of your collaboration with Sven Nykvist.

B: Yes, but he was only one of four cameramen working on that film. It was made in the mess of that circus at a studio which was doing five other films while I was shooting mine. Sometimes other pictures were in my playing area; other times, I was in theirs.

S: How much of an effect has Nykvist had on your films?

B: Little at that time. It started with *Winter Light,* when we began together to examine light. From early morning until late evening, we stayed in that church registering every gradation of the light. Our common passion—and I feel this even on the stage—is to create light: light and faces surrounded by shadows. This is what fascinates me!

S: Yet *The Naked Night* already shows one of your greatest triumphs in lighting: during the scene when the clown is humiliated by his wife's bathing before the soldiers. How was that effect obtained?

B: That was not Nykvist; it was another cameraman.

S: Was it done with overexposure?

B: They thought I was crazy. We made a negative of the print, and then from that negative we made a new print and then a new negative. Eventually we effaced every grain of the image until we got true black and white—and only black and white.

S: There is a related moment in the film that I feel is Strindbergian because—

B: I never thought of it, but perhaps it is Strindbergian unconsciously. If you live in a Strindberg tradition, you are breathing Strindberg air. After all, I have been seeing Strindberg at the theater since I was ten years old, so it is difficult to say what belongs to him and what to me.

S: One of my favorite lines from *The Ghost Sonata*, which is my favorite Strindberg play—

B: Mine, too.

S: —is the young girl's about "the drudgery of keeping oneself above the dirt of life." This I don't see in your films: the dirt, the mere physical act of going on, of tending to things etc.

B: [Very very softly.] That's true.

S: Why? Why, where there is so much life, is the simple dirt absent? Even in *The Touch*, where it could have been, we don't see it.

B: You're right. . . . I select. . . . First of all, I don't know very much about the dirt of life. I have always rejected it . . . and it's not. . . . I have lived under very bad conditions in my life. I have been very hungry and very sick and sometimes very dirty. With four wives and nine children, you can imagine! But in my pictures I always select, and I find—if you mean real dirt—that it is uninteresting to me. My mind has never been infected by it.

S: One film of yours has dirt, and I love this film: *Monika*.

B: Yes.

S: It's very good.

B: Very good!

S: Very underrated. It has several superb things: the sequence in which they leave Stockholm, the opening shot of Harriet Andersson that also closes the film. How did you get that? She's listening to a phonograph record, smoking a cigarette, and looking directly into the camera.

B: It just happened.

S: And then you decided to use it at the beginning and end?

B: It isn't in the beginning.

S: In America, it appears under the credits.

B: That is a mistake. At that time, they made a mess of my pictures outside Sweden. I intended that shot only to appear toward the end. When I made it, everyone said I was crazy; suddenly she looks directly at us!

S: Why did you use something like this again in *Hour of the Wolf?*

B: Because television has made it less difficult to accept. Therefore, I have Liv Ullmann tell the story directly to us.

S: Why do you end the film in mid-sentence?

B: Because the whole picture is half-spoken sentences. It is . . . an unsuccessful attempt—

S: Of hers?

B: Of mine, too.

S: Another personal film.

B: Too personal.

S: Indeed, I can't understand what's going on.

B: [Laughter.] Me, too. It's very strange to me.

S: What does the scene with the boy mean? What are the demons doing to the husband? Why does the wife also see them? I have questions and questions.

B: Me, too. To me, however, the picture is extremely real. The demons and the boy. . . . Do you know French? In French, it is called *folie à deux.* The wife is also ill.

S: But we see her as a kind of earth mother, next to a bowl of apples, and—

B: Yes, that's true. But she is also ill.

S: You should tell us that earlier in the film.

B: No. I wouldn't like that. We discussed it, and I decided not to. But she is infected by him. She is really an earth mother, but she becomes infected and will never return to her former self.

S: But she misinterprets her illness. She doesn't realize that she's infected; she thinks the problem was that she was too weak to help her husband.

B: The difficulty with the picture is that I couldn't make up my mind who it was about. Had I made it from her point of view it would have been very interesting. But, no, I made it the wrong way.

After it was finished, I tried to turn it over to her; we even reshot some scenes, but it was too late. To see a man who is already mad become crazier is boring. What would have been interesting would have been to see an absolutely sane woman go crazy because she loves the madman she married. She enters his world of unreality, and that infects her. Suddenly, she finds out that she is lost. I understood this only when the picture was finished.

S: Do you ever make a film to correct another film?

B: Only with *The Passion of Anna*—

S: Which corrects *Shame*.

B: Yes. And, a little bit, *Winter Light* was made to correct *Through a Glass Darkly*.

S: Yes, and one of the problems—

B: And *The Magician* corrects *The Naked Night*.

S: In—

B: But not consciously. For heaven's sake, it wasn't conscious.

S: You felt it was wrong and—

B: Now I have to go.

S: So we end in midsentence?

[Much laughter.]

II

Perspectives on Individual Films

8

THE EARLY FILMS
Ingmar Bergman and the Devil

Erik Ulrichsen

It seems only yesterday that we were calling him the *enfant terrible* of the Swedish cinema and criticizing his films for being immature, apparently for ever bogged down in the problems of puberty. Perhaps it is characteristic of the Nordic artist that he is slow to mature (and sometimes never does). In any case, although Ingmar Bergman's talent was obvious from the beginning, he has developed by way of so many detours and cul-de-sacs that now and then one has felt tempted to give him up. And it is greatly to the credit of Carl Anders Dymling, of Svensk Filmindustri, that he did not give him up. Bergman's career illustrates the value of a far-sighted producer who is wise enough to allow for experiments and mistakes in the belief that the talented director will learn from them.

Bergman is now forty (on July 14, 1958), and the faults of his most recent films are not primarily due to immaturity. No longer does the director identify himself directly and without detachment with his worried young men; and the pious boys in *Smiles of a Summer Night* and *Wild Strawberries* are, I think, caricatures of the young Bergman.

Ingmar Bergman's work is at once terribly Swedish and terribly personal. In his films, an exceptionally sensitive and highly-strung personality highlights typically Swedish problems.

I

The 'forties were a hectic, experimental, sometimes hysterical period in Swedish literature. A group of writers found their main themes in different aspects of *Angst*. Their works had a paradoxical connection

From *Sight and Sound*, Vol. 27, No. 5 (Summer 1958), pp. 224-30. Reprinted by permission of *Sight and Sound*.

with the fact that during the war Sweden was a neutral country. A sort of "neutrality complex" bothered the Swedes; and perhaps a certain masochism was a kind of "moral compensation" for not fighting Hitler. The suicide of the playwright Stig Dagerman tells us something about the literary climate in Sweden during these years. And in several of Bergman's films—particularly Fängelse (Prison) in which one of the characters is a poet—we find reflections of this pessimism of the 'forties.

Older traditions have influenced Bergman, notably the plays of Strindberg. The demoniacal element in Strindberg appeals to Bergman and he has produced his plays in the theatre. In contrast to these traditions—or as a complementary aspect of them—is the love of nature, the search for purity, moral beauty and belief that can be found so often in Swedish art—in, for instance, Pär Lagerkvist's novel Barabbas and in Sucksdorff's films. Sometimes, as in Molander and Bergman's film Eva, these elements degenerate into naive puritanism.

The Christian faith (and doubt) is a part of Bergman's world. His father is a pastor and his upbringing was severe. Once he broke with his family, and several times during his youth he isolated himself in Stockholm's Gamla Stan, the old quarter of the city. I once asked him if he did this in order to study the milieu, but he said no. "At that time everything revolved around myself and my crises. Only later [in Fängelse] did I use some of my experiences."

This was in the late 'thirties. Bergman studied literature and art at the university of Stockholm and began directing plays with amateurs. In 1942 he produced his own first play with a student cast, and a year later he directed Kaj Munk's anti-Nazi play Niels Ebbesen for a professional theatre. Since then, he has continued to work regularly for the theatre—in Hälsingborg, Göteborg, Stockholm and Malmö, where he is now artistic director of the city's beautiful modern theatre. On the stage he has produced Camus, Ibsen, Pirandello, Molière and his own brutal play The Murder in Barjärna. As a theatre director, he is almost always interesting and inventive; his own plays, however, are unremarkable.

In 1944 Alf Sjöberg made Hets (Frenzy) from Bergman's first film script, and the second international epoch of the Swedish cinema had begun. Although Sjöberg had done some interesting work in the early 'forties, Frenzy was a turning point, a production which gave the Swedish film-makers self-confidence. In it, the world is seen through the eyes of an adolescent, Jan-Erik. Unhappy at school, where he is terrorized by the sadistic Latin master "Caligula," he falls in love with

Bertha, a shop-girl; too late, he realizes that she is another of "Caligula's" victims. One day Jan-Erik finds her dead. "Caligula" is in the apartment. Bertha has had a heart attack after drinking too much. Later, "Caligula" explains his presence: he knew about Jan-Erik and Bertha and wanted to stop their affair. Jan-Erik is expelled from school, but in the end finds the courage to cope with life.

Stig Jarrel as the teacher Caligula torments Alf Kjellin as Jan Erik Widgren in *Torment,* which was written by Ingmar Bergman and directed by Alf Sjoberg.

The film gave at once too much and too little. Interwoven in it are many themes: the tyranny of the conventional school system, the gulf between parents and children, the hypocrisy of official morality, the troubles of adolescence and the war (for "Caligula" is a Himmler opposed to the humane teacher Pippi, and the symbolism is clear). But as an attack on the system the film misfired, though it often brilliantly evoked the school atmosphere. The case of "Caligula" was too abnormal for general conclusions to be drawn from it; Bertha's dependence on him remained unexplored and unexplained; and it seemed improbable that "Caligula" should get away with it in the end. The film's exaggerations are deliberate and stylish—the influences both of expressionism and of the American thriller were evident—and Sjöberg made an effort to match the highly subjective anger in the young writer's script. Many tricks and shocks, in fact. But the film's most convincing passages were the quiet ones, in which the pupils talked as young people really do. Also notable was the playing of Stig Olin, who had some wonderful lines and acted with great charm as the Strindberg enthusiast Sandman. It is not surprising that he became one of Bergman's favourite actors, although he remains at his best in minor parts like that of Sandman.

Already in *Frenzy* the early Bergman world was almost complete: here are the poor prospects for genuine young love, the conflicts between the generations, the lack of imagination in the Swedish *bourgeois* and the somewhat schematic conception of the place of good and evil in the world. "Caligula" is less stylized than Bergman's later devils, but the invincible, inexplicable wickedness is already there.

II

Frenzy made a strong impression at the time (not least in occupied Denmark) and it showed that Bergman had passion and a certain talent for realistic dialogue. But for his first writer-director assignment Bergman used a poor play, and *Kris* (*Crisis*; 1946) was mediocre. Bergman was interested in the character of the villain (played by Stig Olin) and transformed him into a partly demoniacal, partly comic fellow who knows all about his own corruption but finds his way out only in suicide. Here Bergman tried to blend realism and fantasy; he was not successful, and this approach has spoiled many of his later films. It handicapped the two films he made next, *Det Regnar på vår kärlek* (*It Rains on Our Love*; 1946) and *Skepp till Indialand* (*Ship to Dreamland*; 1947), both stories about young love and the obstacles it encounters. The first film had slight elements of social satire; the second was an unreal and melodramatic piece after the style of the Carné of the 'thirties.

After writing the script for *Kvinna utan ansikte* (*Woman Without a Face*; 1947), a rather inhuman study of a nymphomaniac directed by the veteran Gustaf Molander, Bergman touched bottom as a director with *Musik i Mörker* (*Music in the Dark*; 1948), a novelettish affair about a blind young man and his girl. Then, suddenly, he made in *Hamnstad* (*Sea-port*; 1948) a straight naturalistic film. Bergman was now thirty, and the period of uncertainty, if not of immaturity, was for the time being over.

Hamnstad was the first film made by Bergman for Svensk Filmindustri, the company for which he has since mainly worked. It is the story of a young sailor who finds work in Göteborg as a docker. In a restaurant, he meets a young girl who has tried to drown herself. He likes her, but she wants to be honest with him and reveals her past. In flashbacks we learn that she spent a year in a reform school and of the moral ruin of her life. The young man is revolted, gets drunk, but finally returns to her. Working for the first time effectively on location, Bergman made a film less theatrical, and more convincing in its "black" scenes, than his previous ventures. The actors adapted themselves well to the realistic surroundings, with a particularly true and touching performance by Nine-Christine Jönsson as the forlorn girl. Despite some characteristic excesses, the direction was often effective. But the film's dialogue was too high-pitched, too literary, and too often Bergman used his characters as mouthpieces to express his own views on the world. These seem recurrent flaws in his pictures: the good dialogue in many sections of *Frenzy* was due to Bergman's own direct experience of the *milieu*.

Bergman followed *Hamnstad* with another script for Gustaf Molander, *Eva* (also 1948). Another over-dramatized piece, the story of a jazz musician unable to find meaning in his married life, it also ended happily on a reconciliation. Perhaps the happy endings of *Hamnstad*, *Kvinna utan ansikte* and *Eva* did not satisfy Bergman. At any rate, he now made for another company the most desperate of his films. *Fängelse* (1949) was free (too free) cinema.

It opens with a meeting between an old schoolmaster and a film director. The teacher has an idea for a film: its theme is that Hell is on this earth, and it begins with the Devil proclaiming that now he is going to rule the world. He forbids the atom bomb—the human race ought not to be let off so easily. The conclusion is that suicide or the Church are the only alternatives open to the younger generation. The director tells a friend, the poet Thomas, about the teacher's idea. Thomas in return describes a meeting with a prostitute from Gamla Stan, and *Fängelse* then turns to the story of this girl, mixing cruel naturalism and nightmarish dream sequences. Her child is killed by her pimp, and she finally commits suicide. But the film is also concerned with Thomas himself, a man at the end of his tether. He tries to kill his wife, but fails. He falls in love with the prostitute, and in a poetic intermezzo he projects for her an old burlesque film in which (as in *Fängelse* itself) people are chased by the police and by Death. But this relationship does not last, and Thomas goes back to his wife. Finally, we return to the director in the studio: the teacher arrives to ask his opinion of the original idea. The director answers that you cannot make a film like that. It would have to end on a question mark, and to whom should the question be put? "That's true," answers the teacher, "there is nobody—unless you believe in God." "And you don't," is the director's answer. "Then there is no way out."

Smiles are rare—on the screen. But for the spectator it was difficult to take all this very seriously. Even to many Christians, the final alternatives must have seemed too crudely stated. The burlesque was agreeable and the scenes in the film studio entertaining. But the film never really explained the reasons either for Thomas's despair or for the break-up of his marriage. It was sincere, certainly, but Bergman had not achieved a fusion of his own obsessions with the "real" objective world. This "real" world was much too selectively adjusted to fit Bergman's feelings; and the technical invention could not disguise this fundamental narrowness (and was itself rather gleeful for the film's sombre content). Bergman is aware of this. As early as 1950 he said: "*Fängelse* represents a point of view that I have been forced to give up. I needed a severe and schematic conception of the world to get away from the formless, the vague and the obscure, in which I was stuck. So I turned to the dogmatic Christianity of the Middle Ages with its clear dividing lines between Good and Evil. Later I felt tied by it, I felt as though I were imprisoned." The director has called *Fängelse* "a morality play for the cinema," and its affinities with *The Seventh Seal* are easily seen. But so are the differences. In *The Seventh Seal* the *Weltanschauung* is much more comprehensive and the film comes much closer to the old morality plays in its fight between Good and Evil. *Fängelse* was a failure, but perhaps Bergman could not have made *The Seventh Seal* if he had not made this film first.

III

Törst (*Thirst*; 1949) is the film in which Bergman gets closest to real human beings and moves us most. As usual, he made a compilation of different kinds of suffering, but this time his neurotic characters were treated more tenderly than before. In these films, he is relentlessly seeking out the causes and symptoms of pain and evil, preferably those typical of his age and society. He feels (sometimes too prudishly) that we are not sufficiently shocked by them. Sadism, nymphomania, feminine homosexuality (he has never tackled male homosexuality), criminal abortion, suicide, libertinage, horrible accidents, blindness, the war, the atom bomb, feelings of guilt and fear—for a long period he did not tire of turning over the leaves of this catalogue, without ever managing to match the analytical power of Buñuel. The edge of his subjects is blunted by repetition and over-statement; but there is something sympathetic, even pathetic, in the young man's capacity to go on being shocked. Behind the disgust in these films is a strong craving for honesty, harmony and decency in human relationships. And the films remain somehow likeable in spite of their sordidness. It is only later, when the excuse of youth no longer exists, and the more or less indirect suggestion of how things ought to be has gone, that Bergman becomes dislikeable.

He is of the opinion that intellect cannot cope effectively with the urgent problems. In *Törst* the doctor is the Devil; and his films are full of intellectuals who do not understand their wives and make a mess of their marriages. Erotic tenderness, moral and religious feeling, are found to be more helpful than intellect. It is not unfair, I think, to find a certain anti-intellectualism in Bergman's films. At chess, Death and the Devil cheat, so why bother much about chess?

Törst was based on some short stories by Birgit Tengroth, who also played the part of Viola in the film. The stories themselves seemed made for Bergman: the scriptwriter, Herbert Grevenius, took the last one in the collection as a frame for the film, using some others to illuminate it. This made for an interesting experiment rather than a tight dramatic structure. Except for an unbelievable dream sequence and a cheaply fantastic portrait of the devil-doctor, *Törst* was realistic in treatment.

In it a young couple, Ruth and Bertil, travel through Europe. They fight and fight, though—as in *Fängelse*—these conjugal clashes sometimes seem rather unnecessary. She has had a criminal abortion and cannot now have a child; he is still remembering an affair with the now bitterly lonely Viola. The doctor and a girl friend both try to seduce Viola; and—a characteristically exaggerated Bergman reaction—she drowns herself. Her story is used as a counterpoint to the main theme, that of Ruth and Bertil and their eventual reconciliation, but a weakness is that they do not themselves experience it—it is merely shown to the spectator. Some genuine acting covered up some of the flaws in the script of *Törst*. And Bergman's direction was here becoming more fluent, more discreet, less convulsive; he even allowed a little humour to creep in.

But the young Swede did not yet try his hand at comedy, although he considered a project for a film with Nils Poppe (the clown who got his first serious part in *The Seventh Seal*) about a burlesque director who becomes tired of burlesque. Instead, Bergman next wrote and directed *Till glädje* (*To Joy*; 1950). Here we encountered the familiar

Bergman (a bitch and her depraved lover, a bickering couple, a dia-
bolical Don Juan) and also a new one (attempts at the idyllic and a
strong affirmation of joy). The synthesis between old and new, however, was not really achieved and the film as a whole was very slight.
The juxtaposition of the musician-hero's grief and the orchestra playing Beethoven's "An die Freude" is rather grand opera, but in its context an over-formalised expression of human feelings. Too often with
Bergman, the single scene is too formal and the whole drama too
formless.

Eva, Törst, Fängelse and *Till glädje* are all about marriage, and yet
the worries of adolescence are in the films as well. This can be explained and perhaps to some degree defended by the fact that most
of the main characters are exceptionally sensitive Swedes, artists (the
people Bergman knows best). This also gives him opportunities to
introduce "bits of art" into the films; and like Renoir he uses them
as commentaries upon his story.

The writer-director was now becoming less and less afraid of
"beauty." After a routine political thriller, *Sånt händer inte här* (*It
Couldn't Happen Here*; 1950), he made in *Sommarlek* (*Summerplay*;
1951) the most "beautiful" of his films to date. Although written
when Bergman was quite young, the story develops the relatively resigned and adult approach of *Till glädje*. But again the old and the
new were not integrated. The "beauty" was too sweet and external
to be set effectively against the death of the young lover, the blasphemy
and the Devil cliché (a ballet master), though Bergman tried to salt it
with premonitions of death and quarrels. As in *Hamnstad* and *Törst*,
the construction was elaborate, an intricate system of flashbacks
through which Bergman sought to illuminate the present and to give
a melancholy impression of the passage of time. A ballerina visits the
skärgård, where thirteen years ago she was wonderfully happy with a
student who died in a cliff fall. Today, a rather dull and unimaginative
journalist wants to marry her; and in telling him of the past she somehow strengthens their relationship.

As the ballerina, Maj-Britt Nilsson gave a performance of somewhat
forced charm and humour. This was unfortunate, since from about
1950 Bergman began increasingly to look at the situations in his films
through the eyes of his feminine characters. It is easy to see how he
loves to work with actresses like Maj-Britt Nilsson, Eva Dahlbeck,
Harriet Andersson, Ulla Jacobsson and Bibi Andersson. He seems
more or less in love with them all, and as a consequence some of his
later films are thrown off balance. A great actress might have saved

Sommarlek; as it was, we had to be content to admire Bergman's growing skill in the handling of images, helped by the technical resources of Svensk Filmindustri. But *Sommarlek* won considerable praise in Scandinavia, where the critics have never been very helpful to Bergman and have generally tended to be either too enthusiastic or too hostile.

He followed the somewhat mannered *Sommarlek* with *Kvinnors väntan (Women Waiting;* 1952), also mannered in style and in subject a trivial and anecdotal concoction of five stories about five women. Had his creative development stopped, and was he now only interested in perfecting his technique? In fact not even the technique was of interest in *Sommaren med Monika (Summer with Monica)*, which he made the next year. Harry and Monika, lovers on a lower social level than the ballerina and the student of *Sommarlek*, escape from Stockholm and go to the *skärgård*, where for a short time they are happy. But the film contained more melodrama than analysis, and it was becoming increasingly apparent that Bergman rarely created living human beings in his films, that he was relying on his undeniable talent for directing actors and was using visual effects to cover up artificial situations. Harry and Monika were just a nice guy and a bad doll—and that was all.

IV

But Bergman's ambitions were not dead, and in *Gycklarnas Afton (Sawdust and Tinsel)*, made in the same year, he came much closer to creating an interesting portrait. This film was made for Sandrews, and as in the case of the same company's *Miss Julie* the producer was Rune Waldekranz. It is a film which I personally dislike; but it must be admitted that there is some truth and feeling and pity in the characterization of the circus director, Johansson. (Perhaps it is partly self-pity: the film director seems almost to identify himself with the circus director. I am sure that in moments of doubt and anxiety Bergman feels that he is not a poet, only an entertainer.) Johansson is rootless, humiliated by his mistress, Anne, and *declassé* in relation to the actors who despise him. The circus goes badly, and the director is no longer much interested in show business. He feels guilty because he has left his wife, but he cannot go back to her; he tries to kill himself, but fails. He will have to continue with the circus. Ake Grönberg gave an honest if somewhat monotonous performance in the part, and it was unnecessary to elaborate the theme as Bergman did in the sado-masochistic scenes. You could take out the showy flashback, the seduction scene with Anne and the fight at the end without losing any of the important points. These scenes made pain too picturesque; they spoilt the film's feeling; and they were not convincing in themselves. Again, the subjective and the real worlds remained separate.

Ake Gronberg as Albert Johansson, and Harriet Andersson as Anne in *The Naked Night*.

Bergman continued with show business in *En lektion i kärlek* (*A Lesson in Love*; 1954), his first comedy. About a quarrelsome couple (its starting point was an episode from *Kvinnors väntan* about a quarrelling, middle-aged couple stuck in a lift) it did not take humour seriously enough and tottered between sophisticated and low comedy. Neither of these elements had charm. In *Kvinnodröm* (*Woman-dream;* 1955) he took up another familiar theme. *Sommaren med Monika* and *Gycklarnas Afton* had dealt with the humiliation of the male in sexual relationships, not entirely innocently. *Kvinnors väntan*, *En lektion i kärlek* and the later *Smiles of a Summer Night* play more lightly with the same subject. In *Kvinnodröm*, the theme is handled painfully in an account of an elderly consul's infatuation with a young model. He can only make a sentimental, aesthetic adventure of the meeting, and Bergman cruelly dwells on his failings. Suddenly the consul's daughter —a sort of female werewolf—is introduced, and we long for the more real world of James Whale.

V

Then something exciting happened. Bergman found a style and held to it. The style of *Sommarnattens leende (Smiles of a Summer Night;* 1955) was a curious one. To be successfully decadent a cold-blooded detachment from "life" is necessary, and Bergman's temperament is such that he cannot retreat from "life." In a sense the style suited him, because he was not obliged to create realistic characters; in a sense it was a misfit, since wit, extreme detachment and hedonistic pleasure are not for him. So the film was not exciting because of the fact that it worked—it did not—but for the self-knowledge it revealed. Bergman must have perceived that in almost all his earlier pictures he had mixed too many styles, that he had rarely been successful in creating real people. He now recognizes the need for discipline, for working within his own limits. *Smiles of a Summer Night, The Seventh Seal* and his new film *Nära livet* all testify to this.

Smiles of a Summer Night contains the loveliest sequence ever made by the director, that in which Eva Dahlbeck sings *"Freut Euch des Lebens . . ."* and the image is frozen as if to illustrate Faust's cry to the *Augenblick:* "Verweile doch! du bist so schön!" The old Naima Wifstrand is exactly right, and the younger women are beautiful. Although Bergman is no Ophuls the images often have true glamour. But the dialogue lets the film down: it is not sufficiently light and pointed and the frivolity is too determined.

As so often, after trying to renew himself, Bergman next fell back on an old subject. He returned virtually to *Frenzy*, trying to bring it up to date in his development. The script of this film, *Sista paret ut* (1956), was again taken over by Sjöberg and the results were none too happy. A young man has trouble with his girl and his mother is seeking a divorce. He is desperate but finds some comfort with another girl. A laconic old teacher, who first ironically advises him to commit suicide, later tells him that you survive only through will-power and intelligence. This sounds like Sjöberg's ending. At any rate, the film-makers fought over it and the film is not rounded off. But Sjöberg—who does better than Bergman at analyzing people—produced a work which was an interesting failure and had several moments of truth and some touching scenes between the boy and the second girl. For a change, this was a film which tried to come to grips with Swedish life without recourse to symbolism, expressionism or metaphysics.

The subject of Bergman's next and most ambitious work, *Det sjunde inseglet* (*The Seventh Seal*), was life on the whole planet. Although he was immensely helped by using the traditions of the old morality play, the film emerged as cold and a little remote. It is an illustration of the biblical "The meek shall inherit the Earth," and it succeeded to an unpredictable degree. But can we accept the visionary actor and his family as the meek who ought to survive? Are they not ideals of a puritanism which seems almost indecent in relation to the menaces of war and the H-bomb? Is it good Christianity (not to mention good humanism) to let Death take all the normal, "unclean" people without much concern? Nils Poppe has scarcely the stature for the poet in the common man, the whole man in harmony with nature. As the knight, Max von Sydow marvellously combines the human and the allegorical and almost all the emotion in the film is concentrated on him—a pointer to its lack of proportion. Gunnar Björnstrand seems too modern and realistic as the squire, Death is theatrically conceived, and some of the dialogue has a pseudo-poetical flavour. Otherwise, the film was certainly well-made, visually imaginative and handsome, and to a greater extent than before Bergman transcended his solipsism. But it was at the expense of feeling and humanity. The knight plays for nothing less than the salvation of mankind, and we ought to be more gripped and moved. But Bergman's own disgust prevents him from being sufficiently "engaged" to view Death's onslaughts as very tragic. He can be profoundly pained by the death of one of his characters, but the more general "love of mankind" scarcely seems to mean much to him.

Yet compared with *The Seventh Seal,* Bergman's two most recent films, *Smultronstället* (*Wild Strawberries;* 1957) and *Nära livet* (*Brink of Life;* 1958) seem very minor. The portrait of the old doctor (Victor Sjöström) in the first is too incomplete, as are the sensation-seeking descriptions of the women in a maternity hospital in the second. *Nära livet* never leaves the hospital, uses very long takes with close-ups, and dispenses altogether with music. In its concentration on the faces of suffering women, it reminds the spectator of Dreyer.

VI

Throughout his career Bergman has been influenced by many film-makers, as a rule absorbing and transforming these impulses in a personal way. Perhaps only Sjöberg's desire to give his films an extra dimension, Dreyer's torture technique and the masochism in some German pictures have been really harmful for him. Yet Bergman is an original. He is now a brilliant *metteur en scène*; and he is something more than that, though he has not yet proved himself a great poet of the cinema. He has written and directed eleven completely original films. Of the twenty-three films he has collaborated on or created, all but three—*Sawdust and Tinsel, Smiles of a Summer Night* and *The Seventh Seal*—are set in the present. By going back in time in these films, he has reached a new degree of detachment; and through these experiences he may arrive at detachment in a work directly concerned with the contemporary scene. He has never leaned on a classic. He is a poor writer, and has never produced a classic film himself. But it now seems possible that he will one day—perhaps from a script by someone else.

You could be unpleasant and call him the best German director of the post-war period, but this simplification would leave out the many important nuances that make the Swedes Swedish. In contra-distinction to many of the famous German films, Bergman's pictures usually relate their bad dreams directly to contemporary life. His dream sequences may be stilted and heavy but at least they are used in order to illuminate—they do not "stand alone." The interpretation is not left to a Kracauer: Bergman interprets for himself.

He has not only learned from German artists. Anouilh's contrasts between young and old, and other themes of his, have also been important to Bergman. It is also true, however, that Thomas Mann's *Doctor Faustus* impressed and shocked him greatly. In Adrian Leverkühn, the modern Faust, the egocentric artist whose life is a constant striving, Bergman has presumably seen reflected his own aspirations. And there is a Faust and a Mephisto in Ingmar Bergman. They have a constant debate and we should be interested in it, although it is not always easy.

9

THE SEVENTH SEAL
A Director's View

Jorn Donner

. . . .

Of Bergman's films, *The Seventh Seal* is the least immediate, the most rhetorical. It is therefore understandable that the critics who dismiss his art use this very picture as an object lesson. A characteristic essay about Bergman is written by Caroline Blackwood,[1] who is of the opinion that instead of Cecil B. deMille's "Religion and Sex" Bergman has given the public the "Supernatural and Sex, decked out with Symbols." The impact of Bergman's brilliant, skillful fragments and vignettes is often lost, according to this critic, in "all the messy smörgasbord of his hysterical whimsical ideas." *The Seventh Seal* can indeed appear to be overloaded with scenes in which the symbolic meaning, the many-faceted ornamental function, prevents the narrative, analytical material from coming into its own. This arises from the nature of Bergman's inspiration, on the long and difficult road from original artistic vision to finished film. Bergman has often wished for "a sort of notation which would give me a chance to translate all the nuances of the vision, the product's innermost structure, into distinct mnemonic symbols."[2] Something of the spontaneous inspiration that seems to characterize *The Naked Night* has been lost in *The Seventh Seal*. The film's single images may appear as too calculated, too beautiful, too harmonious an impression which makes one regard as almost a parody the caption on a laudatory Swedish review: "A New Swedish Film Classicist."[3]

In Bergman's ability to adjust himself there lies a danger. It is possible that he makes himself the interpreter of his manuscript to the

From *The Films of Ingmar Bergman* (Bloomington: Indiana University Press) pp. 135-51. Copyright © 1964 by Indiana University Press. Reprinted by permission of the publisher.

extent of self-immolation. But such a criticism of the style of *The Seventh Seal* can concern only certain sequences. One must remember that this film poses the greatest of questions, and that among Bergman's films it is the one that perhaps most exactly formulates something akin to a philosophical credo.

Since the end of World War II there has been a strange transformation in the willingness of the Western cultural world to accept works of art of this kind, as Andrew Sarris points out in a brilliant analysis of the film's structure and philosophy.[4] "The individual's situation in an indifferent universe would have struck an artist as a meaningless subject a generation ago, when man's striving hardly extended farther than the next bread line." During the years between the wars, social illusions lived on in undisturbed peace, whether their stamp was Liberal, Marxist, or Christian. To be sure, the break-through in modern art and literature had taken place under the shadow of a disillusionment with the belief in man's chance of a future as a collective creature. Time, however, was not yet ripe for an art which, like *The Seventh Seal*, was modern in its conception of man, while at the same time posing the central questions about the purpose of life and death. The second World War, nuclear weapons, anxiety about a continued life on earth, and the self-destroying development of technology have made people wonder about the meaning of progress, the meaning of the future. In this situation of crisis, *The Seventh Seal* appears as a mature philosophic declaration.

The film has been described as a morality play, a designation which has been used, with more or less justice, in several of Bergman's works. "Moralities" was the title of three plays by Bergman which were published in book form in 1948. One of them. *The Day Ends Early*, tells of a Mrs. Åström, a patient in an insane asylum. She manages to escape. She visits a number of people, telling them that they are to die at a certain hour. One of the persons is a Pastor Broms. His faith is too weak to allay his fears. Prayer is the only help. He pictures "God and the Devil wrestling in a life-and-death struggle. We like to imagine that God is the stronger. Unfortunately, that is wrong. God is about to be killed. And it depends on each and every one of us, however unimportant and ridiculous we are."[5] Exactly the same basic feeling is found in *The Seventh Seal*. This feeling, even among people who call themselves Christians, that they have lost their direction-giving moral and spiritual center, is probably more common today than in the fourteenth century, in spite of the fact that the Black Death was ravaging the province in which the Knight and Jöns find themselves. But to the Knight, the great fatigue after the crusade, combined with what he has experienced of plague and spiritual intolerance, are a counterpart to the feeling of meaninglessness that has met modern man because of the depths of human bestiality he has witnessed. The Knight is a symbol of modern Western man. Not all of the bestialities of modern times can be traced to something evil, to a will that lays evil plans, to a Hitler, a Hoess, or a Himmler. One can also experience evil as ever present, as a ferment in the life we are living. In that case, the interest turns from the outside inward, from the community to the individual, from the individual's condition to his soul. These are the questions posed in *The Seventh Seal*. The accusations against others die away in those who utter them. The feeling of powerlessness is paralyzing. But, as the film demonstrates, there is an escape from these troubles, too. The trouble with the analyses that have been made of the film's structure is that attention has been too one-sidedly concentrated on the Knight, without suspecting that the Knight and Jöns complement each other, are parts of the same spectrum, like Vogler and Dr. Vergérus in *The Magician*.

Bergman has told how in his childhood he accompanied his father on preaching trips to country churches. Many of the single bits in the film are echoes of the old church paintings, for instance, the Knight's chess game with Death, the Holy Virgin in the field (in Jof's vision), the dance across the hills into death. While his father preached, Bergman followed these paintings with his eyes. In one of the sequences in the film, the Knight and Jöns enter a church where an artist is busy painting pictures aimed to frighten and edify the congregation. But Bergman too, wants to emphasize that *The Seventh Seal* is not a realistic description of Sweden in the Middle Ages: "It is a modern poem, presented with medieval material that has been very freely handled. The Knight of the film returns from a crusade as a soldier in our times returns from a war."[6]

This shows how pregnant Bergman's world of imagination is with Christian ideas. The film also builds on the Book of Revelation, on the selection the Knight's wife Karin reads to her returned husband and his entourage. The action is thought to take place during the half hour of silence that occurred when the Lamb has opened the seventh seal: "Woe, woe, woe, to the inhabiters of the earth by reason of the other voices of the trumpet of the three angels, which are yet to sound!" It is easy to draw the parallels between this vision of destruction and the threat of destruction that today seems to hover over humanity. The religious criticism of the film's success in rewriting the

Apocalypse has swung between unreserved approval and clear rejection. According to one critic, Revelation finds its grandeur "in the colossal perspective, which reaches all the way to the throne of God and the Lamb, and where the individual torments have their place in God's cosmic system. If these torments are eliminated, the result is in every sense terrible."[7] For a criticism that only looks at the film, it is difficult to accept this conclusion. The question that has to be answered is this: Has Bergman succeeded in giving the drama of the Knight and Jöns an artistically convincing form? Is *The Seventh Seal* tenable as cinema? It is not theological discussion that can answer this question, but an analysis of the film's structure.

The Seventh Seal is built on a one-act play by Bergman, *Painting on Wood*. The action in this short piece is more taut, more concentrated than in the film. Many critics have regarded it as Bergman's foremost dramatic work. Strindberg has earlier treated similar subjects, especially in *The Tale of the Folkungs*, regarded by some as a prototype.

The film's action is very simple. The Knight Antonius Block returns, after a long crusade, to the Sweden of the fourteenth century, devastated by the Black Death. He is accompanied by his squire, Jöns. On a desolate shore, he engages in a game of chess with Death. The prize for the Knight's victory is to be his life. While the game is in progress, the Knight manages to perform a meaningful act. He saves a couple of traveling jugglers, Jof and Mia, from death. The Knight arrives home and finds his wife. Then enters Death. All present are compelled to join in his dance, while the jugglers look on.

The most interesting figure is Jöns, a refutation of the often advanced statement that "The only villains in any of his films are always men of science and intellect."[8] It has been maintained that Bergman has one-sidedly presented an irrational philosophy. It has been said that his penetration into the world of women is an expression of this, since to live seems more important to women than to think, to act. I cannot entirely accept this theory, because that would mean to deny the root and origin of Bergman's art: the Swedish community. The questions of society have not been finally settled, to be sure, but in most cases they have been changed into queries that concern the technical application. Bergman emphasizes the irrational in man's nature. He turns attention inward, to the individual. This seems to correspond to a tendency in the community itself, that the Swedish citizen "is able to devote too much spare time on self-reflection, which often leads to confused eschatologies or an abuse of moral freedom."[9]

Perhaps Bergman is seeking a consolation which is too simple for one who, like Freud, wants to heal civilization. But to regard him exclusively as an irrationalist does not correspond to the image his films give us.

In *The Seventh Seal* Jöns acts and lives in conscious opposition to the other persons in the film. The Church is busy with persecutions and witch-burning. The Knight unceasingly asks questions, which rebound against emptiness. When the Knight's game with Death begins, Jöns is asleep. He then "opens his eyes, and grunts pig-like, yawns widely, but rises and saddles his horse, lifts up the heavy pack. The Knight rides slowly away from the sea, through the forest by the shore, up toward the road. He pretends not to hear the squire's morning prayer." This morning prayer is a particularly blasphemous song, which Jöns recites to the Knight's rising indignation. The riders pass a human form. Jöns dismounts. But when he takes hold of it, an empty skull is grinning at him. He wasn't mute, Jöns answers to the Knight's question. He was highly eloquent.

One of the clearest scenes takes place in a church where the Knight is at his prayers. Jöns begins to talk to the painter while he is waiting for his master. He becomes so shaken by the artist's tale of mankind's self-torment and stupidity that he asks to have a little brandy. This is interwoven with the Knight's questions. The parallel action in Bergman's films is always illuminating, as, for instance, in *The Naked Night*. The Knight's questions remind us of the confession the minister Tomas Ericsson delivers in *Winter Light:* "How are we going to believe in the believers, when we ourselves do not believe? What will happen to us who wish to believe but cannot? And what will become of those who neither wish to nor can believe?" The Knight demands an answer, knowledge, not faith. In a moment of fright he discovers that the unknown who stands behind the bars is Death himself. In the meantime Jöns continues his conversation with the painter. In his description of the crusade, he renders the background to the Knight's questions:

"Ten years we sat in the Holy Land and let the snakes bite us, insects prick us, wild animals nip us, heathen slaughter us, the wine poison us, women give us lice, fleas feed on us, and fevers consume us all to the glory of God. I'll tell you, our crusade was so stupid that only a real idealist could have invented it."

Jöns has not much use for the doctrines of the Church. Outside the church he spies a young woman who has had "fleshly intercourse with the Evil One." She will be burned. Critics have offered the information that no witches were burned in medieval Sweden, and have advanced this as an artistic argument against the film.[10] Strindberg's historical dramas could very well be condemned with the same argument. His portrait of *Master Olof*, which is historically inexact and faulty, has become the prototype for the picture the Swedish people have made for themselves of the great Reformer.

In a shop Jöns runs into Raval, a thief and a grave robber. Raval was the doctor from the theological seminary in Roskilde who ten years earlier convinced the Knight of the "necessity to go to the Holy Land on a splendid crusade." Jöns announces that he has suddenly come to understand the purpose of the wasted years. "We were too well off, we were too satisfied, and the Lord wanted to chastise our contented pride. Therefore he came and spewed his celestial venom and poisoned the Knight." Jöns is a materialist and a skeptic. He doubts that the big questions have a meaning. Still he is not insensible to the sufferings of others. The Knight continues his questioning. But Jöns helps other people.

Juggler Jof has entered the Tavern Embarrassment. Suspected by the smith Plog of having seduced his wife, Jof is forced by Raval to execute a bear dance on the table. These dark pictures are frightfully, nauseatingly cruel. There is a directness there which otherwise is expressed too seldom in the film. The sequence in the tavern is perhaps the best in the film. It brings to mind the exposure and the absence of disguise that we find in *The Naked Night*.[11] Jöns has promised to get Raval if they ever meet again. Jöns enters the tavern and rescues Jof.

Once more Jöns appears as a helper, when he tries to console the smith for the loss of his wife. But Jöns' words are then spoken on a level that would be more justified in some of the cynically tired train-sequences in *A Lesson in Love*. On their way through the nocturnal forest the group meets eight servants who are taking the witch to be burned. The Knight wants to see the face of the Devil to ask him about God. He, if any, should know. Ironic before the servants, Jöns is trying to think up a practical plan to rescue the girl. He is moved in her presence. But he does not want to use his stirred-up emotions as an excuse for propounding his own questions. The person is the main issue, regardless of how much he tries to hide his sympathy behind a mask of cynicism.

The group meets one more person (aside from Death, with whom the Knight finishes his chess game). It is Raval, now infected by the plague. He wants something to drink. Jöns holds back the girl who accompanies him, not because of hatred toward Raval, but because help is futile. Raval is doomed to die in any case. Jöns' actions are practical. The Knight performs his actions as if there were another task beyond that of living. Jöns is prepared to enjoy life as long as possible. He curses his fate. Jöns is no philosopher: to live is to live is to live. Viewed in this perspective, the foolishness is not found in Jof and Mia ("the golden virgin and her idiot husband"[12]) but in the Knight, because he went on a crusade, and because he is still asking his meaningless questions.

Nils Poppe as Jof, and Bibi Andersson as Mia in *The Seventh Seal*.

Jöns has been called "a modern agnostic, himself not a little cruel, but not indiscriminately so, skeptical toward everything and everybody, not least himself, at the same time candid with his fellow man, aware of his inadequacy passive up to a certain point, but beyond that full of energy and responsibility."[13] The difference between Jöns and the rest finds its clearest expression in the final sequence. The group has reached the home of the Knight. The morning gets lighter. Karin receives her husband. When seated at their breakfast she reads from

Revelation, eighth chapter. Death enters. He is the unknown one who
has come to take them away. They speak to Death. The Knight continues to call upon the God that *must* exist. Jöns remains sarcastic. All
he knows is that his body exists, that he himself is. The girl whom he
has saved from Raval, bids him to be silent. And he answers: "I shall
be quiet, but under protest."

Jöns is a realist. We are reminded of the ballet master's admonition
to Marie in *Illicit Interlude*. The dance is her profession. We remember the laborious and masterly cinematographic strategy that makes
possible the final picture in *The Naked Night*. The solution, that of
protest and action, that Jöns chooses does not appear as the film's only
ideal, but as its most dignified. The persons who remain alive are Jof
and Mia and their son Mikael. Their solution is in privacy, in the
happiness of marital communion. They find their satisfaction in the
knowledge that the family will perpetuate itself. But in any world at
all, a Jof and a Mia have the chance to escape. Jöns, on the other hand,
is a character who aims at a militant, active relationship with the world
around him.

The squire's part is played by Gunnar Björnstrand, who by now
has appeared in more than a dozen of Bergman's films. In *Torment*
his role was very small, while in *A Lesson in Love* he was one of the
dominating figures. The most typical portrait was delineated in *The
Magician*, as the medical counselor Vergérus, who proposes to prove
the sorcerer's incompetence, but becomes frightened by the unknown
powers. With Bergman's conception of the film medium, it is obvious
that he has preferred to use the same actors in picture after picture,
for instance, the romantic hero Birger Malmsten during the forties, or
Harriet Andersson from *Monika* on. (In *While the City Sleeps* she has
a walk-on bit.)

Bergman wants to create an artistic instrument which he can fully
master. He has seldom changed cameramen, designer, cutter, composer. He has worked in the same surroundings, with a crew he knows
well. This analysis of his films is built on the conception that he is one
of the few artists who has succeeded in realizing his personal vision.
He has achieved this through the intermediary of closely associated
artists and technicians. The films are analyzed here as the final result,
the completed work. It is evident that a great deal of the credit for
this result, for the films' inner richness of meaning, belongs to Bergman's collaborators. They are instruments in his hand, nothing more,
nothing less.

"There are many film makers who forget that the human face is the starting point in our work. To be sure, we can become absorbed by the esthetic of the picture montage, we can blend objects and still lifes into wonderful rhythms, we can fashion nature studies of astonishing beauty, but the proximity of the human face is without doubt the film's distinguishing mark and patent of nobility. . . . In order to give the greatest possible power to the actor's expression, the movement of the camera must be simple and uncomplicated, in addition to being carefully synchronized with the action. The camera must appear as a completely objective observer and should only on rare occasions participate in what is going on. We must also consider that the actor's finest means of expression is his eyes."[14]

The choice of actors corresponds to the change and the shading that have taken place in Bergman's films. The romantic heroes were superseded by persons with greater intellectual complications. The idea content in Bergman's pictures achieved a deeper form and was interpreted by such actors as Ingrid Thulin, Max von Sydow, and Gunnar Björnstrand. Still it seems to me a grossly mechanical conception to lump together, for instance, Gunnar Björnstrand's roles and consider that his character remains the same in film after film, as Béranger has done in his book about Bergman. The artist's creative imagination works with the material of reality. A part of the reality that surrounds Bergman is the world of the film, his actors. It is obvious that he creates his characters and writes his parts with a consideration, among other things, of the qualifications he finds among his interpreters. Perhaps the squire Jöns has something of Gunnar Björnstrand, a dignity and a vulnerability found in this actor. This is, however, as irrelevant to the analysis of films as to combine the facts of private life with the fiction of art. It suffices to note the importance of Jöns to the action of *The Seventh Seal:* "Here we perceive the outline of Camus' modern hero, a symbol of man's, of the individual's, integrity. The portrait is not fully rounded. Bergman apparently has not dared to give it the central place it deserves in modern drama. But the fate of the squire intimates in any case modern man's dramatic relationship to the world around him. Man's sluggish hopelessness is contrasted without any religious embellishment with his courage and dignity. This is more than social consciousness: this is the most urgent social message."[15]

The film's main parallel action is between the Knight-Jöns and Jof-Mia. These are the poles around which the action revolves, Jof dreams that his son Mikael will achieve the impossible: that is, to make the juggling balls stand still in the air. Their story begins with the awakening, shown in another light than Albert Johansson's awaken-

ing in *The Naked Night*. Albert, too, has sons, but they do not wish
to join the circus. While Albert must pass through darkness and suffering before he is freed, Jof slips away from all questions despite the
moments of terror he experiences in the tavern.

It is the Knight's meeting with the jugglers that changes his action
and gives these characters another meaning. Before this, however,
the juggler's appearance in the market place has been interrupted by
the passing procession of the flagellants, a vision of man's folly and the
Last Judgment. The scene takes place on a sunny slope. At first, Mia
is alone with Mikael. Jof is at the tavern.

The scene, in Bergman's construction, has the simple, magnificent
seriousness of a consecration, a religious rite. The play of light in *The
Seventh Seal* shows plainly the contrasts between the contemporary
patterns of action. In the lighting of the Knight's story, the dark, the
black, dominates. Above Jof and Mia there almost always hovers a
brightness of grace, as if the action took place in another reality. Jos
Burvenich[16] believes that the image Bergman makes for himself of a
God represents a higher being to whom one should dedicate himself
with pain, like a sacrifice. The dream of paradise and purity in *The
Seventh Seal* cannot become dramatically (Catholic) correct before
Bergman speaks of evil by its rightful name, which is the sin that lives
in the hearts of men. Accordingly, one should not seek a religious interpretation of the film outside of Jof and Mia: their mutual love is
God. The Catholic interpretation presupposes that the paradise of innocence cannot be found here on earth in the momentary, but only
in God's love, which is the Realm, the Kingdom.

As I look at the film, I find it an exact expression of earthly dreams
of paradise, of a philosophical materialism. One may answer Burvenich, with Colin Young, that both the Knight and Jöns are, "by their
philosophical positions, unable to dispatch the problems presented
by death, but Mary and Joseph never commit themselves to this argument and are, in fact, aloof from it and from the double scourge of
pestilence and a reactionary church. Calm and serene, they are the
only ones who in the end are saved."[17] If we place Jof's and Mia's fate
in a social connection, the solution is unsatisfactory. It is just about as
purposeful as to flee to a desert island to escape a nuclear war. Philo-
sophically, however, the solution is the right one. The juggler couple
ask only the small questions. Their existence acquires depth from the
power of being together.

"Sex, art, and imagination" are, according to Eugene Archer, the
consolation that is offered in Bergman's films for the inescapable

loneliness of existence. He who proceeds further, like the Knight, is on the wrong track. With Jof and Mia the world is clearly self-evident —an existence for themselves. "The supreme value toward which consciousness, by its very nature, is constantly transcending itself is the absolute being of the self, with its qualities of identity, purity, permanence."[18] This is according to Sartre's philosophy. It is not in the search for meaning that life is decided, but in the choice of action.

In Bergman's films a mental breakdown is expressed that could be loosely described thus: The persons imagine a belief in Fate, History, God, Happiness, or something else. They cannot, however, live according to these premises, since reality constantly revises their view. In practical, everyday life they discover that such guidelines cannot be followed. Therefore they are forced to deny God's existence. They still leave evil and the devil as a force in life, a power opposed to themselves. Without, however, throwing the major questions overboard, the question that possesses them can never be solved—the question of happiness and fellowship, of practical daily life.

The only certainty that remains is the certainty of death. The question does not concern Jof and Mia, since it is meaningless to discuss it. Joachim in the radio play *The City* says that there is only one thing "that is really true, and that is that I shall die. Even this, that I live, is doubtful, but death is certain."[19] To this Burvenich might have objected that the problem of evil is still not solved. Before one can ask for a settlement with God (depose him), one must search one's own heart. According to this interpretation, Töre in *The Virgin Spring* is, from a religious point of view, the most satisfactory of Bergman's characters. He confesses his sin.

Jof and Mia just live. In the evening, the Knight finds his way to Mia, who is alone, playing with her child. A while later Jof appears, limping and hurt from the ill treatment at the tavern. Finally he is joined by his rescuer, Jöns. Mia offers wild strawberries from a big bowl, and milk for the berries. The berries, here as before and later, symbolize "the warmth of life, the human values, undamaged by metaphysical fear."[20] The Knight asks to be informed about the plans of the juggler couple. He dissuades them from continuing on to Helsingör, and suggests they accompany him through the forest. He warns them about the plague. This scene with the wild strawberries is the nucleus of the Knight's impulse to sacrifice himself in order to save them. During the night, when the chess game is to be finished, the Knight sweeps the chessmen from the board, and succeeds in detaining Death so long that the jugglers escape safely.

Mia has described their existence to the Knight: "One day is like the other. There's nothing strange about that. Summer is better than winter, of course, for then we don't have to freeze. But spring is best of all."

The core of the dialogue comes at the end:

The Knight: Faith is a heavy suffering, do you know that? It is like loving somebody who is out there in the darkness and who never reveals himself, however loudly we call.

Mia: I don't understand what you mean.

The questions asked by the Knight do not exist for Mia.

The Knight: How meaningless and unreal everything seems to me when I sit here with you and your husband. How unimportant it suddenly is . . . I shall remember this moment. The stillness, the dusk, the bowl with strawberries, the bowl with milk, your faces in the evening light. Mikael asleep, Jof with his fiddle. I shall carry this in my memory between my hands, as carefully as if it were a bowl, filled to the brim with fresh milk. . . . And this shall be for me a sign and a great sufficiency.

The scene has been subjected to completely opposite analyses. The visual content corresponds to the one the Knight voices in his final words. Harry Schein[21] emphasizes the contrast between literary and narrative dialogue. The literary dialogue must "in literature and the theater suggest the visions and moods which the film interprets by its own means." He seems to find a great deal of narrative power in *The Seventh Seal*. Important bits, however, are spoiled because the words too obviously underscore the meaning of the pictures.

This opinion seems to be based on a certain cinematographic purism, related to that of Arnheim and Kracauer.[22] Arnheim dismisses as a corruption the development of the film art after the advent of sound. The sequence with the strawberries is, of course, double. The literary mood-creating does not carry the action forward. It means instead that Bergman lets the picture appeal directly to the emotion, to the viewing, while the words communicate the philosophic debate which is the idea of the story. The scene with the strawberries is one of the moments that "man has at his disposal to manifest his moral center."[23] It comprises the center around which the entire film revolves.

We know that the picture ends in the death of everybody except the juggler family. The first one to succumb is the actor Skat, who in a grotesquely comical scene manages to do away with his tormentor, the smith Plog. Skat has eloped with Plog's wife. This happens in the forest during the night. Skat climbs up in a tree, but Death saws it off.

On the stump appears a squirrel, to indicate life's continuity. Skat is a failure, and all except the jugglers have at some time in their lives failed.[24] The Knight has left his wife for a meaningless crusade. He goes with Jöns to the clearing in the woods where the servants have built a pyre for Tyan, the woman we saw outside the church. He interrogates Tyan. Since the Devil is with her, perhaps he knows something about God. He sees the emptiness in her eyes, nothing else, and receives no answer. He consoles her; she cannot console him. She goes calmly to her death, for the Devil will protect her from all evil.

"I believe at times that to ask questions is the most important thing," says the Knight in the frightful scene with Tyan. He thereby intimates his faith in intellectual aspiration. But what remains purposeful in his life is still the one action, namely, that he saves Jof and Mia. The Knight, in other words, gets a chance for a creative action. His life has had a meaning.

The Seventh Seal opens itself slowly to the viewer. This is partly due to the many planes the story touches on, the polyphonic structure of the work. The framework of the narrative is, of course, the chess game with Death, a threatening vision, underscored by the desolate seashore, where the game begins. *The Seventh Seal* has a plastic effect which few of Bergman's films possess, a harmonious rhythm, in spite of the fact that one may detect such different stylistic sources as German expressionism, the Japanese film (Kurosawa), and the Swedish tradition.

Bergman's greatness lies in the fact that he is able to give to terror and insecurity such a dramatic and urgent molding. That I find Jöns to be the film's most interesting and commanding figure is a subjective evaluation, since *The Seventh Seal* "will continue to be a source of discussion for many years to come and—this concerns all the classics of thought—the interpretations will change with the ideas and the era of the critics."[25] In order to survive, man must be able to conquer death. It is a matter of escaping both the inner death of feeling and the threat that looms from without. The film lets this attempt end in success and failure, but the important element is the salute to human dignity, the longing for justice, for life in peace, which constitute the movement of the film. The picture contains a great wisdom and a great naïveté. However: "it is a naïveté that characterizes the eras in art—here the Middle Ages—the spirit of which Bergman has succeeded in transmitting, without spoiling it with pedantry, thanks to his incomparable artistry when it comes to transferring to the language of the film the motifs in the iconography that has inspired him. The shape and forms he shows us are never insignificant, but the fruit of a constantly original creation. His art is so genuine, so new, that we forget art for the questions' questions and the endless series of conclusions. Seldom has the film managed to aim so high and so completely realize its ambitions."[26]

NOTES

1. Carolina Blackwood, "The Mystique of Ingmar Bergman," *Encounter*, XVI, No. 91 (April 1961), pp. 54-57.
2. "Varje film är min sista film."
3. Marianne Höök in *Svenska Dagbladet*, February 17, 1957.
4. Andrew Sarris, "The Seventh Seal," *Film Culture*, No. 19 (1959).
5. *Moraliteter*, 1948.
6. Uttalande om det sjunde inseglet i filmens utländska programblad, Stockholm: Svensk Filmindustri, 1957.
7. Johan Chydenius, "Det sjunde inseglet," *Nya Pressen*, October 6, 1958.
8. Blackwood, "The Mystique of Ingmar Bergman," p. 55.
9. Napolitano, "Dal settimo sigillo alle soglie della vita."
10. Ivar Harrie, "Ingmar Bergman vill vara Sveriges Kaj Munk" (Ingmar Bergman wants to be the Kaj Munk of Sweden), *Expressen*, March 2, 1957.
11. Sarris, "The Seventh Seal."
12. Blackwood, "The Mystique of Ingmar Bergman," p. 55.
13. Harry Schein, "Poeten Bergman," BLM, No. 4 (April 1957).
14. "Varje film är min sista film."
15. The conception that an art which discusses man's conditions for existence is the social art of our time is advanced with great brilliance by Villy Sörenson in his collection of essays, *Hverken—eller* (Copenhagen: Gyldendal, 1961). I have not, however, been able to work it into my book.
16. Jos Burvenich, "Ingmar Bergman à la trace de Dieu," *Art d'Eglise*, No. 113 (1960).
17. Colin Young's review of the film in *Film Quarterly*, XIII, No. 3 (Spring 1959), pp. 42 ff.
18. From Sartre's *Le Etre et le Néant*, p. 137; quoted in Iris Murdoch, *Sartre: Romantic Rationalist* (New Haven, Conn.: Yale University Press, 1953), pp. 43-44.
19. "Staden. Hörspel" (The City: A radio play). In *Svenska Radiopjäser 1951* (Stockholm: Sveriges Radio, 1951), pp. 49 ff.
20. Napolitano, "Dal settimo sigillo alle soglie della vita."
21. Schein, "Poeten Bergman."
22. Rudolf Arnheim, *Film as Art* (Berkeley: University of California Press, 1958), particularly the last essay, "A New Laocoön: Artistic Composites

and the Talking Film," and also Siegfried Kracauer's *Theory of Film*
(New York: Oxford University Press, 1961). Unfortunately, too much in
our contemporary film esthetics discussion is based on Arnheim's opinions.
23. Napolitano, "Dal settimo sigillo alle soglie della vita."
24. Sarris, "The Seventh Seal."
25. *Ibid.*
26. Eric Rohmer in *Arts*, April 23, 1958.

10

WILD STRAWBERRIES
Theology and Psychology

SALVATION WITHOUT GOD   Richard A. Blake, S.J.
. . . .

Ever since Janus Films released *The Seventh Seal* to American audiences in 1958, Ingmar Bergman has been a constant cause of theological questioning in this country. Whether he writes of a medieval pilgrimage or of modern debauchery, his words and images seem to touch the nerve endings of religious sensibilities. Contemporary man, in search of meaningful experience, reads himself in the tortured face of Antonius Block; the medieval imagery gives the illusion of distance while the meaning crowds tight upon the modern conscience. In *Winterlight* (1963) the pastor gags on the clichés he must mouth and his discomfort reaches out from the screen to grip many adherents to institutional religions. Perhaps it is as Bergman suggests in *The Silence* (1963); all the meaning man can really expect out of life is a brief message from a dying woman written in a language he cannot understand. Perhaps all God gives to modern man is a long journey home and a few mysterious words which do not direct, but merely whisper. In these films, and in others as well, Bergman seems to uncover the religious problems which torture the modern intellectual, and, like the victim modern man, he finds little respite.

In addition to the uncertainty of religious beliefs, Bergman strikes another central issue by stating his questions in terms of persons rather than dogmas or institutions. In *Winterlight*, church ritual becomes a hollow routine and the audience is drawn to the personal agony of the pastor as he grapples with the ultimate questions of faith. Only in *The Virgin Spring* (1959) does Bergman consider religious practice, the pilgrimage and the holy candles, as a possible means of attaining

From *Encounter*, Vol. 28, No. 4 (Autumn 1967), pp. 313-26. Reprinted by permission of Christian Theological Seminary.

grace, but even there religious practice is inadequate to erase the evil of rape and murder. The father turns to his pagan background and his personal strength to right the wrong done to his daughter; the church remains a mystery, a miraculous spring, recognized only after the work of man is complete. Moreover, Bergman people face their religious crisis in a state of turmoil and flux, so characteristic of this age. Even in *Wild Strawberries*, the most serene of his films, Isak Borg, the hero, is traveling to a distant city and on the way confronts his past with terror and confusion; in his case the turmoil is interior.

The journey theme in Bergman, as in other religious authors through the ages, points to the essentially transitory state of man's life on earth. By making his journey, man gains an identity, as did the Jewish nation in the Exodus and as Odysseus in his voyage. Again and again in Christian literature the theme occurs: in Dante, Chaucer, St. John of the Cross, Bunyan, and *Everyman*. In *The Sacred and the Profane* Mircea Eliade tries to explain the significance of this theme of pilgrimage:

> The road and walking can be transfigured into religious values, for every road can symbolize the "road of life" and any walk a "pilgrimage," a peregrination to the center of the world. . . . Those who have chosen the Quest, the road that leads to the center, must . . . devote themselves wholly to "walking" toward the supreme truth, which in highly evolved religions is synonomous with the Hidden God, the *Deus Absconditus*.[1]

The "Hidden God," or as Bergman would have it, the God of the Silence, is remote and precisely as unknown cannot be sought after; more important is the matter at hand, man's discovery of himself in the journey. As he travels through life to his destination, the pilgrim grows in awareness of himself in relation to the other-than-self world of persons and things. At journey's end, if he has learned to understand and to love, he achieves meaning; he is saved. Bergman, as will be shown, is not sure that the journey leads to God, but it must lead to reconciliation.[2]

Although Bergman writes of religious problems and even uses the traditional images of religious authors, it would be somewhat misleading to read his scripts as though they were specifically Christian or even purely religious works. Biographers and film critics point eagerly to his being the "son of an Evangelical Lutheran pastor," as though somehow that fact holds the key to unlock all the deep mystery of his films.[3] Lines from *The Seventh Seal* are truly inspirational, but, in the context of the film they fall from the lips of a man facing death with doubt. The last scene, the knight's apparent "reward," is extremely dubious: Death leads him away to an uncertain afterlife, hand in hand with a graverobber, a cynic, a fickle woman, and her brutish husband. Certainly, if this were a morality play in the usual sense of the term, the end of life would not have come upon Antonius in the midst of such as these; the noble character should have been duly rewarded. Bergman does not use his religious images to preach.

His stature as a theologian is further diminished by reports of his personal code of ethics. Carl Dymling, a colleague and president of Svensk Filmindustri says:

> He was a very angry young man—long before they became the fashion a writer looking at the world through the eyes of a teenage rebel, harshly criticizing his parents, offending his teachers, making love to prostitutes, fighting everything and everybody in order to preserve his integrity and his right to be unhappy. . . . Ingmar Bergman has continued to be the rebel child.[4]

Another acquaintance remarks, "there is no tenderness or consideration in the man. Sometimes you feel that there is no one at home."[5] No one, of course, would make personal morality either a prerequisite or a result of theology, but, in fact, Bergman hardly appears to be living in the shadow of a God whose very mystery possesses him.

Despite the doubt which fills his scripts and his apparent lack of commitment to a Christian code of ethics, he writes, "To me, religious problems are continuously alive. I never cease to concern myself with them; it goes on at every hour of the day."[6] The recurrence of apparently religious themes and clearly religious imagery is then no accident. Bergman's inquiry is set in a religious context; he is the man of quest, not the man of dogma or faith. He asks questions about crucial issues, and hence the pertinence of our times, but as a child of this century he withdraws from definite or dogmatic answers. For him importance seems to lie rather in the honest quest than in the goal.

Salvation, the object of the quest for a religious thinker, is clear only in *Wild Strawberries*. After the doubt and confusion of viewing his past on his journey through life, Isak Borg enters into a scene of tranquility and happiness where he is reunited with his parents and the pleasant and timeless memories of childhood. It is a scene as close to paradise as anything Bergman has ever created. Since Borg does gain ultimate "salvation" a brief analysis of how he did so might reveal the connection in Bergman's mind between the journey and the destination, between life and salvation.

Since Bergman was supposedly influenced by his father, the "Evangelical Lutheran minister," a study of some classical Lutheran notions of salvation as found in Luther's *Freedom of a Christian* and in a few contemporary commentators might provide some norm for the assessment of his thought. An analysis of *Wild Strawberries* may point out the extent of Lutheran influence; that is, by seeing how closely he conformed or how widely he separated himself from his Christian background, we can evaluate his contribution as a religious thinker.

I

THE CONTEXT FOR THE ARTIST

To uncover Luther's thinking on the question of salvation, one could do worse than begin with *The Freedom of the Christian*. Luther himself claims that the "little treatise . . . contains the whole of Christian life in a brief form. . . ."[7] The editor of his work agrees: "If one were to single out one short document representing the content and spirit of Luther's faith, *The Freedom of the Christian* would undoubtedly be at the top" (p. 42). In this work, Luther approaches the central problem of *Wild Strawberries* by asking, as does Bergman, what must a man do to be saved.

Luther claims that the Christian lives in a state of paradox: he is "perfectly free lord of all" and "perfectly dutiful servant of all" (p. 53). The key to the paradox is the duality of man's nature; the inner man, which is "spiritual, new and righteous," is free, and the outer man, which is "carnal," is slave (p. 53). From this dualistic perch, Luther can look scornfully down upon the works of man as coming from the outer man alone. Such works are merely peripheral to the inner man: "It is evident that no external thing has any influence in producing righteousness or freedom" (p. 54). Later, he reiterates the theme in another context by stating, "But works, being inanimate things, cannot glorify God" (p. 62). Salvation is the work of the inner man and external works are meaningless; faith alone brings salvation.

Yet his viewpoint is not so horribly simplistic as to force him to say that once a person opens himself to faith in "The Word of God" he is free to ignore all external norms of morality. Of the components of man's dual nature, primacy must go to the inner man, it is true, but man is also carnal at the same time, and will be perfectly free of the flesh only on "the last day, the day of the resurrection of the dead" (p. 67). Surprisingly then, Luther's ideas on asceticism sound quite traditional: "He must take care to discipline his body by fastings, watchings, labors, and other reasonable discipline and subject it to the Spirit, so that it will obey and conform to the inner man and faith" (p. 67). Lest the reader misunderstand the priority of faith as the sole condition for salvation, Luther repeats his warning: "Man, however, needs none of these things [ascetical practices] for his righteousness and salvation" (p. 73). It seems then that personal asceticism is necessary, but only inasmuch as it helps to preserve the faith of the inner man.

Good works, while needed to safeguard faith, do not of themselves bring salvation, since, according to Luther, it is presumptuous to believe that man can ever do anything to justify himself:

> We do not therefore reject good works; on the contrary we cherished and teach them as much as possible. We do not condemn them for their own sake, but on account of this godless addition to them and the perverse idea that righteousness is to be sought through them (p. 72).

Hence, the act of faith is of the inner man and it alone brings salvation; works serve only to subdue the carnal man and to "reduce it to submission" (p. 68).

One particular type of good work stands out as especially significant for the Christian, and that is "things which he does toward his neighbor" (p. 73). Since charity, or love of neighbor, holds the central position in many ethical systems, including, as we shall see, Ingmar Bergman's, it is important to see what Luther says about charity. He writes, "Man does not live for himself alone, but lives for all men on earth; rather, he lives only for others and not for himself" (p. 73). Furthermore, all men's actions should be guided to the "need and advantage of his neighbor" (p. 73). Such works toward the neighbor are expressions of faith, and must follow upon faith. The motive for performing acts of love is the imitation of Christ, which is, we might say, an overflow of Christ's presence in us through faith: "I will give myself as a Christ to my neighbor just as Christ offered himself to me . . . since through faith, I have an abundance of all good things in Christ" (p. 75).

As we have seen, the "freedom of the faith" and justification by faith alone can be open to simplistic misunderstanding; Luther denies that now "all things are allowed" (p. 80). Personal asceticism is needed to subdue the outer man and charity to extend the faith of Christ to others. The Christian "lives in Christ through faith, and in his neighbor through love" (p. 80). Man is the medium between

Christ and the neighbor; without faith in Christ love would be impossible.

CONTEMPORARY LUTHERAN COMMENTARY

Important as it was to begin with a survey of the place of love and faith in Luther's own writings, we realize that the Lutheranism that Bergman imbibed on his father's "confessional couch" had undergone centuries of interpretation and evolution. While his father had undoubtedly studied *The Freedom of the Christian*, there is no evidence that Bergman himself had ever pondered the sources of Lutheran theology. He is a man of the theater, not a scholar. As a sign of his being out of the mainstream of European theology, he refers to the reading of Eiono Kaila's *Psychology of the Personality* as a "tremendous experience"; this is a book of so little impact on Western thought that it has not yet been translated from the Scandinavian languages, although it was published in 1951.[8] Bergman's teachers are not Kierkegaard, Luther, and Kant; they are Ibsen, Strindberg, and Sjoberg.

We can, however, speculate that his religious questions were at least partially formulated by what he heard from his father and from other pastors of his childhood. In notes to *The Seventh Seal* he recalls travelling with his father, listening to sermons and studying church decorations.[9] The headwaters of his thought might well be Luther, but Luther as filtered through the men of Bergman's childhood. Thus, a brief sampling of some contemporary Lutheran commentary might reveal more accurately what Bergman heard and what contribution these ideas made to his thinking.

Undoubtedly, the connection between a personal experience of guilt and justification would have been made clear by Lutheran pastors. Many trace Luther's belief in salvation by faith alone back to his monastic scruples; despite his best efforts he could never feel that his actions were pleasing to God. The attraction of the "old man" was an intolerable burden to him.[10] He needed the certainty of his own salvation, yet his personal failings prevented this. Only an unconditioned act of faith could bring freedom from his guilt and that act was purely a free gift from God. The burden for salvation then rests on God. Man recognizes his sinfulness, confesses, and opens himself to God's mercy and grace; he does nothing to merit grace, for as a sinful creature he cannot.

In turn, God accepts the Christian without any qualification and the Christian realizes it.[11] Luther's tenacity in opposing ecclesiastical

authority and his continuing his journey through hostile territory to
Worms in 1522 are referred to as proofs of the absolute freedom and
confidence he received from God in turn for his act of faith.[12] Strength
comes from Christ working in the soul: "Christ is a living active fruitful Being who does not rest but works unceasingly wherever he is," as
Luther would put it.[13] By using Luther as an example, modern Lu-
therans reflect upon the experience of personal sin, realize their helplessness, confess, and then open themselves to the presence of Christ
by faith, from whom all strength flows.

Faith is a "leap from the safe shore of this life over the abyss where
we feel nothing, see nothing, and have no footing, but entirely at God's
suggestion and with his support."[14] Following this insight, the Lutheran pastor must exhort his flock to leap without stressing the reasonable quality of the move. From experience of sin to confidence in
justification . . . and no syllogisms can help them span the abyss.
Rudolf Otto catches the nature of Lutheran faith well when he writes
in *The Idea of the Holy:*

> Faith for Luther plays the same essential part, *mutatis mutandis,* as
> knowledge and love for the earlier mystics: it is the unique power of the
> soul, the *adhaesio Dei,* that unites man with God: and unity is the very
> signature of the mystical . . . . faith makes man one cake [Ein Kuche]
> with God . . . . Faith for Luther . . . is something that cannot be ex-
> haustively comprised in rational concepts . . . to him faith is the center
> of the soul . . . in which the union of man with God fulfills itself.[15]

Since for so many the central issue in ethics is charity, Lutheran
scholars have returned to the works of the Reformer to clarify his notions on love of neighbor. In the early years, they tell us, his lectures
on the Psalms (1512) seem to confuse charity for all men with the
brotherly love which must be shown among members of the religious
community; at this point Luther is still very much the monk and he
seems to show little compulsion to extend his love to all mankind.[16]
Yet God's will is supreme, and in creating all men he has shown love
to them; the Christian, therefore, with the spirit of Christ acting in
his soul, must conform to his will and like him meet the neighbor in
love.[17] Love does not have any independent meaning, but is merely
part of the demand for conformity with the presence of Christ in the
soul.

By 1519, Luther's idea of love had expanded to embrace all men.
His sermons reflect an interest in the church as the Body of Christ,
and so men are united by membership in the same Body and participa-

tion in the same Eucharist even more closely that they are by mere conformity to the presence of Christ within them.[18] This idea of actual unity of Christians is explicated in the Sermons on *Two Kinds of Righteousness* (1519) and *The Foundation of Consolation* (1519) in which he writes:

> Just as the bread is made out of many grains which have been ground and mixed together, and out of many bodies of grain there comes the one body of bread, in which each grain loses its form and body and acquires the common body of the bread, and as the drops of wine, losing their own form, become the body of the one wine: so it should be with us, and is, indeed, if we use the sacrament aright.[19]

Love is no longer then merely the sense of community for Luther, but is directed completely to the alleviation of the needs of others: food, clothing, shelter.[20] Yet even at this point, good works have no value but as a manifestation of man's incorporation into the Body of Christ; good works are not only dependent upon faith, but actually flow out of it; they are faith in action.[21] The commandments to love the neighbor are all linked by the virtue of faith, which is, for Luther, the first commandment. Love for man derives from love for God.

This brief survey of the relationship between faith and charity, both in the works of Luther himself and as some contemporary Lutheran theologians try to interpret him attempts to show that in both cases faith is prior to charity. Without an act of faith, good works or love of the neighbor would be meaningless to the orthodox Lutheran. With this established as an important element in Lutheran ethics, we can turn to *Wild Strawberries* to measure the degree of Bergman's use of the tradition he received from his father and other pastors he knew in his childhood.

II

GOOD WORKS—SONGS FOR A DEAF MAN

In *Wild Strawberries* Bergman presents through dream sequence and recollection the biography of an elderly bacteriologist, Isak Borg. As the doctor travels to his final reward, he looks back over his life and discovers that his works are dust and his achievement ashes. The climax of his career is to be his installation as jubilee-doctor of the University of Lund, but he is not sure that he does not rather deserve the title of "jubilee-idiot." On one level, the action is completed in twenty-four hours, but on the more significant level, the journey is one of a life time and the destination is salvation.

The opening dream sequence sets the double theme in motion. The old man is writing in a diary and recalls a dream in which he passes beneath the huge broken eyes of an oculist's sign. The giant eyes are reminiscent of F. Scott Fitzgerald's device in *The Great Gatsby* where the all seeing eyes survey the ash heaps of wasted dreams, but since the eyes in *Wild Strawberries* are broken it may well indicate that Borg does not yet see reality clearly. The hands have fallen from the clock in the sign and from his own pocket watch, showing that time has run out for the doctor. He is alone, as all men must be at the end, and the wheel from a hearse, rolling toward him and smashing against a wall, indicates that the wheel of time has ceased turning for him. A coffin falls to the sidewalk and the corpse, a mirror image of himself, reaches up to pull him into death. Borg taps a stranger on the shoulder only to find that it is a spectre of death which collapses under his touch. From the first scene, Bergman has built a split level stage: actual time, a strange dream, and a man's confrontation with death and eternity.

Borg's journey then also has a double dimension: it is a journey to a reward, one as jubilee-doctor at the University and the other the just reward of his life on earth. As he passes the various stages of his trip, he weighs good against evil in an attempt to evaluate his life. Much remains mystery to him, as it must to every man.

According to Luther, man can make this journey to his reward with confidence only after an act of faith, but Isak Borg does not make that act. His ultimate salvation will be a human salvation; the good works of the doctor are not the life of Christ functioning in him, nor is his charity a conformity to God's will or a sharing of the Body of Christ with members of the church. Through his dreams Borg analyzes his relationships to men on their own merits, and reproaches himself for failing to respond to human values. The brief analysis of *Wild Strawberries* which follows is an attempt to substantiate the claim that Bergman, despite an occasional use of Lutheran vocabulary, does not offer Lutheran criteria for salvation. Isak Borg is saved, but he does not make any act of faith; his good works are based on love, not faith.

As shown above, Luther's liberating act of faith follows upon a sinner's recognizing his own hopeless state. Bergman at least goes through the motions of bringing Borg to such a confession during the dream-examination. When he cannot remember a doctor's first duty, the examiner reminds him that it is "to ask forgiveness." Borg does not understand and the examiner tries to explain, "Moreover, you are guilty of a guilt." Once again, Borg does not understand and asks, "Is it serious?" The examiner answers, "Unfortunately, professor." Since Borg is given the opportunity to recognize his guilt and confess, but does not and yet, in the closing scenes is saved, apparently Bergman is explicitly denying this Lutheran condition for salvation. Bergman seems to be saying that a man can seldom be aware of the extent of his guilt; perhaps this awareness is not even necessary.

And if one must throw himself on the mercy of a personal God, Bergman does not commit himself. Borg's relationship to a personal God is somewhat vague. In the restaurant scene, he falls silent and a young girl asks him, "You're religious, aren't you, professor?" Borg replies simply by reciting a line of poetry, "I see his trace of glory and power, in an ear of corn and the fragrance of flower." Borg seems to hold some sort of a belief in a transcendent power, but Bergman does not tell us if this is anything like the traditional Christian notion of a God.

Anders and Viktor, two young men hitch-hiking their way to Italy, seem to represent two poles in Bergman's thought about the traditional God, and it may be significant that neither of them eventually wins the affection of their travelling companion Sara or convinces the other of his philosophic position. They argue:

> VIKTOR: In my opinion modern man looks at his insignificance straight in the eye and believes in himself and his biological death. Everything else is nonsense.
> ANDERS: And in my opinion modern man exists only in your imagination. Because man looks at his death with horror and cannot bear his own insignificance.

Even when asked, Borg refuses to make an act of faith in God and his relationship with man. Perhaps Bergman is showing the indissolubility of the argument and confusion by having the young men resort to a futile fist fight to settle their theological controversy.

Another glaring divergence between Luther and Bergman is their opinion on the need for a personal asceticism. Luther felt that it was necessary to preserve the life of faith in the inner man, but Bergman seems to believe that self-discipline can shrivel the vitality of the soul. The asceticism which Bergman portrays is not the spiritual discipline of "fastings, watching, labors" (p. 67), but rather the painfully demanding discipline of a man of science. In *Wild Strawberries* Borg is the man of science, the bacteriologist and teacher, who sacrifices his humanity to science and who looks at his fellow men as though they were specimens on a slide. His daughter-in-law, Marianne, quotes him as saying that he has "no respect for problems of the soul," and that he regards any attempt to cure such problems merely "masturbation for the soul." Borg sought self-fulfillment as a scientist, and as he reflects upon his career he realizes that he has been a failure. In the dream-examination, he finds that he cannot recall the first duty of a doctor, he cannot read the print on the classroom board, and he cannot recognize the specimen under the microscope; the coarse laughter of the cadaver reminds him that he cannot ever distinguish life from death. He is pronounced "incompetent" not only as a scientist, but as a human being; his punishment is loneliness, which he recognizes as evil on this journey as never before.

His failure in these dream-examinations cheapens his reward at the University, for he recalls that "this strange rite with its heavy symbolism [is] as meaningless as a passing dream." The reward for fifty years of dedication to science leaves no elation, but only the memory that "even our behinds, which have long withstood long academic services, lectures, dusty dissertations and dull dinners, started to become numb and ache in silent protest."

The loved one of his youth, his cousin Sara, returns in the dreams to tell him that his refinement and self restraint are really forms of death. After a family squabble at the breakfast table, a dream of the distant past, Cousin Sara cries into her sister's lap:

> Isak is so refined. He is so enormously refined and moral and sensitive and he wants us to read poetry together and talks about the afterlife and wants to play duets on the piano and he likes to kiss only in the dark and he talks about sinfulness. I think he is extremely intellectual and morally aloof.

Marianne also points out the death behind the facade of refinement, when she says, "You are an old egoist, Father. You are as hard as nails even though everyone depicts you as a great humanitarian. We who have seen you at close range, we know what you really are."

While Luther tells us that fasts and watchings are needed to bring the outer man into submission, so that the inner man may grow freely in the life of faith (p. 68), Bergman seems to say that self-control, at least when carried to the extent of Borg's, smothers the inner man. Science is something he can hide behind without having to expose himself to others. In this Bergman finds fault. As the examiner puts it, Borg's life is a "surgical masterpiece. There is no pain, no bleeding, no quivering," and we might add, no humanity.

Only in the scene with the gas station attendant and his wife does there seem to be any connection between Borg's medical practice and real life. Mrs. Akerman's advanced pregnancy is itself a sign of life, and as they refuse money for the gas and oil, Mr. Akerman says that he cannot forget what Borg did for them. When he offers to name the next boy "Isak," the doctor boasts that he will return to act as godfather. Borg muses, "Perhaps I should have remained here," but when questioned about it, he becomes flustered and prepares to leave.

With these simple people, his life seems to have some meaning. From this scene it becomes apparent that if Borg is saved, if his life is to have any meaning, love and acts of charity, rather than faith or discipline will bring salvation. Without love, his labor will be as meaningless as the song the twins wrote for Uncle Aron in the childhood dream; with love, his life, like their song, will have impenetrable depths of meaning.

LOVE—THE KISS IN THE BERRY PATCH

Isak Borg, like each of us, must approach each interpersonal relationship as a unique experience and, like each of us, he cannot love all men at all times. In fact, he finds it hard to love at all. His salvation will come not so much from his ability to offer love to others, for in fact he loves little, but from his recognition of its importance and his failure. In the closing scenes, as he lies in bed, he says to his daughter-in-law, "I like you, Marianne." For him this statement is a true accomplishment.

Borg's family life militated against love. His mother confuses her children and speaks of them in terms of the toys they played with as children. Her family no longer visits her and she suspects perhaps correctly, that they hate her for failing to die on schedule. The family relationship is continued through thank you notes and an annual visit from Isak's son Evald. During Isak's visit, his mother hands him a gold watch without hands, another reminder that time is ending for him. Perhaps this device is simply Bergman's way of summarizing in image the impact of his mother's age upon him.

Coldness was always characteristic of Borg's nuclear family. In the scene in the summer house, the bustle of activity and the affection shown to deaf Uncle Aron seems to stir Borg with memories of lost possibilities. He is, significantly, missing from the scene; he remains the silent spectator at the doorway. From the discussion around the breakfast table we learn that Borg, as a young boy, is out fishing with his father. Paradise in the closing scene will consist in his reunion with his parents, and in recalling his parents, and in recalling this early scene, Bergman pictures the father as fishing. During his journey to eternity Borg must recapture the lost warmth and brightness of these early scenes.

The family tendency toward aloofness reaches its natural climax in Evald, the tight-lipped middle aged son of Isak. Marianne says of this chain of coldness:

> I thought here is his mother. A very ancient woman, completely ice cold, in some ways more frightening than death itself. And here is her son, and there are light years of distance between them. And he himself says that he is living death. And Evald is on the verge of becoming just as lonely and cold—and dead. And then I thought that there is only coldness and death, death and loneliness, all the way. Somewhere it must end.

Evald is an image of the dark side of Isak's character without the charm and dignity of old age; he is merely pompous. He greets his father with an incredibly bland and formal greeting, saying "Hello, father. Welcome." Immediately, he flees behind the protective armor of small talk by commenting about the "nice looking children in the car." After the ceremonies at the University, when Isak's reflection had mellowed his outlook on human relationships, he tries to approach Evald on the subject of a sum of money which the young Borg still owes his father. Isak may well want to rescind the debt, but Evald cuts off the conversation saying, "Don't worry, you'll get your money." Isak protests and tries to explain, but Evald snaps again, "You'll get your money all right."

Since Evald is so closed off from human love, and consequently from human life, his demanding an abortion for his wife Marianne is perfectly fitting. He says, "It is absurd to live in this world, but it is even more ridiculous to populate it with new victims and it is most absurd of all to believe that they will be any better off than us." Bergman's dislike for Evald is clear; unlike Evald, he believes that man does have a value, and the audience must admire Marianne's decision to have the baby even though it means leaving her husband.

Isak found even less joy in his wife than in his son. Evald comments on the home life of the Borg family, "Personally, I was an unwanted child in a marriage which was a nice imitation of hell. Is the old man really that sure that I am his son? Indifference, fear, infidelity and guilt feelings, these were my nurses." The sole appearance of Isak's wife is after his failure to pass the series of dream-examinations; he passes with the examiner into a garden where he watches his wife and her lover as he had several years before. He overhears her say that her adultery brings no fear of her husband, because he will merely say, "I have nothing to forgive. But he doesn't mean a word of it, because he is completely cold." Borg hears and is silent, and by his silence he fails his examination as a human being; he does not weep or rage, he merely accepts and this is unforgiveable. He asks, "Is there no grace?" The examiner replies, "I know nothing about such things." Even the Almans, a couple who quarrel constantly and violently and who return in the dream-examination to play the parts of the examiner and the cadaver, are more alive than Borg. They have managed to form a meaningful relationship out of hate; Borg is too closed upon himself even to hate his wife.

Marianne, by contrast to Borg's wife, is the most human and feeling of characters. She is vulnerable; she weeps and expresses hatred of Evald. She leaves him, realizes her love for him and returns. During their trip to Lund together she teaches Borg concern for others; after her narrative of her last discussion of the abortion with Evald, Borg comments, "I suddenly felt shaken in a way I had never experienced before." When she meets Evald again, she forgets her bitterness, and despite his coldness makes a joking reference to their sharing a bedroom again for a night. Of course, Evald is embarrassed and shows his displeasure, but later admits to his father, "I can't be without her"; he is willing even to accept the condition that she have the baby. "It will be as she wants," he says. Bergman has made her a warm character through her contagious humanity; she can be hurt, she loves and teaches others to love. Faith does not enter into her life as a source of her love for others; it is a perfectly natural womanly response to another person, particularly to those most in need of her love, like Isak and Evald. There is no reference to a Lutheran desire to share the life of Christ in her soul.

While Marianne scrapes the icy crust from Isak's personality, it is his cousin Sara whose love warms him from within. Sara in the form of the young girl travelling to Italy with the two boys and played by the same actress, Bibi Andersson, is a constant reminder of Cousin Sara and Isak's nearly forgotten love for her. Sadly, before this journey, he never realized the love he had lost.

Cousin Sara first appears in the dreams as a young girl picking wild strawberries, which are always some sort of symbol of life for Bergman. The exuberant young Sigfrid kisses her hard and skillfully, and significantly, her apron is stained with berries as though she will always be a sign of life and vitality for Isak. She becomes with age not cold, like Isak and his mother, but a "lovely old lady of seventy-five years," and the mother of seven children. At the time of the kiss in the berry patch, she is secretly engaged to marry Isak, but, as she admits to her sister Charlotta, she finds him cold. Her dilemma is mirrored by the younger Sara, who must choose between Anders and Viktor, one who will go far and the other who "has nice legs" but will be a minister.

In a later scene in the berry patch, Cousin Sara holds up a mirror to Isak's face, asks him to contemplate his age and tells him that she had decided to marry Sigfrid. He admits pain at the news, but she rebukes him, "You, a professor-emeritus, ought to know why it hurts, but you do not." When confronted with this accusation, Isak correctly identifies his love for her as the cause of his pain, but he cannot communicate his feelings. He pleads, "Don't leave me," and she answers, "You stammer so much that I can't hear your words. Besides, they don't really matter." She turns to her child, another image of life, and rejoins Sigfrid. The sight of their happiness so wounds Isak that it is symbolized by his cutting his hand on the window of their home.

After the series of dream-examinations, Cousin Sara returns once again. This time Isak recognizes his loss, and says, "If only you had stayed with me." In her vitality, she runs away and tells Isak to follow, but he cannot; he is too old and slow. She calls out to him and then vanishes as he awakes from his dream. He confides to Marianne that in his dreams, "I am trying to say something to myself which I don't want to hear when I am awake. . . . That I am dead, although I live." His dream of Cousin Sara has given him insight into his own stifled capacity for love to the extent that in the following scene he can listen with compassion to the narration of the separation of Marianne and Evald.

Cousin Sara returns once more in the final scene. She tells Isak, in his last dream, "Isak darling, there are no more wild strawberries left." The clock has struck its last chime for Isak Borg and he must depart to join his father and mother. He realizes that he cannot reach them alone, and she assures him, "I will help you." Isak's love for Sara sustains him on the journey; his love for her has given meaning to his life, and she will lead him to his reward. He reaches a tranquility touched with uncertainty, fittingly a paradise of human peace, not divine revelation.

I dreamed that I stood by the water and shouted toward the bay, but the warm summer breeze carried away my cries and they could not reach their destination. Yet I didn't feel sorry about that; I felt on the contrary rather light-hearted.

NOTES

1. Mircea Eliade, *The Sacred and the Profane* (New York, 1957), pp. 183-4. Harvey Cox, *The Secular City* (New York, 1965), pp. 47 ff. explains that "themes of mobility and homelessness, of wandering and pilgrimage informed the self-understanding of the earliest Christian community."
2. William Hamilton, "Ingmar Bergman on the Silence of God," *Motive*, XXVII (1966), 37-41. By analyzing the three films usually classed together in the "God Trilogy," *Through a Glass Darkly* (1961), *Winterlight* (1963), and *The Silence* (1963), the author argues convincingly that Bergman's central quest is one not for God, but rather for communication between persons.
3. "I am a Conjurer," *Time* (March 14, 1961), p. 61.
4. Ingmar Bergman, *Four Screenplays* (New York, 1960), "The Introduction," by Carl Dymling, p. viii.
5. *Time*, p. 61.
6. Quoted by Richard Duprey, "Man on a Quest: Ingmar Bergman," *The Critic*, XIX (April-May 1961), 13.
7. Martin Luther, *Martin Luther*, ed. John Dillenberger (New York, 1961), p. 42. All subsequent page references in the text to *The Freedom of the Christian* will correspond to the Dillenberger translation.
8. *Screenplays*, p. xxi.
9. Norman Holland, "*The Seventh Seal*: The film as iconography," *Hudson Review* (Summer 1959), p. 266.
10. Stepher Pfurtner, O. P., *Luther and Aquinas on Salvation* (New York, 1964), pp. 31 ff.
11. Heinrich Bornkamm, *Luther's World of Thought* (St. Louis, 1958), pp. 76 ff.
12. Bornkamm, p. 88.
13. Bornkamm, p. 90, quoting Luther's *Adventpostille* (1522).
14. Bornkamm, p. 87, quoting Luther's *Jonah Exegesis* (1526).
15. Rudolf Otto, *The Idea of the Holy* (New York, 1958), p. 104.
16. Donald Ziemke, *Love for the Neighbor in Luther's* Theology (Minneapolis, 1963), p. 22.
17. Ziemke, p. 27.
18. Ziemke, p. 48.
19. Ziemke, p. 47.
20. Ziemke, p. 49.

21. Ziemke, p. 57. Also, Joseph Sittler, *The Structure of Christian Ethics* (Baton Rouge, La., 1958) explains this concept of faith in action through love, pp. 72 ff.

THE RAGS OF TIME   Harvey R. Greenberg, M.D.

. . . .

While upheavals in adolescence and middle life are favored themes of contemporary authors, crises of the senium have been far less frequently portrayed. Nevertheless, within the past century we have been given three masterful studies of aging men who, on the brink of the grave, experience profound psychic change—Tolstoy's "Death of Ivan Illytch," Mann's "Death in Venice," and "Wild Strawberries," a motion picture by the Swedish *auteur*, Ingmar Bergman.

"Wild Strawberries" occurs within one day in the life, and in another sense the entire life of Isak Borg, a 76-year-old Emeritus Professor of Medicine. The actual day is that on which his half-century of service is to be recognized by raising him to the honored post of Jubilee Doctor.

As the film opens, Borg is discovered in his study, setting down "the events, dreams, and thoughts" of this memorable occasion. His voice tells us that he is a widower, living alone save for an old housekeeper. His only son, also a physician, is childless. His 96-year-old mother is still active. He is grateful for his work. He is an old pedant, "quite trying to myself and to the people who have to be around me." He detests emotional displays.

After this spare self-appraisal, the titles are presented against a neutral background. Then in sharp contrast, we are plunged into a world of nightmare. Borg walks through an empty city in absolute silence. He comes to a watchmaker's shop, whose sign is an enormous clock, under which hangs a pair of giant eyeglasses. The hands of the clock are gone, the lenses smashed. Reflexively, Borg checks his own watch: its hands are missing! The silence is broken by the crescendo pounding of his heart, which ceases abruptly as he glimpses a man dressed in black. Reassured, Borg touches the man's shoulder; he turns, showing

From *American Imago*. Vol. 27, No. 1 (Spring 1970), pp. 66-82. Copyright © 1970 by The Association for Applied Psychoanalysis, Inc. Reprinted by permission of the Wayne State University Press.

Victor Sjostrom as Isak Borg, with Bjorn Bjelvenstam as Viktor, and Bibi Andersson as Sara, Folke Sundquist as Anders in *Wild Strawberries*.

a horribly withered face, with eyes and mouth compressed into pencil-thin lines (in the script, the man is "faceless").

The figure collapses and a foul looking fluid oozes from empty clothing. Bells toll mournfully, and a horsedrawn riderless hearse thunders by. As its rear wheel catches against a lamp post, the horses back and pull until the wheel drops off and rolls away, narrowly missing Borg, and splinters into pieces against a wall. The hearse sways and tilts until the coffin tumbles out, cracking apart. The horses gallop away.

Borg approaches the broken coffin, from which a hand protrudes. As he leans over, it stirs, seizes his arm in an iron grip and drags him inexorably down. Panic-stricken, he realizes that the corpse is himself, and awakens.

This remarkable vision, the stimulus for all that follows, is the culmination of several months of "evil and frightening nightmares." By juxtaposing it against a calm beginning, Bergman adroitly establishes Borg's composed façade and the shattering depression it conceals.

The dream occurs on the eve of unparalleled honor, yet its images speak unrelentingly of futility and decay. The empty city is a powerful metaphor of the protagonist's spiritual condition (Borg = City). The shattered hearsewheel and broken coffin, the clock without hands, the smashed glasses, are externalizations of an ego that is losing its sense of instrumentality and is on the verge of dissolution. Anxiety mounts as Borg discovers that *his* watch is handless. He turns for solace to a man who crumbles at his touch. Symbols of death grow more undisguised until the dreamer is placed in his own coffin, dragging himself into the grave. The dream work cannot bind this moment of supreme terror: like many depressives, Borg awakens fearfully and early.

He calls Miss Agda, his housekeeper of many years. He has decided not to fly to Lund, where his son Evald lives, and where Borg is to receive his award. Instead, he will travel by car, starting immediately. Miss Agda opposes this change, and says that she will not attend the ceremony. She accuses him of meanness and egocentricity, yet packs his things. He tries unsuccessfully to soothe her; her bruised feelings puzzle and discomfit him, for he is unaware of how he wounds through self-absorption.

Marianne, Borg's daughter-in-law, is disturbed by the bickering. Estranged from her husband, she has been living with the old doctor for the past month. Now, she asks him to take her to rejoin Evald. Borg wonders at her decision, the suddenness of which, in fact, parallels his own. This is the beginning of two journeys, one that will take him to his honoring, and of another, far more painful inner journey. Throughout both, Marianne will play an odd sort of Beatrice to his Dante, a sympathetic but not always comforting voice of uncompromising honesty.

In the car, Borg immediately assumes a patronizing tone, bidding her not to smoke, for this is a "manly" vice. He asks her why she has decided on a reconciliation. She does not tell him, and he grows uneasy. Evald and he are much alike, he declares, in their unswerving adherence to principle. Borg gave his son a loan to complete his studies and feels that it is a matter of honor to repay him. Marianne says that the restrictions of this indebtedness are absurd, since Borg is wealthy. But, he replies, a bargain is a bargain, and his son respects him. "But he also hates you," Marianne states flatly.

Borg's expression, caught in full closeup, is one of sudden, total horror. He tries to preserve a semblance of imperturbability. What can she have against him?

> MARIANNE: You are an old egotist . . . completely inconsiderate. All this is well hidden beneath your mask of old fashioned charm . . . but you are hard as nails, even though everyone depicts you as a great humanitarian . . .

She reminds him that when she first arrived, she told him about her floundering marriage, and he cruelly rejected her pleas for emotional support. Although he has completely forgotten his indifference, Borg is not moved to make an apology. But he admits that she is a fine young woman, whose company he has enjoyed. He tries to tell her of his morning's dream, but she is not interested. He has performed true to form: again, he has ignored her pain, and tried to engage her in *his* dreams, *his* feelings. Although he is haltingly reaching out, she cannot regard him without rancor.

Directly after this confrontation, Borg is seized by another impulse and leaves the highway for a side road. He parks, and leads Marianne to a boarded-up house, where he lived with his nine siblings for the first generation of his life. Marianne leaves to take a swim; Borg walks to a wild strawberry patch near the house, sits and eats. As the taste of tea-sweetened *madeleine* sent Proust's hero searching down the corridors of memory, the strawberries move Borg to recapture his own past. He slips into a second dream.

Suddenly the house is sunlit, alive with sounds of music and children. He discovers a lively young girl next to him: his cousin Sara, to whom he was once secretly engaged. She is unaware of his presence. While Borg watches, a handsome youth flirts with her: this is Sigfrid, his next oldest brother. He speaks contemptuously of Isak, Sara defends him and berates Sigfrid for cigar smoking* and loose conduct with a local girl. Sigfrid embraces her; Sara responds impulsively, then pushes him away, overwhelmed by guilt for betraying her fiancé.

A bell sounds and Borg's siblings appear. There is general shouting for Isak. Borg is unable to answer. Then his twin sisters notify everyone that Isak is fishing with his father. Borg feels a "secret and completely inexplicable happiness" and enters the house.

From the shadows, he observes a bustling table at which an imperious aunt presides over the birthday celebration for deaf old Uncle Aron. The festive spirit is disturbed when the twins taunt Sara and Sigfrid with what they witnessed from hiding. Sara rushes from the table into the adjoining room, where Isak is standing. She is joined by Charlotta, a comforting older sister, and blurts out her misgivings about her engagement: "(Isak) is enormously refined, moral and sensitive . . . talks about the after life and likes to kiss only in the

---

* Sigfrid rejoins: "That's a man's smell"—recalling Borg's allusion to "the manly vice." The preoccupation with smoking is found throughout the film. His mother, too, does not tolerate smoking.

dark . . ." She perceives his aloofness, feels small in his presence, yet
also finds him childish compared to the exciting Sigfrid.

The meal ends with cheers for Uncle Aron (so does the dream in
the film). Another sister sees father returning. Sara runs from the
house, Borg follows but loses sight of her. He stands, desolate, at the
wild strawberry patch, to be awakened by a young girl's voice.

The geography of the first dream was stark, devoid of life; the second teems with humanity. Family relations are tumultuous and abra-
sive, but there pervades a binding warmth from which Borg is excluded.
He is absent within the structure of the dream, but as its creator,
he is also its observer. He watches helplessly while his virile older
brother seduces Sara. He regards her criticism of him (Marianne's de-
nunciation is the impetus for Sara's speech to Charlotta) as adoles-
cently ascetic, his character already warped by detachment and
isolation.

His parents are also absent. By placing him securely with father, the
dream attempts to ameliorate the desolation that apparently informed
his alienated adolescence and young manhood. The repair is unsuccessful. Having lost Sara at the dream's opening, he is abandoned
again by her as it ends.

He awakens to regain her, by a marvelous coincidence. *This* Sara
(the same actress plays both roles) is a student, hitchhiking to Italy.
After a bantering introduction (in which Borg rather wistfully corrects
her misimpression that the biblical Sara was married to Isak: it was
Abraham, his father!), with a spontaneity that is a hallmark of the
film's forward movement, he invites her to travel with him.

Marianne rejoins them and, back at the car, they meet Anders and
Viktor, Sara's companions. She is semi-engaged to Anders; Viktor also
loves her, and is the chaperone. (Her father arranged this triangle to
protect her virginity.) Anders studies for the ministry, Viktor will be
a physician. Bergman counterposes, in these two, the man of feeling
and faith against the cold, rational scientist with whom Borg is implicitly identified. Echoes of the second dream reverberate: Viktor is
a frustrated witness to Sara's closeness with Anders, and Borg—*watching* the youngsters from the front of the car, tells Sara of his first love:

> ISAK: She was rather like you . . . she married my brother Sigfrid
> and had six children. Now she's 75 and a rather beautiful old
> lady.
> SARA: I can't imagine anything worse than getting old.

Instead of taking offense, Borg bursts into laughter with the others. At this moment, a car speeds up on the wrong side of the road. Borg swerves desperately, and the other vehicle disappears into a ditch. The occupants, Alman and his wife, Berit climb out. They have been arguing, and within minutes after apologizing for their carelessness, attack each other anew. When Alman's car fails to start after being retrieved from the ditch, Borg offers them a lift with misgivings.

Marianne drives. A heavy silence is broken by Berit's weeping. She shakes off her husband's arm. He cynically describes her manipulations by hypochondrical symptoms and fabricated tears. Marianne asks him to stop, but he derides Berit until she strikes him full in the face. Still he mocks on: even this assault is part of her act! Marianne pulls over; she will not play captive audience to the Almans' sadomasochistic exhibitionism. She orders them from the car, and as they drive away, Berit calls: "Please forgive us, if you can . . ."

Now Borg comes to the town of Huskvarna, where his mother lives and where he practiced as a beloved country doctor for fifteen years, before the teaching career that brought him fame. He stops for gas. The station owner greets him warmly, praises his accomplishments and offers to name his unborn child after Borg. Stirred by this simple man's tribute, he murmurs, half-unaware: "Perhaps I should have remained here . . ."

Borg dines with his friends on a terrace with a magnificent view of lake and sky. He is in a mellow, nostalgic mood, and entertains the company with stories of his doctoring days. Anders recites a poem extolling natural beauty and its Author. Viktor attacks Anders's lyricism and faith; the two get embroiled in a bitter argument over God's existence. Seeking an appropriate ally, Viktor asks Borg for an opinion.

Borg demurs: anything he could say would be greeted by "ironic indulgence." Marianne laughs and lights his cigar, warming up to the old man. Then, Isak answers Viktor after all, by reciting a few verses of poetry. When his memory falters, first Anders, then Marianne take up the stanza:

> Where is the friend I seek everywhere?
> Dawn is the time of loneliness and care . . .
> I see his trace of glory and power,
> In an ear of grain and fragrance of flower.
> In every sign and breath of air
> His love is there . . .

Sara is moved, comments that he *is* religious. In fact, Borg is undergoing a painful conversion. He has made common cause with Anders and Marianne against the fatuousness of Viktor's desiccated atheism. Slowly and subtly, he is being revealed as a man of troubled, long suppressed sensitivity, in tentative touch with the wellsprings of his feelings.

Borg goes to pay respect to his mother, accompanied by Marianne. The atmosphere in her house is still sombre. She accepts her youngest son's kiss, congratulates him, then denounces Marianne, mistaking her for Karin, Borg's faithless wife. Even after he corrects the mistake, the mother is still critical and competitive, noting Marianne's childless condition with obvious disapproval and triumph.

She takes up a large box and, rummaging through battered mementoes of her family's past, broods over her loneliness. Ten children she bore, all dead save Isak, innumerable grandchildren and great-grandchildren, and only Evald visits her. The rest call only when they want money. She is a tiresome person who has the effrontery not to die. As she fingers the relics, she comments unpleasantly on the children who owned them. She shows ancient photographs—she and her husband, Sigfrid and Isak as infants. Borg wants to look at one, and she hands it to him disinterestedly: "It's only trash." She complains that she has felt cold as long as she can remember—"mostly in the stomach . . ."

Borg grows restive, but his mother detains him: she is thinking of giving her daughter Sigbritt's son her dead husband's watch for his fiftieth brithday. It has no hands, but is beautiful and reparable. What does Isak think of her decision? As the camera focuses down on the handless watch, the thudding of a heart sounds familiarly. Borg, distressed, obviously recalling his nightmare, looks at his mother whose face is wizened, imponderable, as she speaks:

> I remember when Sigbritt's boy had just been born and lay there in his basket in the lilac arbor at the summer house. Now he will be fifty, and little cousin Sara, who always went around cradling him, and who married Sigfrid, that no good. Now you have to go . . .

Their strained, solemn encounter is over. Marianne takes his arm, and he is suddenly "filled with gratitude towards this quiet independent girl with her naked, observant face." When they return to the inn, they discover Sara at the car, near tears. Anders and Viktor have continued their quarrel, and are now off settling their differences forceably. While Marianne fetches them, Sara tells Borg of her difficulty in choosing between the two boys. The journey recommences. A storm comes up and Borg, lulled by the rain, falls into restless sleep, and there follows the third, longest, and most complex dream of the film:

Again, he sits at the wild strawberry patch with Sara. She shows him his reflection in a mirror, says he is a worried old man who will die soon. She has been too considerate with him; now she will marry Sigfrid. She asks him to smile, and he makes a painful grimace.

> SARA: You, a Professor Emeritus, ought to know why it hurts. But . . . in spite of all your knowledge, you don't really know anything.

A child—Sigbritt's little boy—cries in the distance. Sara rises, Isak implores her not to leave, but she runs to the arbor and cradles the baby in her arms. A door in the house opens, and Sigfrid beckons to her. She enters, giving him the child. Darkness falls. Isak peers into a window and sees Sara, playing a Bach fugue on the piano. The fugue motif metamorphoses into the film's theme, one of inexpressible longing, as Sigfrid approaches, kisses her, and they move away to the dinner table.

The windows turn opaque. Borg looks up at the lightening sky, then raps impatiently on the windowpane. No one responds. He raps harder with his left hand, and as the heartbeat, mimed by a kettledrum, resounds, he impales his right hand on a nail!

Abruptly, the door is opened by Alman, who leads him to the amphitheatre where once he lectured and gave examinations. In the spare audience are Sara, Viktor, and Anders. Alman directs him to identify a microscopic specimen. Borg peers into the instrument but can only see his own eye staring back.

Alman commands him to interpret a cryptic sentence on the blackboard—supposedly the first duty of a doctor. Borg declares testily that he is not a linguist, falters, and Alman reminds him that the first duty of a doctor is *to ask forgiveness*—and that he is guilty of guilt.

He is next required to diagnose a woman sprawled lifelessly in a chair. Borg pronounces her dead; she opens her eyes and laughs mockingly. It is Berit Alman. Wearily, Alman records his conclusions: Borg is incompetent, indifferent, inconsiderate. These accusations have been made by his wife.

Alman then leads Borg out of the examination hall, through a forest and into a clearing, where he watches Karin provoke a powerful man to take her violently. Alman observes that Borg actually witnessed this scene of savage sexuality, indeed, it is the principle memory he now bears of his dead wife. She speaks to her lover:

KARIN: Now I will tell this to Isak, and I know exactly what he'll say: how I pity you . . . and then I'll ask if he can forgive me. And then he'll say: You shouldn't ask forgiveness from me . . . But he doesn't mean a word of it, because he's completely cold. And then he'll suddenly be very tender . . . and then I'll say it's his fault . . . he'll look very sad, and will say he is to blame. But he doesn't care about anything, because he is completely cold.

She laughs madly and vanishes.

ALMAN: She is gone. Everyone is gone . . . everything has been dissected . . . a surgical masterpiece. There is no pain . . . a perfect achievement . . .

ISAK: What is the penalty?

ALMAN: The usual one, I suppose. Loneliness.

Alman disappears (the dream ends here, in the film) and Sara is beside him.

SARA: Didn't you have to go with them to get your father?

ISAK: Sara . . . it wasn't always like this . . . if only you could have had a little patience.

She too runs from him and he wants to cry with "wild, childish sorrow" but cannot, as he awakens.

The occurrences after Borg is roused from his slumber by the old house, comprise the residue for this remarkable dream, which opens as Sara cruelly taunts him. In the second dream, Borg depicts her as she probably existed: a simple, vital girl confused and angry with his adolescent puritanism. But now the pitiless face she shows is that of the mother, monumentally self-absorbed, and glacially aloof. Isak is her only surviving child. Their relationship in old age is preternaturally reserved, yet one intuits his overwhelming sense of duty towards this terrifying indifferent creature.

She describes Sara's affection for Sigbritt's child; now grown, he will receive her gift, the damaged watch, not Isak. And, in the dream Sara abandons him for this child, denying his desire for maternal sustenance. Next, she moves towards Sigfrid. The second rejection, with an unmistakable oedipal referent, is all the more devastating, because it occurs against the background of Borg's frustrated oral-dependent strivings (as an outsider, he views scenes of dining in two of the dreams).

The impalement that follows is symbolic of his castrated, impotent state. He has been severely wounded in his masculine identity at the mother's hands, but out of loyalty and fear of the maternal superego, he suppresses his rage against her. Instead, a restitutive identification with her disdainful obsessionalism has taken place.

Borg dealt with the real Sara as if she were the mother, to whom intimacy was anathema. By his unyielding, guilt-provoking and distancing behavior, he exacted talion vengeance against his mother, displaced on to all the innocent women of his life. But a healthier part of him, astir throughout this day, now also speaks through Sara, reproving him for his ignorance, ignorance both of human tenderness and the dark forces that have robbed him of pleasure and made him a lonely, pathetic old man.

The theme of ignorance is vividly amplified in the harrowing examination administered by Alman, whose masochistic provocation of his wife grotesquely parallels Borg's relationships with women. The audience of youngsters indicates his own unfulfilled youth, crying out for explanation and release from neurotic bondage.

On examining the microscopic specimen, he sees his own eye, a concretization of merciless self-scrutiny. He cannot decipher the message, complaining he is no linguist; indeed the wish to communicate with others has withered.

The first duty of a doctor is to ask forgiveness—but for what? Sara spoke both for his mother and his own interests; there is an analogous ambiguity in the cryptic inscription. He must ask forgiveness from the mother for ever defying her constraints, for ever presuming to seek warmth at her chill breast. He must subjugate himself, do endless humiliating penance to placate her destructiveness, and by masochistic abasement maintain the illusion that some shred of love will fall his way.

Now he dimly intuits a different order of forgiving. He must ask forgiveness of those he injured by his misdirected spite. The burden of meaningless shame must be cast off if ever he is to learn kindness towards himself. "You are guilty of guilt" says Alman: out of this inexplicable sense of guilt—as if he sinned by being born—he has tortured himself.

Berit Alman asked forgiveness in reality; her figure in the dream is a condensation of the vicious shrew, and the wife whose self-esteem has been destroyed by a hostile husband. Her resurrection—the second time the dead have awakened in his dreams—betokens the reawakening of the painful ambivalent feelings towards women he has striven mightily to disavow.

Borg is finally confronted with Karin, in a setting suggestive of the primal scene. He has been repeatedly cast as an observer of intimacy. Now he is forced to watch his own wife submit to the advances of a brutal male. Afterwards, she describes his insulting solicitude, his coldness, and also his queasy tenderness, as if he could only possess his woman after the oedipal rival has been satisfied. And we recall Sara, ashamed of her need for the enticing Sigfrid, a need Isak encouraged by his withdrawal.

Loneliness is the price of the stillness that follows; the peace in the dream is as illusory as that purchased through decades of denial and isolation. Once more Sara appears, reminding him to seek his father. She disregards his pleas for patience and leaves him as the dream ends. Again, the double mask: she frustrates, yet enigmatically encourages relatedness—with the father.

I have theorized that Borg's obsessional defenses against depressive affect are precipitates of an inadequate, frankly hostile mothering. But what of the father? Is the powerful competitor of the dreams struck in his image? We are given only the briefest allusions to the man, fleeting references which, in fact, may be paradigmatic of the son's perception of him.

If the faceless figure with back turned in the first dream is the father, one may speculate that Borg saw him as distant and unsupportive. The father's handless watch may provide another image of paternal ineffectiveness. In the second dream, in which the parents are absent, their replacements are the domineering, critical aunt, and a foolish deaf uncle!

Although he was the last, youngest male child, under other circumstances Borg might have forged a resolution of his oedipus, and found an adequate identification with the father who may have been experienced as distant simply because he had to be shared with so many others. Two factors prevented this: the mother intensified the oedipal conflict, her openly rejecting behavior implying that young Isak was a poor sort of rival. Then, his next sibling was another male, older by only a year, and although the mother was evidently not fond of him, he was still seen as a sadistic, frightening competitor for her dubious affection.

In any large family, siblings, acting as parental substitutes, are immensely important shapers of personal destiny. In this family, given the mother's pathology, their destructive or reparative influence is crucial. Matters conceivably might have stood quite differently had the next older sibling been a boy more warmly disposed towards Borg, or even a girl more protective of his needs, instead of Sigfrid, who minimized his younger brother openly, perhaps out of envy for an infant he believed was preferred.

We are almost totally ignorant of Isak's feelings towards his other brothers and sisters. There is a hint of warmth for Charlotta, Sara's comforter, but she obviously did not provide Borg with the nurturing the mother denied him. He stands isolated from the rest of the siblings as from everyone else in his life.

I have been considering issues and conflicts that are known—yet unknown. But now, at last, Isak Borg is prepared to recognize the insights his unconscious has been urging upon him for months. He awakens to find himself alone with Marianne. The youngsters are off picking flowers to pay him homage, for she has told them of his elevation. She too is ready to listen, as he speaks of his dreams and what they portend:

> ISAK: It's as if I were trying to say something to myself which I don't want to hear . . . that I'm dead although I live.

She blanches; her husband feels much the same! The scene dissolves to Marianne and Evald sitting in the place occupied a moment ago by his father. They are parked near the sea; Marianne has brought him here unwillingly, and he treats her with a well known sad mixture of irony, aloofness and resentment. She reveals that she is pregnant and will have her child (the inference is that previous pregnancies were terminated at Evald's insistence). He angrily submits that she will have to choose between him and the unborn infant:

> EVALD: It's absurd to live in this world, but it's even more ridiculous to populate it with new victims . . . I was an unwelcome child in a marriage which was a nice imitation of hell. Is the old man really sure I'm his son? . . . this life disgusts me and I don't think I need a responsibility which will force me to exist another day longer than I want to . . . You have a damned need to live . . . and create life . . . my need is to be dead. Absolutely, totally dead.

The dreadful similarities between father and son are painfully evident: Evald's despair is simply closer to the surface. He too experienced a distant father, but Borg's remoteness was a function of unresolved oedipal rivalry, the son bearing the brunt of Borg's long suppressed competitiveness with his brother, as well as the father's innate horror of intimacy. Evald too suffered maternal deprivation, but whatever else compelled her, we know that Karin was driven by her husband to enact the role of a treacherous slut. And Evald too employs the baleful obsessional defenses that are the legacy of the frightful old lady of Huskvarna.

After Marianne finishes, Borg permits her to smoke. When one recalls his peremptory injunction earlier in the day, this small stiff gesture obviously presages potent change:

> MARIANNE: When I saw you together with your mother, I was gripped by a strange fear . . . I thought, here is his mother, completely ice cold, in some ways more frightening than death . . . and here is her son, and there are light years of distance between them. And he himself says that he is living death. And Evald is on the verge of becoming just as lonely and cold —and dead. And then I thought there is only coldness and death and death and loneliness . . . somewhere it must end . . . (I am returnin) to tell him that I can't agree to his conditions. I want my child, no one can take it from me. Not even the person I love more than anyone else.

She stares at him with a "black, accusing, desperate" gaze, and he is shaken to the roots of his being. In one stroke, she has laid bare the chain of interpersonal devastation; her integrity, the life of her child have been endangered by the destructiveness in Evald and his progenitors.

This, then, is the turning point of "Wild Strawberries." Borg asks: "Can I help you?", surely the first time in his adult life the old and honored physician has asked the question of someone near him, and truly meant it.

Marianne is too troubled to notice what she has done. No one can help her, nevertheless she will try to bring Evald back to some semblance of life. At this moment, Sara appears, bearing a bouquet and salutation:

> SARA: We want to pay our respects . . . and to tell you that we are very impressed . . . we know, of course, that you are a wise and venerated old man . . . who knows all about life and who has learned all the prescriptions by heart . . .

Gentle mockery in her voice, yet these young people are also revivers of Isak's parched spirit. Realizing now that he has denied the heart, he is wiser and deserves her gift.

At Lund, Borg is surprised and delighted to be met by Miss Agda. Evald is painfully cordial to Isak. As he unpacks, he overhears his son express a cautious pleasure at seeing Marianne.

Bergman deleted the next scene from the film, but it is instructive of his intentions.* The three old men who are to be honored await the ceremony's beginning. Borg chats with Jacob Hovelius, a bishop, and discovers that the third man is Tiger, a once famed jurist, now far advanced in age and unrecognizeable in his decrepitude.

> ISAK: Do you think we are like that?
> JACOB: What's your opinion? As Schopenhauer says, somewhere: "Dreams are a kind of lunacy and lunacy a kind of dream." But life is also supposed to be a kind of dream, isn't it?

Borg's dreams have accurately reflected the desperate condition of his soul and catalyzed a profound revolution in his inner life. But this point has been made amply; the scene therefore is redundant, the quotation too obvious. Thus, without it, the action proceeds to the Jubilee Rite itself, accelerated as a newsreel, the events of hours compressed into a few moments. The journey to this summit of excellence is what has mattered, not the reward. It is during the ceremony that Borg, seeing his young friends, Evald, Marianne and Miss Agda in the audience, discovers a "remarkable causality" in the day's "unexpected, entangled" events, and decides to record his experiences.

He returns home to find Miss Agda making his bed. He has a surge of warmth for the faithful old woman, and asks forgiveness (sic!) for his rudeness. Amazed, she inquires after his health. He requests that they drop their formality of two generations and address each other as "du." Absolutely not, says she—one must think of one's reputation! He is about to retire when he hears singing in the garden. It is the youngsters, come to bid him adieu.

> SARA: Hey, Father Isak! You were fantastic when you marched in the procession. We were real proud we knew you . . . Goodbye . . . do you know that it is really you I love, today, tomorrow and forever?

They disappear into the night. Marianne and Evald return unexpectedly, because her heel has broken. His son stops by the door, and he asks him to remain a moment. Borg inquires what Evald will do about his marriage. Discomfited, Evald declares that he has asked Marianne to remain; he cannot be without her, all will be as she wishes. Hesitantly, Borg mentions the loan, but Evald dismisses him

* The elisions of the second and third dreams are equally revealing. Cinematically, they now work better and also are more condensed, the manifest content furnishing less obvious clues to the elucidation of latent content.

brusquely: he is not to worry, he will get his money. Just then Marianne enters and leans over Isak:

> ISAK: Thanks for your company on the trip.
> MARIANNE: Thank *you.*
> ISAK: I like you, Marianne.
> MARIANNE: I like you too, Father Isak.

A lesser artist would have cast Borg in the likeness of Scrooge, waking from troubled dreams to spread good cheer until the end of his days. But Borg is an ancient man with an extremely rigid character. Miss Agda and Evald, though they have been hurt by him, believe nothing else possible at his hands; they are actually as inflexible after their own fashion as he. Brilliantly, Bergman portrays the rejection of Borg's tentative efforts to soften his behavior towards the old housekeeper and the stinging rebuff he receives from Evald, so much his father's son. People such as these simply do not give up their defenses with such facility. And Borg's self-description in the opening scene is written *after* this memorable day has passed; the mask he turns to the world would not seem to have altered that significantly.

Yet, to underscore the impressive internal shifts that have occurred, Bergman interpolates two visitations of love between the thorny, unsuccessful confrontations with mother surrogate (Miss Agda) and hardened son. The first is by Sara, who speaks for her past namesake of her wholehearted affection. The second is by Marianne who, with her luminous honesty, has penetrated beyond Isak's facade and respects what she has seen, touched by his suffering and achievements, more firmly commited than ever to affirm the life within herself.

After Evald and Marianne leave, Borg has a final dream. For the last time he lingers by the wild strawberry patch. The day blazes with sun; by the dock, his sisters and brothers frolic with Uncle Aron. Sara and his aunt pass by, laden with picnic baskets. Sara warmly bids him search for father while the rest go sailing; they will rejoin him later. But he says he can find neither parent.

Sara takes his hand, and leads him to a hill from which, now alone, he sees a man and woman seated on the beach. The man holds a long, slender bamboo rod between his knees that arcs gracefully into the clean air. The woman sits slightly apart. The scene is perfectly composed, indeed one of the most perfect in cinema, and save for a few shimmering harp chords, is absolutely still.

His father makes a small, cryptic gesture of greeting. Borg's face is suffused with a rare joy. There is a quick dissolve to the old doctor stirring contentedly in his sleep, and the film ends.

Although the protagonist still appears in this final dream as a distant observer, meaningful repair has occurred—all envy and bitterness have vanished. The scene he watches is harmonious, lovely, and to some degree he partakes of it—as if, having finally found the approval of a warm and giving woman, he can be allowed full cognizance of his merit as child and man.

That this healing recognition comes on the brink of the grave is tragic, but that it has come at all to this constricted, tormented figure is nothing short of miraculous. Whatever dreams and days remain to him, one is sure they will pass with a measure of serenity and comfort, for love has finally achieved a small dominion within Isak Borg, and in Donne's words:

> Love, all alike, no season knows, nor clime,
> Nor days, months, years, which are the rags of time.

BIBLIOGRAPHIC NOTE

All quotations from the film are from *Wild Strawberries*, in *Four Screenplays of Ingmar Bergman* (New York: Simon and Schuster, 1960). The passage from Donne is taken from "The Sun Rising," in *Poems* by John Donne. Everyman's Library Edition (New York: Dutton, 1958).

DISCUSSION OF GREENBERG'S PAPER ON BERGMAN'S *WILD STRAWBERRIES*   Seldon Bach

· ·

Although Bergman was later to make films in which the total world structure appears to be disintegrating, this film, made in 1957, is still old-fashioned both in concept and expression.

For example, Miss Agda, Isak's faithful housekeeper, has been in his service for forty years; he himself is being honored as a fifty-year Jubilee Doctor; his son has become not a hippie, but a doctor at the same venerable institution; the young hitch-hikers whom he picks up listen to

From *American Imago*, Vol. 27, No. 1 (Spring 1970), pp. 83-89. Copyright © 1970 by The Association for Applied Psychoanalysis, Inc. Reprinted by permission of the Wayne State University Press.

him with respect for his age, while they themselves are planning their careers as doctor or clergyman or wife, a future which to them still appears eminently conceivable.

In short, there is a past, present and future that forms an uninterruptured life cycle within which something seems to have gone awry for a particular individual and his family. In some way they seem to have gotten unhooked from the life process and the cycle of generations and they must, in the film, become aware of this and find their way back in again.

For although the story is ostensibly about one lonely old man facing death, Dr. Greenberg has made it clear that the other protagonists represent different times and different aspects of Isak's life. Young Sarah and her two boyfriends, cousin Sarah and her two suitors, Isak's wife and her two lovers are all reflections of the same schema.

The relationship between the son Evald and his unborn child mirrors the relationship between Isak and his son Evald and ultimately the relationship between the un-named father and Isak, who must be re-born.

We are dealing with a world of strangely interlocking protagonists whose conflicts are being simultaneously worked out on several levels at once; the people and events move in isomorphic parallelism like the points of a pantograph; conflicts between Isak and his long-dead wife are worked out in reality between Isak and Marianne and in their turn resolve conflicts between Marianne and her husband. We are confronting an internal world that has been mirrored and projected and the movements we witness on the screen are reflections of the movements of internal objects or, as Bergman might say, the movements of the soul.

What then is the conflict with which Isak Borg is faced in his 76th year on the eve of being named a Jubilee Doctor? In the opening scene he summarizes by saying:

"My life has been filled with work for which I am grateful. It began with a struggle for daily bread and developed into the continuous pursuit of a beloved science. I have a son living in Lund who is a physician and has been married for many years. He has no children. My mother is still living and quite active despite her advanced age. [She is ninety-six.] . . . We seldom see each other. My nine sisters and brothers are dead, but they left a number of children and grandchildren. I have very little contact with my relatives. My wife Karin died many years ago. Our marriage was quite unhappy. I am fortunate in having a good housekeeper.

"This is all I have to say about myself . . ."

There are two notable omissions in this account. He mentions work, but he does not speak of love. And he mentions everyone of importance in his life with the outstanding exception of his father. I was thus led to believe that the conflict centers directly in his love for his father, which would make sense in terms of a depression arising at this time; for how can he allow himself to be named a Jubilee Doctor when he, himself, is unable to name his father?

Isak, of course, was the beloved son of Sarah and Abraham, and yet Abraham was prepared to sacrifice his son when he felt that this was the will of God. To my mind, the first dream in the film represents the sacrifice of Isak Borg:

He finds himself walking alone in the streets. There is the coldness and silence of death. He passes a signboard but the clock is blank, the eyes are sightless. He sees a man standing at the corner and rushes toward him for help but the man turns, revealing no face, and then collapses into dust. Isak's father has turned a cold and unyielding face to his pleas for help.

"High above me the sun shone completely white, and light forced its way down between the houses as if it were the blade of a razor-sharp knife. [The sacrificial knife.] I was so cold that my entire body shivered."

The wheel of the hearse comes loose and narrowly misses hitting him. He is pulled into the coffin by his own corpse and struggles to free himself. At the last moment he awakens. His life has been spared, but his fear and hatred still remain.

The wish in this dream, since it is also a dream about the imminence of Isak's death, is that God, the Grim Reaper, should spare his life *now* in the same way that God and his father had spared his life long ago at the very moment of sacrifice. And we shall see that in a peculiar way this wish is destined to be fulfilled.

This theme, that the father must kill, or abort, or deny his love for his son, is repeated on many different levels throughout the film. Two of the more cogent examples are when Isak's son Evald proclaims that he was "an unwelcome child," and when Evald himself wants to abort Marianne's pregnancy and tells her "You'll have to choose between me and the child."

Thus the child, which is normally a link between the parents and a tie with the future, has become a wedge to keep the parents apart and to break the chain of life.

The sin of Isak, which is passed on to his son Evald, is the wish to

abort the child, to split apart the parental couple and to destroy the
union of mother and father in its concrete manifestation, the making
of babies. This man, the youngest male of ten children, has become a
doctor and a bacteriologist, but the reaction-formation breaks down in
his own unwillingness to have children. For God has promised Abraham that his seed will populate the earth, and it is for this sin against
God's commandment that Isak must ask forgiveness and make repara-
tion in order that his mother and father may come together again and
live within him in peace.

This brings us to the title of the film.

What is the meaning of the wild strawberries? They are first mentioned when Isak goes back to the house of his youth, finds the wild
strawberry patch, eats the berries and falls into a dream of childhood.
The strawberry patch here represents the maternal breast to which one
returns with a sense of familiarity and where one feeds, falls asleep and
dreams.

Later the twin sisters are described as being "identical as two wild
strawberries," and Eve Akerman, in an advanced state of pregnancy,
beams at the doctor "like a big strawberry in her red dress." It becomes
clear that the strawberries symbolize the creative breast, the female re-
productive capacity, the fruit of the earth, in a word, babies.

Each time that Isak returns to the wild strawberry patch Sara appears, conjured up as if she were the goddess of the strawberries. We
know, of course, that she is the cousin who rejected him because he
was cold, aloof and preoccupied with sin, but she is also his wife and
his mother who had nine children before him and whose womb he
must destroy by "a surgical masterpiece, no pain, no bleeding, no quivering, a perfect achievement of its kind. Everything has been dissected."

For Isak cannot permit himself to love his father's wife, his own
wife or any woman until he accepts his father, agrees to the union of
the parents and acknowledges himself as their child. In other words,
he must deal with his jealousy of the father and his envy of the mother
before the split can be healed. And, as in so many of Bergman's films,
the way back to this reunion is through the woman, in accepting her
affirmation of life and identifying with her creativity.

Thus, in each of three dreams, it is a woman who urges Isak to look
for his father and he feels "a secret and inexplicable happiness" at the
thought that he and his father are fishing together.

Later he recites a religious hymn: "Where is the friend I seek everywhere? Dawn is the time of loneliness and care. When twilight comes

I am still yearning . . . Though my heart is burning, burning . . . I see His trace of glory and power . . . In an ear of grain and the fragrance of flower . . ." . . . He forgets the lines, and it is Marianne, his daughter-in-law, who finishes: "In every sign and breath of air, His love is there . . ."

Thus, the affirmation of his father's love is expressed through the woman and, indeed, through the pregnant woman, for Marianne is carrying Isak's grandchild and Isak is bringing her back to her husband on this journey through his life that will end by re-uniting him with his parents.

Should this interpretation seem fanciful to you, I want to remind you that in 1957, the same year that he made *Wild Strawberries,* Bergman made another film called *Brink of Life.* This story takes place in a maternity hospital and it concerns three women who are about to give birth. One wants to abort her baby, the second desperately wants her child but miscarries, and the third, played by Ingrid Thulin, who is the Marianne of our film, loses her child because she knows that her husband doesn't want the baby. Since this film was made just after *Wild Strawberries,* it would seem that the conflict had not yet been settled in Bergman's mind. The fact that he can bring *Wild Strawberries* to a satisfying artistic conclusion raises some interesting questions about the relation between an aesthetic and an intrapsychic resolution of conflict.

Be that as it may, it is on the journey homeward with Marianne that Isak begins for the first time to tell someone else about his dreams and his fears. "It's as if I'm trying to say something to myself which I don't want to hear when I'm awake."

"And what would that be?" she asks.

"That I'm dead, although I live," he says.

Marianne is taken aback by her father-in-law's statement, which reminds her so much of her husband. She tells him of her discussion with Evald about the unborn child, and Evald's insistence that she must choose between the child and him.

"But you're going back to Evald," he says.

"Yes, to tell him that I can't agree to his condition. I *want* my child; no one can take it from me. Not even the person I love more than anyone else."

She turns her face toward Isak, and he suddenly feels shaken to the very depths of his being. He asks: "Can I help you?"

Dr. Greenberg has singled out this moment as the turning point of the film, "the first time in his adult life that the old and honored physician has ever asked that question to anyone near him and truly meant it." It is also the repetition of a scene between Marianne and her husband, as father, mother and unborn child sit together in the automobile and discuss the fate of the child, but *this time* the child *will be spared*.

In offering to help, in sparing this child, Isak permits his son to become a father and his grandchild to be born, and thus seals his identity with the loving patriarch Abraham rather than with the vengeful father of his dreams. Once the mother and father can come together, then babies can be born, and the way is cleared for a fantasy of re-birth.

Isak was terrified of death precisely because he found himself in a position of narcissistic isolation; he was going to die alone and that would be the end of that. But for most of us, death can only have meaning if we identify with a cause or a group that survives the personal accident; and in accepting the continuation of the species, Isak identifies with the child to be born and can find his place once again in the life cycle.

To put this another way: He confronts the inevitability of his death by libidinizing it, by changing his internal perception of death from that of a sacrifice or castration by his father (as in the first dream) to that of an eternal re-union with the loving parents (as in the last dream). Death, as the castrating or aborting father, has been changed to death as the welcoming parental couple to whom one comes as a little child.

All this is contained in his offer of help to Marianne. It then only remains for him to return Marianne and her child physically to her husband, and then to be named Jubilee Doctor.

On returning from the ceremony, he feels a great warmth for Agda, his housekeeper, and he asks her for forgiveness. The youngsters return to serenade him and Sara says she will love him forever. He asks them to keep in touch. He calls Evald in for a talk and, to his own surprise, he attempts a reconciliation. Marianne enters and he thanks her for her company and tells her he likes her. She kisses him and disappears.

He listens to his heartbeat and the tick of his watch. The clock strikes eleven, the last hour before midnight. It begins to rain, quietly and evenly.

His mind returns to the wild strawberry patch on a warm, sunny day with soft summer skies and a mild breeze. We are reminded of the lines of the hymn: "In every sign and breath of air. His love is there. His voice whispers in the summer breeze . . ."

Suddenly Sara spies him and says: "Isak darling, Aunt wants you to search for your father . . ."

He replies: "I have already searched for him, but I can't find either Father or Mother."

"I will help you," she says.

"She took me by the hand and suddenly we found ourselves at a narrow sound with deep, dark water . . . Down at the beach on the other side of the dark water a gentleman sat, dressed in white, with his hat on the back of his head and an old pipe in his mouth. He had a soft, blond beard and a pince-nez. He had taken off his shoes and stockings and between his hands he held a long, slender bamboo pole. A red float lay motionless on the shimmering water.

Farther up the bank sat my mother. She wore a bright summer dress and a big hat which shaded her face. She was reading a book. Sara dropped my hand and pointed to my parents. Then she was gone. I looked for a long time at the pair on the other side of the water. I tried to shout to them but not a word came from my mouth. Then my father raised his head and caught sight of me. He lifted his hand and waved, laughing. My mother looked up from her book. She also laughed and nodded."

In this most poignant scene, Isak has found his parents again, and this time they are together. The father sits with his long pole, a fisher of souls, a symbol of baptism and rebirth through the union of spirit and water. Young Isak has truly come to meet his Maker, for he is present at the primal scene; but how different the feeling from the sadistic and guilt-ridden primal scenes of the earlier dreams.

Here he is reconciled to the union of the parents, to the birth of the child, and to death, for as Uncle Aron, or Charon, ferries the boatload of brothers and sisters who have already died, Sara lifts up a baby boy, the young Moses, for Isak to see. Thus in one magnificent image, we have the symbols of death, birth and the primal re-union woven together by the hands of an artist.

Isak has found his way back into the cycle of life and death, and has been re-born innocent, like a little child.

11

THE MAGICIAN
Finding the Sources

Vernon Young

. . . .

A halt or reversal in the fervor with which critics had been greeting
Bergman's films was noticeable in the reception of *Ansiktet* (literally,
The Face, and so called in England; *The Magician* in the United
States). Not only when the film appeared but on later occasions when
sufficient time had passed in which to reconsider hastily furnished opinions, mystification was stronger than affection and, since mystification
often leads to animosity, an irritated tone informs many futile attempts
to make sense of this film. Rereading many of these reviews today, I
find pure impatience masquerading as common sense and I see critics
fearful of being taken in; in some cases I note a flat refusal to make a
simple effort, and only a simple effort is required, to divine what *The
Magician* is all about—if knowing what it is all about is the only proviso
for a critic's enjoyment of it! A certain kind of poetry, T. S. Eliot said
great poetry, I believe, can communicate before it is fully understood.
In these days of the humbug and the vague-minded, I would not depend on the principle, yet it might be a good one to invoke here. Critical viewers have swallowed, it seems to me, a vast amount of vulgarity
and facile symbolism from, for instance, the films of Pier Paolo Pasolini (that dubious mixture of Catholicism, Marxism, the sacred epi-
cene, and the godlike stud, all of it *mental*). They tend, often the same
viewers, to get thoroughly confused, always at the wrong time, by Bergman or for that matter by Antonioni.

The Magician is an incredibly suggestive work; that it is also defini-
tive is as much to my point, and this very suggestiveness has beguiled

From *Cinema Borealis: Ingmar Bergman and the Swedish Ethos* (New York:
Equinox Books, 1972), pp. 174-87. Reprinted by permission of David Lewis,
Inc.

Max von Sydow as Albert Emannuel Vogler, and Bengt Ekerot as Spegel in
The Magician.

critical opinion into strange interpretations; equally it has tempted certain critics into suspecting Bergman of trifling with them, of indulging
a taste for the occult which he then hopes to endow with a spurious
morality.[1] I believe that Bergman has been many times confused, in
his several films, as to how best to convey a moral or metaphysical ambiguity; I am of the opinion that in his latest films he has lost the
power of discerning what is self-evident to an audience and what is
absurd. I am convinced that he has ultimately unclear ideas about the
nature of moral catastrophe. And it may well be that there are calcu-
latedly hidden meanings in his later films; but I do not believe that he
trades in gratuitous mystification and I do not believe that he manu-
factures effects which have no meaning to him. Frivolity is surely the
last vice with which anyone should charge Bergman.

Above all, *The Magician* is not the film in which to expect irrespon-
sibility, since the conscience of the artist is precisely the burden from
which Vogler, the magician, is suffering. Perhaps I should not say precisely because Vogler is a necessarily imprecise figure, for a very good
personal reason which, at the same time, cannot but lend interest to

the character in the film. I may as well state at the outset of this exploration that when Bergman was working on *The Virgin Spring* he
told me that he had not felt "quite right" about the two films pre-
ceding. As I recall, he was not including *Brink of Life,* which is quite
another matter. With *The Virgin Spring* he felt absolutely sure of
what he was doing. Now, in *Wild Strawberries,* I suggested, he was
unable to see Isak Borg as coolly as the context warranted because of
his respect for Victor Sjöstrom. During the shooting of *The Magician*
I know that he was not altogether decided on the fate of Vogler.
Should he rescue him, should he let him be crushed? His artistic
shrewdness gave him the answer. You can't very well construct a film
in which every appearance is stained with ambiguity, then conclude it
on a note of doom, categorically sounded.

Vogler's fate is left open, as it should be; we have never been quite
sure of his identity; it is fitting that we should feel unsure of his future
although, for the moment, it looks rosy. There may be undertones, in-
tensities, extremities of feeling in this film which cannot rationally be
accounted for, but I sense no fundamental imprecision in the character of the underworld which Bergman was apotheosizing. Obscurity is
one thing, mystery another. At the heart of *The Magician,* as in the
heart of the magician, there is mystery, an onset of fright because people's definitions of each other digress so wildly, and a suspicion de-
moralizing by its enormity that the powers we hold to be most reliable
are just those on which we cannot depend when the hour of exposure
arrives.

Let us, as prosaically as the subject permits, recall the continuity of
the tale. From the depths of a forest, perhaps for the last time in a
Bergman film, comes that cry of players so often materialized before,
usually a token that deeds not altogether savory and not apprehensibly
real are about to transpire. Vogler and his outlaw company, including
his wife disguised as a man, his "grandmother," who has all the appearance and jargon of a professional witch, and his factotum, the ridiculous Tubal, are on their way to Stockholm in the 1840's, where
Vogler hopes to demonstrate his magic at the Royal Palace. We learn,
from brief exchanges of dialogue, that these mercenaries of the occult
art have been fined and jailed in some of the best cities of Europe for
heresy, for blasphemy, for sundry dubious ventures in the realm of the
cure-all. Traveling through the forest, they pick up a dying, or de-
mented, and certainly drunken actor, Spegel. At the entry to Stockholm they are detained at the custom house for approval by Starbeck,
the Chief of Police, and invited by the "liberal" Councillor Egerman

(he is open to proof) to spend the night at his mansion where the royal Doctor of Medicine, Vergerus, hopes to expose Vogler as a charlatan. Bergman's first title for the film was *The Charlatans*, raising the obvious question, "Who are the charlatans?"

During their stay at the mansion, the presence of Vogler and his company stirs up a red-ant colony of frustrations, antipathies, concealed impotence, and buried desires. Ottilia Egerman, wife of the councillor, wants Vogler to requite her loveless life with her husband—their marriage had collapsed after the death of their child, one of the few warmed-over situations in the film—by explaining why the child died and by taking her husband's place in her bed. Egerman overhears her trying to make an assignation with Vogler, reveals to her later that he knows her intention and strikes her. Following which, in true Strindberg-Bergman fashion, he asks her forgiveness. Vergerus too has an itch, for upon discovering that Aman is Manda, a female, he tries to seduce her; when challenged by the irate magician he calms his jealousy by telling him wittily that he has nothing to fear; his wife's fidelity "borders on madness."

Meanwhile, the company downstairs is pursuing its own pleasures and suggestions of supernatural visitors trouble the night; a spectral figure steals the brandy jug. Tubal expresses what share he has of the master's power by bedding the cook; Sara, one of the housemaids, given a magic potion by Tubal makes love in the laundry room (where Antonsson's corpse will later hang) with Simson, the Vogler coachman. Granny shuffles to and fro, murmuring incantations, chalking a sign of exorcism on the courtyard wall, and placating the younger of the two maids, Sanna, who is confused by the whole menagerie, with a lullaby and prophetic mutterings. Some of the nocturnal disquietude is "explained" by the surreptitious return of Spegel who had vanished upon the troupe's arrival in Stockholm. We are so occupied with Bergman flourishing a handkerchief in his right hand that we forget to observe what he's doing with his left. Spegel insists to Vogler that he is not yet dead but decomposing whereupon, soaked in brandy which he stole from the Egerman kitchen, he falls lifeless to the floor. Vogler promptly puts his body into a casket among his stage properties.

The next morning, by invitation, Vogler, by now brought to a pitch of inchoate rage by the demands made on him and by the insensate hypocrisy of his hosts, a rage he dares not publicly express for he is supposed to be speechless, gives his performance. His first trick fails to convince, and to avenge himself he maliciously induces Mrs. Starbeck to disclose in ribald detail the undignified nature of her life with the

Chief of Police. He then picks the Egermans' coachman, Antonsson, to be the victim of his mesmeric specialty, holding the man powerless in an imaginary vice. Antonsson, furious at this humiliating reduction to physical helplessness, flings himself on Vogler and presumably strangles him to death. After which, as we discover later, he hangs himself.

This is the climax of the film. Vergerus takes Vogler's body to the attic, dissects it, decides that there is nothing unusual about the anatomy of this necromancer, and proceeds to write out his report. Suddenly the world turns eerie; a living hand is placed on that of Vergerus, a stopped clock begins to strike, blots appear on the writing paper, a mirror shows unbelievably the face of the freshly carved magician! For Vergerus, a nightmare follows; he is pursued out of the attic by the resurrected Vogler. Of course, the body anatomized by Vergerus is that of Spegel, which Vogler had substituted during the confusion attending his own "death"—a detail which disciples of Vergerus will simply have to accept as theatrical license. A final confusion ends the film. The troupe breaks up. Tubal and Sofia have found each other, i.e., she has commandeered a good provider, and Granny has decided to abandon the twilight career of a spellbinder; she has been hoarding money, she claims, with which to open an apothecary shop. Vogler experiences his final humiliation, begging Vergerus for money with which to leave town; unmasked, vocal, and in need his magnetism vanishes. "I liked *his* face better than yours," Vergerus, with recovered poise, tells him. Egerman is disdainful; even his wife, the hungering Ottilia, tells Vogler: "*I have never seen you before.*" Then, the denouement. Starbeck appears, thoroughly distraught but, in his official person, relieved, for he announces with awe that Vogler has been summoned by the King to give his performance at the palace. Under a beneficent shower of rain, Vogler is rushed off in a coach accompanied by his wife and by Simson with his new bed-warmer, Sara.

I should think that going no further than this synopsis, which I trust will revive the memories of those who saw the film, one would immediately sense the further reaches that lie beyond the bizarre turns of the plot. Previous familiarity with Bergman's films should readily evoke parallel lines of direction and similar conjunctions of profile. The casting, itself, is of assistance here. For to recall that Max von Sydow (Vogler), Gunnar Björnstrand (the skeptical Vergerus), and Bengt Ekerot (Spegel) played, respectively, the Knight, the Squire Jöns, and Death in *The Seventh Seal* is already to be in possession of a clue, if these relationships in *The Magician* are not self-explanatory; of a clue, not of a photocopy. The Knight, infirm believer, was bereft by the want of visible assurance, but he had not made himself responsible for the salvation of others. Vogler is clearly tempted to believe, especially under the stress of confidence placed in him by foolish minds, that his powers may come from an external source, whether diabolic or divine he hasn't the courage to explore; up to now he has only toyed downward, so to speak. Vergerus, unlike Jöns, stakes his life on the positive content of rational demonstration. The Squire was a genial stoic; for him, "Emptiness under the moon, my Lord," yet he was not dehumanized by the insight; one cannot imagine his being more tolerant of a Vergerus than he was of the defrocked priest, Raval, or the witch-burning monk. Vergerus expects a sign, a confirmation that "miracles don't happen," that there are no indefinable forces; his faith, like Vogler's, needs to be ratified.[2] He assures the Egermans, who are prepared to support the opposite view, that it would be fatal if scientists were suddenly led to accept "the inexplicable."

> "Why would it be?" Egerman asks.
> Vergerus tries to explain. "It would mean we should have to take into account—we should be forced to—we should logically have to conceive a—"
> "A God," supplies Egerman.
> "Yes, a God, if you wish."
> And Starbeck concludes for him: "A grotesque thought. Besides, it's not modern."

As to Spegel (the name, of course, like Spiegel in German, means mirror), he has nothing of the aloof dignity of Death, a figure from a masque, in *The Seventh Seal;* he has undergone a radical treatment from Naturalism. But, indeed, he is not the thing itself, he is Death's creature; he is more closely comparable to Frost, vis-à-vis Albert, in *The Naked Night,* a forecast of what another might become—and Vogler is fully aware of that possibility. Spegel confronts him in the forest with the unsparing question, "Are you a charlatan who must hide his real face?" He supplies a terrifying thematic undertone with his weird appearances and disappearances. Has he indeed passed over, one reflects with a shudder, returning as a ghost palpable enough to perish again under the knife of Vergerus? His proclamation to Vogler that he is already decomposing introduces the most disturbing text of the film. "*Step by step we go into the dark. Motion itself is the only truth.*" Without this consent to an underlying incertitude, without his unnerving remark before "dying," "When I thought I was dead I was tormented by horrible dreams," *The Magician* might be thought a harmless, comedic exercise in the perennial Bergman duel of belief and unbelief. During the verbal sparring with Manda over the authenticity of her husband's act, Vergerus has occasion to ask, "Is that true?" and she quickly replies: "Nothing is true." Whatever alternative answers Bergman hopes to imply through one character or another, this, it seems to me, is the key and the burden of the whole film.

I should not argue against the opinion, held by those who are disposed only to see Vogler as himself, that his agitation is forced into a dimension too great for its vehicle, i.e., for the "real" level where a mountebank is on trial before obtuse judges. No question but that this intensity gets close to the creator of the film. Vogler is named Albert Emanuel. Albert is also the name of the circus proprietor in *The Naked Night*, Emanuel the first name of Borg in *Wild Strawberries*. The problem, which to my feeling increases the refractions of the character like planes on a mirror, is that Vogler is simultaneously a faith-healer in 1846 who would like to be genuine and he is the artist—modern, certainly—provoked by the gullibility of his audience into despising it and, alternatively, doubting and probing his own authenticity. Conscious of how much art and how much luck or meticulous timing goes into his act which so impresses otherwise unimpressible mortals, Vogler is intimidated by those who are irreversibly skeptical of his art like Vergerus, those who would like to believe in it for reasons that have nothing to do with art like the Egerman's, those who are merely hypnotized by it like Antonsson, those who exploit it without an inkling of its intrinsic value like Tubal or Starbeck, those who blindly hate it, together with its maker, like Rustan.

The mystery of that touch which produces an effect out of all anticipated proportion to the cause must be a common experience among creative artists in every genre. You stage a farce of which you're so tired after three weeks of rehearsal you can't imagine how anyone might believe it to be funny; yet on opening night and for 136 performances thereafter the audience will have paroxysms of laughter at a sequence of interlocking tricks you feel ashamed to have organized. You introduce a French horn at the unerringly right moment and for two and a half seconds only; 875 inattentive listeners, with a rush of blood to their hearts, become a concerted moan of attention. You bend one outline more acutely, thicken a shadow, or deepen a patch of umber and respectably competent form is preternaturally alive. You accompany a piece of dialogue with a gesture timed to illustrate the point before you have verbalized it and you are credited with "a great reading"!

Call it the magic of art, call it quick thinking; it is the *ding an sich:* intuitive skill, the power of make-believe. Bergman, haunted by this paradox, takes it with an impenitently bad conscience.

> When I show a film I am guilty of deceit. I use an apparatus which is constructed to take advantage of a certain human weakness, an apparatus with which I can sway my audience in a highly emotional manner—make them laugh, scream with fright, smile, believe in fairy stories. . . . Thus I am either an impostor or, when the audience is willing to be taken in, a conjuror. . . .[3]

Kierkegaard said of Martin Luther that he always spoke as if lightning were about to strike behind him! More contingently, however, Bergman's words suggest a paraphrase of Luigi Pirandello on the same subject, an example to which I will return when we reach the film, *Persona,* since there the whole question of apparatus, by which Bergman claims to be embarrassed, is involved to the hilt. In this context I'll just say that Bergman is begging the question; dourly and impossibly he seeks to refute the irrefutable. However, his instinct is often more sophisticated than his misgivings. In *The Magician,* which is about imposture, once you have accepted the ambivalent character of Vogler, you will see that the tone is right, the tenebrous atmosphere in which Bergman conjures and mocks his own conjuring has an awful symmetry.

Within this penumbra, the Bergman ensemble, whether or not it has played the same roles before, is totally interrelated and the performers display a marvelous reciprocity. Max von Sydow, as Vogler, has never been better in film. There is about him sometimes for my taste a touch too much of the unblastable pine tree; in this film he bends to the wind; he is properly tortured, he gnaws on his knuckles, he twists his handkerchief, he has the style of his role—I should say the styles of his role, for the poor man is many—beside the inner compulsions. His readings are of the essence. One of the most electrical moments in the film is his first articulation. Shortly before this moment, we have heard a servant of the Egermans saying viciously, "There's something about magicians—their faces make you mad . . . You want to smash them, tread on them! Faces like Vogler's . . .". Then we are in the Voglers' bedroom. He is lying sleepless, his back to his wife. He stirs, tries to make himself more comfortable, and he speaks, he who has never spoken before in our sight. He puts no undue pressure on the words. "I hate them. I hate their faces—(pause)—their bodies, their movements, their voices." Another pause, and a sigh. "But I'm afraid, too. . . ."

Equally resourceful at playing a part which, with an infinite number of modulations he had so often played, was Gunnar Björnstrand; and all the other supporters, Toivo Pawlo, Naima Wifstrand, Gertrud Fridh, Erland Josephson, are completely tucked into the things they are. But sometimes you pause to ask, *"Who are they?"* Granny, for instance, seemingly a stock figure of senile clairvoyance, babbling such stuff as madmen tongue and brain not: "Wound in the eye, blood in the mouth, fingers gone and neck broken, he calls you down, he calls you forth, beyond the dead, the living and the living dead . . .". She has the gift of foresight, she has an odor of the charnelhouse, she is vatic, and she is in the business. She is, within the scheme of *The Magician*, I would say, decaying religion as Spegel is decaying art. When religion decomposes it becomes mysticism and is often taken for profundity because it does, sometimes, arise from the depths; in such a state, the subject may well feel that he is an ark of revelation. "Mysticism is the most primitive of feelings and only visits formed minds in moments of intellectual arrest and dissolution."[4] Granny is thus a mixture of diabolic superstition, fakery and memories of Christian love, with which she sings the frightened Sanni to sleep:

> "Love is trust and love is rest,
> Love gives strength to the cowardly breast. . . ."

All the same, she has an eye to the self-preserving future, what for her remains; she is advancing into the age of science for she will become an apothecary. In her Vergerus will triumph. Tubal sums up her status shrewdly when he says that her tricks are old hat. "They're not fun any more; they can't be explained. Granny, you should be dead."

Tubal himself (Ake Fridell, with every mannerism in place) is the eternal sacristan who lights the candles and knows nothing of the mystery that is reenacted at the altar; the press agent who guards the personality of the artist; the film distributor who stands knowingly at the screening-room door and tells the more receptive exhibitor that "Of course you know this movie is really about the Loneliness of Modern Man"; the filmmaker who infallibly misconstrues the example of the master by translating his visions of outrage or depravity, for example, those of *The Virgin Spring* and *The Silence*, into salaciousness for its own sake. Tubal explains everything to the others but he is as little astute about his own genitalic "power" over the widow, as the others are when faced by the magician. To steal a line from another movie, he is impotent everywhere but in bed.[5]

One returns to Spegel because he is, despite the scarcity of his appearances, as central to the mood as Vogler, himself, and for this Bengt Ekerot is in no incidental way responsible; he is almost unbearably outstanding; he is in such a convincing state of disintegration that you fear for his, Ekerot's, life before the film is well under way; you swear he will break up before your eyes and that someone else will have to play the part in the later stage of the story. To be sure, Ekerot is one of the most steadfast character actors in Swedish film, so infernally subdued to the role he plays that you forget how many times you've seen him and how unalterably alterable he is.

Concerning analogies with and sources of *The Magician* the fluffier moments, when the company backstairs recapitulates the sexual manoeuvres of those above-stairs, reminded many critics of Renoir's *Rules of the Game,* an observation made also when Bergman produced *Smiles of a Summer Night.* Since, on the first occasion, he had not seen the Renoir film, I would assume that in *The Magician* he was very likely imitating himself, recognizably with those toothsome housemaids he invents. Among more distant references, Fellini's *Il Bidone* was called upon, with its squad of cheats, its theocentric morality, and the undisclosed ethical intent of the swindler played by Broderick Crawford. The mesmerizing of Antonsson and his "murder" of Vogler recalled to some the explosive killing of the hypnotist-dictator in Thomas Mann's *Mario and the Magician*; Mann is authoritatively the progenitor of a Bergman subsubject, the Janus-face of the artist. However, these are random, if interesting, attempts to locate influences of which I am personally skeptical. Closer to the predicament of Vogler is that of Pirandello's Henry IV in the play of that title, *Enrico Quarto,* forced to continue playing a role he had once assumed arbitrarily. Bergman himself told Sjöman, quoted in *L 136* that the connection between his theatre production and his films was a close one and that, for example, intimations of Pirandello in *The Magician* should not be overlooked. On this occasion he did not, however, divulge the unarguable origin of the film; I don't know on which occasion he did so.

The direct source of the situation, the main-character scheme, is obviously Gilbert K. Chesterton's *Magic,* 1913, his only play, I believe, which Bergman had staged in Gothenburg, 1947.[6] Chesterton's setting is the house of an affable, none-too-bright Duke, where the conjuror, hired to entertain the guests, finds himself pitted against characters who represent attitudes consistent with their professions: a liberal clergyman, a mundane young businessman, an agnostic. The conjurer's face is described as mask-like and he has, it follows, the disconcerting habit of making others feel unmasked. Patricia, the Duke's niece, nonetheless falls in love with him, though he tries to dissuade her from thoughts of marriage by telling her what a rough life his mother had undergone after marrying a wandering peddler. A believer in the supernatural, the Conjurer cannot explain his more lurid feats of magic. When he turns a red lamp green, the company is flabbergasted; Patricia's skeptical brother has a brainstorm. The conjurer, who is nothing if not gallant, assures Morris that there is a natural explanation, which he proceeds to contrive, but in fact he had called on devils! It begins to sound like an early-Bergman play, but my summary tells nothing of the tone, which is that of Oscar Wilde (nobody ever says anything not intended as an epigram) mated with J. B. Priestley. "It is much more marvellous to explain a miracle than to work a miracle," says the Reverend Smith, if I recall. This is a fair sample of the whimsy comprised by the play. It is romantic, too; the Conjurer wins his aristocratic bride.

You can see at a glance what Bergman was able to appropriate from this play: the general bearing of the dialectic and a few diagrammatic stand-ins for worldly reason, science, and religion. He took a cue from Chesterton, an epidermis, if we need an image to suit his eventual subject; he had to supply the vital organs, himself. Chesterton's play is all skin. Typically, his characters speak of heaven and hell without ever, you feel, having glimpsed either. He scarcely distinguishes magic, a technique, from faith, a form of comprehension, and his mouthpiece, the liberal clergyman, is far too genial for Bergman's more sanguinary purpose. "You talk of religious mania!," he chides the Doctor. "Is there so such thing as irreligious mania? . . . Why can't you leave the universe alone and let it mean what it likes?" There are times when such a question might cogently be put to Bergman, himself; if he took it to heart, however, we might not have his best movies. We should certainly not have *The Magician*. He took Chesterton's do-it-yourself paradoxes and brooded on their implications until the borrowed characters, while remaining consistent with their original labels, were warped unendurably by the pressures to which they submit each other.

Like *The Naked Night*, to which it is indebted quite as much as to any extrinsic work, and for more than its circus, *The Magician* is an acrid hyperbole: a *comedie rosse*.[7] In the former, Bergman had first, with any power, split his protagonist into the two aspects of Frost and

Albert; in the latter film, the fission is even more drastic and complex. Vogler sees not only the mirror-face of Spegel who begs, in his half-delirium, half-reminiscence, for a knife to remove his brain and heart, to cut away his tongue and his manhood; he sees also the face of Vergerus, that other colder self, ready to oblige. At the same time he is supplied with a feminine component, Manda—not very carnal, to be sure. In public he has already surrendered his powers of speech; now he delivers his body, i.e. Spegel, to the inquisitive surgery of Vergerus, in order to retain more surely what is incorruptible. The self-mutilation of the artist has seldom been pictured with such audacity and in such a spirit, that of a desperate carnival. The progressive self-division of Bergman, dating theatrically from those early primers, like *Jack Among the Actors*, here reaches a kind of climax.

When you consider the wealth of sources, his own and that of others, from which *The Magician* was shaped, the marvel remains that the film is autonomous, a period fantasia which can be enjoyed, if that isn't twisting a euphemism, for its own sake, without concerning oneself with the subterranean occupants.[8] A world of sharp shadows, I would call it, and the shadows are thrown from the beginning. With frugality of means, the brief monitory sequence in the forest—at first, silence, wind-grieved faces, spaced chords from a guitar, a bird of ill omen, a fox—casts such a spell it is hard to realize that the rest of the film takes place inside one house. The remote forest, by the way, was a clump of trees not five hundred yards from the Svensk Filmindustri lunchroom in suburban Stockholm. And the scherzo that ends the film, the coach disappearing up a ramp and a lantern swinging in the final sunlit silence, was shot outside an official building near the palace where, if Bergman had swiveled his camera forty-five degrees, he would have disclosed a view of contemporary Stockholm. This is part of what Fellini meant when, some years ago, long before meeting Bergman, he remarked to our point: "He is a conjurer—half witch and half showman. I also like his tricks, the spectacle made from nothing. . . ."[9] True, if *The Magician* is about the muffled voices of the dead and the maddening voices of those living, it is just as much about theatre, even as it calls theatre into question.

The joke on the actor is no longer a quip as it was in *Smiles of a Summer Night*, when Mrs. Armfeldt asks, "Who's coming to the party? If they're actors they must sleep in the stables," or again in *Wild Strawberries*, spoken by the same actress (Naima Wifstrand): "I think this is Benjamin's locomotive; he was always so amused by trains and circuses and such things. I suppose that's why he became an actor.

We quarreled about it often because I wanted him to have an honest profession. . . ." The joke on Vogler remains a bitter one. Vergerus is temporarily shattered. Starbeck is stunned. The artist triumphs. Yet, but for the grace of—whom?—he would have been an outcast; he would have been Spegel under a bridge, aging in brandy. The man who rides off in a coach to give a royal performance is the same who begged for a safe-conduct and groveled on the staircase for survival money. Tomorrow he may be a Messiah. Mrs. Egerman said, confidently: "You will explain why my child died. What God meant." One remembers the wealthy and licentious women of fifteenth-century Florence, spellbound by the personality, no doubt erotic, of Savonarola, making bonfires of their velvets and tossing their jewels into the Arno. Little in history changes except the icons: the priest, the political demagogue, the social engineer, the film director.

To wit, an anecdote told me by a Swedish business executive. On one of his trips to India, he was accosted by a Bengelese woman, associated in some way with an emancipation movement, who exclaimed,

"You're from Sweden! I'd love to go to Sweden—for just one purpose!"

"And what would that be?" he asked.

Tense with excitement, she answered. "I would just like to shake Ingmar Bergman's hand! *He understands our problem!*"

NOTES

1. My impression has been mainly formed by Anglo-American criticism. Europeans were far less grudging and hostile. *The Magician* took three prizes at the Venice Film Festival in 1959, which proves nothing about the merits of the film, true; but it points to a susceptible reaction. The best of all interpretations I know was written by M. Siclier. M. Siclier never forgets that he is writing about poetry.
2. To my knowledge, this point was first made by Jacques Siclier.
3. *Four Screenplays*. Introduction.
4. *Reason in Religion*. Vol. 3 of *The Life of Reason* by George Santayana. Collier Books, N.Y., 1962.
5. The line was addressed to Laurence Harvey by Julie Christie, in John Schlesinger's *Darling*, 1965.
6. The source was first called to my attention by George Simpson. Marianne Höök, in *Ingmar Bergman* (1962), also mentions the play and further suggests that a work by Hjalmar Bergman, *An Experiment*, unknown to me, has certain parallels with the situation in *Ansiktet*.

7. *Comedie rosse*—i.e., corrosive comedy, wherein virtue is unrewarded and vice unpunished. The term seems to have arisen in the nineteenth century, to describe the plays of Karl Sternheim in Germany and those of Julien Becque, for example, in France.

8. History is sometimes artistic. Royal intercession is not a myth. A famous Commedia del'Arte company, captured by Huguenots, was ransomed by the French ruler who awaited a performance at Blois. The great Molière was involved in a more abstractly gratifying rescue. Refused local burial by the Paris clergy, he was secretly interred by special request of Louis XIV.

9. See *Juliet of the Spirits*. Interview with Fellini conducted by Tullio Kezich. Orion Press, N.Y.

12

THE VIRGIN SPRING
Pro and Con

THE VIRGIN SPRING   Birgitta Steene
· ·

In *The Virgin Spring* (*Jungfrukällan*, 1960) Bergman returned once
more to the world of the Middle Ages. The basis of the script was a
thirteenth-century ballad titled "The Daughter of Töre in Vänge,"
which Bergman had read as a student at the University of Stockholm.
At first he attempted to write a play on the subject; later he tried to
shape the legendary material into a ballet. But when he finally decided
to make a film instead, he asked Ulla Isaksson to write the script. He
felt that he was unable to approach the subject matter with the stylized
detachment of the balladeer.[1] What he wanted was a direct and simple
rendering of the original. Ulla Isaksson, who like himself came from a
religious milieu, had impressed him by her ability to recreate a historical period in her novel about witchcraft trials in Sweden, *Dit du icke
vill.*

The plot: The title of Bergman's film alludes to the central event in
the old ballad: the miraculous welling forth of a healing spring on the
spot where a young virgin, the daughter of Töre in Vänge, has been
raped and killed by three goatherds on her way to church. Like the
original, the film also tells of how Töre avenges the crime by murdering the three men as they come to his farm and unwittingly try to sell
the expensive clothes of the young girl (Karin) to her mother, Märeta.
To atone for his gilt Töre then promises to build a church of limestone,
a gigantic task in thirteenth-century Sweden.

The student of folklore can easily show that the ballad of Töre's
daughter exists in many versions, both verse and prose. Although Bergman's source of inspiration refers to an actual spring in the churchyard

From *Ingmar Bergman* (New York: Twayne Publishers, 1968), pp. 89-95. Reprinted by permission of Twayne Publishers, Inc.

Max von Sydow as Herr Tore in *The Virgin Spring*.

of Kärna parish in Östergötland, which was thought to have healing powers and around which the ballad was danced and sung, the literary prototype is to be found in the Romance languages. Not until the story reached Scandinavia, however, did it become connected with a spring of water and a church building. The Christian themes of the need for reconciliation and the certainty of God's mercy were then added to the original drama of violence and revenge. The ballad which fascinated Bergman had taken on the quality of a religious miracle play.

In filming *The Virgin Spring*, Bergman seems to have had the stylized original in mind. Ulla Isaksson, on the other hand, has above all wanted to furnish motivation for the characters: "The film must in quite another manner [than that of the ballad] make the story of young Karin and her parents realistically understandable, credible as to continuity, psychology, and milieu."[2] The result is, at times, a strange hybrid of a film, in which psychological modernisms—as for instance the Freudian approach to Märeta, Karin's mother, whose religiosity has a strong sensual quality—jars with the director's ritual conception of the story. Bergman's approach does not exclude individualized portraits of the participants in the drama, but it does not permit scenes of verbalized self-consciousness. It has been suggested that in *The Virgin Spring* the spoken word is almost completely irrelevant.[3] This is not entirely true, for although the dialogue is often stilted and over-explicit (i.e., has exactly those qualities for which reviewers have most frequently criticized Bergman's own scripts), "spoken scenes" can be made part of and even support the ritual pattern when placed in the right context. While Märeta's confession of jealousy as she and her family set out to search for Karin, whom they know to be dead, seems like an obtrusive anachronism, Töre's desperate prayer at the end of the film is quite acceptable because of its direct reference to the film's central message. Besides, the speech is such that the *realization* of the promise it contains can in part be suggested in gesture:

> You see it God, you see it! The death of the innocent child and my vengeance. You permitted it. I don't understand you. I don't understand you. Still I ask you now for forgiveness—I know of no other way to *be reconciled with my own hands*. I know of no other way to live. I promise you God, here, by the dead body of my only child, I promise you that in penance for my sin *I will build you a church, I shall build it here*. Of lime and stone and *with these two hands of mine*.[4]

As Jörn Donner has observed, the speech underscores literally that Töre wants to reconcile his hands with Christianity. "He wishes to perform the penance not only of the word, but also of the deed, in order to prove his changed state of mind."[5]

The juxtaposition of good and evil, innocence and rape in the old ballad is amplified by Bergman and Ulla Isaksson to include a tension between paganism and Christianity. They present a picture of a transitional period in Scandinavia, not unlike that conveyed by Sigrid Undset in her medieval novel *Kristin Lavransdaughter*, a world in which Christianity "has not yet moved into people's understanding but . . . already involves rituals and submissions which are accepted."[6] At the same time, powerful remnants of the old heathen beliefs are still at work in the film, especially in the characters who exist outside a community of love and fellowship: in Ingeri, Karin's foster-sister who, pregnant and unmarried, is a mistrusted outcast; in the two goatherds who rape Karin; in the lonely bridge keeper who practices secret rites deep in the woods.

The portrait of Ingeri is an addition to the original. The film opens on a long, slow shot showing the dark-haired girl as she presses her belly against a post in the large manor hall at Töre's place and invokes the pagan god Odin. It is in keeping with the film's ambivalent ap-

218

proach that Ingeri is conceived as both a primitive folklore archetype, the evil stepsister in touch with superstition and black magic, and as a victim of sibling rivalry and social injustice. Jealous of her fair-haired foster sister, who is treated like a princess, and following a sudden impulse, Ingeri puts a toad into a large piece of bread which is to be part of Karin's food sack for her ride to church. Ingeri desires to be Karin's equal. She cannot rise; hence, she must wish Karin to fall, to be violated as she herself has been. The toad she puts into the bread is an ancient symbol of sexuality ("the toads jump in the springtime") and of evil ("When food is turned into frogs and toads, the Devil is frisking around").[7]

Accompanying Karin on her ride to church, Ingeri leaves her foster sister at the edge of the woods to enter the bridge keeper's shack. Although fearful of the old man's fey qualities, she nevertheless becomes associated with them: moments later when she flees in panic into the woods, she is so spellbound by evil wishes that she fails to intervene in the goatherds' violation of Karin, which she watches, hidden behind some bushes with a large stone in her hand. Yet, Ingeri is not the epitome of evil, for she is haunted by guilt. In the end, she is thus prepared to receive absolution at the virgin spring.

Ingeri is indeed a contrast to Karin, who, when we first meet her, lies in bed reveling in the memory of her success on the dance floor the night before. Contrary to the old ballad, Karin is presented in the film as both vain and capricious. In the original she is given the standard ballad epithet "stolts" (noble and proud), but this as well as the enumeration of her pieces of clothing (her skirt being "the work of fifteen young maids") serves to indicate her privileged status rather than her vanity. Nor is there any trace in the original of the unconscious cruelty with which Karin hurts her mother in giving all her affection to her father or kindles Ingeri's hatred by flirting with a man who is probably the cause of her foster sister's pregnancy.

Throughout the first half of the film, Ingeri's dark experiences bring Karin's sexual innocence and her upper-class position into sharper relief. The difference between the two sisters obtains an immediate visual impact during their ride to church.[8] Karin rides delicately side-saddle, beautifully dressed; Ingeri in tattered clothes slumps astride an old mare. The contrast between beauty and ugliness is reinforced as the two girls approach the woods, where lyrical shots of nature frame the sun-worshiping face of Karin and are set off against the darkness that envelops Ingeri as she enters the bridge keeper's shack. The landscape itself partakes of the same ambiguity; it contains a magic beauty and an equally magic evil; sweet birds caw and loathsome toads boggle in enormous close-ups. In this sylvan landscape hideous, yet Pan-like goatherds lie in wait for the young virgin. Hungrily they invite her to a woodland picnic, and we see "beauty and monsters side by side, beauty too rarefied for reality, ugliness too violent for normality."[9]

The rape and murder scene was cut in part for the release of the film in the United States. In Sweden it created an intense debate. The sequence has a far more immediate emotional impact than the lines in the original ballad in which the crime is described:

> First she was three herdsmen's wife
> Then she gave up her young life.
>
> They took her by the golden lock,
> and placed her 'gainst a birchtree stock.
>
> They severed then her lovely head—
> A spring welled up upon that stead.

But as Bengt Idestam-Almquist (Robin Hood) has remarked, the film could have made Karin's death even more gory, had it followed the details given in the last two stanzas above.[10] It was perhaps this part of the legend that Ulla Isaksson had in mind when she argued that it was not possible "to reproduce with entire realism the . . . attitudes of such a distant time, and expect modern men to understand them."[11]

Karin's death brings the first half of the film to an end. The rest of the picture is Töre's and deals with his revenge. The camera moves first to Töre's manor hall. The three goatherds come and ask for lodging for the night. In the ballad they are conceived as an abstract group; in the film they are individualized: one of them is extremely lean and talkative; another is tongueless and inarticulate; the third is a teen-age boy. The aim of this characterization was, according to Ulla Isaksson, to create pathos around the murderers and make us regard them with ambivalent feelings: "The three criminals are not totally evil. On the whole we emphasize that the spectators have pity for all people in this film."[12]

The goatherds are invited to share a meal with the family. Töre presides over the supper and the entire sequence has the ceremonial buildup of an altar painting of Christ's last supper. None of the people in the household knows anything of Karin's fate. Of the goatherds only the young boy realizes that they have come to the home of the violated girl; he recognizes Töre's prayer as the same that Karin had said at the meal in the woods. Remembering the crime, the boy begins to vomit but is subdued into silence by his older companions. Later, during the night, one of them tries to sell Karin's cape to Mä-reta, who, controlling her sorrow, goes to inform Töre. His revenge is ruthless; it is preceded by a ritual during which he pulls down a birch sapling for his steam bath, a scene that is almost a parody of rape although, isolated, it is beautiful in its visual richness.[13]

As the morning sun penetrates through the opening in the roof, Töre sits at the table waiting with a slaughtering knife to kill the murderers. His code of behavior is stark and violent: an eye for an eye, a tooth for a tooth. Cinematically, the scene is balanced against the rape scene: in both cases a largely static camera registers the movements of murderers and victims. In neither sequence is the spectator spared the cruel details. To make Töre's crime fully as evil as the violation of his daughter, Bergman has Töre kill also the one goatherd who is innocent, the young boy.

After the vengeance the entire household goes to find Karin. Up until then Töre has struck us as a man of primitive emotions. Now, however, he is called upon to display Christian repentance. Marianne Höök finds Töre's reaction before his daughter's ravaged body to be rather unbelievable: "Had a new fury welled up in him, or an uncontrollable sorrow, one would have been convinced. But it is psychologically preposterous that he should fall down and thank God at such a moment."[14] It is debatable, however, whether Töre is not so stylized a character as to make realistic criteria meaningless in judging him. More puzzling to the spectator is perhaps the philosophical ambiguity that Töre displays: he prays to God but doubts his goodness; he confesses his inability to understand a divine being who permits such cruelty as rape and murder, but he promises to build him a church.

The film ends with Töre's prayer and the miraculous appearance of the virgin spring (unfortunately accompanied by symbolic hymn singing). The ending constitutes Bergman's most radical departure from the original. The ballad falls into four parts: 1) Karin's preparation for the journey; 2) her rape, murder, and burial, and the miraculous appearance of a spring on the spot where her head was chopped off; 3) the arrival and murder of the three goatherds at Töre's place; 4) Töre's atonement.

It is inevitable that Bergman's transposition of the miracle to the end of the story, and placing it *after* Töre's promise to God, takes on the quality of a bargain. According to Ulla Isaksson the final scene is "Lutheran" (although it is a cornerstone in Luther's teachings that we cannot point to our deeds and ask for grace):

The final words of the film imply that we are not able, by our own power, to live our lives as human beings. The last scene when Töre kneels down and asks forgiveness, occurs because forgiveness is the only possibility. It is also of great importance that the spring wells forth when all need it. In that sense the film is very Lutheran. That this possibility exists is the very meaning of the film.[15]

But contained in the transplantation of the miracle to the end of the film lies not only a theological question but a broader, religious difference between a universe conceived in terms of total faith, and one of subtle meanings and symbolic justice. "In the film, the spring comes as a poetic apotheosis and an emblem of goodness; in the ballad it is simply there; God is not only someone who answers when called upon; he works full time."[16]

Bergman himself has indicated that the welling up of the spring was not meant as simply "the tidy expression of a religious miracle." He considered the scene a cathartic necessity: "I didn't see how it was possible to allow the picture to end without the spring, for if the father had merely gone home, and there had been a great silence, there would have been no release for the feelings of the people of the story, nor for those of the audience."[17]

In *The Virgin Spring* setting and milieu are captured with great photographic beauty and subtlety. Yet, the approach to the story is direct and simple. In crucial scenes the camera suggests no symbolic level of response. It is a recorder rather than an interpreter and it is often quite still in a way that suggests an earlier film art. The inflexible position of the camera creates a mood of cruel spectatorship, and it is likely that the rape and murder scenes shock our sensibilities, not because of Bergman's "conscious dwelling" upon them,[18] but because his static technique pinpoints our own position as passive observers: we are locked in a visual display of horror. At the same time, however, we sense the director's distance from the subject matter. Bergman approaches the story with an objectivity and a subordination of personal feelings that he usually reserves for his stage productions. *The Virgin Spring* is, in fact, closer in cinematic style to the earlier Bergman-Isaksson film *Brink of Life* than to *The Seventh Seal*, even though the former film is set in our time and the action of the latter takes place in the Middle Ages.

NOTES

1. Marianne Höök, *Ingmar Bergman* (1962), p. 146.
2. Ulla Isaksson, *The Virgin Spring* (New York: Ballantine Books, 1960), p. vi.
3. Cf. Jörn Donner, *The Personal Vision of Ingmar Bergman*, p. 189.
4. Italics mine.
5. Jörn Donner, *The Personal Vision of Ingmar Bergman*, p. 189.
6. Colin Young, "The Virgin Spring," *The Art Film*, 1961, n.p.
7. Quoted in Donner, *The Personal Vision of Ingmar Bergman*, p. 193.
8. Peter Cowie, *Antonioni, Bergman, Resnais*, p. 98.
9. Isabel Quigly, "The Light that Never Was," *Spectator*, June 9, 1961, p. 839.
10. Robin Hood, "Jungfrukällan främst regikonst," *Stockholms-Tidningen*, February 9, 1960.
11. Ulla Isaksson, *The Virgin Spring*, p. vi.
12. Quoted in Sven Stolpe, "Jungfrukälan än en gång," *Aftonbladet*, February 26, 1960.
13. In his review of the film, Bengt Idestam-Almquist suggests that in this sequence Töre frees himself of his own lust for Karin. Robin Hood, "Jungfrukällan främstregikonst," *Stockholms-Tidningen*, February 9, 1960.
14. Marianne Höök, *Ingmar Bergman*, p. 151.
15. Quoted in Sven Stolpe, "Jungfrukällan än en gång," *Aftonbladet*, February 26, 1960.
16. William S. Pechter, "The Ballad and the Source," *The Kenyon Review*, XXIII (Spring 1961), p. 334.
17. Statement quoted in Hollis Alpert, "Style is the Director," *The Saturday Review of Literature*, December 23, 1961, p. 40.
18. Norman S. Holland, "Bergman Springs Again," *The Hudson Review*, XIV (Spring 1961), p. 110.

THE VIRGIN SPRING   Stanley Kauffmann
. . . .

A failure by Ingmar Bergman is always welcome. All of his pictures seen here have been to some degree failures, yet almost all have contrib-

From *A World on Film* (New York: Harper & Row), pp. 277-79. © 1960 by Stanley Kauffmann. Reprinted by permission of Harper & Row, Publishers, Inc., and Brandt & Brandt.

uted to his deserved reputation as one of the most stimulating of contemporary film-makers. Even his best work to date, *Wild Strawberries*,
leaves much unresolved in symbol and theme, but so much of it is so
beautiful that no viewer can be ungrateful for its existence. When
Bergman fails, he does it at a level quite beyond most directors' suc-
cesses.

He has failed again in *The Virgin Spring*, rather more seriously than
in *Wild Strawberries* or *The Magician*. But he has once more hurled
himself against towering questions; and again he has created a film of
extraordinary minute-by-minute texture. It is neither paradoxical nor
perverse to add that the film is sometimes tedious, occasionally senten-
tious, and architecturally flawed. Those are some of Bergman's hallmarks.

With a screenplay by Ulla Isaksson, who collaborated on *Brink of
Life*, Bergman here retells a fourteenth century Swedish legend about
an innocent girl, traveling through the forest on her way to church,
who is raped and murdered; when her body is later lifted from the
ground by her grieving parents, a spring of fresh water starts from the
spot. Into this legend Bergman has woven the conflict of stubborn
paganism fighting the revealed truth; the girl's jealous pregnant maid-
servant invokes Odin's curse on her, which is seemingly fulfilled. Bergman demonstrates, too, the inseparability of light and shadow, good
and evil. The innocent victim is a spoiled and vain girl. The young
brother of the two rapists, who watches their actions dumfoundedly
and is sickened, is vindictively slain along with them. The girl's father,
who kills the trio when he discovers their guilt, is struck immediately
with the inutility of his act and vows to build a church on the murder
site in repentance. And the spring flows from the ground at the end
as if to certify that God has witnessed all and that the contradictions
have all taken place within his knowledge.

Max von Sydow, the stalwart of so many Bergman pictures, is stately
as the father, Birgitta Valberg appropriately troubled as the mother.
Birgitta Petterson has the right pettish, round-cheeked prettiness for
the daughter, and Gunnel Lindblom smolders with saturnine, sensual
hate as the maid. The two murderers, Axel Düberg and Tor Isedal, are
credibly cruel, therefore frightening. Bergman has helped Ove Porath,
as their younger brother, to give a moving little performance.

As might be expected, the sense of medieval life is excellently maintained. For a split second or two, you can find a portion of your mind
asking: "How in the world could a camera have been present?" The
scenes of violence are superbly done. (An interesting comparison might

be made between the rape-murder here and the bathtub murder in *Psycho*. Bergman horrifies us at the act; Hitchcock horrifies us at himself—his cynically adroit exploitation of the act.)

But the bulk of the picture is a religious-moral charade. It is like looking at a series of scenes of a large medieval tapestry, each well composed, each representing a station on the way to the point of the parable, all of it (except for the visceral moments of sex and blood) rarefied and abstract. We are left with the sense that a lesson has been spelled out—in huge, cloudy symbols of a high romance with God.

Intrinsically, too, there are faults. The frog which the maid encloses in a loaf of bread is either too obvious a symbol of the persistence of hate or too obscure a symbol of persistent paganism to be effective. The maid's encounter with the bridge-keeper seems irrelevant. The silence of the maid about the daughter's fate is unexplained. If she feared what the father would do to her, why did she return? If she returned, why didn't she speak? The vengeance scene is so long that it verges on the ridiculous. The father and mother enter the murderers' chamber, fasten locks, take bags from one man's arms, slam a knife into a table, yet the sleepers never stir. Then the father wakes them and has to kill them separately. Theatrically and otherwise, it is an irrational scene.

Still the film is valuable because of its concerns. In the introduction to his recently published screenplays, Bergman, the son of a Lutheran minister, says, "My father and mother were certainly of vital importance not only in themselves but because they created a world for me to revolt against." Subsequently he says, "Regardless of my own beliefs and my own doubts, which are unimportant in this connection, it is my opinion that art lost its basic creative drive the moment it was separated from worship." Apropos of the rebuilding of Chartres Cathedral and a figurative contemporary parallel, he says, "Regardless of whether I believe or not, whether I am a Christian or not, I would play my part in the collective building of the cathedral." These quotations support a view of Bergman as a Protestant's Protestant, rebelling that he may love, attempting (particularly in this new film) to shear away modern preoccupation with good deeds in the hope that he may find again the pure strength of Luther's "justification by faith"—salvation by belief alone. He is a kind of cinema Kierkegaard, who sees everyone trying to make life easier and has set out to do what he can to make it harder.

The hazard, which he has by no means escaped, is that his films have become essentially arenas of spiritual wrestling for the author through his characters, rather than disciplined artistic experiences whose prime purpose is emotional involvement of the audience. Even for the most serious viewer, the final result—in this new film as in others—must be called a failure in relation to the totality of its existence as art work; but it is a failure that serious film-goers will not want to miss.

13

WINTER LIGHT
Symbolism and Preparation of a Concept

HOW WARM IS THE COLD, HOW LIGHT THE DARKNESS?
Robert H. Adams

. . . .

What do Ingmar Bergman's "cold" films—*Through a Glass Darkly, Winter Light* and *The Silence*—mean? Are they just a terrifying diagnosis, or are they something more?

Treatment afforded *Winter Light* by Britain's film journal *Sight and Sound* is typical of the secular film enthusiasts' response; refusing to give the movie a full review, it observed tersely that "Bergman has little to say" (Summer 1963). Arthur Schlesinger, Jr., writing for a wider audience in *Show* (July 1963), noted of the same film, "I must confess my bafflement as to the point Bergman is trying to make."

More disturbing, reviewers for *The Christian Century* have said little more. "Bergman's vision of the divine [in *Through a Glass Darkly*] leaves us in doubt" (Oct. 3, 1962). "The meaning is ambiguous [in *Winter Light*]" (Nov. 20, 1963). Bergman "describes with admirable and vivid clarity [in *The Silence* and the trilogy as a whole], but we search in vain . . . for prescription" (July 8, 1964).

If one is to go beyond these meager conclusions—and I believe the films demand it—one must first abandon what appear to have been inadequate methods of analysis. Specifically, pieces must be put in context. A character and what he says must be considered in terms of the entire film. And with each successive film it becomes clearer that all three must be viewed as a whole; Bergman published the works as a unit (in Swedish) and designated them a trilogy, certain elements have appeared in more than one film (e.g., uses of music by Bach, ref-

From *The Christian Century*, Vol. 81, No. 38, pp. 1144-45. Copyright 1964 by Christian Century Foundation. Reprinted by permission of the Sept. 16, 1964 issue of *The Christian Century*.

erences to God as a spider) and characters have reappeared again and again (the person loved but unable to love in return—Karin, Tomas, Anna; the person capable of some commitment but doomed to find it unreturned—Martin, Märta, Ester; and the innocent who is destroyed by others—Minus, Jonas, Johan).

Finally, we must *look at* as well as listen to the films. Many have complained that Bergman has stripped his cinematic style so bare that he has ended with stage plays. This is just not so. Important parts of the stories are told through the medium of the selective and analyzing eye of the camera.

Put simply, the so-called cold films of Bergman are, I believe, filled with both light and warmth. Each is concerned with the transforming insight experienced by King Lear on the heath (a place of desolate and chilling blackness): the discovery that man must "show the heavens more just."

Through a Glass Darkly appeared first and is crucial in that it gives us the terms of the trilogy. For this reason it is particularly unfortunate that it was widely misinterpreted. The prevalent reaction, expressed in *The Christian Century*, the *Hudson Review* and elsewhere, was to object to the film as a sentimentally positive statement made in a non-dramatic and hence unconvincing manner. The father, David, says "God is love" at the end of the film and this, the reviews maintained, is hardly what is demonstrated by the film. The daughter, Karin, has found God a spider. Because the father's orthodox pronouncement comes at the close of the story, however, many critics took it to be Bergman's message.

That such an interpretation was hasty became embarrassingly clear in *Winter Light* when, at the end of that film, Bergman apparently mocks remarks such as David's when he has a church organist tell Märta, "God is love. Love is God. Love proves God's existence. . . . Tripe."

Clearly, what was neglected by critics of *Through a Glass Darkly* was the composite dramatic statement. In terms of the entire film, God *can* be love (David finally shows an interest in and concern for his son, Minus, and the movie closes with the son's joyous and multi-level line "Father spoke to me"), or God can be ugly, inhuman and spider-like (it appears that David also created this God as he neglected his daughter and contributed to her mental illness). The fact is that man has a certain freedom to define immanent God for others. Apparently sensing this, the son remarks at the close, "Anything can happen now, Father. Anything." However, this statement, like all the others in the film, must be put in context. In this case, the context includes Karin's husband, Martin, who loves her (in a humanly imperfect way, though genuinely) but can do nothing to help her. As she indicates to him, she simply does not love him in return.

As the title would suggest, then, no one person isolates the full truth of his situation in *Through a Glass Darkly*. The total artistic statement, however, is clear: man is free, within severe limits that are not always explicable, to construe God for others as love or indifference or worse.

Winter Light, though commercially unsuccessful, seems to me the strongest of the three films. Directly related to its predecessor, it is again a story of the way God is destroyed. The opening scene takes place in a church. Tomas Ericsson, the pastor, prays, ". . . Thy will be done on earth as it is in heaven . . . ," and the camera shifts to a series of exterior scenes in snow and cold. This is the condition "on earth"; this is the climate of the human heart. In the same opening sequence other symbols that indict are suggested. One of the first views of the congregation is of a figure coughing, and in the course of the story we learn that Tomas and others are sick. There is something in man that is diseased. The service concludes with the snap of a lady's purse. Shortly afterward there is another close-up, this time of a few coins being shaken from a collection bag, with the cross in the background. For Tomas the church is a business, and a rather unfortunate one.

Bergman's depiction of the bad priest—the weakling shepherd—is thorough and pointed. Here the man who professes to serve as Christ served turns away the cripple (when the sexton first tries to speak to Tomas, the pastor cuts him off with a "Yes, yes") and cannot reach the fisherman Jonas (he tells the despairing man, "If God does not exist, what does it matter?"). After brutally sending the fisherman to his death he repeats with horrible irony lines that Christ spoke as he gave himself sacrificially: "God, why hast thou forsaken me?" Later he attends the fisherman's corpse with more diligence than he had his spirit (he stays with it, by the thunderous silence of the river rapids, as the police bring a truck).

Tomas emerges as the man who defines love not after I Corinthians but as devotion to what is attractive. Love does not include commitment beyond condition. Märta describes their past: "[My] sores disgusted you. . . . I understand you now. . . . The disease broke out

on my hands and feet and that was the end of our affair." In a sense
Tomas' moral size is measured when, trying to stop his harsh tirade
against her, she says to him through tears, "I can't see you without my
glasses."

In this film too, when the spirit of a man responsible to others de-
cays, he takes away the faith of those others. The fisherman's wife
had watched the pastor's first limp attempts to reconcile her husband,
and had withdrawn in the belief he might do more with her gone.
When Tomas reports to her that her husband has killed himself, the
conversation is brief. Mrs. Persson: "I'm alone then." Tomas: "Shall
we pray?" Mrs. Persson: "No."

As in *Through a Class Darkly*, sentimentality is eschewed. Freedom
is limited (Tomas acts this out symbolically and in a way that suggests
Providence when, after abandoning Jonas, he asserts "I'm free," only
to cough so severely that he sinks until his head touches the floor before the cross). Märta, like Martin, finds that her love can change
nothing. When Tomas mocks her by asking if he is to learn to love
from her, she replies in defeat, "That is beyond my power." We learn
later of her prayer: "God—you don't put my strength to any use."

In *Winter Light* there is no positive example of conversion such as
Minus constitutes in the prior film. But for the person who will *watch*
the closing sequence, there can be no doubt where Bergman places his
hope. The church, the sanctuary of which is faced with angels rather
than a crucifix as in the first building, is readied. The sexton, who has
demonstrated a profound understanding of the suffering involved in
the crucifixion (suffering most closely approximated by Märta's),
smiles affirmatively as Tomas tells him the service will be held despite
the fact that there are only four of them. In the back pews the organist
tells Märta she should leave Tomas, but she refuses to listen. Then, in
one of the most indescribably beautiful close-ups that Bergman's camera has ever recorded, the scene moves to Märta's face against the back
lighting of a window. The ugly glasses are taken off and her eyes, which
have appeared swollen and bleary at other times, are clear. The artist
could not have made a stronger visual statement of faith.

The Silence concludes the trilogy—a trilogy begun with an examination
of the nature and obligations of human freedom, continued with a
story about a man's failure to use that freedom, and finished with a
depiction of the hell to which such a failure leads. We have moved
from a kind of simple and Edenic island to the complex sounds and
rubble of urban Europe. *The Silence* is, however, the simplest of the

three works because its terms are so nearly absolute (as much so as the gray and relative natures of credible characters allow.) The final statement is the same; parents are not conducting themselves as parents. The boy in the film is orphaned out into the surrealistic corridors of the hotel where he, his mother and his aunt are staying. He has no earthly father present and, fittingly, the film makes almost no mention of God. The Father is silent because fathers are absent.

This last film suggests, perhaps more than the others, that basic to any examination of the trilogy is a recognition of the importance and validity of negative witness. It could be argued, I suppose, that the center of Dante's hell is the murkiest and most frigid dead end in the history of man's imagination. But of course it is this dead end that points Dante and centuries of readers toward light and warmth. Bergman's trilogy is itself concerned extensively with the components of despair: darkness, cold, silence. But the subtitle that Bergman appends to the Swedish script for *The Silence—The Photographic Negative—*is apt in relation to all three films. As any photographer knows, a negative cannot be made without light, and once it is made, a carefully measured amount of light must pass through it to produce a positive image.

FROM L 136: A DIARY OF INGMAR BERGMAN'S *WINTER LIGHT*   Vilgot Sjoman

MAY 1961: What is it about? He doesn't say, except to talk about his uneasiness:

"Imagine how it feels: I am going to make a new film this fall, and I still haven't written a line of it. The whole thing exists only in my head."

From *The Literary Review*, Vol. 9, No. 2 (Winter 1965-66), published by Fairleigh Dickinson University, Rutherford, N.J. Reprinted by permission of *The Literary Review* and the author. The article also appeared in *Cinema Journal* (Spring 1974).

These excerpts from *L-136* are a drastic condensation representing the process of Bergman's mind as *Winter Light* took shape, not merely in its own right but as a stage between *Through a Glass Darkly* and *The Silence*. *L-136* is rich in many other things including the technical details of rehearsal, set construction, camera work, cutting, and so on.

Ingrid Thulin as Marta Lundberg, and Gunnar Björnstrand as Thomas Ericsson in *Winter Light*.

The only things he reveals is that it will constitute the final step in a trilogy: *The Virgin Spring, Through a Glass Darkly*, plus the new one.**

Therefore it ought to have a religious theme.

WEDNESDAY, 14 JUNE: Bergman discusses the idea for the new film:

"A minister shuts himself up in his church. And says to God: I will wait here now until you reveal yourself. Take as much time as you want. I am not going away until you have revealed yourself."

And so the minister waits, day after day, week after week. That was the original idea for the new film, he says.

"Then I awoke one morning—well, you know that state when one wakes up and has dreamt something. Then I felt that the minister's

---

** He likes to work with the trilogy plan. Later, he advances the trilogy forward one step: the first hurdle drops, when a new one appears. By the time we do the TV interview on Torö on 12 August 1961, *The Virgin Spring* has been left out. Now *Through a Glass Darkly* is the first part of the trilogy. [All footnotes Sjöman's.]

waiting needn't continue as long as I had first thought. Just as much can happen in one and one-half hours—the actual running time of the film.

"So now I am beginning, straight away, by depicting a communion service. Only six communicants—one of them is the minister's wife. After the service, the pastor remains behind in the church. He is waiting for a man who is to appear at a specified time. The man doesn't come because he has hanged himself."

He adds that this film is a chamber play, with a small cast: the minister, his wife, a few more. "The chamber play has been neglected by the films."†

He is going to depict the whole empty, dead, hollow routine of the communion.

"How will you handle it?"

"Oh, one need only go out to a country church in Uppland and show everything exactly as it is. I have gone around for several Sundays now and looked."

"With Käbi? [his wife]

"No, with my father." [The Reverend Erik Bergman]

"Do you discuss the ideas for your films with him?"

"No, never. But he helps me with the practical details of portrayal."

Bergman doesn't tell enough for me to get any concept of the film. And I blanch at the prospect of having to see yet another movie priest who staggers beneath the weight of doubt. How many similar cases has one suffered through? Is Ingmar really capable of reinvigorating this theme? Then he adds something that really makes me prick up my ears.

"You see: this minister has a hatred for Christ that he doesn't want to admit to anyone. He is envious of Christ."

"Envious?"

"Yes, and jealous. He feels somewhat the same hatred that the son who remains at home felt toward the Prodigal Son, the one who gets all the attention when he finally comes home: the fatted calf, etc. I

† I don't know when Bergman began to cultivate the term "chamber play," but ever since he discovered that the film lent itself so well to what Strindberg called "the intimate experience," "the powerfully significant motif," he has been one of the energetic successors to the Strindbergian chamber-play tradition. But it isn't easy to define the "chamber play." Strindberg himself had his difficulties (see "Open Letters to the Intimate Theatre"), and Bergman can refer to films as structurally different as *Wild Strawberries* and *Through a Glass Darkly* as chamber plays.

simply thought of confessing my own envy and jealousy of the Christ figure."

"Envy of Christ"—that awakens thoughts of Bergman's childhood. How is it to be a little child in a parsonage where the father leaves home every Sunday to devote himself to some other completely strange person named Jesus Christ?

A pastor who is envious of Christ: a fascinating theme. And original, in a literary sense. I should guess that it has never been treated before.

"Only it's hard to give it form. But, of course, one only has to project what one finds in oneself—as candidly as one can."

He continues with some remarks on how long a time it has taken him to become at all interested in the figure of Christ. And it certainly shows in his films: as soon as he took up a religious theme, it was the God motif. Is he now going to penetrate into the Christ motif for the first time?

"—because then, when the pastor paces back and forth in the church waiting for the man who doesn't come, then he experiences, for the first time, how it must have been for Christ when he felt himself forsaken on the Cross. It wasn't just that Judas betrayed him and that the disciples fell asleep at Gethsemane. Even God forsook him when he hung on the Cross—"

THURSDAY, 10 JULY 1901

Last Thursday, the minister's wife was still alive. Now she is dead.

"I woke up one morning and killed her. It felt wonderful. And right." He laughs heartily as he tells about it.

"The wife was to have had a significant role, actually. But I couldn't write her. It never went well with her when I began to write."

"Now the pastor has got a mistress instead. An hysterical, lonely, middle-aged, flat-chested country schoolteacher. So now things are moving."

The new film has a name now: *The Guests of the Lord's Supper* [the literal title]. I like it. It has the ring of high Swedish tradition, all the way back to Tegnér's *The Children of the Lord's Supper* . . . Obviously Ingmar has come fairly far along in the writing, for he dares to talk about some of it.

"It is a companion-piece to *Through a Glass Darkly*. An answer to it. When I wrote *Through a Glass Darkly*, I thought I had found a real proof of God's existence: God is love. All kinds of love are God, even perverted forms—and that proof of God's existence gave me great security . . ."

Great security. Those were his exact words.

"—and I let the whole film work itself out in that proof of God, which formed (he uses a musical term) the actual coda in the last movement. But I lost confidence in the idea even as I began to rehearse the film."

"Therefore I destroy that proof of God in this new film. A settling of accounts, in a way. I do away with God the Papa, the God of auto-suggestion, the security God."

Bergman is obviously accustomed to dividing up a text into pedagogically clear sections to get perspective and order. He divides the new film into three parts:

1. THE DESTRUCTION THEME OF THE CODA. Settling of accounts with the God of auto-suggestion. "Difficult to write that part?" "Not so hard."

2. EMPTINESS AFTER THE DESTRUCTION. "Not so difficult to write either."

3. THE FLOWERING OF A NEW BELIEF."That's the most difficult part to write. I think I've found a solution. Have you heard of 'duplication'? Certain Sundays the pastor has two services to perform: the one in the parish church and then one for a mission congregation. Now there is a practice in the Swedish church which says that no service need be held when there are three persons in the church. This is what I do: When Gunnar Björnstrand arrives at the mission church the warden comes forward toward him and says: 'Only one person is here for the service.' Nevertheless, the pastor conducts the service. Nothing more is needed to indicate the new feeling which moves inside the pastor."

The film's opening gives Ingmar, the preacher's son—moralist, a qualm of conscience. He searches himself wondering if it's only a "gimmick," and an "arty gimmick" at that, to open the film with the entire communion service. In such case, he ought resolutely to refrain from it!

"The more I mull over the thing, the more certain it seems that I'm not indulging in an arty device."

Sometimes Bergman has an absolutely Asiatic look. Then his eyes and lips gleam and he looks down upon his co-workers from a height, conscious of his position and his psychological power. A smile like that of some Indian icon. The sharp canine teeth. The dark-green copper nuances of his complexion.

Other times he is helplessly solemn, pleading like a child: his defenses down, all his sensitivity exposed. So it is when he talks about religion; his face is softened by gravity and tension. I note traces of torment and the need for candor.

Those times in the past when we have touched upon religion, we beat around the bush. Today, too, I am on the defensive, encircled by my naturalism. Ingmar scents it and tries to create contact between us by telling how he experiences a distinction between "conviction" and "knowledge":

"I have the same 'conviction' as you, if you see what I mean."

" 'Conviction' is naturalistic: has nothing to do with the supernatural."*

"But I have a 'knowledge' which says just the opposite. Knowledge which is at the same time both distinct and elusive."

" 'Knowledge' says that God exists."

"You understand: I believe that one can cut himself off from God. Or one can say yes, I really believe that." (How many times he has returned to that theme. Now this pastor who cuts himself off from God and love—in the form of a woman, typically enough.)

"And intercession: I am convinced that it is a reality."

WEDNESDAY, 9 AUGUST 1961

Yes, just as I feared. The Christ-envy is gone. At any rate, the theme remains quite undeveloped. It appears in only two speeches now: the first by the pastor, the second time by the schoolteacher.

Why has it been cut so much?

So far as the coda is concerned, I think that the trip to Frostnäs church should embody a choice for Tomas—so that one gets the point that something has really happened inside of him. As it stands now, one doesn't really notice "the flowering of a new belief." Here is a possibility of choice, a dramatic turning point which Ingmar hasn't brought out.

* The naturalistic perspective exists in Tomas' speech to the fisherman in the completed film: "If God doesn't exist, what difference does that make? Life becomes understandable. What a relief. Death becomes an extinction, a dissolution of body and soul." Etc.

THURSDAY, 10 AUGUST 1961 [Four hours of mangling the manuscript. Sjöman and Bergman discuss in detail various points of disagreement in the manuscript.]

"Why have you cut the envy-of-Christ theme?"

"Because it doesn't belong here, not in *this* film. It belongs in the next film. You know that every subject has its specific gravity. All this business of Christ-envy is too much to settle this time; I felt absolutely that I had to save it until the next time. This film is simpler than that. I have had to begin at the beginning again, with a restoration of the God image."

"When Tomas meets the fisherman the first time and later when he meets Märta—I don't know how, but I think there's still a little too much of yourself in those lines. In *Through a Glass Darkly* you succeed in objectifying yourself much better . . ." (Shake of the head.)

"There is much less of myself in the figure of Tomas than you think. I have actually only one thing in common with Tomas: this weeding out of an old image of God and the glimmer of a new image—much more difficult to grasp, explain, and describe . . ."

God himself is a safe, fatherly God, "who loved mankind, to be sure, but who loved me most of all" (says Tomas to the fisherman). "Father talked to me," says the boy at the end of *Through a Glass Darkly* —with an undertone of: "God talked to me." One ought to look more closely at all of the associations of "father" with "God" in these films, for Ingmar has made them intentionally.

Why has Bergman never (before) been interested in Christ? A quick theory: because his religious-emotional world has been poisoned (supersaturated) with the association "father"—"God."

"More objections?"

"The end. One never feels 'the flowering of a new belief' in Tomas. He just goes in and does the service . . ."

"Exactly. He is the packmule that plods on. Much too weak to be of any use in God's work. God can't instill any strength in him—but in Märta, quite the contrary! It is Märta who takes over the struggle for faith in the end, don't you see?"

11 AUGUST 1961 [Bergman discusses his marriage to Käbi, how the romantic relationship gave way to a more concrete and real relationship.]

"That first romantic time, *that* corresponds to Tomas' marriage in the film."

Through a Glass Darkly was conceived during that first romantic phase—and became the only one of his films to bear the dedication: "To Käbi, my wife." Therefore this mysticism in the final coda: Love exists. Love is real. Love is God. A mysticism which (I suppose) absorbed the difficulties, cruelties, conflicts in life in a much too simple way—that's why it had to be contradicted and shattered, in anticipation of a greater concept of God. The beautiful Karin-mysticism in *Through a Glass Darkly* had to be succeeded by the stern Märta-Lundberg-demand in *Winter Light*.

MONDAY, 2 OCTOBER 1961 [Bergman explains Thomas' hatred of Christ.]

"In a strange way, the hatred of Christ and a father-and-son relationship between Tomas Ericsson and his self-fashioned God are integral parts of this concept of God, so that there is no room for Christ. He has simply not studied the Evangelists very closely, a fact which Algot Frövik teaches him in a terrible way at the end."

"Does Tomas become in some way converted through Algot Frövik?" asks Allan [Allan Edwall plays Algot Frövik in the film.]

"Yes. No. Not so much. Now we have to dig into the character of Märta Lundberg, because Tomas Ericsson is already destroyed when the film begins. He is an industrious and proper person—he even writes his own sermons. Märta's case is like this: the passion is played out in her, in a double sense. Märta is a nonbeliever. She has a good and happy environment from the beginning. She is shy. They find each other, Tomas and she—that's how I've envisioned it all—because they are both so bored."

[The fisherman's visit to the pastor is discussed.]

"Isn't this a dream episode?" asks Gunnar Björnstrand.

"I'll tell you truthfully," answers Ingmar. "When I wrote this, I thought that no one could speak this openly except in a dream. I don't know if it has happened to you, but it has very often happened to me that if I have a very hard task ahead of me—something very pressing, psychologically—I can wake up in a terrible anxiety and then I can suddenly fall asleep again. And then I am in the midst of this task and tackle it in an emotional way, in terrible nakedness and pain; you know, utilize all my strength. And then I waken, tired unto death and taut in every limb. I have something like that in mind. We both ought to be able to imagine something like this: we won't have a bit of dream atmosphere. We will view it exactly as if it were reality. Only Märta has never seen Jonas Persson [the fisherman]. Because that moment of slumber—it can just as well have come after Jonas Persson's visit as before. I mean, it's of no importance which way it is."

> GUNNAR BJÖRNSTRAND: He has thought about this man's problems and now he is preparing what he is going to say?
> INGMAR: This is a moment of terrible anguish. So that the whole drama leads up to this—the whole course of events leads unfalteringly from the beginning of the film, past the letter, and here comes the culmination, the drama's first culmination. The dramatic line rises to this point.

Now I finally begin to understand why Ingmar doesn't want to decide whether it is a dream or not. For me it's a mystification; for him a necessity.

The fisherman disappears. The minister is alone. He experiences God's silence. God is dead.

[Now the pastor's visit to the fisherman's widow is discussed.]
"Is Tomas further influenced by this visit?" asks Gunnel Lindblom. [Gunnel Lindblom plays the fisherman's wife.]
"No. You see, he is beyond all influence just then. The visit to Mrs. Persson is only a station on the road of suffering. He moves as if in an atmosphere of God's abandonment; there are spots of self-insight and despair."
Where is Tomas in the final scene, religiously speaking? Here, says Ingmar:
"The mirror is clean. There stands a newly scoured vessel that can be filled by mercy. By a new image of God."

14

THE SILENCE
Problems of Evaluation

THE WORD, THE IMAGE,
AND "THE SILENCE"   Carol Brightman

. . . .

In contemporary criticism, particularly when it "pans," it becomes increasingly obvious that the words of seeming description just don't stick—at least not to what happens on the screen. Instead, it is the paper wars which are supported, the sectarian skirmishes of critics whose periodic schedules encourage newsy jurisdiction at the price of understanding. Film criticism has, in effect, largely become an awkward series of maneuvers between camps, by which critics can distinguish themselves not according to their singular perceptions, but simply *from* each other. That they fail even in that is obvious from the surprising coincidence of fault-finding phrases which, in the hands of many serious critics, only exceeds Crowther's anxious preoccupation with "negativism" by a degree of literacy, or by a matter of taste. It would appear, from a cursory reading of such regular critics as Kauffmann, Simon, and then Sarris, that they are often intent upon resisting those cinematic impressions which *cannot* be subsumed beneath a single word or phrase which judges, while it presumes to describe. Yet it is just these impressions of which the best of modern cinema is made.

Truffaut, Godard, Antonioni, and Bergman in *The Silence* may be analyzed according to a literary principle of dislocation, for example; but to superimpose on that a suspicion of formlessness which slips easily into charges of deliberate obscurantism, or irreverence for the "fullness of life" (a novelistic ideal we've clung to long after the frag-

From *Film Quarterly*, Vol. 17, No. 4 (Summer 1964) pp. 3-11. © 1964 by The Regents of the University of California. Reprinted by permission of The Regents.

Ingrid Thulin as Ester, Gunnel Lindblom as Anna, and Birger Malmsten as the bartender in *The Silence*.

mentations of modern life have undermined it), is a tricky pastime of critics who have inherited movies largely by default, in place of the new novels which have abandoned them. Like much of recent European literature these films defeat the pundit; their meanings (or apparent lack thereof) cannot be paraphrased, much less used as sticks to beat or tame the very animals from which they are wrenched. Whenever meaning is attributed to man or deed within these films, it characteristically presents itself as simply a further phenomenological routine: we take it or leave it depending on whether or not it is displaced by another, or left hanging. But first we note its presence on its own peculiar terms. Recognition without judgment, unfortunately, has always been rare in the West; only in our time we have forgotten that it is the essential distinction which would make the critic's imperative a worthwhile one.

"Ingmar Bergman's *The Silence*," John Simon submits, "is, I am sorry to say, a disappointing film" (*New Leader*, Feb. 17). I maintain it is not, but my first concern here is to question the *technique* of Simon's judgment. I choose his review because it so effectively spans the

gap between the news hacks, bedeviled with messages of promise, and
those critics who know better than to freight movies with an irrelevant
duty to console—but who nevertheless have not eluded that vocabulary
which scales their plus and minus value according to vague normative
assumptions of what "says" something, and what does not. Essentially
there is no difference between the affirmative mania, bored in the face
of gratuitous invention, and the splenetic disaffection of critics such
as Simon who can't put up with [Godard's] "attitudinizing and maundering about the human crisis" (*NL*, Sept. 30, 1963) at the expense
—of *what?* Of succinct statement presumably, direct narration, content
unencumbered by stylistic options. It is hard to guess the alternative
because it forces us to stop talking about modern films and begin talking about drama perhaps, or nineteenth-century novels—some art
where, alas, the blind of the camera is absent.

We do know, however, what happens to the critic when a modern
film is found "maundering"; so will his attention. "Emptiness, boredom and lack of transcendental values" will, by virtue of a peculiarly
anxious empathizing, guarantee the emptiness, boredom, and lack of
a transcendental response from the spectator. As if these emotions
projected in the film are merely projections of living tensions, the spectator suffers accordingly, mistaking art for life. He is accustomed to the
abreactions of their more positive or tragic counterparts. These latter
emotions, he finds, do *not* tend to drag, without happy end or any
end at all; conventionally, they respond to objective stimuli as well as
ultimately transform the given world in their own images. The emotions born of frustration, on the other hand, endure for the very reason
that the given environment cannot be assimilated or overwhelmed; it
remains in the rough: the fractious residue of a world cut off from
human use which survives to remind its inhabitants of their uselessness.
A character in this case doesn't interact; he does not develop in time—
but in space. His being expands, gesture by gesture, until by the end
he has revealed himself within the configuration of objects (including
the human) into which he is thrown. The emotional content of his
existence arises from a crisis without solution. But our critic won't
have one without the other; hence he is doubly confused. He wants an
out, an alternative to the apparent submission, a proper measure of
experience which might attribute motive to that existence, giving it
the causal necessity he likes to find in life.

"Like Antonioni, Bergman chose to make a trilogy about the emptiness, boredom and lack of transcendental values in life; like Antonioni's, Bergman's third installment stringently divests itself of narra-

tive content and shifts the burden of communication from incident to implication, from statement to symbol." The comparison with Antonioni is apt, but the analysis is wrong.

Let me first suggest that if Simon insists upon bracketing this formidable assembly beneath such worn and depreciable labels, better he simply say these "trilogies" (if the term itself is anything more than a critical expediency) are about lives which *happen* to be empty, bored, and bereft of transcendental values. There is a difference, and not a negligible one for a face-to-face encounter with these films. What preserves them all from being thematic tracts in the first place (with the partial exception of *Through a Glass Darkly*) is the fact that character is applied to idea, not idea to character. (When the latter occurs, Simon may be right: "Bergman, whatever his greatness, does not have enough 'ideas' for a film of ideas." *NL*, May 27, 1963—on *Winter Light*.)

Simon seriously errs when he automatically introduces an *evaluative* discrimination between the effectiveness of "communication" shifted from "incident" to "implication," from "statement" to "symbol." He assumes a gradual weakening—or dissolution—of expression in its passage from statement to symbol ("symbol" in a sense the Symbolists would have abjured). Just so, does Kauffmann find *The Silence* "patently a symbolic work about alienation . . . its symbolism is its defect; it breaks down into a series of discernible metaphors" which he scrupulously itemizes; he then concludes imperturbably, "it almost seems to have been contrived as an exercise for that school that looks on *criticism* as cryptography" (*New Republic*, Feb. 22, 1964. Italics mine: curious that Kauffmann faults the critic not the film, which would seal his case.) The well is poisoned, no wonder it yields an unsavory draught.

Such semantic malpractice cannot be cured by a dictionary or thesaurus. Only a new look at the films themselves will suffice. Kauffmann's charming synopsis demonstrates how irrelevant the old, letterbent eye can be to these films. "Two sisters are traveling through Europe. . . . Ester is unmarried, Anna is married and is accompanied by her eleven-year-old son. Ester suffers a violent attack of an unnamed but obviously grave illness. They must stay overnight in the capital of a fictitious country . . . in a *luxe* hotel . . ." It all happens, but something's wrong (and it's not the fact that this would seem to make even duller watching than it does reading). The missing factor upon which the whole power of the film depends is that *The Silence* makes sense not according to what happens, but to *how* it happens. The plot synopsis is irrelevant because the film is not "about" a plot, but about certain emotions, about character. Events serve to provoke characters to certain quintessential routines through which we see their existences circumscribed.

Film like any art has a number of parts, none of which are expendable but any of which can be exploited to serve varying purposes. It is unfortunate, and not entirely coincidental, in a time when the director's function as technician is frequently exploited far more than his (or his screenwriter's) function as storyteller, that critics should tax that part of stylistic invention with the losses accrued by the part of direct narration. Hence Kauffmann: "Bergman so easily creates such an atmosphere of import that, in fact, its excellence only emphasizes the vacuousness of the piece." The resulting exegeses are not only misleading but useless to a true reception of the film.

Consider Simon: "Like *Eclipse*, *The Silence* deals with non-communication." (Non-communication, like in vacuousness.) But what are the silences, punctured by natural sounds and only abortively by vague, erratic monosyllables in both films, if they are not forms of communication? Because these characters do not speak in paragraphs, are they not communicating? (This, I fear, is the plaint of the literary man.) A muttered "No-no," a blank or searching stare, is as much an act of communication in film as a mouthful of whys and wherefores. Bergman's "implication" may be as declarative as Wayne's whip, it only says something else. A mum female is not a trussed symbol of man's inability to communicate, but a mum female. It's the least we owe her, without holding her or her director to promises they never made. We might listen to our Vittis, Moreaus, and Thulins for what they do say, not for what they fail to say. *Eclipse*, finally, isn't "about non-communication," but a certain kind of communication; the same holds for *The Silence*. If what is communicated is boredom, emptiness, etc., so be it, but let us not fall into a Panglossian trap and prate about an "inability to communicate": the happier emotions just aren't there; meanwhile, a great deal, including some acute intelligence concerning the nature of women, happens in their absence.

In his review of *Eclipse* (NL, Feb. 4, 1963), Simon called it a "luminous failure," a phrase which might better describe his own critical response to the film. After a brilliantly perceptive description of *Eclipse* as a "metaphor made up of many smaller metaphors," he nevertheless asks—and we must demand the same of him—"Why should so many superb details add up to an unsatisfactory film?" "Because," he replies, "we cannot care for people who will not even put up a fight against boredom, because we are not allowed to go inside characters, because no possible alternative to defeat is offered." But why can't we care? Won't our *amour propre* allow it? Or is it a commitment to that "fullness of life" properly delineated in novels? Are we free to care only when these characters become somehow hopeful? Is their acquiescence too strong a tonic for us, a sense of loss which poisons our attentiveness? It is our loss, of course, if that is the case. But despite Simon's oddly arbitrary conclusion, it would appear he cared very much, at least enough to notice a great deal more in the film than most.

It may well be that an obdurate impatience with such hopelessness begins with a critical confusion over the purpose of a film—a confusion which is more than semantic. There is no reason why film or any art should be freighted with a "burden of communication." People may frequently address each other for that purpose, but artists are rarely so singlemindedly inclined. In art such communication is a contingency of the essential production. A film is composed of parts of which "communication" is one, but one inextricably bound to the visual structure of the whole; and in the modern film moreover, one which is often incidental, as spectacle to a tragedy. It is the propagandist, however enlightened or enlightening, who will use his characters, incidents, and symbols primarily to communicate certain messages, rather than to objectify them. Imagine for a moment some natural mystery (a man's fate, perhaps, driven to term by an accident): suppose we were asked to choose between belief and comprehension; comparably, we can distinguish art from propaganda. In neither case are we fooled, but in the latter the sense is merely conveyed rather than created.

For critics suffering from an undue preoccupation with film as communication, style, or formal coherence, will frequently go unnoticed or misconstrued. "Like *Eclipse*, *The Silence* will have no truck with a middle. And there is no end either . . ." Unless one walks in after the beginning, such an observation is irresponsible. Again Simon barks up other trees. Very possibly for any film whatsoever, no matter how conventionally narrated, the beginning, end and middle must be first considered as just those points before which nothing happens, after which nothing happens, and then, everywhere in between. Even with a causal propulsion from one event to another, the movement of "plot" in cinema is uniquely a succession of images—not incidents; and the expressive content of an image or sequence, contributive to the total plot, is not necessarily proportionate to its apparent activity or relevance to the solution of plot. It is indeed extremely difficult when speaking of film to dissociate the function of incident itself from the function of its component images (angle, lighting, sound properties, etc., which determine their net effect). Simon manages so easily because he is simply looking for—and so, naturally misses—action, the action which leads the spectator from one time and place and statement, to another.

First in the consequent "threefold inadequacy" Simon finds in *The Silence*, is "not enough forward thrust, not enough momentum to unite the specific points, the complementary but discrete images.". Presumably he will take his images only if they are ornamental to action which moves neatly if thrustingly forward. It is undoubtedly a problem of the imagist films of today (to risk another expedient label) that we must respond *specifically* to the cinematic environment: that our attention must be delicately tuned to the tensions in visual as well as sound montage, and finally that the beginnings and ends of these contrapuntal sequences be initially observed in montage as well as in *mise en scène*, rather than in the origin and solution of narrative action. Such attention is nothing new, and we know too well how blindly it can be pressed into the service of the most egregious examples of New American Cinema. But *The Silence* is no such film. Like many an imagist film it is static in that there is no significant development of plot.[1] Action is synchronous; the dramatic whole emerges in the overall pattern of juxtaposition. Should the film begin anywhere else but in the clammy heat of the train compartment, where again it ends, the whole would collapse. We would lose the thematic unity which seals the three lives in an inescapable vise at each end: from their emergence out of a mutually debilitating past into a foreign city, to the return of the two back to the same past, without future, by the same route, while the third surrenders to an actual death, locked in the middling labyrinth of the strange hotel. Importantly, we would lose Bergman's favored myth of the journey which, although it proves elliptical in *The Silence*, in many of his earlier films serves to draw character along an arduous path of discovery and development, for better or worse.

[1] Godard is the exception here, since images in his hands are themselves set in motion. Through jumpcuts, swift panning, and the "snapshot" cutting used in *Le Petit Soldat*, action is not accreted through successive visual impressions, but is propelled on a linear plane, frame by frame; like the full life of the Absurd which it reflects, it affords no regret, no flashback nostalgia for the consequences of actions already spent in a present severed from successive moments of consciousness; its *happening* is all, and is complete.

Simon submits as the second aspect of the "threefold inadequacy":
"There is not enough human content; there are hints of the past . . .
but the characters do not have enough space in which to develop, precisely because what space there is must remain empty to convey the
message." We are reminded of his impatience with *Eclipse* for not
allowing us "to go inside the characters." Just why he should demand
further entrance (if indeed any "inside" exists) is unclear, but it's clear
enough that Simon is not alone among critics dissatisfied with appearances unbuttressed by explicit motivation. The point of *The Silence*
and *Eclipse* is that the emptiness, the preoccupation with objects, *is*
the "human content" of each film. When the objects take over (in
Eclipse) they displace a quality of human content, not "human content" itself. Man must remain responsible, even for his displacement.
Again, it is the least we owe him.

Perhaps if critics ceased snapping at messages ("Why does this well-
bred, intelligent boy pee in the corridor of this posh hotel? Obviously,
that means *something*."—Kauffmann), this deductive trap could be
avoided.[2] Simon has considered only that space where he finds his
"message," and obviously, finding it less than earthshaking he wants
more, more filler material. The ladies are too disturbed, the boy a
sphinx without a riddle; there must be some explanation! Clearly *The
Silence* does not offer us full-blown case studies, or even spare ones.
We are confronted with the effects of disturbance, of the supine obei-
sance of the boy, not the causes; the symptoms, not the disease. But
why demand more?

We might introduce a very respectable argument here for the timely
realism of Bergman's assemblage, but this isn't the point. Simon resembles the art critic who looks at a Gris and complains there is no
substance there, only surfaces. By now we should know that the "in-
sides" of things, as well as minds, can only be viably described from
the outsides. There are many ways to accomplish this. A psychoanalytic
inter-penetration of behavioral symbols is only a more frantic manipu-
lation of surfaces, and in film particularly this preoccupation tends to
be least interesting (e.g., *David and Lisa*, along with the plurality of

[2] "The dwarfs are just symbols. . . . The tank in the street is a symbol. . . .
The few words in the foreign language are a symbol. Even the wild sex is a
symbol." (Sarris, *Village Voice*, Feb. 20, 1964). So goes the ridiculous extreme of this kind of criticism—a kind of madness, assuredly, where either
everything's a symbol, or nothing is.

Hollywood's psychodynamic whodunits). Bergman in fact deserves credit here for controlling his impulse to explain, an impulse which has burdened many of his films with themes they strain overmuch to deliver. No doubt it is this very reserve which led Truffaut to allude to *The Silence* as his best film—a reserve which in effect leads Bergman to engage in the same dislocation of action from its customary emotional, judicative responses which Truffaut himself used so effectively in *Shoot the Piano Player.*

Only when Ester's breakdown seems imminent and we are shocked by our incomprehension of her disease ("symbol" says lung cancer) does she exclaim: "We try out many attitudes; but the forces are too strong, the dark forces." And these lines do provide a clue, in depth, of the existential imperatives. Ester has wagered without profit. They underline the psychical evidence of her torment without diminishing it by abstraction. She exclaims, she does not explain, and it comes as revelation: Ester *would* say that on her deathbed. Unlike the tag line, "God is love, love in all its forms," in *Through a Glass Darkly,* Ester's recognition provides us with only a skeleton key to her schizophrenia, a schizophrenia which is, fundamentally, as ordinary as it is alarming. Her monologue (for the sympathetic old waiter can't understand a word) is simply a tentative summation, which happens to be final, under which her previous misadventures might be reckoned. As apologia it is equally vulnerable to reason and passing sensation, like all last-ditch acts of personal vengeance. We find ourselves still observing her phenomenologically, with no real explanation of the origin of her breakdown, no real expectation of a solution, but waiting nevertheless for the act of recognition which will seal her fate. That is the tension which ultimately is unrelieved in a dramatic sense; it is merely superceded when our attention is shifted to the boy troubling over the foreign words she has passed on to him.

As it happens Ester knows perhaps a little more about herself than we can, but not enough to convert herself conveniently to symbol. From the intellectual pride (a pride, as well, in the appurtenances of intellect) which we observe manifested so coolly before the typewriter, we can deduce a long history of such "attitudes" desperately assumed —but none the less authentic for that—to withstand the invasion of irrational forces which will fracture not only the attitudes but the human will-to-assume itself. The "forces"—the incestuous attraction for father, then sister, finally for self—achieve their proper magnitude as the shriek of flesh, once repressed, or exiled by disjunctive demands

of intellect, becomes intolerably mean and animalistic. The forces of
the body, finally, its "secretions and excretions," prove too strong for
the assumptions of the will.

Could this be the Message? And is the leap to faith to follow? Perhaps the words which Johan doggedly pursues on the retreating train
do forge a link between Ester's last will and testament to the powers
of comprehension and the ongoing, pre-reflective life of the boy.
"Spirit," he reads (in the dubbed version, although we are denied this
last-minute tip in the subtitles). Simon concludes that this final act of
communication suggests "Art is universal, and so, potentially, is language." Such a leap does befit the customary reduction of Bergman's
plots to Intellect *v.* Art, Reason *v.* Faith, etc. Even better, we could
snare a happy synthesis here, since it is the intellectual's submission to
faith in the endurance of language as source of communion among
men which carries the day. (The fact that, as Simon observes, language shared by the sisters is used solely to poison each other further
against themselves, and can only fall comfortably upon the uncompre-
hending ears of the old waiter, could merely add a note of heroic desperation to Ester's testament.)

If Ester's sudden volubility is also Bergman's, the screenwriter finally
possessing the screen, then perhaps the mesmeric oscillations between
Ester's unsure intellectualism and Anna's unsure voluptuosity (linked
by Johan's dutiful passage from one to the other) have merely been
enforced to set up reverberations in our mind ("implications"), which
Bergman can manipulate, even fulfill, in the single verbal dialogue between the "attitudes" and the "dark forces."

Not bad. Silence could make sense after all: it's been communicated.
The polar personae of the two women, locked in a baleful embrace,
cancel each other out dramatically. The dilemma can only be resolved
in the timely confession of the more articulate, rising from her heated
couch to speak for a director who simply hung around with a camera
until this moment, when he would finally say what just can't be said
any other way.

So runs the risk of reading a movie. If this should satisfy we should
not be surprised to catch ourselves a moment later echoing Sarris, for
one, whose critical job is relieved by the "evidence of an irreversible
decline" he finds so generously supported in the symbolic obviousness
of *The Silence.* Or like Kauffmann and Simon (on *Winter Light*),
how easy it will be to wonder why Bergman has to make films when
his messages are carried so economically in a few lines, in a few static
sets. But it *doesn't* satisfy. For one reason, as Colin Young observes in

his review of *The Fiancés*, because "Ester and Anna must finally say
to each other what their conduct has said already to us. This is not
dramatic redundancy—exposition in the eighth reel—unless you look at
these films as being conventionally about action which grows continually in a straight line instead of proceeding in circles which never
really close."

Words speak while images only appear, and words are our business
(don't we all share them?) while images are thrust upon us in the pure
state, from a source compounded of artifice and raw being, leagued in
the elusive interests of the director's imagination. So we find ourselves
surrendering to the faintest appeal of language which explains, at the
expense of a visual language which simply presents. We find it hard to
see the sudden burst of speech as just another phenomenalist event.

Even Anna explains (earlier): "You hate me because you hate yourself—and all I have!" Her revelation probes the surface of their enmity
like a periscope. But nothing follows: Ester dismisses her with a tricky
condescension still left to her. Nevertheless the words may linger. Our
first clue—first among the many with which we would later challenge
Bergman's cinematic integrity, concluding perhaps, with Kauffmann,
that the fact "the film is a rebus, with clues to be hunted in it, indicates its limitations" (not our own, of course). But Anna's words do
echo throughout the succeeding silence. Ultimately, the two women do
mirror each other; the dichotomy can be resolved only if they fuse,
intellect with animality. Until then (until another film) Anna will find
Ester's eye in the mirror watching her feed on her reflection, and Ester
will find Anna's sex eating at her own body in despair of ever claiming
that sex; and each will hate what she lacks, and love, needing the loss
to heal the open wound. There can be no fusion, just as there is no
explanation in *The Silence* but merely image straining to achieve a coherence through the dwindling resources of meaning which words
provide. Anna catches a further symptom, not a solution. The silence
in the film, as much as the grate of natural and unnatural sounds, perpetually threatens to swallow the human voice. Not unreasonably do
these characters often halt mid-sentence, overwhelmed by their vulnerability.

It is hardly surprising that Simon should find his third inadequacy in
the physicality of the film (although it should be noted that this physicality, which Sarris believes pitches *The Silence* into the nudie circuit,
is as scaring a display of wounded intellect—not sex—imaginable).
"For a film which proceeds by metaphors and implications," says Si-

mon, "certain sensual details are too strong." The question arises, Even
if we could support this distinction between implication and incident,
metaphor and statement, why single out "certain sensual details" as
somehow "stronger" than what seems to be the nonsensual details of
the rest of the film? This is a confession of taste, or of a proclivity to
register the more obvious functions of sex on a higher frequency than
other demonstrations of instinct, thought, or emotion. What really
unsettles Simon is likely to be that Bergman has isolated sensual details
from their customary contexts. Even when Anna takes the café waiter,
sex is still somehow onanistic; more important, these details are reported naturalistically without any interest in causes or effect.[3]

But the real issue here is that Johan's adventures in the hotel corridor, or Ester's assault upon cigarette, bottle, and later, upon her translations (safe cinematic proof of the Female Intellectual), are no more
nor less "implication" or "metaphor" than Ester or Anna indulging
themselves (much to their dissatisfaction). To me, these indulgences
are less sensual. Anna moving through the streets, the bathroom, or
just moving, is far more so. It is not the degree of exertion which ani-
mates these latter scenes; it is their resonance, their suggestiveness,
cinematically enforced in close-ups which amplify the minutest gestures into actions of resounding significance. Walking back and forth
in the room becomes the pacing of a trapped animal. Lighting a cigarette, getting a fix. Ester's grimace, a spellbound shriek without issue.
Anna putting on a dress, an act of self-immolation. The old man eating a frank to lure the boy, nothing less, or less ludicrous, than castration. Johan being frocked by the dwarfs, a defloration. True passion
resides in the charged gesture, not the overt act.

Not the least curious aspect of these close-ups is the fact that instead of creating a sense of intimacy with the characters, they effectu-
ally alienate them from us. We are continually rearing back from the
massive circumstances of their narrow lives. Faces, fingers, hair, appear
too close—they get *in the way*. Ester's naked face imprisons her, but it
is all there is. The only difference between these three faces filling the
screen and the painted masks of earlier films whereby Bergman obscures
the human countenance from simple view, is that these faces mask
themselves, without artifice. Sven Nykvist's camera imprisons them by
liberating them from any background. Just so, the spare details of en-

[3] Kauffmann is led by the details to quibble, "Foe of censorship as I presume
to be, I have not yet seen explicit sexual details in any film that were necessary
to it. Whatever was cut of *The Silence* has not hurt it" (an interesting admission coming from one of our more venerated weekly reviewers).

vironment themselves encroach. Rather than provide the objects by
which a man passes out of himself into a concrete world, these corridors, damask curtains, featherbeds appear as obstacles, like the glass
windows through which an infrequent view of the world outside is
gained—sealing the inhabitants away from any real encounter with that
world. Like the earliest of Bergman's films, *The Silence* is an *huis clos*
but not on principle, simply because if one looks so close, it appears
that way. Stripped to its inessentials, the human condition itself is
claustrophobic.

Every visual incident amplifies the frustration of instinct caught at
cross-purposes with reality, until by the end, instinct appears resound-
ingly solipsistic. Reality remains a tank, lumbering prehistoric monster,
phallus erect but extinct like the spine of a dead horseshoe crab. Escape appears for the boy as an interminable chase through the laby-
rinthine corridors: for his mother, it is the bought relief of the café
and theater, reached through a street pinched by men and machines.
For Ester everything she finds herself doing is a futile escape.

Johan *is* the sphinx; his blank face compels interpretation, but it
repels every attempt to read. When the old waiter attempts to "talk"
to Johan (after the misfire of his sudden, frightful embrace) he fum-
bles for a worn photo of himself taken at the same age standing behind
the open coffin of his father. The boy responds with interest; with less
interest he later slips it beneath the carpet, unseen. Brief displays of
affection are native to his youth; an over-all impression of cool reticence
is more native to his character. Johan is involved in a crisis without
solution; he may be the product of it, but he promises no salvation; in
effect he is unformed enough to be the product of other worlds the
sisters have forgotten or never known. His remains the one existence
which bridges the shrill edge of *The Silence* with the world of possibility beyond, but he has not yet stepped beyond. So far, he too only
perceives the world through glass. And when he does his attention is
swiftly marshalled, as by the trainload of tanks which jerk his round
eyes back and forth, uncomprehendingly (while telling us clearly
enough that the town we are entering is sealed off from the rest of the
world—and from its own freedom—by military rule). The sun which
Johan watches rising over the mountains, a white heat resembling Antonioni's ultramodern "eclipse," is unnatural. All of the pastimes open
to Johan are unnatural; only his curiosity is not. When he looks out at
us, it is as if he sees as far as the flat screen which delimits him, no
further. His eyes never really focus. He has the terrifying innocence
which comes once in a lifetime from knowing the worst without un-

derstanding either the worst or the best life may offer. Should he never mature to understand, he might be one of the bemused Exterminators of the coming generation. Like the depthless Anna who stares at mirrors, Johan stares and finds things staring back at him, all equally detached from any knowledge he might have of their use. All three are hemmed in by a web of anxiety spun from the unconscious recesses of their frustration, which forbids natural engagement.

Bergman has transformed his three favorite themes into a new film, quite superior to his others. Notably, the Big Questions do not function in *The Silence* as excuses for the big answers. There is indeed no exit in life's game, but hell is hardly rendered more bearable in togetherness. Women do scrape the bottom of human experience, but for that very reason theirs is the more pitiful lot. (Unlike the women in *Brink of Life,* Ester and Anna are not awaiting men. In fact, the absence of men—except for the dumb and solely functionary waiters—in *The Silence* is a curious thing; Ester tries hard to assume the masculine principle, but cracks embarrassingly.) Lastly, man's quest for knowledge is, in truth, a bitter one, so much so that the twin horns of reason and impulse which he is condemned to ride do eventually impale him. Life itself is a dying-in; any other form of protest would bore these three travelers who at least know how to make more out of their "lack of transcendental values" in less time and space than a host of busier characters marked for deliverance.

15

PERSONA
The Film in Depth

Susan Sontag

. . . .

One impulse is to take Bergman's masterpiece for granted. Since 1960 at least, with the breakthrough into new narrative forms propagated with most notoriety (if not greatest distinction) by *Last Year in Marienbad*, audiences have continued to be educated by even more elliptical and complex work. As Resnais's imagination was subsequently to surpass itself in *Muriel*, a succession of ever more difficult and rewarding films has turned up in recent years. But that good fortune releases nobody who cares about films from acclaiming work as original and triumphant as *Persona*. It is depressing that the film has thus far received only a fraction of the attention it deserves—at least in New York and Paris. (At the moment of writing, it hasn't yet opened in London.)

Of course, some of the paltriness of the critics' reaction may be more a response to the signature *Persona* carries than to the film itself. That signature has come to mean a prodigal, tirelessly productive career; a rather facile, often merely beautiful, by now (it seemed) almost oversize body of work; a lavishly inventive, sensual, yet somewhat melodramatic talent, employed with what appeared to be a certain complacency, and prone to embarrassing displays of intellectual bad taste. From the Fellini of the North, exacting filmgoers could hardly be blamed for not expecting, ever, a truly great film. But *Persona* happily forces one to put aside such dismissive preconceptions about its author.

The rest of the neglect of *Persona* may be set down to emotional squeamishness; the film, like much of Bergman's recent work, bears an

From *Styles of Radical Will* (New York: Farrar, Straus & Giroux). Copyright © 1966, 1967, 1968, 1969 by Susan Sontag. Reprinted by permission of Farrar, Straus & Giroux, Inc., and Martin Secker & Warburg Ltd. The article also appeared in *Sight and Sound* (Autumn 1967).

Bibi Andersson as Alma, and Liv Ullmann as Elisabeth Vogler in *Persona*.

almost defiling charge of personal agony. I'm thinking particularly of *The Silence*—most accomplished, by far, of the films made before this one. And *Persona* draws heavily on the themes and schematic cast established in *The Silence*. (The principal characters in both films are two women bound together in a passionate agonised relationship, one of them the mother of a drastically neglected small boy. Both films take up the themes of the scandal of the erotic; the polarities of violence and powerlessness, reason and unreason, language and silence, the intelligible and the unintelligible.) But the new film ventures at least as much beyond *The Silence* as the distance separating that film, by its emotional power and subtlety, from Bergman's entire previous work.

That distance gives, for the present moment, the measure of a work which is undeniably "difficult." *Persona* is bound to trouble, perplex and frustrate most filmgoers—at least as much as *Marienbad* did in its day. Or so one would suppose. But, heaping imperturbability upon relative neglect, critical reaction has shied away from associating anything very baffling with the film. The critics have allowed, mildly, that the latest Bergman is unnecessarily obscure. Some add that this time he's overdone the mood of unremitting bleakness. It's intimated that with this film he has ventured out of his depth, exchanging art for artiness. But the difficulties and rewards of *Persona* are much more formidable than such banal objections would suggest.

Of course, evidence of these difficulties is available anyway. Why else all the discrepancies—plain misrepresentations—in critics' accounts of what actually happens during the film? Like *Marienbad*, *Persona* seems to be full of obscurity. Its general look has nothing of the built-in, abstract evocativeness of the château in Resnais's film: the space and furnishings of *Persona* are anti-romantic, cool, clinical, and bourgeois-modern. But there's no less of a mystery lodged in this setting. Images and dialogue are given which the viewer cannot help but find puzzling, not being able to decipher whether certain scenes take place in the past, present or future; and whether certain images and episodes belong to "reality" or "fantasy."

One common approach to a film presenting difficulties of this now fairly familiar sort is to declare such distinctions to be irrelevant, and the film to be actually all of one piece. What's happened is that its action has been situated in a merely (or wholly) "mental" universe. But this approach merely postpones the difficulty, it seems to me. *Within* the structure of what is shown, the elements continue being related to each other in the ways that might have led the viewer to settle for supposing some events to be "real" and others visionary (whether dream, fantasy, hallucination or extra-worldly visitation). For example: causal connections observed in one portion of the film are flouted in another part; several equally persuasive but mutually exclusive explanations are given of the same event. These discordant internal relations are only transposed, intact, when the whole film is relocated in the mind.

Actually, it's no more helpful to describe *Persona* as a wholly subjective film, one taking place entirely within someone's head, than it was (how easy to see that now) in elucidating *Marienbad*, a film whose disregard for conventional chronology and a clearly delineated border between fantasy and reality could scarcely have constituted more of a provocation than *Persona*.

What first needs to be made clear about *Persona* is what can't be done with it. The most skilful attempt to arrange a single, plausible anecdote out of the film must leave out or contradict some of its key sections, images and procedures. It's the failure to perceive this critical rule that has led to the flat, impoverished and partly inaccurate account of the film promulgated almost unanimously by reviewers.

According to this account, *Persona* tells the story of two women. One is a successful actress, evidently in her mid-thirties, named Elizabeth Vogler (Liv Ullmann), now suffering from an enigmatic mental collapse whose chief symptoms are muteness and a near-catatonic lassitude. The other is the pretty young nurse of twenty-five named Alma (Bibi Andersson) charged with caring for Elizabeth—first at the mental hospital, then at the beach cottage loaned to them by the woman psychiatrist who is Elizabeth's doctor and Alma's supervisor. What happens in the course of the film, according to the critics' consensus, is that, through some mysterious process, each of the two women becomes the other. The officially stronger one, Alma, gradually assumes the problems and confusions of her patient, while the sick woman, felled by despair and/or psychosis, regains her power of speech and returns to her former life. (The viewer doesn't see this exchange consummated: what he sees at the end of *Persona* looks like an agonised stalemate. But it was widely reported that the film, until shortly before it was released, contained a brief closing scene which showed Elizabeth on the stage again, apparently completely recovered. From this, presumably, the viewer was to infer that the nurse is now mute and has taken on the burden of her despair.)

Proceeding from this constructed version, half "story" and half "meaning," critics have read off a number of further meanings. Some regard the transaction between Elizabeth and Alma as illustrating some impersonal law which operates intermittently in human affairs; no ultimate responsibility pertains to either of them. Others posit a conscious cannibalism of the innocent Alma by the actress—and thus read the film as a parable of the predatory energies of the artist, forever scavenging life for "material." Other critics move quickly to an even more general plane, and extract from *Persona* a diagnosis of the contemporary dissociation of personality, a demonstration of the inevitable failure of good will and trust, and predictably correct views on such matters as the alienated affluent society, the nature of madness, psychiatry and its limitations, the American war in Vietnam, the Western legacy of sexual guilt, and the Six Million. (Then they often go on, as Michel Cournot did in *Le Nouvel Observateur*, to chide Bergman for this vulgar didacticism which they have imputed to him.)

My own view is that, even when turned into a "story," this prevailing account of *Persona* grossly oversimplifies and misrepresents. True, Alma does seem to grow progressively more vulnerable; in the course of the film she is reduced to fits of hysteria, cruelty, childish dependence and (probably) delusion. It's also true that Elizabeth gradually becomes stronger, that is, more active, more responsive; though her change is far subtler and, until virtually the end, she still refuses to speak. But all this is hardly tantamount to an "exchange" of attributes and identities. Nor is it established that Alma, however much she does come, with pain and longing, to identify herself with the actress, takes on Elizabeth's dilemmas, whatever these may be. (They're far from made clear.)

With *Persona*, it's the temptation to invent more "story" that has to be resisted. Take, for instance, the scene which starts with the abrupt presence of a middle-aged man wearing dark glasses (Gunnar Bjornstrand) near the beach cottage. All we see is that he approaches Alma, addressing her and continuing to call her, despite her protests, by the name of Elizabeth; that he tries to embrace her; that throughout this scene Elizabeth's impassive face is never more than a few inches away; that Alma suddenly yields to his embraces, saying "Yes, I am Elizabeth" (Elizabeth is still watching intently), and goes to bed with him amid a torrent of endearments. Then we see the two women together (shortly after?); they are alone, behaving as if nothing has happened. This sequence can be taken as illustrating Alma's growing identification with Elizabeth, and gauging the extent of the process by which she is learning (really? in her imagination?) to become Elizabeth. While Elizabeth has voluntarily (?) renounced being an actress, by becoming mute, Alma is involuntarily and painfully engaged in becoming that Elizabeth Vogler, the performer, who no longer exists. Still, nothing we see justifies describing this scene as most critics have done as a "real" event—something that happens in the course of the plot on the same level as the initial removal of the two women to the cottage. But neither can we be absolutely sure that this, or something like it, isn't taking place. After all, we do see it happening. (And it's in the nature of cinema to confer on all events, without indications to the contrary, an equivalent degree of reality: everything shown on the screen is "there," present.)

The difficulty is that Bergman withholds the kind of clear signals for sorting out what's fantasy from what is "real" offered, for example, by Buñuel in *Belle de Jour*. Buñuel has put the clues there; he wants the viewer to be able to decipher his film. The insufficiency of the clues Bergman has planted must be taken to indicate that he intends the film to remain partly encoded. The viewer can only move towards, but never achieve, certainty about the action. However, so far as the distinction between fantasy and reality has any use in understanding

Persona, I should argue that much more than critics have allowed of what happens in and around the beach cottage is most plausibly understood as Alma's fantasy. One prime piece of evidence is a sequence occurring soon after the two women arrive at the seaside. It's the sequence in which, after we have seen (i.e., the camera has shown) Elizabeth enter Alma's room and stand beside her and stroke her hair, we see Alma, pale, troubled, asking Elizabeth the next morning "Did you come to my room last night?" And Elizabeth, slightly quizzical, anxious, shaking her head No.

Now, there seems no reason to doubt Elizabeth's answer. The viewer isn't given any evidence of a malevolent plan on her part to undermine Alma's confidence in her own sanity, nor for doubting Elizabeth's memory or sanity in the ordinary sense. But if that is so, two important points may be taken as established early in the film. One is that Alma is hallucinating—and, presumably, will continue doing so. The other is that hallucinations or visions will appear on the screen with the same rhythms, the same look of objective reality, as something "real." (However, some clues, too complex to describe here, are given in the lighting of certain scenes.) And once these points are granted, it seems highly plausible to take at least the scene with Elizabeth's husband as Alma's fantasy, as well as several scenes in which there is a charged, trance-like physical contact between the two women.

But even to make any headway sorting out what Alma imagines from what may be taken as really happening is a minor achievement. And it quickly becomes a misleading one, unless subsumed under the larger issue of the form of exposition employed by the film. As I have suggested, *Persona* is constructed according to a form that resists being reduced to a "story"—say, the story about the relation (however ambiguous and abstract) between two women named Elizabeth and Alma, a patient and a nurse, a star and an ingenue, *alma* (soul) and *persona* (mask). The reason is that reduction to a "story" means, in the end, a reduction of Bergman's film to the single dimension of psychology. Not that the psychological dimension isn't there. It is. But a correct understanding of *Persona* must go beyond the psychological point of view.

This seems clear from the fact that Bergman allows the audience to interpret Elizabeth's mute condition in several ways—as involuntary mental breakdown, and as voluntary moral decision leading either towards self-purification or suicide. But whatever the background of her condition, it is much more in the sheer fact of it than in its causes that Bergman wishes to involve the viewer. In *Persona*, muteness is first of all a fact with a certain psychic and moral weight, a fact which initiates its own kind of causality upon an "other."

I am inclined to impute a privileged status to the speech the psychiatrist makes to Elizabeth, before she departs with Alma to the cottage. The psychiatrist tells the silent, stony-faced Elizabeth that she has understood her case. She has grasped that Elizabeth wants to be sincere, not to play a role; to make the inner and the outer come together. And that, having rejected suicide as a solution, she has decided to be mute. She advises Elizabeth to bide her time, to live her experience through; and at the end of that time, she predicts, the actress will return to the world . . . But even if one treats this speech as setting forth a privileged view, it would be a mistake to assume that it's the key to *Persona;* or even to assume that the psychiatrist's thesis wholly explains Elizabeth's condition. (The doctor could be wrong, or at least be simplifying the matter.) By placing this speech early in the film, and by never referring explicitly to this "explanation" again, Bergman has, in effect, both taken account of psychology and dispensed with it. Without indicating that he regards psychological explanation as unimportant, he clearly consigns to a relatively minor place any consideration of the role the actress's *motives* have in the action.

In a sense, *Persona* takes a position beyond psychology. As it does, in an analogous sense, beyond eroticism. The materials of an erotic subject are certainly present, such as the "visit" of Elizabeth's husband. There is, above all, the connection between the two women themselves which, in its feverish proximity, its caresses, its sheer passionateness (avowed by Alma in word, gesture and fantasy) could hardly fail, it would seem, to suggest a powerful, if largely inhibited, sexual involvement. But in fact, what might be sexual in feeling is largely transposed into something beyond sexuality, beyond eroticism even. The only purely sexual episode is the scene in which Alma, sitting across the room from Elizabeth, tells the story of the beach orgy. Alma speaks, transfixed, reliving the memory and at the same time consciously delivering up this shameful secret to Elizabeth as her greatest gift of love. Entirely through discourse, without any recourse to images (through a flashback), a violent sexual atmosphere is generated. But this sexuality has nothing to do with the "present" of the film, and the relationship between the two women.

In this respect, *Persona* makes a remarkable modification of the structure of *The Silence,* where the love-hate relationship between the sisters had an unmistakable sexual energy. In *Persona,* Bergman has achieved a more interesting situation by delicately excising or transcending the possible sexual implications of the tie between the two women. It is a remarkable feat of moral and psychological poise. While maintaining the indeterminacy of the situation Bergman can't give the impression of evading the issue, and he mustn't present anything that is psychologically improbable.

The advantages of keeping the phychological aspects indeterminate (while internally credible) are that Bergman can do many other things besides tell a "story." Instead of having a full-blown "story" on his hands, he has something that is in one sense cruder, and in another more abstract: a body of material, a subject. The function of the "subject" or "material" may be as much its opacity, its multiplicity, as the manner in which it yields itself up to being incarnated in a determinate plot. One predictable result of a work constituted along these principles is that the action would appear intermittent, porous, shot through with intimations of absence, of what could not be univocally said.

This procedure doesn't mean that a narration of this type has forfeited "sense." But it does mean that "sense" isn't necessarily tied to a determinate plot. What is envisaged instead is the possibility of an extended narration composed of events which are not (wholly) explicated, but which are nevertheless possible. The "forward" movement of such a narrative might be measured by reciprocal relations between its parts—e.g. *displacements*—rather than by ordinary realistic (mainly psychological) causality. Often, there might exist what could be called a dormant plot. Still, critics have better things to do than ferreting out the story line as if the author had—through mere clumsiness or error or frivolity or lack of craft—concealed it. In such narratives, it isn't a question of a plot that has been mislaid but of one that has been (at least in part) annulled. That intention, whether conscious on the artist's part or merely implicit in the work, should be taken at face value and respected.

Take the matter of information. One tactic upheld by traditional narrative is to give "full" information, so that the ending of the viewing or reading experience coincides, ideally, with full satisfaction of one's desire to "know," to understand what happened and why. (This is, of course, a highly manipulated quest for knowledge. It's the business of the artist to convince his audience that what they haven't learned at the end they *can't* know, or shouldn't *care* about knowing.) But one of the salient features of new narratives is a deliberate, calculated frustration of the desire to "know." Did anything happen last

year at Marienbad? What did become of the girl in *L'Avventura?*
Where is Alma going when she boards a bus alone in one of the final
shots of *Persona?*

Once it is conceived that the desire to "know" may be (in part)
systematically thwarted, the old expectations about plotting can no
longer hold. At first, it may seem that a plot in the old sense is still
there; only it's being related at an oblique, uncomfortable angle, where
vision is obscured, Eventually, though, it needs to be seen that the
plot isn't there at all in the old sense; and therefore that the point
isn't to tantalise but to involve the audience more directly in other
matters, for instance in the very processes of "knowing" and "seeing."
(A great precursor of this conception of narration is Flaubert. And the
method can be seen in *Madame Bovary,* in the persistent use of the
off-center detail in description.)

The result of the new narration, then, is a tendency to de-dramatise.
In, for example, *Journey to Italy* or *L'Avventura,* we are told what is
ostensibly a story. But it is a story which proceeds by omissions. The
audience is being haunted, as it were, by the sense of a lost or absent
meaning to which even the artist himself has no access.

The avowal of agnosticism on the artist's part may look like un-
seriousness or contempt for the audience. But when the artist declares
that he doesn't "know" any more than the audience knows, what he
is saying is that all the meaning resides in the work itself. There is no
surplus, nothing "behind" it. Such works seem to lack sense or meaning only to the extent that entrenched critical attitudes have established as a dictum for the narrative arts that meaning resides solely in
this surplus of 'reference" outside the work—to the "real world" or to
the artist's intention. But this is, at best, an arbitrary ruling. The
meaning of a narration is not the same as a paraphrase of the values
associated by an ideal audience with the "real-life" equivalents or
sources of the plot elements, nor with the attitudes projected by the
artist towards them. And there are other kinds of narration besides
those based on a "story."

For instance, the material can be treated as a *thematic resource*—
from which different, perhaps concurrent, narrative structures can be
derived as variations. Once this possibility is consciously entertained, it
becomes clear that the formal mandates of such a construction must
differ from those of a "story" (or even a set of parallel stories). The
difference will probably appear most striking in the treatment of time.

A "story" involves the audience in what happens, how it comes out.
The movement is strongly linear, whatever the meanderings and di-

gressions. One moves from A to B, only to look forward to C, whereupon C (if the affair is satisfactorily managed) points one's interest in the direction of D. Each link in the chain is, so to speak, self-abolishing—since it has served its turn.

But the development of a theme-and-variation narrative is much less linear. The linear movement can't be altogether suppressed, since the experience of the audience remains a movement in time. But this forward movement can be sharply qualified by a competing retrograde principle, which could take the form, say, of continual backward- and cross-references. Such a work would invite re-experiencing, multiple viewing. It would ask the spectator, ideally, to be able to position himself at several points in the narrative simultaneously. Time may appear in the form of a perpetual present, or as a conundrum in which it's made impossible to establish exactly the distinction between past, present and future (*Marienbad* and Robbe-Grillet's *L'Immortelle* are fairly pure examples of the latter procedure). In *Persona*, Bergman uses a mixed approach. The treatment of sequences in the centre of the film seems realistically chronological, while distinctions of "before" and "after" are drastically bleached out, almost indecipherable at the beginning and close of the film.

But despite this more moderate use of the procedure of temporal dislocation, the construction of *Persona* is best described in terms of the form: variations on a theme. The theme is that of *doubling*; and the variations are those that follow from its leading possibilities—duplication, inversion, reciprocal exchange, repetition. Once again, it would be a serious misunderstanding to demand to know exactly what happens in *Personna*; for what is narrated is only deceptively, secondarily, a "story" at all. It's correct to speak of the film in terms of the fortunes of two characters named Elizabeth and Alma who are engaged in a desperate duel of identities. But it is no less true, or relevant, to treat *Persona* as what might be misleadingly called an allegory: as relating the duel between two mythical parts of a single "person," the corrupted person who acts (Elizabeth) and the ingenuous soul (Alma) who founders in contact with corruption.

Bergman is not just telling a "story" about the psychic ordeal of two women: he is using that ordeal as a constituent element of his theme. And that theme, for which I've used the name of *doubling*, is no less a formal idea than a psychological one.

We know this in two ways. First, by the fact already stressed that Bergman has withheld enough information about the "story" of the two women to make it impossible to determine clearly the main outlines, much less all, of what passes between them. Second, by the fact that he has introduced a number of reflections about the nature of representation (the status of the image, of the word, of action, of the film medium itself). *Persona* is not just a representation of transactions between the two characters, Alma and Elizabeth, but a meditation on the film which is "about" them.

The most explicit vehicle for this meditation is the opening and closing sequence, in which Bergman tries to create the film as an object: a finite object, a made object, a fragile perishable object, and therefore existing in space as well as time.

Persona begins with darkness. Then two points of light gradually gain in brightness, until we see that they're the two carbons of the arc lamp; after this, a portion of the leader flashes by. Then follows a suite of rapid images, some barely identifiable—a chase from a slapstick silent film; an erect penis; a nail being hammered into the palm of a hand; a shot from the rear of a stage of a heavily made-up actress declaiming to the footlights and darkness beyond (we see this image soon again and know that it's Elizabeth playing her last role, that of Electra); the immolation of a Buddhist monk in Vietnam; assorted dead bodies in a morgue. All these images go by very rapidly, mostly too fast to see; but gradually they're slowing down, as if consenting to adjust to the time in which the viewer can comfortably perceive them. Then follows a final set of images, run off at normal speed. We see a thin, unhealthy-looking boy around eleven lying under a sheet on a hospital cot against the wall of a bare room; the viewer, at first, is bound to associate to the corpses he's just seen. But the boy stirs, awkwardly kicks off the sheet, puts on a pair of large round glasses, takes out a book and begins to read. Then we see that ahead of him is an indecipherable blur, very faint, but on its way to becoming an image. It's the face of a beautiful woman. As if in a trance, the boy slowly reaches up and begins to caress it. (The surface he touches suggests a movie screen, but also a portrait and a mirror.)

Who is the boy? It seems easy for most people to say he's Elizabeth's son, because we learn later on that she does have a son, and because the face on the screen is the actress's face. But is it? Although the image is far from clear (this is obviously deliberate), I'm almost sure that Bergman is modulating it from Elizabeth's face to Alma's to Elizabeth's again. And if that is the case, does it change anything about the boy's identity? Or is his identity, perhaps, something we shouldn't expect to know?

In any case, the abandoned "son" (if that's who he is) is never seen again until the close of the film, when again, more briefly, there is a complementary montage of fragmented images, ending with the child again reaching tentatively, caressingly, towards the huge blurry blow-up of the woman's face. And then Bergman cuts to the shot of the incandescent arc lamp; the carbons fade; the light slowly goes out. The film dies, as it were, before our eyes. It dies as an object or a thing does, declaring itself to be "used up" and thus virtually outside the volition of the maker.

Any account which leaves out or dismisses as incidental the way *Persona* begins and ends hasn't been talking about the film that Bergman made. Far from being extraneous (or pretentious), as many reviewers found it, this so-called "frame" of *Persona* is, it seems to me, only the most explicit statement of a motif of aesthetic self-reflexiveness that runs through the entire film. This element of self-reflexiveness in the construction of *Persona* is anything but an arbitrary concern, one superadded to the "dramatic" action. For one thing, it states on the formal level the theme of doubling or duplication that is present on a psychological level in the transactions between Alma and Elizabeth. The formal "doublings" are the largest extension of the theme which furnishes the material of the film.

Perhaps the most striking episode, in which the formal and psychological resonances of the double theme are played out most starkly, is the monologue in which Alma describes Elizabeth's relation to her son. This is repeated twice in its entirety, the first time showing Elizabeth's face as she listens, the second time Alma's face as she speaks. The sequence closes spectacularly, terrifyingly, with the appearance of a double or composite face, half Elizabeth's and half Alma's.

Here, in the very strongest terms, Bergman is playing with the paradoxical nature of film—namely, that it always gives us the illusion of having a voyeuristic access to an untampered reality, a neutral view of things as they are. But what contemporary film-makers more and more often propose to show is the process of seeing itself—giving the viewer grounds or evidence for several different ways of seeing the same thing, which he may entertain concurrently or successively.

Bergman's use of this idea here seems to me strikingly original, but the larger intention is certainly a familiar one. In the ways that Bergman made his film self-reflexive, self-regarding, ultimately self-engorging, we should recognize not a private whim but an example of a well-established tendency. For it is precisely the energy for this sort of "formalist" concern with the nature and paradoxes of the medium itself which was unleashed when the 19th century formal structures of "plot" and "characters" were demoted. What is commonly patronized as the over-exquisite self-consciousness in contemporary art, leading to a species of auto-cannibalism, can be seen—less pejoratively—as the liberation of new energies of thought and sensibility.

This, for me, is the promise behind the familiar thesis that locates the difference between traditional and so-called new cinema in the altered status of the camera—"the felt presence of the camera," as Pasolini has said. But Bergman goes beyond Pasolini's criterion, inserting into the viewer's consciousness the felt presence of the film as an object. He does this not only at the beginning and end but in the middle of Persona, when the image—it is a shot of Alma's horrified face—cracks like a mirror, then burns. When the next scene immediately begins (again, as if nothing had happened) the viewer has not only an almost indelible after-image of Alma's anguish but an added sense of shock, a formal-magical apprehension of the film—as if it had collapsed under the weight of registering such drastic suffering and then had been, as it were, magically reconstituted.

Bergman's procedure, with the beginning and end of Persona and with this terrifying caesura in the middle, is more complex than the Brechtian strategy of alienating the audience by supplying continual reminders that what they are watching is theater (i.e., artifice rather than reality). Rather, it is a statement about the complexity of what can be seen and the way in which, in the end, the deep, unflinching knowledge of anything is destructive. To know (perceive) something intensely is eventually to consume what is known, to use it up, to be forced to move on to other things.

This principle of intensity lies at the heart of Bergman's sensibility, and determines the specific ways in which he uses the new narrative forms. Anything like the vivacity of Godard, the intellectual innocence of Jules et Jim, the lyricism of Bertolucci's Before the Revolution and Skolimowski's Le Départ, is far from Bergman's range. His work is characterised by its slowness, its deliberateness of pacing; something like the heaviness of Flaubert. And this sensibility makes for the excruciatingly unmodulated quality of Persona (and of The Silence before it), a quality only very superficially described as pessimism.

What is emotionally darkest in Bergman's film is connected particularly with a sub-theme of the main theme of doubling: the contrast between hiding or concealing and showing forth. The Latin word persona means the mask worn by an actor. To be a person, then, is to possess a mask; and in *Persona* both women wear masks. Elizabeth's mask is her muteness. Alma's mask is her health, her optimism, her normal life (she is engaged; she likes and is good at her work). But in the course of the film, both masks crack.

One way of putting this is to say that the violence the actress has done to herself is transferred to Alma. But that's too simple. Violence and the sense of horror and impotence are, more truly, the residual experiences of consciousness subjected to an ordeal. It isn't, as I have suggested, that Bergman is pessimistic about the human situation—as if it were a question of certain opinions. It's that the quality of his sensibility has only one true subject: the depths in which consciousness drowns. If the maintenance of personality requires the safeguarding of the integrity of masks, and the truth about a person is always the cracking of the mask, then the truth about life as a whole is the shattering of the total façade behind which lies an absolute cruelty.

It is here, I think, that one must locate the ostensibly political allusions in *Persona*. I do not find Bergman's references to Vietnam and the Six Million genuinely topical, in the manner of seemingly similar references in Godard's films. Unlike Godard, Bergman is not an historically-oriented film-maker. The TV newsreel of a Buddhist immolating himself, and the famous photograph of the little boy from the Warsaw Ghetto, are for Bergman, above all, images of total violence, of unredeemed cruelty. It's as images of what cannot be imaginatively encompassed or digested that they occur in *Persona* and are pondered by Elizabeth—rather than as occasions for right political and moral thoughts. History or politics enters *Persona* only in the form of pure violence. Bergman makes an "aesthetic" use of violence—far from ordinary left-liberal propaganda.

His subject is, if you will, the violence of the spirit. If each of the two women violates the other in the course of *Persona*, they can be said to have at least as profoundly violated themselves. More generally the film itself seems to be violated—to merge out of and descend back into the chaos of "cinema" and film-as-object.

Bergman's film is profoundly upsetting, at moments terrifying. It relates the horror of the dissolution of personality (Alma crying out to Elizabeth at one point, "I'm not you!"). And it depicts the complementary horror of the theft (whether voluntary or involuntary is left unclear) of personality, what is rendered mythically as vampirism: at one point, Alma sucks Elizabeth's blood. But it is worth noting that this theme need not necessarily be treated as a horror story. Think of the very different emotional range in which this material is situated in Henry James's late novel, *The Sacred Fount*. The vampiristic exchanges between the characters in James's book, for all their undeniably disagreeable aura, are represented as partly voluntary and, in some obscure way, just. But the realm of justice (in which characters get what they "deserve") is rigorously excluded by Bergman. The spectator isn't furnished (from some reliable outside point of view) with any idea of the true moral standing of the two women; their enmeshment is a *donnée*, not the result of some prior situation we are allowed to understand. The mood is one of desperation: all we are shown is a set of compulsions or gravitations, in which they founder, exchanging "strength" and "weakness."

But perhaps the main contrast between Bergman and James on this theme derives from their differing positions with respect to language. As long as discourse continues in the James novel, the texture of the person continues. The continuity of language, of discourse, constitutes a bridge over the abyss of loss of personality, the foundering of the personality in absolute despair. But in *Persona* it is precisely language—its continuity—which is in question.

It might really have been anticipated. Cinema is the natural home of those who don't trust language, a natural index of the weight of suspicion lodged in the contemporary sensibility against "the word." As the purification of language has been envisaged as the peculiar task of modernist poetry and of prose writers like Stein and Beckett and Robbe-Grillet, so much of the new cinema has become a forum for those wishing to demonstrate the futility and duplicities of language.

In Bergman's work, the theme had already appeared in *The Silence*, with the incomprehensible language into which the translator sister descends, unable to communicate with the old porter who attends her when she lies ill, perhaps dying, in the empty hotel in the imaginary garrison city. But Bergman did not take the theme beyond the fairly banal range of the "failure of communication" of the soul isolated and in pain, and the "silence" that constitutes abandonment and death. In *Persona*, the notion of the burden and the failure of language is developed in a much more complex way.

Persona takes the form of a virtual monologue. Besides Alma, there are only two other speaking characters, the psychiatrist and Elizabeth's husband: they appear very briefly. For most of the film we are with the two women, in isolation at the beach—and only one of them,

Alma, is talking, talking shyly but incessantly. Though the verbalisation of the world in which she is engaged always has something uncanny about it, it is at the beginning a wholly generous act, conceived for the benefit of her patient who has withdrawn from speech as some sort of contaminating activity. But the situation begins to change rapidly. The actress's silence becomes a provocation, a temptation, a trap. For what Bergman shows us is a situation reminiscent of Strindberg's famous one-act play *The Stronger*, a duel between two people, one of whom is aggressively silent. And, as in the Strindberg play, the one who talks, who spills her soul, turns out to be weaker than the one who keeps silent. (The quality of that silence is changing all the time, becoming more and more potent: the mute woman keeps changing.) As real gestures—like Alma's trustful affection—appear, they are voided by Elizabeth's relentless silence.

Alma is also betrayed by speech itself. Language is presented as an instrument of fraud and cruelty (the blaring newscast; Elizabeth's cruel letter to the psychiatrist which Alma reads); as an instrument of unmasking (Alma's excoriating portrait of the secrets of Elizabeth's motherhood); as an intrument of self-revelation (Alma's confessional narrative of the beach orgy) and as art and artifice (the lines of Electra that Elizabeth is delivering on stage when she suddenly goes silent; the radio drama Alma turns on in her hospital room that makes the actress smile). What *Persona* demonstrates is the lack of an appropriate language, a language that's genuinely full. All that is left is a language of lacunae, befitting a narrative strung along a set of lacunae or gaps in the "explanation." It is these absences of sense or lacunae of speech which become, in *Persona*, more potent than words, while the person who places faith in words is brought down from relative composure and confidence to hysterical anguish.

Here, indeed, is the most powerful instance of the motif of exchange. The actress creates a void by her silence. The nurse, by speaking, falls into it—depleting herself. Sickened almost by the vertigo opened up by the absence of language, Alma at one point begs Elizabeth just to repeat nonsense phrases that she hurls at her. But during all the time at the beach, despite every kind of tact, cajolery and anguished pleading, Elizabeth refuses (obstinately? maliciously? helplessly?) to speak. She has only one lapse. This happens when Alma, in a fury, threatens her with a pot of scalding water. The terrified Elizabeth backs against the wall screaming "No, don't hurt me!" and for the moment Alma is triumphant. But Elizabeth instantly resumes her silence. The only other time the actress speaks is late in the film—here, the time is ambiguous—when, in the bare hospital room (again?), Alma is shown bending over her bed, begging her to say just one word. Impassively, Elizabeth complies. The word is "Nothing."

At the end of *Persona*, mask and person, speech and silence, actor and "soul" remain divided—however parasitically, even vampiristically, they are shown to be intertwined.

16

HOUR OF THE WOLF
Two Views

POEMS OF SQUARE PEGS   Penelope Gilliatt

. . . .

Preserve the out-of-step. Our newshounds and public nannies may generally manage to deride and mutilate the meaning of the singular man's existence, but at least our fiction grasps it. The late-eighteenth-century Romantics celebrated oddity for baroque reasons and drew lonely madmen as if they were animals, but we see something else. The wry new films lately made by Bergman and by Buñuel are tales of the peculiar only if they are taken literally; the obsessions of their chief characters are really images for the measures that people take to thrash their way out of comatose lives. In Bergman's *Hour of the Wolf*, a painter apparently goes mad, but he isn't much more beset or isolated than most of us, and his flight from a life of vanishing contact with his wife and from sterile social chatter about art seems less than lunatic. The hallucinated way he sees and hears things is a means of energizing a world that has gone stale in his own head. In Buñuel's *Belle de Jour*, a highbred girl is packed away in a marriage that is happy enough but leaves her sexually ravenous, so she turns herself into a tart in the late afternoons (either in objective reality or perhaps only in the reality within her mind). She does it not as any didactic blow against the bourgeoisie, or against the stingy dole of eroticism allowed to nicely born young Frenchwomen, but because she can feel her life sending her into a stupor of masochistic daydreams through sheer boredom.

The act of performing some private and willful act of defacement on the self that everyone else knows—by having a breakdown, or adopting unapproved characteristics, or suddenly reviling everything that was

From *The New Yorker*, Vol. 44, No. 9 (April, 1968), pp. 163-66. © 1968 by The New Yorker Magazine, Inc. Reprinted by permission.

ever nourishing, for the grim interest of seeing how shriveled a remnant can survive—has been the foundation of a great number of films, plays, and novels in the West since the Second World War. The painter and the young wife of the picture by Bergman and Buñuel use affronting behavior as a kind of dynamite upon their lives—out of desperation, because they feel inert and too smoothly understood. Bergman's painter isn't simply a mad artist in torment, and Buñuel's girl isn't simply a frosty beauty capable of Genet's freedoms as soon as she escapes from couture clothes. One responds to them because they stand for a troubled sort of person: urgent, modern, scared of the mid-twentieth century's particular sin of numbness, and hugely skeptical of the soft cant that says human life is forging ahead when it is so evidently turning to stone in their own nerve ends. The mad painter's disappearance at the close of the picture and the well-dressed girl's wild fantasies of whoring are symbols of torpor defeated. They express the possibility of winning some freakish victory over a society so congealed and generalized that to quit it by psychosis or idiosyncrasy has become, in art, a poetic act.

The hour of the wolf, in Swedish folklore is the time when most people die and most babies are born. It is the time when one sees what one is afraid of: the time that everyone in hospital dreads and the time when it is hardest not to give up. The painter must once have been less haunted, but now the bad hour engulfs him all the time. He draws people with muddled genders and the faces of monsters, and he has such a sense of decay-in-life that he sees a vision of an old woman at a dinner party in a castle peeling off the skin of her face like a surgical rubber glove. The other guests at the castle smile, cackle, agonize over nothing, stroke their own beautiful bare shoulders as they talk, and make brutish sexual boasts. Max von Sydow, as the painter, twists his head away and sees them like cartoons by George Grosz. His pregnant wife—Liv Ullmann, who played the actress in *Persona*—watches him endlessly and gets drawn into his hallucinations. Once, in their cottage, he suddenly counts out a minute as if it could never be over, holding his breath like a man in a poisonous crypt. The more she understands him, the more suffocated he seems to feel. She knows that the awful gang of art lovers up at the castle seem to him to be cannibalizing his flesh; she knows that he is terrified of the dark and gruesomely drawn to accepting punishment; but her intuition that he is being consumed is no help to him, and when she hysterically promises never to be scared into desertion he pulls away from the impossible liability of her unfailing kind of love. He knows more of Judas's sort. He has a hardboiled mistress who flourishes a ravishing bruise at him when he is trying to paint, and then he has to go through the wretched experience of meeting the man whom he has cuckolded, a glumly open soul who says that he knows every detail of their lovemaking. Von Sydow's guilt then makes more phantoms. To his horror, he sees the cause of his remorse walk up a wall of the castle and then across the ceiling. The man courteously asks him to take no notice. "It's only jealousy," he says, hanging like a stalactite.

Behind the credits of the film there are the sounds of cheery voices and hammering. It seems to be the racket between setups on a movie stage. The device is like the tearing of the film in *Persona*, the masterpiece that came before this picture; it says that what we are about to see is not a piece of life but a thing made. Films usually imply that they know the whole truth, and that selection is due to some Olympian whim of aesthetics playing peekaboo with what is told, but Bergman is beginning to do something else. In *Hour of the Wolf*, the form says that he is telling all he understands of a situation and that it is not very much. His film plays the part of an interlocutor and a witness, a sort of man in the middle who knows no more of the two people he is looking at than any third person knows of a couple in reality. The film, like *Persona* and *The Silence*, is about the inroads of two identities into one another. The impingement of temperaments can almost be seen. Bergman sometimes shows the flowing and merging as easy, but not often. There is usually an imbalance that makes something jam. The painter is open to pain only from the phantom projections of his superstitious ego, but the wife's range is more limited still, and her anguish is always a replica of his. She sometimes seems to be drumming for entry on the walls of his skull, as though becoming lost in another person were her only hope of sanctuary. His passion to remain intact is just as clamorous. Like the equivalent character in *Persona*, he uses every system of apathy and madness to stave off invasion.

Bergman tells the harsh story with a flicked switch of tense. The marriage was "some time ago." At the start of the film, Miss Ullmann walks out of the satanic little Hansel-and-Gretel cottage with a basket on her arm and sits down in closeup for a long, long take in which she tries to put together the evidence of the past. The only testimony, Bergman says in the titles, is the diary that the painter left and what the wife remembers. The rest of the picture has the tinge of a past inflection. There are slips and gaps and exaggerations. The wife's unbroken prologue has the mood of someone obsessed with unfinished business. What happened to their lives? She seems to have gone over everything that follows again and again. There was a time—we see a scene that is like some romantic rhapsody in the middle of electronic music—when her bilious husband was fond and less unhappy. In the sun outside their cottage, he has a flash of contentment. He makes a drawing of her, curled up with her arms on her knees and her hair up to show the nape of her neck. Maybe her memory falsifies, but she doesn't seem sentimental or self-justifying; she may simply be too ready to refract the personality of someone else. She asks the camera whether she did too much or too little; she can't see, as we can, that she had a third choice, and that doing nothing at all might have preserved more, at least of herself. "Isn't it true that old people who have been living together for a long time come to resemble one another?" she says to her husband, and then, later in the film, she asks him the same question directly, instead of wrapping it up as one about the aged. Her imagination fills with his, and his with the demons of the paranoid. I don't admire trumpery shots like the cut to an old lady's eyeball being dropped into a glass, but the acted part of the movie is filled with a more grown-up and authentic distaste for humankind. There are images of the painter in flight from company that are like scraps of the music for the world of Chaos and Old Night in "The Magic Flute." The formal organization of the film is beautiful, and it happens to knit into it some bars of opera ("Die Zauberflöte" itself: Tamino and the chorus) as exquisitely as I can remember anywhere in the cinema. Most snatches of great music in films seem not earned, a draft on reserves of feeling built up by other things; the Bach in Pasolini's pictures, for example, is colossal cheek—especially when the picture is about a ponce, like *Accattone*. Using it is like shoving seriousness into a war picture by using newsreel stock of Hiroshima. Bergman has an interesting ear. He said once that he always starts with the sound: "If you hear the right things, you also see the right things."

HOUR OF THE WOLF   Philip Strick
· ·

"I turn souls inside out," observes the psychiatrist to the artist who is grimly striving to avoid him, "and what do I see? But you'd know, of course—you and your self-portraits." The only reply he gets is a punch

From *Sight and Sound*, Vol. 37, No. 4 (Autumn 1968), pp. 203-4. Reprinted by permission of *Sight and Sound*.

on the nose (which, scientific detachment being what it is, he later returns with interest when his assailant is safely outnumbered). But his point—and Bergman's—is stingingly accurate. Like psychiatrists, artists can only work on the basis of what is inside themselves, and the truths that they uncover are as much personal as general. What amuses Bergman, however, is that the array of truth in *his* self-portraits is so complex and elusive that his would-be analysts can lose even themselves in the attempt to ferret them out.

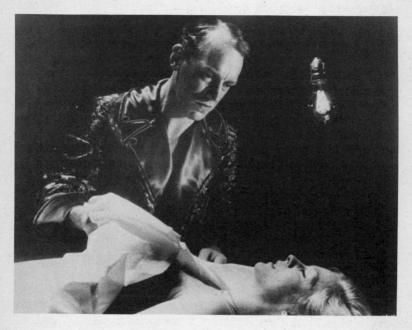

Max von Sydow as Johan Borg, and Ingrid Thulin as Veronica Vogler in *Hour of the Wolf.*

As with *Persona*, he challenges us in *Hour of the Wolf* (United Artists) to detect what is real in an indigenously unreal situation, and absolves himself from any responsibility towards providing a solution by confronting us at the conclusion as at the beginning with Liv Ullmann's appealing expression of contrite and inarticulate bewilderment. Bergman has always been at pains to establish that within the arch of his own proscenium anything can happen, and that when it does it will be, in several senses, his own affair. His method might be a game of charades, a cartoon on an ancient projector, a circus act, a medieval roadshow, an opening and closing on flaring carbons, but there has rarely been a Bergman film without at some point a miniature curtain being raised to reveal posturing souls in torment. The purpose is two-fold: on the one hand to remind his audience that even a one-act play requires a *deus ex machina,* on the other to stress that just as words are inadequate communication symbols for pure thought, so drama is merely an attempt to formulate for easier comprehension concepts normally too abstract to be defined.

Films and theatre cannot help but allegorise, for they involve contrivance and artificiality; but the joke, as Bergman sees it, is that through artifice they are nevertheless capable of getting closer to reality than any other medium. The joke is better still when that reality turns out to be nebulous or, like the logic of Aquinas, perversely illogical. For all that the artist may proclaim the unimportance of his work in the world of man, it is only through that work that the world can be revealed, an endless paradox.

So Bergman turns *Hour of the Wolf* into a succession of deceptive curtain-raisings, each leading us into deeper darkness until, like the exhausted couple keeping each other awake until dawn, we can conjure demons out of nothing. To start, the Bergman proscenium. Behind simple credits, the racket of stagehands at work, dwindling to a hush as the scene is set. Added alienation and insulation, as a narrator (Bergman himself?) puts the whole thing on the level of a dry report; then, as yet another complication, Alma Borg gives *her* version of the circumstances of her husband's disappearance.

Not until the flashbacks do we eventually come to grips with what appear to be the basic facts, and these in turn convey a speedy unreliability. Did Alma really receive a visit from an old lady in white whose hand she might have held and whose words were sometimes lost in the roar of the sea, or did she invent her (based on a fantastic sketch by her husband) to conceal her guilty intrusion into the secrets of Johann's diary? Worse, although we can assume that her recollection of the diary entries is accurate, does the diary itself report truths or inventions, genuine or imagined hallucinations? One can prowl through *Hour of the Wolf* with pedantic schematism and deduce from the evidence provided by husband or wife or both (and taking roughly into account the stages of their mental disintegration) what is "real" (all their scenes together), what is distorted "reality" (most of the scenes at the castle), and what is totally "unreal" (for the sake of argument, all scenes described only in Johann's diary plus the murder of the boy)—although whichever way one interlocks the jigsaw there are awkward pieces (the assault on Heerbrand, the arrival of the gun, and the final scene of Johann's disappearance).

But to sift through the film in this way is to imply that parts of it can be disregarded or discarded altogether in favour of a tidy narrative of psychopathic degeneration. They can't. *Hour of the Wolf* contrives to be another step forward on the path that could imaginably, and honourably, have reached its destination with *Persona;* and it does so both by approaching the *Persona* argument from an entirely new (and healthily sardonic) tangent, and by enriching it with several layers of illustration. The richest, perhaps Bergman's richest yet, is the link with "The Magic Flute." Controlled by the satanic impresario Lindhorst (on whose face a shadow flings a clown's smile), yet another curtain rises, to reveal Tamino with the song of mingled despair and hope (*O ew'ge Nacht*) that is at the same time a hymn to a love worth seeking and an apology for unfamiliarity with the rules of Freemasonry (representing, one might interpret, the established society from which Johann is an outcast).

It's a hefty clue, and there's a case to be made for relating everyone from Bergman downwards to the dying Mozart and his chameleon-like characters, whether or not one can strain this further than the astonishing scene in which Lindhorst/Papageno conducts Johann/Tamino along a corridor thick with wings to the room of Veronica/Pamina. "You see what you want to see," calls the Bird Man, feathers and all. However, the subsequent destruction of Johann by his jealous admirers, who having laughed him to scorn proceed to tear him to bits (they have, after all, found his replacement already in the pallid form of Kapellmeister Kreisler), is hardly vintage Mozart so much as undiluted contemporary Bergman, for whom critics were ever a fickle bunch . . .

Twenty-two years ago (*Crisis*) Bergman was telling the story of a man torn between two women; ten years ago (*The Face*) he was showing a performer being stripped of his mask, and five years ago (*The Silence*) he was revealing a single human coin by the examination of both its sides. All these were present in *Persona*, and they recur again in *Hour of the Wolf*, augmented on the immediate visual level by such familiar Bergman phrases as the bleached flashback (*Sawdust and Tinsel*), the errant eyeball (*The Face*), and the corpse that rises laughing from its slab (*Wild Strawberries*).

Yet there are new departures, too—the dizzying revolve by Nykvist's camera around the dinner-table, the hideous ambivalence of the murder scene, the startling levitation of the Baron (a joke that is delicately capped by von Sydow's nervous glance at the ceiling as he hurries on his way), the jump-cuts with the firing of the gun, the rapturous Lester-style burst of sunlight on the lens as Veronica flings herself into her lover's arms. "Awful things can happen," she murmurs. "Dreams can be revealed." Nightmares as well, it seems. In the hour before dawn, Bergman's imagination remains the finest, and the most disturbing, of all the cinema's modern visionaries.

17

SHAME
Film and Philosophy

**BERGMAN'S "SHAME" AND
SARTRE'S "STARE"**   Robert E. Lauder

· ·

It seems generally agreed that *Shame* is one of Ingmar Bergman's
finest films. Both director and film have been widely acclaimed and
applauded by the critics. What has been disturbing is the lack of accurate detailed analysis that the film, though hailed as a masterpiece,
has received. Many critics have divorced the film from Bergman's previous work and have looked upon *Shame* as merely an excellent anti-
war film. In their reviews such distinguished critics as Renata Adler,
Philip Hartung, Pauline Kael and Moira Walsh did not sufficiently relate *Shame* to Bergman's earlier films. In one of the better reviews of
Shame the National Catholic Office of Motion Pictures, in its bi-
monthly newsletter (January 30, 1969), correctly related *Shame* to existentialism by comparing the film to Albert Camus' *The Fall*.

Though there are strong resemblances between *Shame* and *The Fall*
and between Camus and Bergman, I think that Bergman can more
fruitfully be compared to the existential phenomenologist, Jean-Paul
Sartre. It is my thesis that *Shame* can best be understood in relation to
Bergman's earlier films and that the entire corpus of Bergman's serious
films can be illuminated by comparing and contrasting Bergman with
Sartre.

The story of *Shame* concerns a husband and wife who live on an island in 1971. A terrible civil war is raging on the mainland. The sym-
phony orchestra in which the couple played has been dissolved. The
couple, Jan and Eva, perfectly played by Max von Sydow and Liv
Ullmann have never paid much attention to the war. When the hor-

From *New Catholic World*, Vol. 209, No. 1254 (September 1969), pp. 247-
50. Reprinted by permission of *New Catholic World*.

rors of war are visited upon them, Bergman explores their relationship in order to make comments not only about them but about all human relationships. Though an anti-war film, *Shame* is much more.

It is my contention that every serious film that Bergman has made in the last thirteen years deals with either one of two aspects of a basic problem. Bergman's films concern the problem of the silence of God and the possibility of human love. For clarity's sake, Bergman's basic problem might be formulated as: "Given the silence of God, can human beings achieve enough self-identity to enter into meaningful love relationships?" In his earlier films Bergman focuses on the silence of God; in his later films he centers his attention on interpersonal relationships. There are two meanings with which Bergman has been obsessed: God and man. How do they interact? Can they communicate? What happens when they don't? For Bergman, the absence of evidence of Divine Love leads to the near impossibility of human love; the absence of human love reveals the absence of God.

Before using Sartre to understand Bergman and *Shame* a brief review of some of Bergman's previous films is necessary. The basic conflicts which preoccupy Bergman can be found as far back as 1956 in *The Seventh Seal*. This film can serve as an introduction to all Bergman's successive films. The Crusades having ended, a knight is returning home after battling for the Christian faith in a foreign land. He wonders what the meaning of life is, what significance his own life has. Engaging in a chess game with Death, the knight strives to perform one significant act, one meaningful action before he dies. He sees that if there is no God and no life after death, then life on earth is an absurdity. His squire, used by Bergman as an alterego, is constantly tempting the knight to despairing, cynical nihilism. The knight in describing faith says, "To believe is to suffer. It is like loving someone in the dark who never answers." The knight comes upon a young couple, Joseph and Mary, and their small baby boy. Joseph is a juggler and he says that some day his son will perform the one impossible trick, a juggling trick that will defy the natural laws of the universe.

Bergman makes clear that the family is a symbol of the Holy Family. In what has been described as the most tenderly wrought scene in Swedish cinema, the knight sitting on a hillside with the young family accepts gifts of food and drink from the family. Holding the drinking cup before him in an elevated fashion, the knight confesses that the love of the couple will be a sign for him that he will never forget. Later in the film, he performs the one significant act: he saves the family from Death. The film ends with the knight about to die still calling

to a God who is silent, still being tempted to despair by his cynical alterego, still wondering if, in the face of Death, life can have a meaning.

In an interview Bergman confessed: "Whenever I am in doubt, I
take refuge in the vision of a simple and pure love." Given the entire
context of the film, the love of Joseph and Mary can be seen as a sign
of God's love. It is this Divine Love of which the knight is finding so
little evidence in the world. God is present in the love of this family.
There is hope for mankind in the baby boy who will perform the one
impossible trick. Because of hope for the future, death can be faced.
The film ends on a note of hope.

The basic themes of the presence of God, of human self-identity and
love are brilliantly replayed by Bergman in the films following *The
Seventh Seal*. In *Wild Strawberries*, the elderly doctor, riding in a
hearse-like car on a long, winding road is like the knight in that both
try to find some meaning in their lives as they move toward death. In
The Virgin Spring, Bergman using much of the medieval symbolism of
The Seventh Seal struggles with the meaning of a loving God in light
of human cruelty and unjust suffering. *Through A Glass Darkly*, one
of Bergman's clearest films, explicitly states that we find God through
human love. The daughter who has not known the love of her father,
lives in the totally disordered world of the mentally sick and looks upon
God as a spider.

Winter Light and *Silence* are concerned with the meaning of divine
and human love, when either kind of love is absent. In *Winter Light*
when the pastor's first wife is alive, her love is a great support for him
and his faith is alive. After his wife's death he wonders whether God is
alive. The love of the school teacher does not support him, and he feels
that he no longer believes in God. The magnificent talk on the silence
of God by the crippled sacristan sugests that Bergman's God will always be a God Who hides His face.

With *Silence* some critics thought that Bergman had surrendered to
nihilism, but the film's ending rules out a nihilistic interpretation. By
ending the film with the young boy looking at the words in a foreign
language, Bergman is holding out hope for man to find himself though
the hope will be achieved with great difficulty. However, the film does
seem to mark a significant change in Bergman's emphasis. In *Silence*
and the films following it, Bergman no longer seems to be struggling
with God's existence. Bergman takes the silence and absence of God
as a fact and focuses on the difficulty of finding order and human love
in a world without God. Bergman's interests become centered totally

on man. The complete disorientation in the absence of a world-vision, of an ordered universe created by God, is what Bergman probed in *Persona* and *Hour of the Wolf*. In *The Magician* we have a portrait of an artist tormented by the loss of the community of faith but finding no consolation in the world of science.

It is in understanding the meaning of Bergman's most recent film that a consideration of Jean-Paul Sartre can be most helpful. Perhaps more than any philosopher in history, Sartre has constructed his philosophy around human freedom. Man is freedom. So unique is freedom, so different from everything else in experience, that Sartre contrasts it with being, by calling it nothingness. We might paraphrase the title of Sartre's master work, *Being and Nothingness*, as "Every thing Else and Freedom." Man is not a thing, an essence, a being, a substance or a person. He is spontaneity, creativity, freedom on the move.

Man for Sartre is, as more than one commentator has pointed out, so free that he resembles God. Sartre says that man is so free that man is not what he is but rather what he will be. To grasp Sartre we have to see human reality not as "man," which is too substantial a word, but as mercurial freedom. Because human reality is mercurial, human love is impossible. Two freedoms can never successfully love. Sartre says we must keep trying, but we will never succeed. Lovers are doomed to miss one another because they are not persons but rather freedoms. The great temptation is to treat a freedom as another thing. We are doomed to succumb.

In stressing this view, Sartre is the exact opposite of the great Jewish philosopher, Martin Buber. Sartre would say that an I-Thou relationship is metaphysically impossible. Love will ultimately destroy freedom. There are two great temptations that will lure most who try to love: sadism and masochism. In sadism, one of the lovers will try to control the other, make the other a thing, another object in the lover's experience. The lover becomes a stare in relation to the beloved. The stare tries to make the other an object, kill his possibilities and make him what he is during the moment of the stare. As the knower-lover gives meaning to the world, he also tries to give meaning to the human reality he confronts. He tries to control the possibilities of the other because the other's freedom is a threat to his own freedom. In masochism one partner of the love relationship submits, gives up his freedom because it is too great a burden. He wants to be a thing, he wants to be controlled. He cannot bear the anxiety that comes with freedom. Though we must continually try to love because it is the finest human activity, we cannot succeed.

It is because of his view of freedom that Sartre believes God is an impossibility. If God existed He would be an infinite stare. He would know all my possibilities, my future, all my actions before I performed them and consequently my freedom would be an illusion. God's stare would destroy me as freedom. Sartre's phenomenology, his letting-reality-appear-as-it-is, reveals to him that God is a metaphysical impossibility. Human reality's freedom demands the death of God.

Sartre's notion of freedom is powerfully brought out in *No Exit*. The three characters are in hell. They are solidified. They are total facticity, completely bound by their situation. Each is what the stare of the other makes him. When Garcin, the coward, pleads his innocence, Inez tells him:

> You're a coward, Garcin, because I wish it—do you hear?—I wish it. And yet, just look at me, see how weak I am, a mere breath on the air, a gaze observing you, a formless thought that thinks you . . . So you've no choice, you must convince me, and you're at my mercy.

Each character experiences shame at the stare of the other. Garcin is a coward, Estelle is a murderess and Inez is a lesbian because they are not free to be anything else. Each is controlled and limited by the stare of the others. The very order and objectivity created by the stare destroy freedom. Sartre's humans must exist in an absurd, disordered world in order to be free. For Sartre, freedom requires irrationality. The order that an existing God would introduce would destroy freedom. The characters in *No Exit* would rather suffer as objects than endure freedom. The burden of freedom is too great for them. Sartre himself longs for the order, objectivity and rationality that a God would introduce. In a poignant section of his autobiography, *The Words*, Sartre reveals this when he writes:

> I have just related the story of a missed vocation: I needed God, He was given to me, I received Him without realizing that I was seeking Him. Failing to take root in my heart, He vegetated in me for a while, then He died. Whenever anyone speaks to me about Him today, I say with the easy amusement of an old beau who meets a former belle: "Fifty years ago, had it not been for that misunderstanding, that mistake, the accident that separated us, there might have been something between us."

But there is no God and human reality is condemned to be free. Not to be free is to be immoral. Human reality is *abandonée*, adrift in a meaningless universe, but a man must never surrender his freedom.

Liv Ullmann as Eva Rosenberg, and Max von Sydow as Jan Rosenberg in *The Shame*.

Bergman's *Shame* parallels Sartre's philosophy in a number of ways. Also acting as a phenomenologist, Bergman is letting-reality-appear-as-it-is. The phenomenology that results is one pervaded by the silence of God. This silence makes the world a disordered place, a land in which it is impossible for a man to discover his personal identity. Consequently real communication is hopeless. It is a world in which profound intersubjective relationships are precluded.

The lack of communication between God and man and consequently between man and man is indicated early in the film. When Jan hears church bells, he indicates his annoyance that they should ring on any day but Sunday. He asks what they might mean. His wife, Eva, replies that they mean nothing. Then the phone rings. Eva picks it up, but there is no one on the other end. After she replaces the receiver the phone rings again. Eva says "Hello," but there is no reply. A third time the phone rings, but Eva just looks at it. The themes of lack of communication between man and God and between man and man are carried through the film. The church bells are heard a number of times in the film as a background that is meaningless. Before Eva commits adultery she hears the church bells and pauses. It seems as though she's trying to remember what they might mean. The church bells are replaced in the film by the constant noise of guns and bombs. The meaningless sound of church bells is replaced by man's unique way of communicating: the sounds of war.

The relationship between man and man is shown by the war but also by the love relationship between Jan and Eva. He is basically incapable of loving. In this film contemporary man's inability to achieve his self-identity and to love unselfishly and successfully is most evident in Jan. He is self-centered and weak. In the first half of the film, he is reliant on his wife. He is Sartre's masochist. In the second half of the film, he acts the sadist. Bergman's trust in the momentary and fleeting appearances of human love so beautifully expressed in *The Seventh Seal* is present though not emphasized in *Shame*. There are a few incidents, but the most striking occurs early in the film. After watching his wife for a few moments, Jan tells her, "For a second I loved you." The couple are Sartre's lovers in a meaningless, absurd universe, inhabitants of a nameless island off a nameless mainland, victims of a war between nameless powers. Jan loves his wife for a second. But in *Shame* the fleeting moment of love is not redemptive.

The most striking Sartrian scenes occur at the end of the film. Jan and Eva are in a lifeboat with other survivors of the war. They are *abandonée*, adrift at sea. Their boat moves by the floating bodies of hundreds of dead soldiers. The shame of war, of failures in loving, is almost unbearable. As Jan totally unmoved by anything human is dozing off, he stares at the man steering the boat. Experiencing the shame of being human, apparently unable to bear the presence of human beings, the navigator climbs over the side of the boat and slips into the water. Jan completely unperturbed returns to sleep. Bergman's closing shot of the boat adrift in the sea is the perfect symbol for atheistic existentialism.

The phenomenology of man constructed by Bergman in *Shame* is basically the same as Sartre's. Human love fails. Jan and Eva do not know an I-Thou relationship but rather a sadistic-masochistic relationship. Love is not redemptive as it is in *The Seventh Seal* or other Bergman films. Nor is it creative. Jan and Eva have no children, though she dreams of having them. Bergman and Sartre both present a phenomenology that presumes God's silence. For Sartre there is no God, no eternal establisher of values; man must grope with his freedom to achieve values through love, though love is doomed to ultimate failure. For Bergman the silence of God means that the world has no order, that man has no self-identity, and that human love is terribly fragile and fleeting. Bergman wants the order and security of a world in which man can achieve self-identity, and successfully enter into love relationships. As he lets-reality-appear-as-it-is, Bergman does not see that world. However, he is still asking, still searching.

Perhaps Bergman's phenomenology is not to our liking. It may be too dismal, its images too pessimistic. We are forced, however, to admit that—in his genius—Bergman often asks his questions better than we provide our answers.

18

A PASSION
Analysis

Peter Harcourt

· ·

A *Passion* opens with the sense of a slightly disabled, crippled, uncertain world, a world of diffused light, of burnt-out colour—a world in which we might feel strong moral certainties will prove to be impossible, where distinctions may be unclear. Behind the titles, we hear the sound of tiny bells, suggesting Chinese wind-chimes but blending imperceptibly into the sound of sheep bells that accompany the opening image of the film. It is an image of apparently serene animal life, a serenity, of course, that proves to be superficial.

Andreas Winkelman is attempting to repair his damaged house, his island retreat from the legal and emotional failures (the narrator explains to us) in the world outside. The first images we see of him suggest, through the continued close-ups of him tiling the roof and then hammering down below, a kind of physical energy which we will later see can erupt into a most destructive rage. But we also get the sense of a man suspended in time, as the twin dissolves of the sun might suggest. The sense of suspended time is carried on throughout the rest of the film in the alternation between snow-covered and snow-clear scenes, a device that both suggests an extended stretch of time and conveys a sense of uncertain seasons, part of the diffused quality that characterizes almost every element in the film.

Present in these first scenes is also the sense of Andreas Winkelman's tenderness in his concern with Johan Andersson. Andreas gets off his bicycle just to talk to him and to ask about his health. Yet this kind of concern is probably most active in situations where there is

From *Six European Directors* (England, Penguin Books) pp. 176-82. Copyright © 1974 by Peter Harcourt. Reprinted by permission of Penguin Books Ltd.

least demand. This might make us think of old Borg's relationship with the petrol attendant in *Wild Strawberries* where there was a similar sense of kindness offered to friends at a distance while emotional cruelty was inflicted on those close to home.

But in *A Passion*, the compassion is very real and a strong part of Andreas's withdrawn character, a hint perhaps of the kind of man he would like to be. As well as the scenes with the puppy and with Eva, I retain a vivid memory of the detailed attention that Bergman gave to Andreas's visit to the self-hanged Johan's house. Andreas lays his own live hand on the dead carter's folded hands. This gesture is not only affirmative in itself, an act of helpless compassion, but it also implies a recognition on Andreas's part of their sense of kinship. They have both been defeated by misfortune and driven back upon themselves. Through this gesture Andreas seems to recognize that he too might have been singled out as scapegoat for all the violence on the island, that he too shares such guilt as we all must share for the latent violence in us all—for the "forces from underneath," as the narrator calls them at the beginning of Anna's *Shame*-ful dream.

Anna's first appearance in the film presents her on a crutch, reinforcing our sense, already gathered from Andreas's broken-down house and from Johan's bronchitis, of a diseased and crippled world. Her distress over the phone-call seems very real, and Andreas's eavesdropping somewhat ambiguous. Perhaps his simple curiosity is part of his tentative feeling outwards towards other people. It is certainly a necessary plot device, prompting him as it does to read his namesake's letter, a letter to which the film returns again and again as if in Andreas's memory, the remembered lines giving the lie to all Anna's assertions about the honesty and truthfulness of her past marriage. Yet her lies are not *just* lies. They represent as well an aspiration towards a truthfulness which, the film finally brings home to us, none of the characters can ever hope to attain.

Though it is difficult to convey in words the sensations received from the total aural and visual impact of a film as finely achieved as this, I'd like to draw attention to this eavesdropping moment as an indication of the delicacy of nuance that characterizes the entire film. As we hear Anna talking, we move in on Andreas and can hear a clock ticking—a sound heard in many Bergman films but insistently in this one, emphasizing the stretching out of time referred to a moment ago yet creating also a kind of suspense, as if of someone counting, measuring out the moments yet left to live. When Andreas realizes the extent of Anna's distress and slips out to leave her alone with her grief, we are left with a coloured pattern on the wall caused by the sun coming in through the stained-glass window. As I responded to it, I felt it was not just a "pretty" effect: it conveyed in a purely visual and abstract way a sense of the delicacy that Andreas strives to bring to others in his relationship with them.

Somewhat similar is the moment after the silhouetted kiss between Andreas and Eva when they begin to make love. The camera focuses in on the window-pane, bringing to our attention the soft pink blur of a farm house, still out-of-focus, across the yard. Even more effective as a tiny visual detail is the orange lens flare just to the left of Andreas's face caused by the flasher on the police car that had come to announce Johan's suicide—a slight effect on the screen (possibly not even intended) that is in keeping with the sense the scene conveys of the fleeting precariousness of human life.

The central concern of *A Passion* seems to be with what I have already called the essential isolation of the human spirit. In this way the film is the summation of all of Bergman's work so far. Every detail in it contributes to this concern, even the magnificently staged dinner sequence at the Vergeruses' that shows the characters attempting to break through this isolation (like the ferry sequence in *Shame*). Even here, however, except for the closing four-shot and the moments when we hear them all chattering together, Bergman presents the bulk of the scene through single faces in close-up, separate from each other, each telling his own story. Similarly, the opening talk between Andreas and Johan is presented largely in action/reaction shots. At the very moment that we most feel Andreas's concern for the carter, through the editing Bergman emphasizes their essential separateness.

Related to this concern is the recognition of how unstable our sense of self is, our sense of who we really are. This is why the direct comments of the actors on the characters they are portraying work so well in the film. They not only distance us from the action slightly, in a Brechtian/Godardian way, reminding us that we are after all only watching a film, but they also give us the sense that even the actors cannot fully comprehend the characters they are portraying. This seems especially true of Bibi Andersson, who talks about her role in the same slightly over-sweet, over-sympathetic way that she, as Alma in *Persona*, talked about her life.

Sometimes this identity uncertainty is stated directly. Andreas wanders out into the wintry woodscape, screaming out his own name. But generally, it is more dramatically embodied within the discrepancies between what we see about the characters and what they say: *least* of

all with Elis, whose cynical acceptance of his self and the meaninglessness of life gives him his kind of eerie power over the other characters
in the film; *most* of all with Anna, whose problem seems the most serious in the film. After every scene with her when she talks about her
marriage and her great need for commitment and truth, we return to
that letter that Andreas has read, to Anna's husband's recognition of
the failure of their marriage (at least from *his* point of view) and of
his fear of the "physical and psychical acts of violence" that they
might inflict upon one another unless they part. Anna who in her talk
can seem most certain is in fact most insecure; or, put another way,
her assertions of certainty bring in their wake the very "physical and
psychical acts of violence" that her husband had feared. It would be
too simple to say that, on a metaphorical level, it is Anna's passion for
the certainty of truth that brings about the violence on the island, for
in varying degrees it is brought about by them all. But as the film is
presented to us, hers does seem to be the most destructive of the character dilemmas, and she has quite unambiguously been responsible for
the death of her husband and her own son.

The violence on the island, inexplicable as it is in terms of plot, is
clearly related to Bergman's concern with the theme of isolation. People who cannot reach one another and who are not certain who they
themselves are flail out at one another. This psychological insight, implicit in this film, may also have political ramifications and be part of
the cause of the persecution of the Jews or of the Vietnam war. But to
utilize political references in the way Bergman has done in *Persona* and
Shame (as I have already argued) seems to me simplistic and offensive,
considering the political reality of these issues today, a reality that
Bergman has nowhere shown he understands.

In *A Passion* Bergman seems to recognize this. Once again he shows
Andreas and Anna watching atrocities on television. But the scene is
immediately followed by the accident involving a little bird, which
they then have to kill together, to put it out of its misery, and bury.
Afterwards, they wash their hands together—he clean of the blood, she
of the earth in which they have buried it. The juxtaposition of these
two scenes seems to imply a recognition on Bergman's part that the
real violence that we have to concern ourselves with is the violence
closest to home, the violence that is directly a part of our own domestic
lives. Certainly this is the only kind of violence that Bergman, the artist, as he once again seems to realize, intimately understands.

When I write about *A Passion* in this way, so much of what I most
admire remains undescribed—the actual texture of the images and the

meaningful juxtaposition of scene against scene. Andreas's scream on his bed after his night with Eva is immediately followed by the blood-red scenes of the gratuitously slaughtered sheep, suggesting that this act of destruction is in some way connected with the (would it have been?) violence towards Eva that, in his efforts to be kind to her, he has repressed within himself. Similarly, the red of the blood is most tellingly and sensitively recapitulated by Anna's bright red kerchief left in the snow after their angry fight together, the fluttering spot of red suggesting in this way the blood that might have flowed from her as well.

The final sequences form a most masterful conclusion for this most masterly of all Bergman's films. The burning horse that would not die might well stand as emblem for the desperate clinging to life of all the characters in the film, no matter how great their disease or pain. In this way even this image provides a kind of affirmation, the affirmation of blind animal energy within despair.

The drive back along the rainy road that Anna and Andreas take to-

Max von Sydow as Andreas Winkelman, and Liv Ullmann as Anna Fromm in *The Passion of Anna.*

gether, a drive punctuated at two key moments by flash shots from outside the car and the single stroke of timpani (the only non-naturalistic sound in this film), recalls similarly cloistered moments of truth in other Bergman films, especially Marianne and Evald's talk in the rain in *Wild Strawberries*. At the same time, the little key-chain dog dangling from the windshield recalls the hanging puppy which we saw towards the opening of the film. It thus prepares us for Anna's attempted violence to come.

Anna, who claims to believe in truth, when confronted by the *conflicting* truth about her marriage represented by that letter, is driven towards an act of destruction as she had been once before on a similarly rainy road. Yet she is not totally blind to her own part in the failure of their relationship, to her own way of provoking the violence that, a few scenes before, we saw Andreas inflicting upon her.

"Why did you come for me at the fire?" Andreas asks her, after he has prevented her from crashing the car. "To ask for forgiveness," she replies. This comment conveys her recognition of her own kind of failing and also recalls *Wild Strawberries* in the juxtaposition that we have in this scene of the need for forgiveness—a doctor's first duty, as it was put in that film—with the punishment of *ensamhet*, of loneliness. "I want my solitude back," as Andreas had previously said.

But this time, at this moment in *A Passion*, it is Andreas who seems unable to forgive. He gets out of the car and lets her drive away, leaving himself alone with his own uncertainty concerning who he is and what he can do. Even his name is presented through the narrator as if somewhat provisional: "This time he was called Andreas Winkelman." He could be somebody else in another situation. He could be any one of the characters portrayed in other Bergman films by Max von Sydow; or indeed, he could be all of us.

We believe that when we look more closely at something we see it more clearly, even when we look at another person's identity. The very form of Bergman's film gives the lie to this, certainly the form of the ending. In what is one of the most remarkable shots in the history of the cinema (if I may be allowed this enthusiasm), we move in on Andreas pacing back and forth and then falling to his knees, as the grain swells up and the light increases until the image literally disintegrates before our eyes. Then another stroke on the timpani provides the final punctuation to this most extraordinary film.

19

THE TOUCH
The Role of Religion

BERGMAN'S ODYSSEY   Robert E. Lauder

. . . .

Like metaphysics with its undertakers, Ingmar Bergman is a good bet
to outlast his critics. Occasionally in the past a reviewer has indicated
fatigue with Bergman's alleged obscurity or his unintelligible symbols
or his heavy brooding attitude toward life. Word went out that Bergman was on the decline, that he was obscurantist or esoteric or narcissistic. But no sooner had it been announced that the master was slipping when a new masterpiece appeared. Though not a masterpiece,
Bergman's latest film *The Touch* supports his reputation as a cinematic genius.

The less than enthusiastic response of many critics to *The Touch*
should be viewed against what critics have come to expect from Bergman. For most directors *The Touch* would be hailed as a first-rate
accomplishment.

The plot centers around a love triangle. Though the marriage of
Dr. Andreas Vergerus (Max von Sydow) and Karin (Bibi Andersson)
is outwardly happy, Karin enters into a long love affair with an American archeologist, David (Elliott Gould), who is doing excavation
among religious ruins. Though Bergman has described it as a love
story, the film essentially is neither more nor less of a love story than
the director's other major works. With *The Touch* students of Bergman will be on familiar ground. The film is the latest signpost of an
odyssey that can be traced back to *The Seventh Seal* (1956). Marking
the extremely neurotic archeologist who discovers a lost Madonna and
Child from a more stable age of faith, the doctor who cannot heal the
wounds in his own love relationship and the wife who feels she may be

From *America*, Vol. 125, No. 5 (September 1971), pp. 119-20. © 1971 by
America Press, Inc. Reprinted by permission of *America*. All rights reserved.

able to successfully love both men, Bergman fans will experience a distinct sense of *déjà vu*.

The general theme of the film is presented visually before the credits appear. Karin is rushing to a hopsital to see her dying mother. Upon arrival she is told that her mother has died peacefully. As Karin gazes at her dead mother, Bergman intercuts shots of articles in the room with shots of the dead woman's hand. The mother's wedding ring is evident. The battle of human touch against death, of affection against coldness and closedness, has been stated, and the remainder of the film is an exploration of frail, faltering people trying to make contact with each other.

The role of religion in Bergman's world has been a source of disagreement among commentators. While some claimed that with *The Silence* (1963) Bergman opted for nihilism, others such as Fr. Arthur Gibson in his excellent book, *The Silence of God* (New York: Harper and Row, 1969), interpret Bergman's films as principally exploring the relation between God and man. My own thesis is that the basic question in all Bergman's major films is whether persons can relate and communicate with one another—more particularly whether they can relate in love to one another. Religious questions, allusions and symbols form a background for Bergman's most basic question. In Bergman's vision when people do not love, God is at best a memory and at worst an attacking spider. The basic search is for love.

The central position that the problem of interpersonal relationships has for Bergman is clearly evident in his famous trilogy: *Through a Glass Darkly* (1961), *Winter Light* (1962) and *The Silence* (1963). At the end of the first film, David the father confesses to his confused and questioning son Minus that his one hope is in the presence of love in the world of man: "Every sort of love, Minus. The highest and the lowest, the poorest and the richest, the most ridiculous and the most sublime. The obsessive and the banal. All sorts of love. . . . We can't know whether love proves God's existence or whether love is itself God. After all, it doesn't make very much difference."

After the dialogue Minus, genuinely moved by his father's sincerity, says "Daddy spoke to me."

More than merely a study of the minister's struggle with faith, *Winter Light* is the story of the schoolteacher's attempt to call the minister in love to be fully human. At the end of the film in the empty church before Vespers the schoolteacher prays to no clearly defined god: "If only we could dare to show each other tenderness." While her words continue on the soundtrack Bergman cuts to a shot of the minister in the vestry. There is a suggestion of some kind of communion between them. When the minister begins Vespers for a congregation, which consists only of the schoolteacher, the suggestion is strengthened. The Swedish title of the film, *The Communicants*, adds emphasis to this interpretation.

In *The Silence* Bergman explores the loveless relationship between the two sisters, Esther and Anna. When Esther is dying, she gives her small nephew a message she considers extremely important. The message consists of two words written in the foreign language of the country in which they have stopped. The film ends with the nephew pondering the foreign words—the words for "hand" and "face." The words are an admission of her own failure to be touched, to be loved, and state her hope that her nephew will succeed in loving.

The importance of love in the trilogy receives emphasis from Bergman's comments in an interview: "Each film, you see, has its moment of contact, of human communication. . . . A tiny moment in each film—but the crucial one. What matters most of all in life is being able to make that contact with another human. Otherwise you are dead, like so many people today are dead. But if you can take that first step toward communication, toward understanding, toward love, then no matter how difficult the future may be . . . then you are saved."

This concern with communication and human love could be traced in the films that came before *Through a Glass Darkly* and becomes more obvious in the films which followed *The Silence: Persona* (1966); the island trilogy *Hour of The Wolf* (1968); *Shame* (1968) and *Passion of Anna* (1970); and in the seventy-five-minute *The Ritual* (1969) made for television. The ending of the *Passion of Anna* is extremely significant for seeing a unifying theme in all of Bergman's major works. The main character, Andreas Winkleman, incapable of loving, is alone on a road. As the camera in a long shot focuses in on him, a telephone pole is seen a short distance from him, highlighting the theme of non-communication. The camera zooms in, and the texture gets more and more grainy. As Andreas paces back and forth aimlessly, we hear the narrator's voice: "This time he was called Andreas Winkleman." On the brink of pedantry, Bergman informs us that Andreas is everyman, that Andreas is every major character in Bergman's films from the knight in *The Seventh Seal* to the loveless couple in *Shame* and the actors in *The Ritual*.

At the end of *The Touch* when David, angrily walking away from Karin, leaves her alone on a country road, we almost expect to hear

Bergman's voice saying: "This time she was called Karin Vergerus."
Karin is the latest member of Bergman's troupe of searchers for love.
The title and theme of the film relate, of course, to Esther's message
at the end of *The Silence*. Brilliantly portrayed by Bibi Andersson,
Warin strives to be one who touches, though she succeeds with neither
her lover nor her husband.

Elliott Gould as David Kovac, and Bibi Andersson as Karin in *The Touch*.

At one point in the film David and Karin hold hands while they are
standing outside the church where he has discovered the ancient Madonna and Child. He says to her that at this moment they are really
close, really meeting one another. The church bells chime seemingly as
both a sign of their success and a reference to another age, more ordered and secure, when personal relationships were attainable. However, the I-Thou relationship is brief. Eventually it is discovered that
larvae have been eating away the Madonna and Child from the inside.
The neurotic David, incapable of opening himself to love, comments
that the insects are beautiful, at least as beautiful as the images. Berg-

man's spider-god has returned. Later, when Karin learns that David suffers from a mysterious arthritic condition in his hands, Bergman is offering a physical symbol of David's failure to love.

The film's concluding scenes form less a conclusion than a gradual fade-out. Pregnant Karin remarks that whether the father of her child is David or Andreas does not really matter. She is less concerned with the identity of the physical father than with the impossibility of making loving contact. Out of a new sense of duty Karin returns to Andreas, and their relationship is marvelously depicted when in the middle of the night Karin, facing camera, calls into her husband's darkened bedroom "Andreas! Andreas!" and no answer is given. Though Karin in her relationship with her husband has progressed to the level of duty, whether any "touch" will happen between them is left in doubt. The final shot of Karin, alone on the road after the rejected David has departed, leaves the viewer with the feeling that the drama has not really been concluded. One feels that, though the names and situations may be different in future films, Bergman has not finished probing the problem of loving.

Whatever its weaknesses, *The Touch* is a fascinating film. Admittedly Bergman is an acquired taste. But for those filmgoers who like metaphysics in their movies, the Swedish director remains in a class by himself.

20

CRIES AND WHISPERS
Bergman and Women

Joan Mellen

· ·

It is often claimed that Bergman, like Antonioni, is a director whose subject is Woman, that he has a unique affinity for portraying and understanding the female psyche. It is certainly true that many of Bergman's films focus particularly on women and the manner in which they come to terms with their lot in life. This applies to early works like *Monika* (1952), films of his middle period like *The Silence* (1963), and more recent films like *Persona* (1966), *The Passion of Anna* (1969), and *The Touch* (1970). Bergman's view of woman and her capacities for fulfillment is most explicit in his latest film, *Cries and Whispers* (1972).

Women are indeed frequently so significant to him as symbols of the dilemma of alienated, suffering human beings that Bergman employs them as spokeswomen to express his personal world-view—colored by a trauma in the absence and silence of a caring God who has coldly abandoned man to a cruel world. His women characters sometimes serve Bergman to express his agony over our ultimate inability to derive meaning from life except in rare moments of sensual ecstasy which are soon contaminated by disgust over the bodily processes in which all experience is rooted. Yet if women occasionally are Bergman's vehicle for locating meaning, it is much more frequently male characters who pursue the ethical issues in his films which are not peculiar to either sex.

What is striking about Bergman's treatment of women is thus not

Women and Their Sexuality in the New Film (New York, Horizon Press), Chapter Four. Copyright © 1973 by Joan Mellen. Reprinted by permission of Horizon Press and the author. The material also appeared in *Film Quarterly* (Fall 1973)

the philosophical role they are called upon to play in his films. It is, rather, his treatment of their characters. Bergman offers a much different explanation for the inability of his female, as opposed to his male, characters to find purpose in a universe without direction. His men fail largely because their pleas go unanswered; his women are ensnared at a much more elementary level of human development. Their lives lack meaning because they are rooted in biology and an inability to choose a style of life independent of the female sexual role. In this sense Bergman is arbitrarily far harder on his women than on his men. They are depicted as if on a lower notch of the evolutionary scale. Although the philosophical quest for an authentic mode of existence should not be influenced by female as opposed to male hormones, Bergman insists that because of their physiology, women are trapped in dry and empty lives within which they wither as the lines begin to appear on their faces.

If the Knight in *The Seventh Seal* fails to achieve a sentient life because the cold abstractions by which he moves lock him into an ethical opacity, Bergman's Ester in *The Silence* lives an empty, futile life because she has not accepted the demands of the female body, because she refuses the female sexual role. Her quest does not fail, like the Knight's, because her intellectual or even emotional gifts are not rich enough, but because her body drags her down and she is punished for her revulsion by the odors of the sexual act. Her "disease," like that of Agnes in *Cries and Whispers*, is unlike those of Knight, of Tomas in *Winter Light* or even that of the old man in *Wild Strawberries*. Ester is fixed in relation to her physiology and in her refusal to assume the primeval, instinctual life of a woman.

Thus Bergman presents us with a double standard. His men move in an ethical realm, his women in a biological one. It is true that his films reveal that these men are frequently found wanting. They contribute little solace or transcendence to a world filled with people who have lost the capacity to care for each other. But the cause of their moral demise does not rest especially in their male physiology. Bergman's men are distorted human beings, but their intrinsic physical characters and the nature of their flesh are not presented as standing in the way of their redemption. They are not irrevocably limited by the nature of their participation in the sexual act, as are his women. Free of limitations which are defined as intrinsic to the species, there is the hope, at least implicitly, that these men can change.

Bergman's women, on the other hand, are creatures whose torment resides in the obligation to submit to the repulsive sexual act. If Bergman's men lack power because there is no ethical imperative rooted outside the individual to which he can respond, his women (like Anna in *The Silence* or Karin in *The Touch*) are powerless before the sway of their lusts. They are passive, almost somnambulistic, in their search for a man with whom they can unite their flesh. This is the *raison d'être* of his *healthy* women—those who are presented as infinitely preferable to women who rebel futilely and self-destructively against this injustice visited upon them by nature.

This is the story of Ester in *The Silence* and Karin in *Cries and Whispers*, both played with hysterical frigidity by Ingrid Thulin, as well she might given the definition of the female Bergman continuously imposes upon her. Rebellion only leaves women like Ester and Karin exhausted and excluded from the flow of normal existence. Ester, in fact, must die for her rebellion. If she refuses to be a woman as Bergman defines woman—instinctual, passive, submissive and trapped within the odors and blood of her genitals—there is no place for her in the world. If a woman director were to present a male equivalent to Ester, most critics would be quick to infer that she hated the sex.

It might be argued that in our stage of cultural and psychological development this is how women are, that Bergman merely depicts what he sees. According to this view, one should not make the mistake of assuming that Bergman endorses this vision of woman as weak, pallid and locked into her physiology. Yet Bergman's point of view is arbitrary, contrary to the long chain of revisions of the misogynist female psychology outlined by Helene Deutsch wherein women are by nature passive, narcissistic and masochistic. Bergman's insistence upon maintaining this stereotype suggests that he has accepted an anachronistic view unquestioning of how his adherence to the spirit of the Northern Protestant culture out of which he springs has shaped his understanding of the potential of women. Absent from Bergman is the sense of how women have transcended and can overcome the norms of the ascetic and rigid 19th century philosophical milieu with which he has burdened himself. Far from understanding and showing compassion for the plight of women, Bergman creates female characters who are given the choice—only as in *Cries and Whispers*—to be a Karin, cold and frigid, or a Maria (mindless and promiscuous) or an Agnes, inexplicably non-heterosexual and insatiably in *angst* or an Anna, servile and bovine. And Bergman implies through the closed microcosm of human existence he presents that these will forever be our alternatives. To say that this is how women are is itself a distortion of reality, for however copiously the world is populated with women like Karin and

Maria, there are other kinds of women as well. Even Robert Altman's
Mrs. Miller, a professional prostitute in *McCabe and Mrs. Miller*, has
an intelligence and vitality absent from the entire range of the Bergman women.

This is not how we are. These basic types of women forever imposed
on us by Bergman, beginning as early as *The Naked Night* (1953)
represent a distinct and jaundiced sensibility. In all cases woman's behavior is arbitrary and axiomatic, inexplicable because it is based upon
an ordained mysticism of the female body, a view which most conscious women today would scorn. Alma, the wife of the clown Frost,
who bathes with a regiment of soldiers, represents the lust of women.
Agda, the bourgeois wife of the circus owner, Albert, finds "peace" in
renouncing her sexual role. She is the prototype of the cold and un-
feeling woman who denies her nature and its imperatives.

In the later films, the motives of women like Agda are clothed in
irrationality and mysticism. All we can observe is distorted behavior
flowing from discontent with their biological natures, a limitation
which Bergman presents as a given, rather than as an eccentricity. The
typical woman of the more recent Bergman is Eva in *Shame* (1967)
who cannot have children and who gives herself gratuitously to the
Mayor out of self-hatred and despair. She is as amoral and disoriented
as Anna in *The Passion* who caused the automobile accident in which
her supposedly "beloved" husband was killed.

Even those women who succumb to the dictates of their biological
role fail to find peace or meaning. Releasing themselves to lust makes
them feel only unsatiated and demeaned. It is through such a false
dichotomy—these two definitions of "woman" as the hot and the cold
—that Bergman continues his theme of the human being as a humiliated, pathetic creature ruled by impulses which he lacks the power to
fulfill.

For Bergman's women in general the body and its demands are insatiable. When bodily urges are unacknowledged, rage and frustration
follow in the denial. When they are gratified, the mind and sense of
middle-class decency are outraged, possessed by feelings of disgust,
low animality and self-hatred. But denied women become stifled, emotionally dead or harsh and perverse. Thus every feeling or emotion in
these women is burdened with the weight of animal lust and a parallel
contempt for that craving within the individual herself. Only grace
from a God who must be cruel and unfathomable or he would not
have so afflicted us could bring respite, and the heart despairs over
such absolution from this deity. Part animal and partially aspiring to

transcend her animal nature, Bergman's woman can never be content.

"I think it's terribly important," Bergman has said, "that art expose humiliation, that art show how human beings humiliate one another, because humiliation is one of the most dreadful companions of humanity and our whole social system is based to an enormous extent on humiliation." It is largely through woman, the creature tied to her flesh, that Bergman pursues the theme of man as a humiliated victim of a cosmic joke whose dictates can never be transcended nor its purpose fully grasped or accepted. The debasing sexuality of his women is fated as long as there is a human race. They are powerless, inherently unable to organize their lives differently, as with the young girl in *The Virgin Spring* (1960) whose rape signifies the destiny of all women. A spring is discovered where the girl was murdered partly because in the morally inexplicable universe which torments Bergman, fertility and the reproduction of the race require the violence visited upon women. It is another harsh paradox of human existence from which Bergman's women can never escape.

Discussing *Cries and Whispers*, Pauline Kael recognized the psychological and clinical distance of Bergman from his woman characters, his sense of "women as the Other, women as the mysterious, sensual goddesses of male fantasy." But this considerably underestimates the meaning of Bergman's distance from his female characters. Seeing women as "different" and "Other" amounts in Bergman's films to their utter dehumanization.

Cries and Whispers particularly carries this emotion and perception of women. Agnes, a dying woman, represents primarily the condition of women, if also that of mankind. She is shown in constant close-up in the sheerest animality of ailment: puking, rending and biting her lips and racked by asthmatic gasping. There are buckets of sweat, vile secretions and contractions. The full ugliness of the body dominates. Bergman's disgust becomes objective and aesthetically repellent to the subject herself, adding to her malaise. Stripped of its cumbersome and portentous metaphysics, this portrayal reveals in Bergman a man for whom not only sexuality or its intimations of need are vile, but most particularly, the female functions.

Woman, whose behavior flows from the mysteries of her organism, is at best patronized by the male director. Bergman's intellectual women are vastly less attractive than his spiritually questing men like the Knight in *The Seventh Seal* or the old man in *Wild Strawberries*. One is ineluctably brought to the conclusion that for Bergman it is not woman's *role* to quest after meaning. When she does, it is forced, unnatural and with far less grace, finesse or hope than with men. The most appealing of his women are those played by Liv Ullmann. Since *Persona* she has represented in his films a sensuality which, while it does not transcend its torments, at least attempts style. But even in the Ullmann characters it is a fate particular to woman that she is locked within the essential vulgarity of her flesh.

Cries and Whispers presents four women ensnared for the time period covered by the film into obsessive relationships with each other, excluding, except in flashback, men, children and parents. It culminates and makes unmistakable for Bergman's entire opus his sense of how women are inexorably and particularly limited by the physical shells in which their souls have been encased by that absent, unintelligible godhead who has left us so alone without communication, solace or release.

The set design of *Cries and Whispers* is a decaying mansion suggestive of a cocoon walled by red velvet and red brocade. The frequent fades to red with which Bergman moves between his characters convey how every woman acts out a facet of the character of each. This red comes to represent not only their shared blood, but the way in which each sister, in enacting aspects of behavior which are potential, or at other moments actual in them all, exhausts the nature of women, her soul colored by her physiological being. "Ever since my childhood," Bergman says in the treatment for the film which he published in *The New Yorker* (October 21, 1972), "I have pictured inside of the soul as a moist membrane in shades of red." In *Cries and Whispers*, this color of blood stands for woman. An image of her biology, like a "moist membrane," it defines her however she struggles to elude its grasp.

The four women are the dying Agnes, her sisters, Karin and Maria gathered at her deathbed, and a servant named Anna. Although Agnes is very emaciated, writes Bergman in the treatment, "her belly has swelled up as though she were in an advanced stage of pregnancy." She is dying of cancer of the womb, at once the disease of being a woman and of not fulfilling a woman's function by bearing a real child.

Karin, the eldest, despises her sexuality. Her husband, writes Bergman, "is repulsive to her physically and mentally." Although she has five children (whom, significantly, we never see, not even in Karin's own flashback), she is tortured by her sexuality and hates being a woman. In the treatment, although not in the final film version, Karin speaks of an affair she is having with another man which she refuses to associate with love: "It's a dirty itch and a few moments' oblivion."

The reference may not have been incorporated into the film because Bergman wishes to stress Karin's frigidity and a total abstention from the physical life of her sex.

Only deceptively an opposite to Karin, Maria promiscuously uses her body to pursue "pleasure." She is utterly unmindful of moral categories or distinctions. Her body is not merely indulged but assimilates all experience to its demands. The doctor with whom she once had an affair has since discarded her. He comments on the deterioration of her physicality. Indifference has caused four wrinkles to appear above each eyebrow, a line from her chin to her ear shows her to be easygoing and indolent. There are wrinkles under her eyes. She stands before the mirror that exposes to all women the pursuit of age. Just as Karin is humiliated by being a woman, the doctor, and Bergman, try to humiliate Maria with the evidence that she is losing what has always defined her: physical perfection as a woman.

The fourth woman is the servant Anna, heavy and silent. Having lost her child, her entire sensual life is devoted to the love and care of Agnes. At no time in the film is she revealed in any physical act of love other than when she climbs into the bed of the dying (or dead, as in one scene) woman and cradles her to her ample breasts. She is the character most capable of loyalty and love in the film, yet her love amounts only to the animal consolation of physical nearness—all, Bergman says, of which woman is capable. Comfort is possible in this film only from another woman, although even this is extremely rare. Most women, like most people for Bergman, cannot reach out and offer any love or kindness to another except in the easiest of circumstances, or out of lust.

All these women suffer deeply. The hurt of all is symbolized by the agony of Agnes, as in torment and struggle she leaves this world. Her lips are bitten, her skin sallow, her hair lank, her teeth yellow and her nostrils distended with pain. She is woman stripped of allure, bared to the repellent essentials of a body in decay. The redness of the walls, chairs, and floor is the diseased body of Agnes exposed to view.

The women are dressed in white, expressing their unconscious wish developed in the course of the film to return to the virginal and to exclude men entirely from their lives. All the men in the film—the pompous, self-satisfied doctor, the sardonic, sadistic husband of Karin and the weak, pallid, plump husband of Maria—are pathetic figures, less physically vibrant than the women. Woman is thus defined at once by being physical and unsatisfiable, a judgment validated by the inadequacy of the men Bergman chooses as their husbands and lovers.

Liv Ullmann as Maria, and Erland Josephson as the doctor in *Cries and Whispers*.

All the women in *Cries and Whispers* yearn to remain children and suffer for being adult women unwillingly. The first shot of Maria shows her as still a small girl lying next to the dollhouse of her childhood with a doll in bed beside her. As she sleeps, she childishly holds her finger to her lips. With Karin, Bergman focusses in close-up on her large white hands, cracked and chapped. They express the price she has paid for refusal to assume her role as a woman foreshadowing the brutal onset of an unattractive middle age. Anna is childlike with a continuing faith in God. She thanks God for his all-knowing kindness in taking her baby daughter and she still prays to him. Agnes has had no man and like a child the primal event of her life centered on her mother who preferred the pretty Maria to the more austere, deeply loving Agnes.

Bergman uses an extreme close-up of each woman to introduce the defining flashback of her life. Simultaneously, if awkwardly, a narrator in voice-over informs us of the lapse in time and why the characters happened to be at the original mansion in which they are now gathered in the present. The first such flashback has Agnes remembering a mother whose love she could never win. Her mother is a woman plagued by "ennui, impatience and longing," who could be "cold," and who always made Agnes feel left out. The high point of Agnes' life was a moment when she was permitted to touch her mother's cheek. Through this gesture she could express how deeply she felt, although only now, too late, can she understand her mother's ennui and loneliness.

Their mother, who doesn't speak a word in the film, is a woman very much like her daughters, and like all of Bergman's women. She felt in the very sight of Agnes the futility of her aspiration to be more than a reproducer. The more Agnes craved her mother's love, the more oppressed her mother felt. Maria, even as a child frivolous and unperceptive, was paradoxically easier for the mother to be with than the daughter who understood too much. To give love in Bergman is to be reminded of one's despair. This is so painful that it is easier not to love. And without love, life is empty. The emotions of Agnes repeat those of her mother, and of all women. This memory, culminating in touching her mother's cheek, is all that remains to the dying woman whose mother has been dead for twenty years. And it is on Agnes, who longed for more love than life offered, that Bergman inflicts a Kierkegaardian sickness unto death. Her disease is almost a direct consequence of her greater perception of God's brutality and man's hopeless self-hatred and sense of futility.

The whisper Agnes hears as she returns to the present is not a cosmic echo, but the entrance of the doctor and former lover of Maria. Like God, this healer cares little for his patients and does not in fact heal at all. In the course of the film two of his patients die—Agnes and the little daughter of Anna. Maria hears her own cries and whispers, the frustrations defining her past, just as Agnes has been tortured by an unuttered cry—her never having had the opportunity to tell her mother how well she understood her. The fade to red (the blood defining them all) returns us to the evening Maria spent alone with the doctor while her husband was away.

The camera focusses on the doctor's animalistic manners as he eats his dinner. As Maria makes small talk, the fork goes up to his mouth. With his head rigid, his mouth opens, his jaws moving up and down. And it is in this repellent act of eating that Maria, watching him, is aroused. While she lusts after him, he, like a cunning animal, is cold and indifferent, contemptuous of her because of his power to arouse. The doctor in him sees her clinically with curiosity, as if he were watching a spider spin a web. His very coldness and indifference, like

God's, attracts her. His inaccessibility makes him desirable. Animal lust in women for Bergman is usually directed toward a man who cares little for them, who in fact mixes his passion with contempt. Selfish and indifferent, both Maria and the doctor deteriorate beneath the weight of their own emptiness.

The next morning Maria's husband Joakim, having returned, perceives her infidelity as she sits whispering to her daughter, the way her mother had whispered to her before the jealous eyes of her plain sister Agnes. This time it is the man who is shut out. Joakim lays his hand on the cheek of his preoccupied wife. In chagrin, unable to live with his wife's infidelity, Joakim the weak stabs himself in the chest with a paper knife. Then, in tears, sobbing pathetically, he cries out for help. His wife eyes him with revulsion as the screen fades to red. Maria's contempt for her husband thus punctuates the flashback, defining the relationship.

In the original treatment Bergman has Maria indulge at this moment in a fantasy of "forcing the knife deeper into her husband's chest with all her strength, in a moment of stinging satisfaction." In the final version we are left with her scorn, the sneering for which the doctor had reproached her only the night before. The hatred of women for men is unabated throughout the course of this film. It is as irrevocable and inevitable as life, as the blood red fades to the "normal," pointing to woman's special shame.

Anna bares her breast to the dying Agnes while the death agonies of Agnes grow louder and deeper. Wheezing and screeching, she expresses Bergman's sense of how humiliated we are by our animal natures. The disease in its vileness conveys the horror of our existence on this "dirty earth" as the Pastor will refer to it. Bergman strongly suggests it is no worse than we deserve, so essentially incapable are we of even gestures of kindness and selflessness. For every scene in the film in which Karin and Maria are gentle toward Agnes, there is a companion scene in which they retreat in revulsion before her yellow hands and insatiable demands for consolation and love. The scene of Maria and Karin washing Agnes and of Maria reading her the *Pickwick Papers* is paralleled by both the refusal of each sister in turn to comfort the dead woman who cries that she cannot yet go to sleep so attached has she become to the living.

The dying cry of Agnes is "Can't someone help me?"—Bergman's metaphysical lament which forever goes unanswered. He sees it as beyond the family or society—as an ungratifiable hunger. Bergman has in fact reified this feeling into a fatality and a principle of the universe;

in this sense Maria and Karin must remain impotent to help their dying sister, despite their partial desire to console.

The dead body of Agnes further depicts Bergman's sense of the repulsiveness of human flesh, that of women included. Her feet are twisted with corns and callouses; her knees are grotesquely bent. The two crones in black who come to lay her out are like witches; they look like twins, like sisters. Shrivelled and parched, they represent the fate awaiting the sisters in the film—and all women.

No stronger than the husbands of Karin and Maria or the doctor is the Pastor who asks the dead Agnes to intercede for him and all the living with the God who has taken her. The Priest, speaking for Bergman, begs her to "pray for us who are left on this dark, dirty earth under a cruel, empty sky . . . to free us from our anxiety." Ask him, the Preacher exhorts Agnes, "for a meaning for our lives . . . plead our cause." The individual woman Agnes is sacrificed in the film by Bergman in a primitive ritual (again explaining the omnipresence of the color of blood) in the hope that this time God will answer. One can only conclude that Bergman was being less than frank when he said after the production *Winter Light* (1962) that he had finished with the theme of the silence of God:

> You know I was still convinced that God was somewhere inside the human being, that he had some answer to give us, and the end of the picture was exactly that. You have to continue; if God is silent you still have to go on with your work, the service, without believing anything. Things are difficult enough without God. They were much more difficult when I had to put God into it. But now it's finished, definitely and I'm happy about it.

Yet *Cries and Whispers* is broken in half by the reiteration of this very theme. It remains as integral to Bergman's work as his sense of the absence of free will afforded by the universe to human beings. It is expressed in his depiction of women as "classical" examples of beings limited by the shape God has given them and powerless to do anything but act in reaction to repellent biological drives.

The flashback to the central memory of Karin comes directly after the Pastor's incantation. Her mouth opens in agony, as if she is about to scream, just as throughout the film she is in constant pain. She hears the cries and whispers which bind her to her own past and the fade to red takes us back to a visit she made to the manor with her husband, Frederik.

Karin's husband is small, yellow, parched and ugly. He is also cold and unsympathetic. When she breaks her wineglass at dinner, his silence conveys more disdain than if he had verbally reproached her for the clumsiness by which both he and Karin's mother had been repelled. Karin's spilling of the red wine expresses her not-so-latent desire to spill his blood.

Karin and her husband are impeccably dressed. Their table manners (unlike those of the doctor)are beyond reproach. Not a hair is out of place, so tightly and primly are they combed and arrayed. Their rigidity and unnaturalness express of course repression and the fear of any spontaneous feeling. Undressing, Karin peels off endless layers of clothing, beautifully symbolic of the layers of convention hiding feeling both in her and in the class of which she is a member. The façade of false identity is represented by her elaborate clothes and is contrasted with the childlike closeness to her own feelings of Anna who helps her. Hating herself, Karin strikes Anna. But Anna, who represents all the simplicity that Karin has lost, denies her forgiveness.

Concealing a shard of jagged, broken glass, Karin murmurs, "it's nothing but a tissue of lies," a statement that could stand for the disillusionment of all of Bergman's characters. Karin's "it" may well stand for "love," her life with her husband, or the holy covenant of marriage itself, and Karin will not easily allow herself to be loved again. The phrase is repeated three times as she thrusts the glass into her vagina, finally drawing the actual blood which has dominated the *mise-en-scène* throughout the film. It is the blood of being a woman drawn with the special perverse satisfaction that comes with a revenge on men. In a scene of gross exaggeration, Bergman has Karin in bed spread her legs exposing the bloody mess to her prissy little husband in his fur-trimmed smoking jacket. Smearing blood on her face, she proceeds to lick it off as she revels in her own degradation and in the degradation of her sex. But revenge involves only self-mutilation. The fade to red comes this time as a kind of humiliation, one impossible to forget because it is accompanied by the inevitable cries and whispers.

The last third of the film posits and then rejects the thesis that women are capable of greater gentleness and feeling than men. It denies that they alone have retained the power to "touch" each other. Two overtures occur. The first is made by Maria to her sister Karin that they "be friends." She is sorry that they never "touch each other." She urges that they "laugh and cry together." The second overture is made by the dead woman toward her two sisters and her friend. Only Anna, the deprived, working class woman who possesses nothing of her own retains the capacity unselfishly to feel concern for another.

Karin finally yields to the embraces of Maria, although hatred has so locked her into her own life that she abhors anyone's touching her. She is deeply aware of the pain of losing contact after yielding to the need for it. Finally, she retreats murmuring, "I can't. I can't. It's like hell." Life is "disgusting, degrading." She tells Maria that she has often thought of suicide and that she even hates Maria with her "coquettishness and wet smiles." Yet she is correct about the "false promises" of Maria, as the film will reveal.

More than the others Karin speaks for Bergman. Her horrid and fought off emotions are the most deeply felt and are presented as the most authentically derived from experience. At last Karin yields to Maria's embraces only to discover her own awakened needs and feelings unreciprocated at the end of the film. And it is only when Karin is physically and sexually aroused by Maria that she responds to her caresses. This summons in her only the return of anxiety, disgust and self-hatred. Feeling for Bergman, between women as between men and women, has its origin in lust, although rejecting such love as unclean brings only loneliness. After much self-torture, Maria and Karin share one brief moment of tenderness and pure feeling, expressed by the haunting cello, the only sound we hear. It is a redeeming moment, all that life can offer. But great agony precedes the experience in which we are made vulnerable. And once the moment passes, despair and self-hatred return with a vengeance.

The second overture is made by the dead Agnes to each of the other women in turn, that they hold her hands and warm her because she can't get to sleep. Because *Cries and Whispers* moves on so non-naturalistic a level of abstraction, so doggedly leading from its *mise-en-scène* to generalizations about the human condition, the scene in which the dead Agnes makes overtures to her co-sufferers does not strain the credibility of the film. The mood of Kierkegaardian despair has so ominously prevailed and the imagery of the film so statically illustrated preconceived values that we do not suffer a shock upon discovering that the corpse, tormented in death as in life, cannot fall asleep. Even in death there is no respite. It is a test contrived by Bergman to measure the supposed humanity of these sisters who seem to have come out of sisterly devotion to comfort the dying Agnes. They are shown to be selfish and unable to respond even at a moment that escapes the boundaries confining us to the normal, the mundane, the pragmatic. Karin, alone with the corpse, refuses her outright: "There isn't a soul who would do what you say," she replies. "Perhaps if I loved you. But I don't love you. What you ask is repulsive." The corpse of Agnes is repulsive to her because, self-hating, she is repulsive to herself and because life as a woman is repulsive to her. Love involves death as well; the risk is too frightening and Karin flees. The corpse begins to cry and asks Anna to bring Maria.

Much more pliant, Maria responds to the corpse's request to touch her. "I feel so terribly sorry for you," she says. But when she is asked to come closer because "Agnes" cannot hear, the real test occurs and the corpse attempts to pull her down and kiss her violently on the lips. Maria, in a spasm, recoils and flees in sobs. Only in death could Agnes fully release her need for love, and it too proves to be of the body, only it is now of putrefaction, nearly expressive of Bergman's fear and revulsion for the physical. The corpse is left on the floor to be comforted by the devoted Anna who again exposes her large breasts and thighs. Like the now spotted hands of Agnes, Karin and Maria, members of a decadent bourgeoisie, have also begun to decay as human beings, although they will not recognize it. Bound both by their biologies and by their ungenerous and exploiting class, they are pathetic and empty.

Yet Anna's warmth also seems to involve an obliviousness to life's horrors, a limited capacity to register what life is. She cannot, for Bergman, represent a viable alternative to the self-centeredness of Maria and Karin. To Anna, Agnes is like the sick child she has lost. Her simplicity is the result of not asking too much of the world, especially of not questing for the purpose of things. It is only she, not the actual, intellectual mother of Agnes, who is capable of mothering. The perpetually dumb, accepting and serving Anna is a symbol of what God's servant has to be.

After the funeral, the two bourgeois couples take their leave. Maria and Joakim are willing to accept Frederik's insistence that they owe Anna nothing because "young and strong" she will survive, an oblique reference by Bergman to the vitality of her class as opposed to the degeneracy of theirs. To the chagrin of Frederik, Anna refuses to accept a keepsake. Only Maria abides by the forms, touching Anna on the cheek. It is another of those touches in the film that reveal not feeling, but convention. The gesture only conceals the absence of generosity and emotional commitment. Maria alone speaks to Anna at the end as well because, animal-like and weak, she is most like her.

Karin now tests the earlier sensual overture of Maria. "Do you mean to keep your resolutions?" she asks. But it has all meant nothing to Maria. She is far from gentle as she carelessly replies "whyever not?" Her mind wanders to Joakim waiting impatiently outside, and when Karin asks about her thoughts, she becomes hostile. For Maria, Karin is asking too much. "You touched me," Karin reminds her, "don't you remember?" "I can't remember every silly thing," is Maria's reply. And when Karin turns away coldly, Maria titters, "what a pity," and makes her exit. She becomes as cold and vengeful as Karin has been throughout the film. Rejecting the perfunctory, superficial embrace Maria offers, unwilling to take less than what she needs, Karin is left as alone at the end as she was at the beginning.

The crowning irony of the film is reserved for the conclusion. As a further expression of her devotion, Anna has secretly chosen her own keepsake—the diary of Agnes. She opens it and we read of the day when Karin and Maria first came to sit by the side of Agnes. The same woman who later, in her greatest need, will be rejected by both her sisters has written:

> . . . the people I'm most fond of in the world were with me. I could hear them chatting round about me; I felt the presence of their bodies, the warmth of their hands. I close my eyes tightly, trying to cling to the moment and thinking, come what may, this is happiness.

Agnes writes, ironically, not of Anna and her love, but of the sisters who will abandon and betray her and who will recoil when her need in death is greatest. And it is Anna and not her sisters who must read these words. Love among these women is not recognized or valued when it is present. After all of Anna's devotion and Agnes' dependence upon her comforting, not a syllable registering her feeling for Anna is present in the diary. She has left Anna as little as her sisters have, and equally rejects her, if by default. Thus Agnes too partakes of the natures of her sisters.

The park around the house is still green as the women in white go out to the swings. "For a few minutes I can experience perfection," Agnes writes; it is only these few moments that will be granted her during her entire life. She feels a gratitude for life that seen in flashback seems to represent a pre-experience, the film before it began and before either we or Agnes learn how little Karin and Maria are capable of giving. That all was illusory is stressed by Bergman in Agnes' words which are juxtaposed with all that has come after. Anna is mentioned in this recorded memory only as swinging the three sisters.

There is a disparity in *Cries and Whispers* between the richness of color, the purity of the white against red, and the absolute degradation visited by and upon these women. The women who are Bergman's supposed subject have been deprived of every savnig grace, even the mythical "gentleness" that is said to belong to females but be denied the male. Far from being his "favorite people," as one feminist critic supposed, Bergman exposes himself once again to be one of those filmmakers most hostile to a vision of women as free, creative, autonomous, self-sufficient, productive, satisfied, or, indeed, gentle. His women, rather, are chained to bodies which leave them little freedom or opportunity to transcend the juices, demonic drives and subordination peculiar to their gender. Paradoxically, their bodies even deprive them of that sensitivity frequently attributed to women. *Cries and Whispers*, in fact, provides one of the most retrograde portrayals of women on the contemporary screen.

Despite the plethora of women inhabiting the director's world, Bergman, as one of the great (if cult) figures in international cinema, stands in the way of a liberated image of women in film through a rigidity that ought not to escape notice because it is rooted in a pseudo-philosophical determinism which passes as profundity. There is something both inauthentic and suspect in an artist who delights in enclosing his women characters in a cycle of pain based on physiology at a time when many women are examining and discovering the means by which they can move beyond what they have been. In fact, Bergman has made victims and martyrs of his women at precisely the moment when they are rapidly rendering obsolete his vision of their "natures."

21

SCENES FROM A MARRIAGE
The Popular Audience

BERGMAN AND THE POPULAR AUDIENCE
Lester J. Keyser

. . . .

Scenes From a Marriage may become Ingmar Bergman's first smash hit in America; the first week of its release, *Variety* was referring to the box office receipts as "boffo" and the American distributor, Cinema V, a company beleaguered recently by financial problems, was lining up more theaters to exhibit the film. Critics gave *Scenes From a Marriage* rave reviews almost unprecedented in the history of New York journalism. Rex Reed, writing for the *Daily News*, hailed the film as "one of the most important films I have ever experienced in my lifetime."[1] Vincent Canby of *The New York Times* pronounced it a film that is "intensely, almost unbearably moving,"[2] while Archer Winsten of the *New York Post* was absolutely euphoric in declaring *Scenes From a Marriage* "from now until eternity, the best, most penetrating, utterly fascinating movie ever made on the subject."[3] Long lines of ticket-holders formed along Third Avenue, the Mecca of New York cinema, which hadn't seen such pushing and shoving nor endured so many traffic jams since the days of *The Godfather* and *The Exorcist*.

Probably no one is happier with this turn of events than Bergman himself. Once a cult figure, the demi-god of the art house clique, Bergman has, in recent years, publicly announced his intention of courting a wider audience, of creating art for the common man, like the inhabitants of Faro, his adopted island home. Film is worthwhile, "it does its job," Bergman now feels, when "one can get ordinary people to shut their mouths for a minute after the curtain has fallen" or

"Bergmen and the Popular Audience" is here published for the first time by arrangement with the author.

Liv Ullmann and Erland Josephson as Marianne and Johan in *Scenes from a Marriage*.

when "ordinary folk make themselves a sandwich and sit together and have a chat in the kitchen for five minutes after seeing a film" or when someone laughs or cries or is the "least bit" moved by what he has seen.[4] Expanding on this idea in an interview with Stig Bjorkman, Bergman mused that anyone who works in film must have the same goal before him: "to try to get as close to the viewer as possible, to affect him as deeply as possible."[5] *Scenes From a Marriage* is Bergman's most successful attempt yet at moving a mass audience. It has pleased both the sophisticated audiences of New York and the rural denizens of Faro.

   Scenes From a Marriage had its genesis in popular culture; the individual episodes, six in number, constituted a weekly series made for Swedish television. The shows were amazingly popular, the whole country was caught up in Bergman's story of a marriage, and the episodes were re-broadcast because of high audience demand. Bergman then prepared a film for international release based on the actual footage used in the television series. His first version condensed the six fifty-minute episodes into apporximately four hours. New World Cinema, which had distributed *Cries and Whispers* after most American companies had rejected it, was offered the American rights to Bergman's new film, but when executives at New World asked that *Scenes From a Marriage* be cut in length or be released as two separate two-hour films, Bergman refused, and negotiations ended. Dan Rugoff of Cinema V then accepted Bergman's conditions, the arrangement was settled, and preview screenings of the four-hour version were held. The screenings garnered unsatisfactory response, however, and Bergman decided to edit the film to the length now in American distribution, one hundred and sixty-eight minutes. Thus, *Scenes From a Marriage* actually has three reductions largely because it is aimed at a wide popular audience: a three-hundred-minute version designed for television, a two-hundred and-forty-minute version, Bergman's original cinematic design now shelved because of adverse reaction, and an American version of one hundred and sixty-eight minutes. Complicating matters somewhat more is the publication in English of the complete television version of *Scenes From a Marriage* by Simon and Schuster; book stores are already touting the text as the book that gives you what the movie left out. There are also persistent trade rumors that the original six episodes will eventually be shown on American television.

Given its origins in television, *Scenes From a Marriage* looks quite different from both traditional popular feature films and from Bergman's other works. The film is, for example, shot almost entirely in close-up. Bergman was well aware of the problems medium, long, and panoramic shots raise for the small television screen; he had confronted them in his work on *The Rite*. In *Scenes From a Marriage* he chose to crowd the cathode tube with faces in extreme close-up. Transferred to the cinema, Bergman's close-ups take on dimensions totally unlike those originally intended; the small screen has become large, and the introspective microscope of the electron beam has been replaced by the exhibitionistic magnifying glass of the movie projector. The small gaps we so naturally fill when the electronic beam dances on its reflective field are totally transformed in cinema, a hot medium. Furthermore, *Scenes From a Marriage* was shot in 16 mm for television and blown up to 35 mm for commercial release. The result is a graininess that superficially recalls cinema-verité, but soon transcends it. Vincent Canby aptly compares the impression of these colored dots flecked with black to "a kind of pointillist" effect.[6] The intimate scenes Bergman limned for television come perilously close to portraiture on the big screen.

The feeling of portraiture in *Scenes From a Marriage* is intensified by the straightforward narrative format that episodic television imposed on Bergman. On television each scene was presented as a separate weekly segment. Because television had divided the scenes one from another, Bergman could not additionally jeopardize the sense of one story, of one marriage, by further fragmenting his tale. Gone, then, in the television series and the resultant film are many of the hallmarks of Bergman's earlier works: the flashbacks and flashforwards, the dream sequences, the lap dissolves, the interior monologues, the surrealistic reveries, and the complex montages. When the serial development of episodic television is transferred to the continuous universe of a feature film, the static visual device of fading in and fading out separates the sequences and makes the scenes look like an orderly row of regular shaped pearls carefully strung together by the most mundane of threads. Stylistic fireworks are totally gone, and with them vanishes much of the dynamism and suggestive ambiguity inherent in the medium of film. Theater audiences are thus forced to look deeper into the frame and focus more sharply on individual pointillist images.

Bergman was acutely aware of the restraints television had imposed and warns in his preface to the teleplay that artistically sensitive people will be aesthetically sick after the very first scene, because *Scenes From a Marriage* is so readily understandable.[7] Apparently, simplicity and straightforwardness were two concessions he gladly made to capture a large audience. Considered in bare outline, even the plot he constructs in *Scenes From a Marriage* seems quite akin to hackneyed soap opera. Scene One, entitled "Innocence and Panic," introduces the main characters, Marianne, a lawyer, and Johan, a professor of science. They seem the most conventional middle class couple imaginable, cozy in their lifestyles, and content in an apparently ideal marriage. Scene Two, with its revealing title, "The Art of Sweeping Under the Rug," begins to strip away some of the veneer. Marianne senses that something is wrong between them although all seems normal on the surface.

In Scene Three, the lightning strikes; Johan tells Marrianne all about his new lover, "Paula," who gives her name to the scene. Johan then leaves Marianne all alone and totally distraught. Scene Four, "The Vale of Tears," presents both Johan and Marianne in a transitional stage, a period of suffering, as Marianne tries to find her identity and take control of her life, and Johan suffers his first serious doubts about Paula. Scene Five plunges the couple into the hell of hatred. The divorce papers are ready to be signed, and Johan and Marianne vent their spleen on each other in a bloody fight over the bloodless document that legally separates them. The last episode, Scene Six, with its somewhat cryptic, indeed almost metaphysical title, "In the Middle of the Night in a Dark House Somewhere in the World," presents the couple five years later, both re-married, but together again on a clandestine basis for a weekend in the country. On this weekend, they discover how much they have changed and grown, and forge a deeper bond than they had known before.

In the hands of a lesser director, this predictable plot might have degenerated into a vulgar tear-jerker, a mellower *Love Story*. Bergman's touch transforms his material into a film of rare beauty; like a cinematic Midas, he turns dross to gold. In the place of sentimental generalities and lachrymose situations, Bergman offers a wealth of fully realized incidents, a treasure hoard of appropriate and beguiling details, which make his romance both realistic and poetic.

Bergman captures the essence of the day to day life of Johan and Marianne by cataloguing the endless array of commonplace concerns which constitute the bulk of their life, concerns Johan and Marianne are oblivious to for far too long. Johan and Marianne don't seem to notice that they are overwhelmed by dinner dates and family obligations, by the house to be painted, the roof to be tiled, the teeth to be fixed, by the parking tickets and the dry cleaners. Even when Marianne and Johan are about to separate, they talk of banalities: of split fingernails and misplaced books, of electric shavers and shoes too heavy to be packed, of mailmen, plumbers, and cars. Each of these seemingly trivial concerns offers a spark of recognition for the audience; as Johan and Marianne are smothered and lost under details, the audience is attracted as though by an electromagnet of everydayness to identify with Bergman's characters, and to examine the details of their own life in the reflected light of the life of Johan and Marianne. In a paradoxical way, the more Johan and Marianne are developed as individuals and linked to specifics, the greater the tendency is for the mass audience to identify with them and generalize upon their experience. By making his *Scenes From a Marriage* so straightforward and so specific, Bergman has taught his "lessons in love" much more effectively than ever and to a much wider audience.

Bergman's lessons in love seem especially appropriate for the mass audience of the seventies. As Molly Haskell acutely observes in her discussion of the film, the modern age has become "an age of communal self-therapy and prescriptive sociology" which cooperate in an effort "to reassure us that we are not alone in our problems."[8] The lines of people on Third Avenue in New York and the clusters of sheepherders around their television sets on Faro can find in the unvarnished saga of Johan and Marianne one more case-study to be pondered, more grist for the mill of psychological analysis.

Scenes From a Marriage seems almost tailor-made for those pseudo-scientists and popularizers who have created a massive industry out of analyzing modern marriages. Advocates of transactional analysis, armed with their vision of personalities as parents, adults, and children, will be able to apply their vocabulary most convincingly to *Scenes From a Marriage*. Johan's voyage can be seen as one from childhood to adulthood, and Marianne's as a liberating transition from parenthood to adulthood. Locked in their cozy marriage, Johan does, in fact, speak of himself as feeling safe, noting that it reminds him of childhood, "when I felt I was protected" (*Scenes*, p. 8). Cast adrift for a while, and given a chance to recognize his limitations and to grow as a result of this recognition, Johan can finally look back and see that he is "a child with genitals. A fabulous combination when it comes to women with maternal feelings" (*Scenes*, p. 187). His self-recognition is, of course, the sign of his final maturity and adult vision. Marianne, at the beginning of the film, can only define herself in terms of her social role, parenthood: "Hmmm, what can I say . . . I'm married to Johan and have two daughters" (*Scenes*, p. 3). By the end of the film, she is puzzling over the meaning of life. Having found her adult identity, she is in quest of an understanding of the world. She has, in Johan's words, perceived "her greatness" (*Scenes*, p. 192).

Other analysts will also be happy with the film and use it as a text for their approach. Communications theory, for example, plays a large role in the film. In the very first scene, Marianne analyzes the problem of another couple as involving a difference in language: "They don't speak the same language. They must translate into a third language they both understand in order to get each other's meaning" (*Scenes*, p. 25). Johan rejects Marianne's notion at first, but years later finds himself echoing her metaphor when he attempts to explain what went wrong in their marriage: "I'll tell you something banal. We're emotional illiterates" (*Scenes*, p. 143). Bergman calls his fifth scene "The Illiterates" and obviously invests further symbolic value in concrete images of communication like Johan's poetry, Marianne's journal, and the repeated critical telephone calls.

Even behavioralists will find much to ponder in *Scenes From a Marriage*. Johan and Marianne are not only the victims of things; they are caught in a web of family relationships and larger social movements, like rats in a maze. They don't like the insipid magazine article about them, for example, but explain that "our mothers and daughters thought it was all wonderful, so we let it go" (*Scenes*, p. 12). Also let go were the obligatory Sunday dinner, the dinner parties with business acquaintances, and the endless round of other social niceties. When the breach in their relationship comes, Johan explodes: "Do you know what I'm most fed up with? All this fucking harping on what we're supposed to do, what we must do, what we must take into consideration" (*Scenes*, p. 85). Bergman counterpoints this idea with a marvelous visual symbol. In the lab, Johan, himself a scientist, has devised a behavioristic experiment where the subject must follow a moving dot with a marker; during the experiment, the subject is registered on a television monitor. The initial results suggest that the longer one tries to follow the pattern of the dot, the more agitated one becomes. Johan and Marianne are themselves unconsciously following the dots as they pursue the ideal marriage; it is Bergman's monitor that records their misadventures. The audience is left to offer its hypothesis.

The danger in all these attempts to dissect *Scenes From a Marriage* is that the search for theme and meaning may obscure the most basic fact of all: for all its realism, and popularity, and social relevance, the film is primarily a work of creative imagination, a fictional artifact resulting from the collaboration of some very gifted professionals. Bergman provided the script, which he indicates in his preface to the teleplay "took three months to write, but rather a long part of my life to experience" (*Scenes*, p. viii). *Scenes From a Marriage* is one of Bergman's finest screenplays, full of terse, economic dialogue, dialogue as true to the ear as Hemingway's best. The screenplay contains some almost incandescent passages as imaginatively rich as the allegorical sequences in *The Hour of the Wolf*. Marianne's journal entries about "the same perpetual dissimulation," Johan's rage over their emotional illiteracy, and the entire last scene, as they "snuggle down" in bed, are among the best writing Bergman has ever done.

To interpret his dialogue, Bergman worked eight weeks shooting his television series with Liv Ullmann, a member of his regular acting company, and Erland Josephson, a stage actor who had appeared briefly as the doctor in *Cries and Whispers*. Ullmann told an interviewer recently that there was "no improvisation" on the set; instead the actors were under Bergman's thumb, and "were not allowed to depart one word from the script."[9] This fidelity to the written word did not, however, curb the creativity of each actor. The remarkable achievement of *Scenes From a Marriage* is, in fact, largely due to the stellar job the two actors do. It is Ullmann and Josephson who give life to Bergman's words, who hold the many realistic details together, and who reflect in their faces and bodies the emotional turmoil of a faltering marriage. The closeups of *Scenes From a Marriage* give them no shelter at all from the camera's probing eye; the film depends on their control of the slightest facial gesture to convey the many subtleties of a complex human relationship.

To capture and convey the nuances of Marianne's character, probably the most challenging role for a woman in film this year and a role destined to go down in cinema history, Liv Ullmann drew inspiration from her own life, including her marriage to Bergman, and the lives of her friends. One reason for the popularity of *Scenes From a Marriage*, and especially for its popularity with women, is, Ullmann confided to Molly Haskell, this very borrowing from real life: "One reason a lot of women relate to it is that I've drawn from so many women; from this friend and that one, I steal bits and pieces like a drawing."[10]

The portrail Liv Ullmann draws depends on her unique ability to capture both small, quite revealing scenes and the big, loud scenes of confrontation without either underplaying an emotion or getting lost in histrionics. One fine example of her understated eloquence is her scene with Mrs. Jacobi, a client who has come to Marianne's law firm to get a divorce. Mrs. Jacobi's visit occurs around the time Marianne is first feeling some disharmony at home; Mrs. Jacobi's quandary thus provides a powerful foil to Marianne's perplexity. The camera focuses quite intensely on Liv Ullmann's reactions as Mrs. Jacobi talks of a marriage without love; Marianne obviously recognizes parallels to her own situation when Mrs. Jacobi declares: "There is no love in the marriage. There never has been" (*Scenes*, p. 52). Marianne must deal with this professionally, however, and she probes for another explanation: maybe the real cause is money or another woman or some other tangible thing. No, replies Mrs. Jacobi, the feeling is that of something "thin and dry" (*Scenes*, p. 55). Ullmann tenses at these words, words that capture Marianne's own thirst for more in marriage. Excusing herself, she quickly telephones Johan, just to talk, just to banish the revelation that Mrs. Jacobi and she are kindred spirits. Ullmann manages to capture both the dawning recognition in Marianne and her innate desire to repress this unwanted knowledge, and she does it without speaking a word.

At the other end of the spectrum, Liv Ullmann can shout Bergman's words with almost more intensity than an audience can bear. In a chilling episode from the Fifth Scene, "The Illiterates," Marianne finally asserts her independence at Johan's expense. The scene is critical since it serves as a prelude to a brutal, bloody battle, the first physi-

cal conflict between Johan and Marianne. There is literally fire in Ullmann's eye and a fighter's tenseness in her body when she pours out
her venom:

> Do you suppose that I've gone through all I have and come out on the
> other side and started a life of my own which every day I'm thankful for,
> just to take charge of you and see that you don't go to the dogs because
> you're so weak and full of self-pity? If I didn't think you were so deplor-
> able I'd laugh at you. When I think of what you've done to me during
> the last few years, I feel sick with fury. Go on, look at me. I'm proof
> against that gaze of yours. I've hardened myself. If you knew how many
> times I've dreamt I battered you to death, that I murdered you, that I
> stabbed you, that I kicked you. If you only knew what a goddamn relief
> it is to say all this to you at last. (*Scenes*, p. 151)

Ullmann's inflection and gesture in this sequence move masterfully
from anger to self-pity to disgust, to end in a feeling of relief that the
burden has been lifted from her and everything is out in the open,
that the hatred is clear. All that remains is for her anger to express itself in blows.

Johan's character also runs a broad gambit of emotions, and Erland
Josephson struggles mightily to make a rather subtle role acceptable to
a large audience. Josephson is hampered by Johan's stuffiness in the
opening scenes; audiences are bound to be somewhat taken back by a
man who tells an interviewer he is "extremely intelligent, successful,
youthful, well-balanced, and sexy. A man with a world conscience,
cultivated, well read, popular, and a good mixer" (*Scenes*, p. 3). Josephson builds on this pomposity and self-righteousness, this insensi-
tivity and crassness, however, as he allows the audience to see more
and more of Johan's insecurities. By Scene Five, Johan is a totally
broken man, full of self-pity and self-hatred, yet he is by this time a
complex enough presence to make his subsequent resurrection in Scene
Six, which takes place five years later, perfectly acceptable. Johan's own
words show his change into a well-balanced, mellower character:
"Someone said I'd grown slack and gave in too easily. That I diminished myself. It's not true. If anything, I think I've found my right
proportions. And that I've accepted my limitations with a certain humility. That makes me kind and a bit mournful" (*Scenes*, p. 182).

It is Josephson's forceful interpretation of Johan that makes all these
changes seem natural and acceptable; his somewhat too formal and
too stiff beginning makes the mellowing of Johan's attitudes all the
more noticeable and effective. It is interesting to note that audiences

in Sweden didn't react well to Johan when the television series was first shown. By the time the series was rebroadcast three times, Johan had become a favorite of the fans; it appears the audiences needed the sense of the whole film to understand the insecurities that plagued Johan throughout, and it is his last scenes that really illuminate the first.

Much of *Scenes From a Marriage* is best understood in retrospect. The five years that lapse between the fifth scene and the last one, while not pictured, are critical ones in Johan's and Marianne's lives. After all the agony and suffering, Bergman's last vision of their relationship and of human relationships in general is an affectionate if not a happy one. In place of the vale of tears, there is quiet laughter in the country. Johan's banter on the telephone as he requests the loan of a friend's cottage for his weekend rendezvous with Marianne brilliantly exposes the shallowness and banality of casual affairs; when he tells his buddy that Marianne is "young" and "very pretty" and "blonde," he and Marianne and the audience laugh knowingly, well aware by now that life is so much more complex than that, so much more entangling.

Although aimed at a mass audience, Bergman's *Scenes From a Marriage* rejects entirely the silly romanticism that usually dominates popular entertainments. There are no easy answers, no clichés, and no cotton candy in the world of Johan and Marianne. Their love is, as Bergman presents it and as Johan analyzes it, the only love that fallible humans can find in the middle of the night in the dark house of the world: "And I think I love you in my imperfect and rather selfish way. And at times I think you love me in your stormy, emotional way. In fact, I think that you and I love one another. In an earthly and imperfect way" (*Scenes*, p. 197). Bergman has obviously come a long way in *Scenes From a Marriage* from the visions of an absent God, or of a universe with a spider in God's place. And in his journeys, he has found a new audience.

NOTES

1. Rex Reed, "Fans: This Is Your Life; Bravo Bergman!" New York *Daily News* (September 20, 1974), p. 80.
2. Vincent Canby, "Superb Bergman," *The New York Times* (September 16, 1974), p. 41.
3. Archer Winsten, "*Scenes From a Marriage* Opens," *New York Post* (September 16, 1974), p. 28.

4. Stig Bjorkman, Torsten Manns, and Jonas Sima, *Bergman on Bergman: Interviews with Ingmar Bergman,* trans, Paul Britten Austin (New York: Simon and Schuster, 1973), p. 130.
5. *Bergman on Bergman,* p. 159.
6. Canby, p. 41.
7. Ingmar Bergman, *Scenes From a Marriage, trans.* Alan Blair (New York: Pantheon Books, 1974), p. vii. Subsequent citations from this volume appear in the text with the notation *Scenes* and the page reference.
8. Molly Haskell, "A Doll's House of Cards," *The Village Voice* (September 26, 1974), p. 84.
9. Molly Haskell, "Liv Ullmann: The Goddess as Ordinary Woman," *The Village Voice* (October 3, 1974), p. 5.
10. Haskell, "Liv Ullman," p. 24.

SELECTED BERGMAN FILMOGRAPHY
(*Principal Credits*)

I. Films for which Bergman wrote the screenplay, but did not direct.

1944: TORMENT/Br. Frenzy (*Hets*)
DIR: Alf Sjoberg
SCR: Ingmar Bergman
D/P: Martin Bodin
MUS: Hilding Rosenberg
SET: Arne Akermark
EDR: Oscar Rosander
PRO: Svensk Filmindustri
CAST: Stig Jarrel (Caligula), Alf Kjellin (Jan-Erik Widgren), Mai Zetterling (Bertha Olsson), Olof Winnerstrand (school principal), Gosta Cederlund (Pippi), Stig Olin (Sandman), Jan Molander (Pettersson), Olav Riego (Widgren), Marta Arbiin (Mrs. Widgren), Hugo Bjorne (doctor), Gunnar Bjornstrand (teacher), Curt Edgard, Anders Nystrom, Birger Malmsten.

1947: WOMAN WITHOUT A FACE (*Kvinna utan ansikte*)
DIR: Gustaf Molander
SCR: Ingmar Bergman
D/P: Ake Dahlqvist
MUS: Erik Nordgren
SET: Arne Akermark
EDR: Oscar Rosander
PRO: Svensk Filmindustri
CAST: Alf Kjellin (Martin Grande), Gunn Wallgren (Rut Kohler), Anita Bjork (Frida Grande), Stig Olin (Ragnar Ekberg), Olof Winnerstrand (Director Grande), Marianne Lofgren

(Charlotte), Georg Funquist (Victor), Ake Gronberg (Sam Svensson), Linnea Hillberg (Mrs. Grande), Calle Reinholdz, Sif Ruud, Ella Lindblom, Artur Rolen, Bjorn Montin.

1948: EVA

DIR: Gustaf Molander
SCR: Ingmar Bergman and Gustaf Molander from a synopsis by Bergman
D/P: Ake Dahlqvist
MUS: Erik Nordgren
SET: Nils Svenwall
EDR: Oscar Rosander
PRO: Svensk Filmindustri
CAST: Birger Malmsten (Bo), Eva Stiberg (Eva), Eva Dahlbeck (Susanne), Stig Olin (Goran), Ake Claesson (Fredriksson), Wanda Rothgardt (Mrs. Fredriksson), Inga Landgre (Frida), Hilda Borgstrom (Maria), Axel Hogel (fisherman), Lasse Sarri (Bo at twelve).

1950: WHILE THE CITY SLEEPS (*Medan staden sover*)

DIR: Lars-Eric Kjellgren
SCR: Lars-Eric Kjellgren from a manuscript by P. A. Fogelstrom based on a synopsis by Bergman
D/P: Martin Bodin
SET: Nils Svenwall
EDR: Oscar Rosander
PRO: Svensk Filmindustri
CAST: Sven-Erik Gamble (Jompa), Inga Landgre (Iris), Adolf Jahr (Iris's father), Elof Ahrle (basen), Ulf Palme (Kalle Lund), Hilding Gavle (halaren), John Elfstrom (Jompa's father), Barbro Hiort af Ornas (Rut), Carl Strom (Portis), Marta Dorff (Iris's mother), Ilse-Nore Tromm, Arne Ragneborn, Hans Sundberg, Lennart Lundh, Hans Dalberg, Ulla Smidje, Mona Geijer-Falkner, Harriet Andersson.

1951: DIVORCED (*Franskild*)

DIR: Gustaf Molander
SCR: Ingmar Bergman and Herbert Grevenius from a synopsis by Bergman
D/P: Ake Dahlqvist
MUS: Erik Nordgren
SET: Nils Svenwall
EDR: Oscar Rosander
PRO: Svensk Filmindustri
CAST: Inga Tidblad (Gertrud Holmgren), Alf Kjellin (Dr. Bertil Nordelius), Doris Svedlund (Marianne Berg), Hjordis Pet-

tersson (Mrs. Nordelius), Hakan Westergren (P. A. Beck-man), Irma Christensen (Dr. Cecilia Lindeman), Holger Lowenadler (Tore Holmgren), Marianne Lofgren (Inge-borg), Stig Olin (Hans), Elsa Prawitz, Birgitta Valberg, Sif Ruud, Carl Strom, Ingrid Borthen, Yvonne Lombard, Einar Axelsson, Ragnar Arvedson, Rune Halvarson, Rudolf Wend-bladh, Guje Lagerwall.

1956: THE LAST COUPLE OUT (*Sista paret ut*)

DIR: Alf Sjoberg
SCR: Ingmar Bergman and Alf Sjoberg from a story by Bergman
D/P: Martin Bodin
MUS: Erik Nordgren, Charles Redland, Bengt Hallberg
SET: Harald Garmland
EDR: Oscar Rosander
PRO: Svensk Filmindustri
CAST: Olof Widgren (Hans Dahlin), Eva Dahlbeck (Susanne Dahlin), Bjorn Bjelvenstam (Bo Dahlin), Johnny Johansson (Sven Dahlin at eight), Marta Arbiin (Grandmother), Jullan Kindahl (Alma, the Dahlins' maid), Jarl Kulle (Dr. Farell), Nancy Dalunde (Mrs. Farell), Bibi Andersson (Kerstin), Aino Taube (Kerstin's mother), Jan-Olof Strand-berg (Claes Berg), Hugo Bjorne (Lecturer), Goran Lund-quist (small boy).

1961: PLEASURE GARDEN (*Lustgarden*)

DIR: Alf Kjellin
SCR: Buntel Eriksson (pseudonym for Ingmar Bergman and Erland Josephson)
D/P: Gunnar Fischer
MUS: Erik Nordgren
SET: P. A. Lundgren
EDR: Ulla Ryghe
PRO: Svensk Filmindustri
CAST: Gunnar Bjornstrand (David), Sickan Carlsson (Fanny), Bibi Andersson (Anna), Per Myrberg (a young pastor), Kristina Adolphson (Astrid), Stig Jarrel (Lundberg), Gosta Cederlund, Torsten Winge, Hjordis Pettersson.

II. Films which Bergman directed.

1946: CRISIS (*Kris*)

DIR: Ingmar Bergman
SCR: Ingmar Bergman from the play *Moderdyret* by Leck Fischer
D/P: Gosta Roosling

MUS: Erland von Koch
SET: Arne Akermark
EDR: Oscar Rosander
PRO: Svensk Filmindustri
CAST: Dagny Lind (Ingeborg), Inga Landgre (Nelly), Stig Olın
      (Jack), Marianne Lofgren (Jenny), Allan Bohlin (Ulf),
      Ernst Eklund (Uncle Edvard), Signe Wirff (Aunt Jessie),
      Svea Holst (Malin), Arne Lindblad (the mayor).

1946: IT RAINS ON OUR LOVE (*Det regnar pa var karlek*)
DIR: Ingmar Bergman
SCR: Ingmar Bergman and Herbert Grevenius from the play *Bra
      mennesker* by Oskar Braathen
D/P: Hilding Bladh, Goran Strindberg
MUS: Erland von Koch
SET: P. A. Lundgren
EDR: Tage Holmberg
PRO: Lorens Marmstedt, Sveriges Folkbiografer
CAST: Barbro Kollberg (Maggi), Birger Malmsten (David), Gosta
      Cederlund (man with umbrella), Ludde Gentzel (Hakans-
      son), Douglas Hage (Andersson), Hjordis Pettersson (Mrs.
      Andersson), Julia Caesar (Hanna Ledin), Gunnar Bjorn-
      strand (Purman), Magnus Kesster (bicycle mechanic), Sif
      Ruud (his wife), Ake Fridell (the pastor), Benkt-Ake
      Benktsson (the Prosecutor), Erik Rosen (the Judge), Sture
      Ericsson (Kangsnoret), Ulf Johansson (Stalvispen).

1947: A SHIP TO INDIA (*Skepp till Indialand*)
DIR: Ingmar Bergman
SCR: Ingmar Bergman from the play *Skepp till Indialand* by
      Martin Soderhjelm
D/P: Goran Strindberg
MUS: Erland von Koch
SET: P. A. Lundgren
EDR: Tage Holmberg
PRO: Lorens Marmstedt, Sveriges Folkbiografer
CAST: Holger Lowenadler (Captain Alexander Blom), Birger
      Malmsten (Johannes Blom), Gertrud Fridh (Sally), Anna
      Lindahl (Alice Blom), Lasse Krantz (Hans), Jan Molander
      (Bertil), Erik Hell (Pekka), Naemi Briese (Selma), Hjordis
      Pettersson (Sofie), Ake Fridell (music hall manager), Peter
      Lindgren (foreign crewman).

1948: NIGHT IS MY FUTURE (*Musik i morker*)
DIR: Ingmar Bergman
SCR: Dagmar Edqvist from her novel of the same title

D/P: Goran Strindberg
MUS: Erland von Koch
SET: P. A. Lundgren
EDR: Lennart Wallen
PRO: Lorens Marmstedt, Terrafilm
CAST: Mai Zetterling (Ingrid), Birger Malmsten (Bengt), Bengt Eklund (Ebbe), Olof Winnerstrand (the pastor), Naima Wifstrand (Mrs. Schroder), Bibi Skoglund (Agneta), Hilda Bergstrom (Lovisa), Douglas Hage (Kruge), Gunnar Bjornstrand (Klasson), John Elfstrom, Sven Lindberg, Bengt Logardt, Marianne Gyllenhammar, Barbro Flodquist, Ulla and Rune Andreasson.

1948: PORT OF CALL (*Hamnstad*)

DIR: Ingmar Bergman
SCR: Ingmar Bergman from a story by Olle Lansberg
D/P: Gunnar Fischer
MUS: Erland von Koch
SET: Nils Svenwall
EDR: Oscar Rosander
PRO: Svensk Filmindustri
CAST: Nine-Christine Jonsson (Berit), Bengt Eklund (Gosta), Berta Hall (Berit's mother), Erik Hell (Berit's father), Mimi Nelson (Gertrud), Hans Straat (Vilander), Birgitta Valberg (Vilander's assistant), Nils Dahlgren (Gertrud's father), Harry Ahlin (Skaningen), Nils Hallberg (Gustav), Stig Olin (Thomas), Sif Ruud (Mrs. Krona), Sven-Eric Gamble.

1949: THE DEVIL'S WANTON/Prison (*Fängelse*)

DIR: Ingmar Bergman
SCR: Ingmar Bergman
D/P: Goran Strindberg
MUS: Erland von Koch
SET: P. A. Lundgren
EDR: Lennart Wallen
PRO: Lorens Marmstedt, Terrafilm
CAST: Doris Svedlund (Birgitta-Carolina), Birger Malmsten (Tomas), Eva Henning (Sofi), Hasse Ekman (Martin Grande, film director), Stig Olin (Peter), Irma Christenson (Linnea), Anders Henrikson (Paul), Marianne Lofgren (Mrs. Bohlin), Carl-Henrik Fant (Arne), Inger Juel (Greta), Curt Masreliez (Alf), Ake Fridell (Magnus), Bibi Lindqvist (Anna), Arne Ragneborn (her lover).

1949: THREE STRANGE LOVES/Thirst (*Torst*)

DIR: Ingmar Bergman
SCR: Herbert Grevenius from the short story *Torst by* Birgit Tengroth
D/P: Gunnar Fischer
MUS: Erik Nordgren
SET: Nils Svenwall
EDR: Oscar Rosander
PRO: Svensk Filmindustri
CAST: Eva Henning (Rut), Birger Malmsten (Bertil), Birgit Tengroth (Viola), Mimi Nelson (Valborg), Hasse Ekman (Dr. Rosengren), Bengt Eklund (Raoul), Gaby Stenberg (Astrid, his wife), Naima Wifstrand (Miss Henriksson, dancing teacher), Sven-Erik Gamble (the worker), Gunnar Nielsen (male nurse), Estrid Hesse (patient), Helge Hagerman (Swedish priest), Calle Flygare (Danish priest), Else-Merete Heiberg (woman on train), Monika Weinzierl (her child), Hermann Greid (guard).

1950: TO JOY (*Till gladje*)

DIR: Ingmar Bergman
SCR: Ingmar Bergman
D/P: Gunnar Fischer
MUS: Mendelssohn, Mozart, Smetana, Beethoven
SET: Nils Svenwall
EDR: Oscar Rosander
PRO: Svensk Filmindustri
CAST: Maj-Britt Nilsson (Martha), Stig Olin (Eriksson), Victor Sjostrom (Sonderby), Birger Malmsten (Marcel), John Ekman (Mikael Bro), Margit Carlquist (Nelly, his wife), Sif Ruud (Stina), Rune Stylander (Persson), Erland Josephson (Bertil), Georg Skarstedt (Anker), Berit Holmstrom (Lisa), Bjorn Montin (Lasse), Carin Swenson, Svea Holm (two women), Svea Holst, Agda Helin (nurses), Maud Hyttenberg (salesgirl).

1950: THIS CAN'T HAPPEN HERE/High Tension (*Sant hander inte har*)

DIR: Ingmar Bergman
SCR: Herbert Grevenius
D/P: Gunnar Fischer
MUS: Erik Nordgren
SET: Nils Svenwall
EDR: Lennart Wallen
PRO: Svensk Filmindustri

CAST: Signe Hasso (Vera), Alf Kjellin (Almkvist), Ulf Palme (Atka Natas), Gosta Cederlund (the doctor), Yngve Nordwall (Lindell), Stig Olin (the young man), Ragnar Klange (Filip Rundblom), Hanno Kompus (the pastor), Sylvia Tael (Vanja), Els Vaarman (woman in the cinema), Edmar Kuus (Leino), Rudolf Lipp ("The Shadow").

1951: ILLICIT INTERLUDE/Br. Summer Interlude (*Sommarlek*)
DIR: Ingmar Bergman
SCR: Ingmar Bergman and Herbert Grevenius from a story by Bergman
D/P: Gunnar Fischer
MUS: Erik Nordgren
SET: Nils Svenwall
EDR: Oscar Rosander
PRO: Svensk Filmindustri
CAST: Maj-Britt Nilsson (Marie), Birger Malmsten (Henrik), Alf Kjellin (David), Annalisa Ericson (Kaj), Georg Funkquist (Uncle Erland), Stig Olin (ballet master), Renee Bjorling (Aunt Elisabeth), Mimi Pollak (Henrik's aunt), John Botvid (Karl), Gunnar Olsson (pastor), Douglas Hage (Nisse), Julia Caesar (Maja), Carl Strom (Sandell), Torsten Lilliecrona (lighting man), Marianne Schuler (Kerstin), Ernst Brunman (Captain), Olav Riego (doctor), Fylgia Zadig (nurse), Sten Mattsson, Carl Axel Elfving, Gosta Strom.

1952: SECRETS OF WOMEN/Br. Waiting Women (*Kvinnors vantan*)
DIR: Ingmar Bergman
SCR: Ingmar Bergman
D/P: Gunnar Fischer
MUS: Erik Nordgren
SET: Nils Svenwall
EDR: Oscar Rosander
PRO: Svensk Filmindustri
CAST: Anita Bjork (Rakel), Maj-Britt Nilsson (Marta), Eva Dahlbeck (Karin), Gunnar Bjornstrand (Fredrik Lobelius), Birger Malmsten (Martin Lobelius), Jarl Kulle (Kaj), Karl-Arne Holmsten (Eugen Lobelius), Gerd Andersson (Maj), Bjorn Bjelvenstam (Henrik), Aino Taube (Anita), Hakan Westergren (Paul), Kjell Nordenskold, Marta Arbiin, Carl Strom.

1953: MONIKA/Br. Summer with Monika (*Sommaren med Monika*)
DIR: Ingmar Bergman
SCR: Ingmar Bergman and P. A. Fogelstrom from the novel by Fogelstrom
D/P: Gunnar Fischer

MUS: Erik Nordgren
SET: P. A. Lundgren
EDR: Tage Holmberg
PRO: Svensk Filmindustri
CAST: Harriet Andersson (Monika), Lars Ekborg (Harry), John Harryson (Lelle), Georg Skarstedt (Harry's father), Dagmar Ebbessen (Harry's aunt), Ake Fridell (Monika's father), Naemi Briese (Monika's mother), Ake Gronberg, Sigge Furst, Gosta Pruzelius, Arthur Fischer, Torsten Lilliecrona, Gustaf Faringborg, Ivar Wahlgren, Renee Bjorling, Catrin Westerlund, Harry Ahlin.

1953: THE NAKED NIGHT/Br. Sawdust and Tinsel (*Gycklarnas afton*)

DIR: Ingmar Bergman
SCR: Ingmar Bergman
D/P: Hilding Bladh, Sven Nykvist
MUS: Karl-Birger Blomdahl
SET: Bibbi Lindstrom
EDR: Carl-Olov Skeppstedt
PRO: Rune Waldekranz, Sandrews
CAST: Harriet Andersson (Anne), Ake Gronberg (Albert Johansson), Hasse Ekman (Frans), Anders Ek (Frost), Gudrun Brost (Alma), Annika Tretow (Agda, Albert's wife), Gunnar Bjornstrand (Sjuberg), Erik Strandmark (Jens), Kiki (the dwarf), Ake Fridell (the officer), Majken Torkeli (Mrs. Ekberg), Vanje Hedberg (Ekberg's son), Curt Lowgren (Blom).

1954: A LESSON IN LOVE (*En lektion i karlek*)

DIR: Ingmar Bergman
SCR: Ingmar Bergman
D/P: Martin Bodin
MUS: Dag Wiren
SET: P. A. Lundgren
EDR: Oscar Rosander
PRO: Svensk Filmindustri
CAST: Eva Dahlbeck (Marianne Erneman), Gunnar Bjornstrand (Dr. David Erneman), Yvonne Lombard (Suzanne), Harriet Andersson (Nix), Ake Gronberg (Carl Adam), Olof Winnerstrand (Professor Henrik Erneman), Renee Bjorling (Svea Erneman, his wife), Birgitta Reimer (Lise), John Elfstrom (Sam), Dagmar Ebbesen (nurse), Helge Hagerman (traveling salesman), Sigge Furst (priest), Gosta Pruzelius (train conductor), Carl Strom (Uncle Axel), Arne Lindblad (hotel manager), Torsten Lilliecrona (porter), Yvonne Brosset (ballerina).

1955: DREAMS/Br. Journey into Autumn (*Kvinnodrom*)
    DIR: Ingmar Bergman
    SCR: Ingmar Bergman
    D/P: Hilding Bladh
    SET: Gittan Gustafsson
    EDR: Carl-Olov Skeppstedt
    PRO: Rune Waldekranz, Sandrews
    CAST: Eva Dahlbeck (Suzanne), Harriet Andersson (Doris), Gunnar Bjornstrand (Sonderby), Ulf Palme (Henrik Lobelius), Inga Landgre (Mrs. Lobelius), Sven Lindberg (Palle), Naima Wifstrand (Mrs. Aren), Benkt-Ake Benktsson (Magnus, director), Git Gay (lady in the studio), Ludde Gentzel (Sundstrom, photographer), Kerstin Hedeby (Marianne), Jessie Flaws, Marianne Nielsen, Siv Eriks, Bengt Schott, Axel Duberg.

1955: SMILES OF A SUMMER NIGHT (*Sommarnattens leende*)
    DIR: Ingmar Bergman
    SCR: Ingmar Bergman
    D/P: Gunnar Fischer
    MUS: Erik Nordgren
    SET: P. A. Lundgren
    EDR: Oscar Rosander
    PRO: Svensk Filmindustri
    CAST: Eva Dahlbeck (Desiree Armfeldt), Ulla Jacobsson (Anne Egerman), Harriet Andersson (Petra), Margit Carlquist (Charlotte Malcolm), Gunnar Bjornstrand (Fredrik Egerman), Jarl Kulle (Count Carl-Magnus Malcolm), Ake Fridell (Frid), Bjorn Bjelvenstam (Henrik Egerman), Naima Wifstrand (Madame Armfeldt), Jullan Kindahl (the cook), Gull Natorp (Malla, Desiree's maid), Birgitta Valberg, Bibi Andersson (actresses), Anders Wulf (Desiree's son), Gunnar Nielsen (Niklas), Gosta Pruzelius, Svea Holst, Hans Straat, Lisa Lundholm, Sigge Furst, Lena Soderblom, Mona Malm, Josef Norman, Sten Gester.

1957: THE SEVENTH SEAL (*Det sjunde inseglet*)
    DIR: Ingmar Bergman
    SCR: Ingmar Bergman
    D/P: Gunnar Fischer
    MUS: Erik Nordgren
    SET: P. A. Lundgren
    EDR: Lennart Wallen
    PRO: Svensk Filmindustri
    CAST: Max von Sydow (Antonius Block, the Knight), Gunnar

Bjornstrand (Jons, the Squire), Nils Poppe (Jof), Bibi Andersson (Mia), Bengt Ekerot (Death), Ake Fridell (Plog, the smith), Inga Gill (Lisa, his wife), Erik Strandmark (Skat), Bertil Anderberg (Raval), Gunnel Lindblom (the girl), Inga Landgre (Knight's wife), Anders Ek (the monk), Gunnar Olsson, (painter), Maud Hansson (the witch), Lars Lind (the young monk), Benkt-Ake Benktsson (merchant), Gudrun Brost (woman in the tavern), Ulf Johansson (leader of the soldiers).

1957: WILD STRAWBERRIES (*Smultronstallet*)

DIR: Ingmar Bergman
SCR: Ingmar Bergman
D/P: Gunnar Fischer
MUS: Erik Nordgren
SET: Gittan Gustafsson
EDR: Oscar Rosander
PRO: Svensk Filmindustri
CAST: Victor Sjostrom (Professor Isak Borg), Bibi Andersson (Sara), Ingrid Thulin (Marianne), Gunnar Bjornstrand (Evald), Folke Sundquist (Anders), Bjorn Bjelvenstam (Viktor), Naima Wifstrand (Isak's mother), Jullan Kindahl (Agda), Gunnar Sjoberg (Alman, an engineer), Gunnel Brostrom (Mrs. Alman), Gertrud Fridh (Isak's wife), Ake Fridell (her lover), Max von Sydow (Akerman), Sif Ruud (Aunt), Yngve Nordwall (Uncle Aron), Per Sjostrand (Sigfrid), Gio Petre (Sigbritt), Gunnel Lindblom (Charlotta), Maud Hansson (Angelica), Anne-Marie Wiman (Mrs. Akerman), Eva Noree (Anna), Lena Bergman, Monica Ehrling (twins), Per Skogsberg (Hagbart), Goran Lundquist (Benjamin), Gunnar Olsson (Bishop), Josef Norman (Professor Tiger).

1958: BRINK OF LIFE/Br. So Close to Life (*Nara livet*)

DIR: Ingmar Bergman
SCR: Ulla Isaksson from her short story "Det vanliga vardiga"
D/P: Max Wilen
SET: Bibi Lindstrom
EDR: Carl-Olov Skeppstedt
PRO: Nordisk Tonefilm
CAST: Eva Dahlbeck (Stina Andersson), Ingrid Thulin (Cecilia Ellius), Bibi Andersson (Hjordis), Barbro Hiort af Ornas (Sister Brita), Erland Josephson (Anders Ellius), Max von Sydow (Harry Andersson), Gunnar Sjoberg (Dr. Nordlander), Anne-Marie Gyllenspetz (Welfare worker), Inga Landgre (Greta Ellius), Margareta Krook (Dr. Larsson),

Lars Lind (Dr. Thylenius), Sissi Kaiser (Sister Marit),
Monica Ekberg (Hjordis' friend), Gun Jonsson (night
nurse), Inga Gill (woman), Gunnar Neilsen (a doctor),
Maud Elfsio, Kristina Adolphson.

1958: THE MAGICIAN/Br. The Face (*Ansiktet*)

DIR: Ingmar Bergman
SCR: Ingmar Bergman
D/P: Gunnar Fischer
MUS: Erik Nordgren
SET: P. A. Lundgren
EDR: Oscar Rosander
PRO: Svensk Filmindustri
CAST: Max von Sydow (Albert Emanuel Vogler, mesmerist), Ingrid
Thulin (Manda Vogler), Ake Fridell (Tubal, Vogler's as-
sistant), Naima Wifstrand (Vogler's grandmother, a sorcer-
ess), Gunnar Bjornstrand (Dr. Vergerus), Bengt Ekerot
(Spegel, an actor), Bibi Andersson (Sara Lindqvist), Gertrud
Fridh (Ottilia Egerman), Lars Ekborg (Simson, Vogler's
coachman), Toivo Pawlo (Starbeck, police chief), Erland
Josephson (Egerman), Sif Ruud (Sofia, Egerman's cook),
Oscar Ljung (Antonsson, Egerman's coachman), Ulla
Sjoblom (Henrietta), Axel Duberg (Rustan, butler), Birgitta
Pettersson (Sanna, maid)

1960: THE VIRGIN SPRING (*Jungfrukallan*)

DIR: Ingmar Bergman
SCR: Ulla Isaksson from 14th-century ballad "Tores dotter i vange"
D/P: Sven Nykvist
MUS: Erik Nordgren
SET: P. A. Lundgren
EDR: Oscar Rosander
PRO: Svensk Filmindustri
CAST: Max von Sydow (Herr Töre), Birgitta Valberg (Fru
Märeta), Gunnel Lindblom (Ingeri), Birgitta Pettersson
(Karin), Axel Duberg (thin herdsman), Tor Isedal (mute
herdsman), Allan Edwall (beggar), Ove Porath (boy), Axel
Slangus (old man), Gudrun Brost (Frida), Oscar Ljung
(Simon), Tor Borong, Leif Forstenberg (farm laborers).

1960: THE DEVIL'S EYE (*Djavulens oga*)

DIR: Ingmar Bergman
SCR: Ingmar Bergman, adapted from a Danish radio play
D/P: Gunnar Fischer
MUS: Motif from Scarlatti
SET: P. A. Lundgren

EDR: Oscar Rosander
PRO: Svensk Filmindustri
CAST: Jarl Kulle (Don Juan), Bibi Andersson (Britt-Marie), Stig
      Jarrel (Satan), Nils Poppe (pastor), Gertrud Fridh (Renata,
      his wife), Sture Lagerwall (Pablo), Gunnar Bjornstrand
      (the actor), Georg Funquist (Count Armand de Roche-
      foucauld), Gunnar Sjoberg (Marquis Guiseppe Maria de
      Macopazza), Axel Duberg (Jonas), Torsten Winge (old
      man), Allan Edwall, Kristina Adolphson, Ragnar Arvedson,
      Borje Lind, Lenn Hjortzberg.

1961: THROUGH A CLASS DARKLY (*Sasom i en spegel*)

DIR: Ingmar Bergman
SCR: Ingmar Bergman
D/P: Sven Nykvist
MUS: J. S. Bach, from Suite No. 2, D minor, for cello
SET: P. A. Lundgren
EDR: Ulla Ryghe
PRO: Svensk Filmindustri
CAST: Harriet Andersson (Karin), Max von Sydow (Martin, her
      husband), Gunnar Bjornstrand (David, her father), Lars
      Passgard (Minus, her brother).

1963: WINTER LIGHT (*Nattvardsgasterna*)

DIR: Ingmar Bergman
SCR: Ingmar Bergman
D/P: Sven Nykvist
SET: P. A. Lundgren
EDR: Ulla Ryghe
PRO: Svensk Filmindustri
CAST: Gunnar Bjornstrand (Thomas Ericsson), Ingrid Thulin
      (Marta Lundberg), Max von Sydow (Jonas Persson), Gun-
      nel Lindblom (Karin Persson), Allan Edwall (Algot Frovik),
      Olof Thunberg (Fredrik Blom), Elsa Ebbeson (old woman),
      Kolbjorn Knudsen (church-warden).

1963: THE SILENCE (*Tystnaden*)

DIR: Ingmar Bergman
SCR: Ingmar Bergman
D/P: Sven Nykvist
MUS: J. S. Bach, Goldberg Variations
SET: P. A. Lundgren
EDR: Ulla Ryghe
PRO: Svensk Filmindustri
CAST: Ingrid Thulin (Ester), Gunnel Lindblom (Anna), Jorgen
      Lindstrom (Johan), Hakan Jahnberg (waiter), Birger

Malmsten (bartender), Eduardo Gutierrez (manager of the dwarfs, the "Eduardini"), Lissi Alandh (woman in cinema), Leif Forstenberg (man in cinema), Birger Lensander (usher), Nils Waldt (cashier), Eskil Kalling (bar proprietor), K. A. Bergman (paper-vendor), Olof Widgren (old man in hotel corridor).

1964: NOW ABOUT ALL THESE WOMEN (*For att inte tala om alla dessa kvinnor*)

DIR: Ingmar Bergman
SCR: Ingmar Bergman and Erland Josephsson under pseudonym Buntel Ericsson
D/P: Sven Nykvist
SET: P. A. Lundgren
EDR: Ulla Ryghe
PRO: Svensk Filmindustri
CAST: Jarl Kulle (Cornelius), Eva Dahlbeck (Adelaide), Bibi Andersson (Humlan), Harriet Andersson (Isolde), Gertrud Fridh (Traviata), Mona Malm (Cecilia), Barbro Hiort af Ornas (Beatrice), Karin Kavli (Mme Tussaud), Georg Funkquist (Tristan), Allan Edwall (Jillker), Gosta Pruzelius (Swedish radio reporter), Jan-Olof Strandberg (German radio reporter), Goran Graffman (French radio reporter), Jan Blomberg (English radio reporter), Ulf Johansson, Axel Duberg, Lars-Erik Liedholm (men in black), Lars-Owe Carlberg (chauffeur), Doris Funcke, Yvonne Igell (waitresses), Carl Billquist (young man).

1966: PERSONA

DIR: Ingmar Bergman
SCR: Ingmar Bergman
D/P: Sven Nykvist
MUS: Lars-Johan Werle
SET: Bibi Lindstrom
EDR: Ulla Ryghe
PRO: Svensk Filmindustri
CAST: Bibi Andersson (Alma), Liv Ullmann (Elisabeth Vogler), Margareta Krook (the doctor), Gunnar Bjornstrand (Mr. Vogler), Jorgen Lindstrom (the boy).

1967: STIMULANTIA
Daniel episode

DIR: Ingmar Bergman
SCR: Ingmar Bergman
D/P: Ingmar Bergman
MUS: Kabi Bergman

EDR: Ulla Ryghe
PRO: Svensk Filmindustri
Other episodes directed by Hans Abramson, Lars Gorling, Arne Arnbom, Jorn Donner, Tage Danielsson and Hans Alfredson, Gustaf Molander, Vilgot Sjoman.

1968: HOUR OF THE WOLF (*Vargtimmen*)

DIR: Ingmar Bergman
SCR: Ingmar Bergman
D/P: Sven Nykvist
MUS: Lars-Johan Werle
SET: Marik Vos-Lundh
EDR: Ulla Ryghe
PRO: Svensk Filmindustri
CAST: Liv Ullmann (Alma), Max von Sydow (Johan Borg), Erland Josephson (Baron von Merkens), Gertrud Fridh (Corinne von Merkens), Bertil Anderberg (Ernst von Merkens), Georg Rydeberg (Lindhorst, archivist), Ulf Johanson (Heerbrand, curator), Naima Wifstrand (old lady), Ingrid Thulin (Veronica Vogler), Lenn Hjortzberg (Kreisler), Agda Helin (maid), Mikael Rundqvist (boy), Mona Seilitz (woman in mortuary), Folke Sundquist.

1968: SHAME (*Skammen*)

DIR: Ingmar Bergman
SCR: Ingmar Bergman
D/P: Sven Nykvist
SET: P. A. Lundgren
EDR: Ulla Ryghe
PRO: Svensk Filmindustri
CAST: Liv Ullmann (Eva Rosenberg), Max von Sydow (Jan Rosenberg), Gunnar Bjornstrand (Colonel Jacobi), Sigge Furst (Filip), Birgitta Valberg (Mrs. Jacobi), Hans Alfredson (Lobelius), Ingvar Kjellson (Oswald), Willy Peters (older officer), Ulf Johansson (the doctor), Vilgot Sjoman (interviewer).

1969: THE RITE (*Riten*)
Written and directed by Ingmar Bergman for Swedish television.

DIR: Ingmar Bergman
SCR: Ingmar Bergman
D/P: Sven Nykvist
SET: Mago, Lennart Blomkvist
EDR: Siv Kanalv
PRO: Cinematograph

CAST: Ingrid Thulin (Thea Winkelmann), Gunnar Bjornstrand (Hans Winkelmann), Anders Ek (Albert Emanuel Sebastian Fisher), Erik Hell (Dr. Abramsson), Ingmar Bergman (the Confessor).

1969: THE PASSION OF ANNA/A Passion (*En passion*)

DIR: Ingmar Bergman
SCR: Ingmar Bergman
D/P: Sven Nykvist
SET: P. A. Lundgren
EDR: Siv Kanalv
PRO: Svensk Filmindustri
CAST: Liv Ullmann (Anna Fromm), Bibi Andersson (Eva Vergerus), Max von Sydow (Andreas Winkelman), Erland Josephson (Elis Vergerus), Erik Hell (Johan Andersson), Sigge Furst (Verner), Svea Holst (Verner's wife), Annika Kronberg (Katarina), Hjordis Pettersson (Johan's sister), Lars-Owe Carlberg and Brian Wikstrom (policemen).

1971: THE TOUCH (*Beroringen*)

DIR: Ingmar Bergman
SCR: Ingmar Bergman
D/P: Sven Nykvist
MUS: Jan Johansson
SET: P. A. Lundgren
EDR: Siv Kanalv-Lundgren
PRO: ABC Pictures Corp.
CAST: Bibi Andersson (Karin, Mrs. Vergerus), Barbro Hiort af Ornas (her mother), Elliott Gould (David Kovac), Staffan Hallerstram (Anders Vergerus), Maria Nolgard (Agnes Vergerus), Max von Sydow (Dr. Andreas Vergerus), Erik Nyhlen (archaeologist), Margareta Bystrom (Dr. Vergerus' secretary), Alan Simon (museum curator), Sheila Reid (Sara, David Kovac's sister).

1973: CRIES AND WHISPERS (*Viskningar och rop*)

DIR: Ingmar Bergman
SCR: Ingmar Bergman
D/P: Sven Nykvist
MUS: Bach (played by Pierre Fournier) and Chopin (played by Kabi Laretei)
SET: Marik Vos
EDR: Siv Lundgren
PRO: Svensk Filmindustri
CAST: Harriet Andersson (Agnes), Ingrid Thulin (Karin), Liv Ullmann (Maria), Kari Sylwan (Anna), Erland Josephson (doc-

tor), George Arlin (Fredrik, Karin's husband), Henning
Moritzen (Joakin).

1973: SCENES FROM A MARRIAGE *(Scener ur ett aktenskap)*
    DIR: Ingmar Bergman
    SCR: Ingmar Bergman
    D/P: Sven Nykvist
    EDR: Siv Lundgren
    PRO: Cinematograph
    CAST: Liv Ullmann (Marianne), Erland Josephson (Johan), Bibi
          Andersson (Katarina), Jan Malmsjo (Peter), Gunnel Lind-
          blom (Eva), Barbro Hiort af Ornas (Mrs. Jacobi), Bertil
          Norstrom (Arne), Wenche Foss (Marianne's mother).